Loosening the Grip

A handbook of alcohol information

JEAN KINNEY, M.S.W.
Assistant Professor of Clinical Psychiatry,
Executive Director, Project Cork Institute,
Dartmouth Medical School,
Hanover, New Hampshire

GWEN LEATON
Private consultant in alcohol education;
formerly Director of Education,
Edgehill/Newport, Inc., Newport, Rhode Island

THIRD EDITION

Illustrated by
Stuart Copans, M.D.

TIMES MIRROR/MOSBY COLLEGE PUBLISHING
ST. LOUIS • TORONTO • SANTA CLARA 1987

Editor: Nancy K. Roberson
Developmental editor: Kathy Sedovic
Project editor: Suzanne Seeley
Production editor: Tim O'Brien
Designer: Susan E. Lane
Production: Publication Services

THIRD EDITION

A division of The C. V. Mosby Company
11830 Westline Industrial Drive
St. Louis, Missouri 63146

Printed in the United States of America

Previous editions copyrighted 1978, 1983

Library of Congress Cataloging-in-Publication Data
Kinney, Jean, 1943–
    Loosening the grip.

    Includes index.
    1. Alcoholism—United States—Handbooks, manuals, etc.
2. Alcoholism—Treatment—United States—Handbooks, manuals, etc.   I. Leaton, Gwen, 1934–   II. Title.
HV5292.K53   1987   362.2'92   86-30058
ISBN 0-8016-2687-0

BIN.
PS/D/D   9 8 7 6   02/A/292

Contributors

FREDRICK BURKLE, Jr., M.D., M.P.H.

Dr. Burkle came to the psychiatry residency program of Dartmouth Medical School after a practice in pediatrics. He has since left chilly New England and is in private psychiatric practice and a consultant in adolescent health care in Maui, Hawaii.

Adolescents, CHAPTER 10

TONY CLAXTON, M.D.

Dr. Claxton, a graduate of the University of Oklahoma College of Medicine, is a third-year resident in psychiatry at Dartmouth Medical School. Having a special interest in alcohol and substance abuse treatment, he has served as therapist and medical director in an intensive weekend, diagnostic and education program conducted at Dartmouth for those convicted of drinking and driving.

Medications, CHAPTER 10

STUART COPANS, M.D.

Dr. Copans (*Illustrator*) was formerly a Fellow in Child Psychiatry at Dartmouth Medical School. During that period, he was a lecturer in the alcohol counselor training program, discussing the effects of alcohol abuse on the family—the first sign of what has since become a major professional interest. He presently is Medical Director, Adolescent Alcohol and Substance Abuse Treatment Program, Brattleboro Retreat, a Dartmouth-affiliated teaching hospital, and Associate Professor of Clinical Psychiatry at Dartmouth.

ILLUSTRATOR
Effects of alcohol problems on the family, CHAPTER 7

RICHARD GOODSTEIN, M.D.

Dr. Goodstein is Vice President for Medical Education of the Carrier Foundation and Clinical Associate Professor of Psychiatry at Rutgers Medical School. The material included here represents lectures to the counselor trainees.

Suicide evaluation and prevention, *The elderly* CHAPTER 10

PETER HAURI, Ph.D.

Dr. Hauri is a Professor of Psychiatry and directs the Behavioral Medicine Section and the Sleep Clinic at the Dartmouth Medical School.

Sleep disturbances, CHAPTER 5

JEAN KINNEY, M.S.W.

Jean Kinney, Assistant Professor of Clinical Psychiatry at Dartmouth Medical School, was the Associate Director of the Alcohol Counselor Training Program conducted at Dartmouth from 1972–1978, the program that was the source of this text. With the completion of the alcohol counselor training program, she joined the staff of Project Cork, a program to develop and implement a model alcohol curriculum for medical student education.

GWEN LEATON

Gwen Leaton was intimately involved in the Alcohol Counselor Training Program as a Research Assistant. Upon its completion she held several positions as Director of Education and Training in both academic and treatment settings, most recently at Edgehill-Newport, Rhode Island. At the moment, while her interest in alcohol and alcoholism continues, she has taken a sabbatical from full-time employment in the field.

HUGH MacNAMEE, M.D.

Adolescents, CHAPTER 10

Dr. MacNamee was an Associate Professor of Clinical Psychiatry in the Division of Child Psychiatry at Dartmouth until his death in 1983. His lectures on adolescents as originally presented and incorporated here have been retained and required little modification. They reflect his eminently practical stance and uncommon common sense; some things really cannot be improved upon.

FRED OSHER, M.D.

Psychiatric illness, CHAPTER 10

Dr. Osher, an Assistant Professor of Psychiatry at Dartmouth Medical School is a community psychiatrist in West Central Mental Health Services of New Hampshire, a community mental health system affiliated with the Dartmouth Medical School. Having served as medical director in an urban detox center before beginning his psychiatry residency at Dartmouth, he entered psychiatry with his "credentials" in alcohol and substance abuse well established.

TREVOR R.P. PRICE, M.D.

Alcohol and the body, CHAPTER 2
Medical complications, CHAPTER 5

Dr. Price is Associate Professor of Clinical Psychiatry at the University of Pennsylvania School of Medicine, an adjunct Associate Professor of Psychiatry at Dartmouth Medical School, and Chair of the Council overseeing the Project Cork Institute at Dartmouth. He entered psychiatry after training in internal medicine. During his tenure at Dartmouth his interest in alcohol was sparked when he became involved in the Alcohol Counselor Training Program.

DONALD WEST, M.D.

Multiple substance abuse, CHAPTER 10

Dr. West, a psychiatrist with a major professional interest in medical education, spent a sabbatical year with the Project Cork Institute in academic year 1985–1986 to focus on the issues of integrating alcohol-substance abuse training into medical training. This introduction ultimately provided a recruit to the alcohol field, and he has since joined Dartmouth's Department of Psychiatry as Director of Alcohol Services.

God of Compassion, if anyone has come to thine altar troubled in spirit, depressed and apprehensive, expecting to go away as he came, with the same haunting heaviness of heart; if anyone is deeply wounded of soul, hardly daring to hope that anything can afford him the relief he seeks, so surprised by the ill that life can do that he is half afraid to pray; O God, surprise him, we beseech thee, by the graciousness of thy help; and enable him to take from thy bounty as ungrudgingly as thou givest, that he may leave here his sorrow and take a song away.

AUTHOR UNKNOWN

Preface

THE PURPOSE OF THIS BOOK

Material on alcohol and alcoholism is mushrooming. Books, articles, scientific reports, pamphlets. On present use, past use, abuse. Around prevention, efforts at early detection, effects on the family, effects on the body. When, where, why....

And yet, if you are in the helping business and reasonably bright and conscientious and can find an occasional half hour to read but don't have all day to search library stacks, then it's probably hard for you to lay your hands on the information you need when it would be most helpful.

This handbook is an attempt to partially remedy the situation. It contains what we believe is the basic information an alcohol counselor or other professional confronted with alcohol problems needs to know and would like to have handy. This work is an effort to synthesize, organize, and sometimes "translate" the information from medicine, psychology, psychiatry, anthropology, sociology, and counseling that applies to alcohol use and alcoholism treatment. This handbook isn't the last word. But we hope it is a starting point.

This handbook originally grew out of an Alcohol Counselor Training Program that was conducted by the Department of Psychiatry at the Dartmouth Medical School between 1972 and 1978. That program was funded by a training grant from the NIAAA. The Counselor Training Program involved many faculty of the Department of Psychiatry and the staff of the Dartmouth-Hitchcock Mental Health Center. Their lectures, presentations, and advice helped shape this handbook. The counselor trainees with whom we worked were also a vital force in the endeavor. They assisted us in separating the important from the trivial, the useful from the useless, and truth from nonsense.

RECENT DEVELOPMENTS

In some respects those days now seem very long ago, definitely the "early days", or even "dark ages" depending upon one's perspective. In the process of undertaking this revision we have come to appreciate the tremendous strides that have been made in the field. If we might share some of the landmarks that we noticed:

- The notion of alcoholism's having a genetic basis is no longer a "recent" finding. The assimilation of this information has certainly helped reinforce the notion of children of alcoholics as being at risk. It has likewise forced us to pay more attention to the significance of a positive family history of alcoholism when dealing with those who experience problems early in their drinking careers.
- Paralleling the above, the recognition that the psychological problems that accompany alcoholism are a symptom and not the source of the disease is a major advance in knowledge.
- Early intervention and use of families in interventions is no longer a novelty, but a mainstay of treatment.
- Addressing the family as part of the alcoholic's treatment is no longer seen as optional or merely a "nice touch." It is now viewed as an essential component of treatment. This represents another major shift in treatment approaches.
- The alcohol field too has begun to attend to more than frank alcoholism. Attention to alcohol problems and alcohol abuse as well as efforts to deal with the negative consequences of acute use are within the clinical domain.
- Clinical work with children of alcoholics, both those in the home and adult children, is a new development.
- Attention to the physical effects of moderate alcohol use is new, rather than the earlier virtually exclusive focus upon the physical toll that accompanies alcoholism and chronic heavy use.

These changes in the alcohol field place demands upon all clinicians, and necessitate as well that those veterans in the field actively work at remaining current.

CHANGES IN THIS EDITION

Beyond the obviously expected changes of updating statistics and references, the third edition reflects changes in the alcohol field described above. Accordingly, there is new or significantly expanded discussion of the following.

- **Clinical approaches to alcohol problems and alcohol abuse:** The alcohol field is no longer confronted exclusively with the treatment of alcoholism. Guidelines are set forth for diagnosing and managing the spectrum of alcohol problems.
- **Diagnostic procedures:** Greater attention is directed to specific tips for interviewing around alcohol, screening techniques and

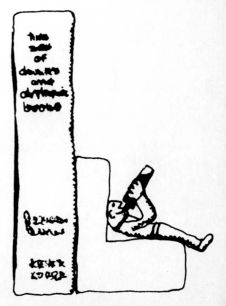

instruments, the core alcohol history, and guidelines for documenting findings in the agency or medical record.

- *The effects of alcohol problems and alcoholism on the family:* Discussion ranges from treatment of family members, to involving family in interventions to initiate treatment for the alcoholic member, to alcohol's impact on children—both the impact on those in the home and the impact continuing into adult life.
- *Adolescent alcohol and substance abuse:* Material includes the signs and symptoms common to adolescent alcohol and substance use, diagnostic criteria, and treatment issues and approaches age-specific to adolescents.
- *Current research:* Within the alcohol field there has been considerable research in a number of areas, particularly the natural history of alcoholism; alcoholism's etiology, both biochemical and cultural influences; and the medical aspects of moderate alcohol use. These are summarized and their clinical implications highlighted.

Illustrations

More than 40 new cartoons have been added in the margins to accompany the narrative.

In closing, we acknowledge the convention of extending appreciation to all those who have been supportive in the preparation of this work. Trusting that those who are a part of our professional lives and our spouses know who they are, we break from that tradition.

Jean Kinney

Gwen Leaton

ACKNOWLEDGMENTS

The publisher would like to acknowledge the assistance of the following reviewers:

Genny Carlin, M.S.
Bruce Larson, C.C.D.D.
Hazelden Foundation
Center City, Minnesota

Iris Heckman, Ph.D.
Washburn University

Debra Portch, M.Ed.
Montana State University

Theresa Powell, Ed.D.
Boston College

Clay Rivers, Ph.D.
University of Nebraska, Lincoln

Contents

Introduction

Remember...

Remember back to the time you wanted to learn to ride a bicycle.... A *real* bicycle. A two-wheeler.

Remember the street you lived on.... How about the big kids who had their own.... Can you feel how eager you were to join them? You could just picture yourself hopping on one of your own and winging off.... Picture that scene.

Continue in your imagination.

Suppose you had decided to seriously pursue your desire to ride a two-wheeler. Off to the town library, signing out a book on *Riding a Two-Wheeler in 20 Easy Steps.* Glossy pictures, diagrams, and sure enough, absolutely everything you'd need to know, to the smallest detail.

Step 1.   Stand beside bicycle.

Step 2.   Place hands on handlebars.

Step 3.   With foot, push up kickstand.

Step 4.   Walk briskly, pushing bicycle.

Step 5.   Place left foot on left pedal (if standing on left side) and simultaneously swing right leg over bicycle and place on right pedal. (*Caution*: It is imperative to maintain forward motion during this step. Also critical to see that center of gravity of the body is properly positioned above bicycle.)

Step 6.   Depress pedal in clockwise motion with ball of foot.

And so forth....

That isn't quite how it happened, is it? Had anyone ever suggested that was how you should go about it, there's no way you would not have spotted the ploy as the super con-job of the year.

So, how did you learn? By trying it! Getting your hands on a bike and simply climbing on! Unless you happened to be the Larry Bird of the cycling set, you didn't smugly cruise down to the playground, either, on that first try. Wobbling along, training wheels, your mom or dad running beside holding the seat...spills, scuffs, tears, despair, forgetting how to brake in the crunch, more spills...and eventually it all clicked!

Working with alcoholics is pretty much like learning to ride that two-wheeler. It's a process. A series of trying things that occurs over a period of time. We hope that *Riding a Two-Wheeler in 20 Easy Steps* has convinced you. That means learning by doing—feeling awkward, going shakily in the beginning, having someone close by for support and to provide advice. It will include some blows to your pride, moments of feeling silly or unknowledgeable.

How does this book fit in? It's not a step-by-step guide that you can read—even memorize—and then be a counselor. If it were, it probably would be of little use. At best it can be a guide. As you recall from the days you tackled that bicycle, experience is a big key to learning. Although things we read may be of some assistance, it is important that they be put to the test of our own experience. To exhaust the bicycle comparison, riding a bicycle requires doing many different things that people already know how to do. Moving their legs up and down, gripping something in their hands, looking around, balancing, and others. But these activities, when uniquely combined and coordinated, are lumped together and called "riding a bicycle".

Counseling, too, involves many familiar activities: talking to people, gathering information, sifting out possibilities, solving problems, and so on. Counseling people about alcohol problems requires some specific knowledge. Alcohol, its uses and associated problems, is a far more complex subject than simply alcoholism itself. To narrow your outlook to a focus on the problems of the alcoholic, however tremendous, could leave you forever using only three of the gears on your ten-speed bike.

Alcohol

ONCE UPON A TIME...

Imagine yourself in what is now Clairvoux, high in the Swiss hills. Stone pots dating from the Old Stone Age have been found that once contained a mild beer or wine. It probably was discovered very much like fire—nature plus curiosity. If any watery mixture of vegetable sugars or starches is allowed to stand long enough in a warm place, alcohol will make itself.

Say you're a caveman named Urg, coming back from a lengthier than usual flight from a dinosaur or some such thing. "Aha!" Some berries or barley left in a bowl in the sun. "Smells a bit funny, but so what! I'm thirsty and hungry and tired." Down it goes. Can you imagine what you might have thought as your first booze went down?

No one knows what kind of liquor was first, wine or beer or mead; but by the Neolithic Age, it was *everywhere*. Tales of liquor abound in the folklore. One relates that at the beginning of time the forces of good and evil contested with each other for domination of the earth. Eventually the forces for good won out. But a great many of them had been killed in the process, and wherever they fell, a vine sprouted from the ground. So it seems

some felt wine to be a good force. Other myths depict the powers of alcohol as gifts from their gods. Some civilizations worshipped specific gods of wine: the Egyptians' god was Osiris; the Greeks', Dionysius; the Romans', Bacchus. Wine was used in early rituals as libations (poured out on the ground, altar, etc.). Priests often drank it as part of the rituals. The Bible, too, is full of references to sacrifices including wine.

From ritual uses it spread to convivial uses, and customs developed. Alcohol was a regular part of the meals, viewed as a staple in the diet, even before ovens were invented for baking bread. The Assyrians received a daily portion from their masters of a "gallon" of bread and a gallon of fermented brew (probably a barley beer). Bread and wine were offered by the Hebrews on their successful return from battle. In Greece and Rome wine was essential at every kind of gathering. Alcohol was found to contribute to fun and games at a party; for example, the Roman orgies. Certainly, its safety over water was a factor, but the effects had something to do with it. It is hard to imagine an orgy where everyone drank water, or welcoming a victorious army with lemonade. By the Middle Ages alcohol permeated everything, accompanying birth, marriage, death, the crowning of kings, diplomatic exchanges, signing treaties, and councils. The monasteries became the taverns and inns of the times, and travelers received the benefit of the grape.

The ancients had figured that what was good in these instances might be good in others, and alcohol came into use as a medicine. It was an antiseptic and an anesthetic and was used in combinations to form salves and tonics. As a cure it ran the

Ramses III distributed beer to his subjects and then told them the tingling they felt radiated from him!

God made yeast, as well as dough, and loves fermentation just as dearly as he loves vegetation.
EMERSON

Food without drink is like a wound without a plaster.
BRULL

In vino veritas.
PLINY

Persia. Malcolm, in his "History of Persia," relates that wine was discovered in that kingdom in the reign of Janisheed. He attempted to preserve grapes in a large vessel. Fermentation ensued and the king believed that the juice was poison and labeled it as such. A lady of the palace, wishing to commit suicide, drank from it. She was pleased with the stupor that followed and repeated the experiment until the supply was exhausted. She imparted the secret to the king and a new quantity was made...Hence wine in Persia is called...delightful poison.

SPOONER, WALTER W. *The Cyclopaedia of Temperance and Prohibition,* 1891.

gamut from black jaundice to pain in the knee and hiccups. St. Paul advised Timothy, "No longer drink only water, but use a little wine for the sake of your stomach and your frequent ailments." Liquor was a recognized mood changer, nature's tranquilizer. The biblical King Lemuel's mother advises, "Give wine to them that be of heavy hearts." The Bible also refers to wine as stimulating and cheering, "Praise to God, that he hath brought forth fruit out of the earth, and wine that maketh glad the heart of man."

FERMENTATION AND DISCOVERY OF DISTILLATION

Nature alone cannot produce stronger stuff than 14% alcohol. Fermentation is a combustive action of yeasts on plants: potatoes, fruit, grain, etc. The sugar is exposed to wild yeasts in the air or commercial yeasts, which produce an enzyme, which in turn converts sugar into alcohol. Fermentive yeast cannot survive in solutions stronger than 14% alcohol. When that level is reached, the yeast, which is a living thing, ceases to produce and dies.

Now imagine the widespread joy when something stronger came along. In the tenth century an Arabian physician, Rhazes, discovered distilled spirits. Actually, he was looking for a way to release "the spirit of the wine." It was welcomed at the time as the "true water of life." European scientists rejoiced in their long-sought "philosopher's stone," or perfect element. A mystique developed, and alcohol was called "the fountain of youth," "eau-de-vie," "aqua vitae." *Usequebaugh* from the Gaelic *usige beath,* meaning breath of life, is the source of the word "whiskey." The word alcohol itself is derived from the Arabic *al kohl.* It originally referred to a fine powder of antimony used for staining the eyelids and gives rise to speculation on the expression, "Here's mud in your eye!" The word evolved to describe any finely ground substance, then the essence of a thing, and eventually came to mean "finely divided spirit," or the essential spirit of the wine. Nineteenth-century temperance advocates tried to prove that alcohol is derived from the Arabic *alghul,* meaning ghost or evil spirit.

Distilled liquor wasn't a popular drink until about the sixteenth century. Before that it was used as *the* basic medicine and cure for all human ailments. Distillation is a simple process that can produce an alcohol content of almost 93% if it is refined enough times. Remember, nature stops at 14%. Start with a fer-

can you find the anachronism in this picture?

Rhazes discovers distilled spirits

mented brew. When it is boiled, the alcohol separates from the juice or whatever as steam. Alcohol boils at a lower temperature than the other liquid. The escaping steam is caught in a cooling tube and turns into a liquid again, leaving the juice, water, etc. behind. Voilà! Stronger stuff, about 50% alcohol!

Proof as a way of measuring the strength of a given liquor came from a practice used by the early settlers of this country to test their brews. They saturated gunpowder with alcohol and ignited it: too strong, it flared up; too weak, it sputtered. A strong blue flame was considered the sign of proper strength. Almost straight alcohol was diluted with water to gain the desired flame. Half and half was considered 100 proof. Thus 86 proof bourbon is 43% alcohol. Because alcohol dilutes itself with water from the air, 200 proof, or 100%, alcohol is not possible. The U.S. standards for spirits are between 195 and 198 proof.

ALCOHOL USE IN THE NEW WORLD

Alcohol came to America with the explorers and colonists. In 1620, the *Mayflower* landed at Plymouth because, it says in the

ship's log, "We could not now take time for further search or consideration, our victuals having been much spent, especially our bere...." The Spanish missionaries brought grapevines to the New World, and before the United States was yet a nation, there was wine making in California. The Dutch opened the first distillery on Staten Island in 1640. In the Massachusetts Bay Colony brewing ranked next in importance after milling and baking. The Puritans did not disdain the use of alcohol as is sometimes supposed. A federal law passed in 1790 gave provisions for each soldier to receive a ration of one-fourth pint of brandy, rum, or whiskey. The colonists imported wine and malt beverages and

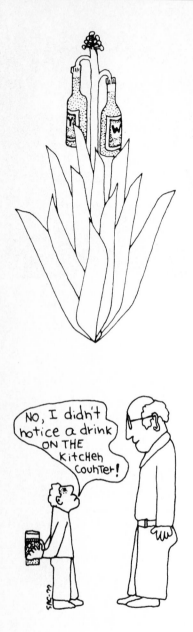

planted vineyards, but it was Jamaican rum that became the answer to the thirst of the new nation. For its sake, New Englanders became the bankers of the slave trade that supplied the molasses needed to produce rum. Eventually whiskey, the backwoods substitute for rum introduced to America by land, superseded rum in popularity. Sour-mash bourbon became the great American drink.

This is a very brief view of alcohol's history. The extent of its uses, the ways in which it has been viewed, and even the amount of writing about it that survives give witness to the value placed on this strange substance. Alcohol has been everywhere, connected to everything that is a part of everyday life. Growing the grapes or grains to produce it is even suspected as the reason for the development of agriculture. Whether making it, using it as a medicine, drinking it, or writing about it, people from early times have devoted much time and energy to alcohol.

WHY BOTHER?

So alcohol happened, why didn't it go the way of the dinosaurs?

Think about the first time *you* ever tasted alcohol....Some people were exposed really early and don't remember the experience of a little sherry in their bottle, or rubbed on their gums when they were teething. Some were allowed a taste of Dad's beer or the Christmas Day champagne at a tender age. Some sneaked sips at the first big wedding or party they were around. Some never even saw it until junior or senior high school. Still others were taught from infancy that it was evil and may not have touched it until college or the army took them away from home. And there are some, who for one reason or another, have never touched the stuff. If you are in the majority, however, you probably encountered it in a variation on one of the above themes.

Maybe you didn't like that first sip of Dad's beer or Aunt Tillie's sherry. Rather than admit it, you decided they must know what was good. So you took a sip every time it was offered. "*As you're fighting your way to the top, it helps to have a taste of what's up there.*"

Perhaps you were around for the preparations for a big do at your house. Ice, soda, and funny-colored stuff in big bottles were lined up with neat things like cherries, oranges, lemons, and sugar. The atmosphere was busy and exciting. When the guests began to arrive, the first thing they got was something from those bottles. Everyone seemed to talk and laugh quite a bit, and after a while no one seemed to see you. Mom left her drink in the kitchen while she served some of those tasty cheese things she let you try earlier. One quick sip. *"To keep the party going, keep the best on hand."*

Perhaps people in your home drank on weekends, but not you. Mom and Dad said things like, "When you're of age" or "Wouldn't want to stunt your growth" or "This is a big people's drink." Anyway, you weren't getting any tastes. Somewhere along the school trail, you wound up at a party you had expected to be like all the others you'd been to. Not this time. Someone brought some beer, and everyone else was having some. There might have been a brief flash of guilt when you thought of the folks, but who wants to stick out in a crowd? So you kept up with the gang. Soon you felt as grown-up as you'd ever been. *"On your night of nights, add that sophisticated touch."*

Or perhaps your folks never touched the stuff. They were really opposed to alcohol. They gave you lots of reasons: "It's evil," "People who drink get into terrible trouble," "Vile stuff, it just eats you up" or even, "God's against it." Well, you admired your folks, or were scared of them, or you really believed the part about God's stand. Anyway, no one pushed you too much. Then came the army or college. It seemed as though everyone drank something, sometime, somewhere. They weren't dropping dead at the first sip or getting into too much trouble that you could see. Even if there was a little trouble, someone said, "Oh, well, he was just drunk, sowing some wild oats." Lightning didn't strike. You didn't see the devil popping out of glasses. Just the opposite, most of your friends seemed to be having a lot of fun. *"When the gang gets together...."* Bowling, fishing, sailing, hiking, beaching, everywhere.

It could be that you grew up with wine being served at meals. At some time you were initiated into the process as a matter of course. You never gave it a second thought.

You might have had a religious background that introduced you to wine as a part of your ritual acceptance into adulthood or as a part of your particular church's worship.

With time, age, and social mobility, the reasons for continuing to drink become more complex. It is not unusual to drink a bit more than one can handle at some point. After one experience of being drunk, and/or sick, and/or hung over, some people

We take a drink only for the sake of the benediction.

PERETZ

decide never to touch the stuff again. For most, however, something they are getting or think they are getting out of alcohol makes them try it again. Despite liquor's real effects on us, most of us search for an experience we have had with it, or want to have with it, or have been led to believe that we can have with its use. *"As an essential part of the Good Life, ————cannot be excelled."*

Theories to explain alcohol use

Those trying to explain drinking behavior have always been more interested in alcohol*ism* than in explaining alcohol use per se. Nonetheless from time to time, various theories have been advanced to explain the basic why behind alcohol use. Probably all contain some truth. To *escape anxiety*—"It calms me down, helps my nerves." "It helps me unwind after a hard day." This explanation can be thought of as the anxiety thesis and was derived from Freud's work. Freud concluded that in times of anxiety and stress, people fall back on things that have worked for them in the past. In theory, the things you will choose to relieve anxiety are those you did when you last felt most secure. That lovely, secure time might last have been at Mom's breast. It has been downhill ever since. In this case, use of the mouth (eating, smoking, drinking) would be chosen to ease stressful situations. This phenomenon is called *oral fixation.*

Another version of the anxiety thesis came from Donald Horton's anthropological studies. He observed that alcohol was used by primitive societies either ritually or socially to relieve the anxiety caused by an unstable environment. Drunken acts are acceptable and not punished. The greater the environmental stress, the heavier the drinking. Therefore, in this view, alcohol's anxiety-reducing property is the one universal key to why people drink alcohol. This theory has by and large been rejected as the sole reason for drinking. Indeed, as biological research advances are made and more is learned of the actual effects of alcohol, the drug, it can no longer even be said that alcohol does reduce anxiety.

Another theory that surfaced was based on the need for a feeling of power over oneself or one's environment. Most people don't talk about this, but take a look at the heavy reliance of the liquor industry on he-man models, executive types, and beautiful women surrounded by adoring males. People in ads celebrate winning anything with a drink of some sort.

The power theory was explored by researchers in the early 1970s, under the direction of David McClelland. They examined folktales from both heavy- and light-drinking societies. Their research indicated that there was no greater concern with relief from tension or anxiety in heavy-drinking societies than in those that consumed less. To look at this further, they conducted a study with college men over a period of 10 years. Without revealing the reasons for the study, they asked the students to write down their fantasies before, during, and after the consumption of liquor. The stories revealed that the students felt bigger, stronger, more influential, more aggressive, and more capable of great sexual conquest the more they drank. The conclusion was that people drink to experience a feeling of power. This power feeling was seen as having two different patterns, depending on the personality of the drinker. What was called *p-power* is a personal powerfulness, uninhibited and carried out at the expense of others. Social power, or *s-power*, is a more altruistic powerfulness, power to help others. This social power was found to predominate after two or three drinks; heavier drinking produced a predominance of p-power.

Another theory arose during the late '60s at the height of the "counterculture" when the use of drugs other than alcohol was extensive. This approach, as discussed by Andrew Weil, claimed that every human being has some need to reach out toward some larger experience. And people will try anything that suggests itself as a way to do that: alcohol, drugs, yoga, meditation. Some drugs are commonly known to "blow your mind" or are even designated as "mind-expanding drugs." Evidence cited for the seeking of altered states of consciousness begins with very young children who whirl, or hyperventilate, or attempt in other ways to produce a change in their experience. When older, people learn that chemicals can produce different states. In pursuit of these states, alcohol is often used because it is the one intoxicant we make legally available. The drug scene was seen as another answer to the same search. Weil suggested that this search arises from the "innate psychological drive arising out of the neurological structure of the human brain." His conclusion was that we have put the cart before the horse in focusing attention on drugs rather than on the states people seek from them. Thus he suggested that society acknowledge the need itself and cope with it in a positive rather than a negative way.

A newer perspective on factors that may contribute to alcohol use focuses on stresses associated with modern everyday life—be it in the executive rat race, the declining economy, the changes in family structure. Use of alcohol is seen as one response to stress that may have long-term harmful consequences. Other responses to stress might include hypertension, ulcer disease, migraine headaches. Accordingly, stress management is a newly emerging field directed toward helping people develop alternative healthy ways of dealing with stress.

Current research is less concerned with identifying factors within the individual that motivate alcohol use. Instead, the interest has turned to the social settings in which people find themselves, in order to identify factors associated with patterns of alcohol use. Accordingly, for example, attention is turning to the role of peer pressure in determining adolescents' decisions to use alcohol, or the influence of parental standards in setting norms for their teenagers' drinking, or the impact of legislative approaches.

In general, the accepted stance now seems to be a "combination of factors" approach. One inescapable fact is that from the very earliest recorded times alcohol has been important to people. Sheldon Bacon, former head of the Rutgers School of Alcohol Studies made a point worth keeping in mind. He called attention to the original needs that alcohol might have served: satisfaction of hunger and thirst, medication or anesthetic, fostering of religious ecstasy. Our modern, complex society has virtually eliminated all these earlier functions. Now all that is left is alcohol the depressant, mood-altering drug, the possible, or believed, reliever of tension, inhibition, and guilt. Therefore, contemporary society has had to create new "needs" that alcohol can meet.

Myths

In thinking about alcohol use, remember that myths are equally important to people. Many think that alcohol makes them warm when they are cold (not so), sexier (in the courting, maybe; in the execution, not so), manlier, womanlier, cured of their ills (not usually), less scared of people (possibly), and better able to function (only if very little is taken). An exercise in asking a lot of people what a drink does for them will expose a heavy reliance on myths for their reasons.

Whatever the truth in the mixture of theory and myth, enough people in this country rely on the use of alcohol to accomplish something for them to support a $66.4 billion per year industry.

ALCOHOL PROBLEMS: THE FLY IN THE OINTMENT

Alcohol is many faceted. With its ritual, medicinal, dietary, and pleasurable uses, alcohol can leave in its wake confusion, pain, disorder, and tragedy. The use and abuse of alcohol has gone hand in hand in all cultures. With the notable exceptions of the Muslims and Buddhists, whose religions forbid drinking, temperance and abstinence have been the exception rather than the rule in most of the world.

As sin or moral failing

Societies have come to grips with alcohol problems in a variety of ways. One of these regards drunkenness as a sin, a moral failing, and the drunk as a moral weakling of some kind. The Greek word for drunk, for example, means literally to "misbehave at the wine." An Egyptian writer admonished his friend with the slightly contemptuous "thou art like a little child." Noah, who undoubtedly had reason to seek relief in drunkenness after getting all those creatures safely through the flood, was not looked on kindly by his children as he lay in his drunken stupor. The complaints have continued through time. A Dutch physician of the sixteenth century criticized the heavy use of alcohol in Germany and Flanders by saying "that freelier than is profitable to health, they take it and drink it." Some of the most forceful sanctions have come from the temperance movements.

An early temperance leader wrote that "alcohol is preeminently a destroyer in every department of life." As late as March 1974, the New Hampshire Christian Civic League devoted an entire issue of its monthly newspaper to a polemic against the idea that alcoholism is a disease. In its view the disease concept gives reprieve to the "odious alcohol sinner."

As a legal issue

Others see the use of liquor as a legislative issue and believe misuse can be solved by laws. Total prohibition is one of the methods used by those who believe that legislation can sober people up. Most legal approaches through history have been piecemeal affairs invoked to deal with specific situations. Excessive drinking was so bad in ancient Greece that "drinking captains" were appointed to supervise drinking. Elaborate rules were devised for drinking at parties. A perennial favorite has been control of supply. In 81 AD, a Roman emperor ordered the destruction of half the British vineyards.

The sin and legal views of drunkenness often go hand in hand. They have as a common denominator the idea that the drunk chooses to be drunk. He is therefore either a sinner or a ne'er-do-well who can be handled by making it illegal to drink. In 1606 intoxication was made a statutory offense in England by an "Act for Repressing the Odious and Loathsome Sin of Drunkenness." In the reign of Charles I, laws were passed to suppress liquor altogether. Settling a new world did not dispense with the problems resulting from alcohol use. The traditional methods of dealing with these problems continued. From around 1600 to the 1800s, attitudes toward alcohol were low key. Laws were passed in various colonies and states to deal with liquor use, such as an early Connecticut law forbidding drinking for more than half an hour at a time. Another law in Virginia in 1760 prohibited ministers from "drinking to excess and inciting riot." But there were no temperance societies, no large-scale prohibitions, no religious bodies fighting.

America's response to alcohol problems

Drinking in the colonies was largely a family affair and remained so until the beginning of the nineteenth century. With increasing immigration, industrialization, and greater social freedoms, drinking became less a family affair. Alcohol abuse became more open and more destructive. The opening of the West brought the saloon into prominence. The old and stable social and family patterns began to change. The frontier hero took to gulping his drinks with his foot on the bar rail. Attitudes began to intensify regarding the use of alcohol.

These developments hold the key to many modern attitudes toward alcohol, the stigma of alcoholism, the wet–dry controversy. Differing views of alcohol began to polarize America. The legal and moral approaches reached their apex in the United States with the growth of the temperance movement and the Prohibition amendment in 1919.

The temperance movement and Prohibition.

The traditional American temperance movement did not begin as a prohibition movement. The temperance movement coincided with the rise of social consciousness, a belief in the efficacy of law to resolve human problems. It was part and parcel of the humanitarian movement, which included child labor and prison reform, women's rights, abolition, and social welfare and poverty legislation. Originally it condemned only excessive drinking and the drinking of distilled liquor, *not all liquor or all drinking.* It was believed that the evils connected with the abuse of alcohol could be remedied through proper legislation. The aims of the original temperance movement were largely moral, uplifting, rehabilitative. Passions grow, however, and before long those who had condemned only the excess use of distilled liquor were condemning all liquor. Those genial, well-meaning physicians, businessmen, and farmers began to organize their social life around their crusade. Fraternal orders, such as the Independent Order of Good Templars of 1850, grew and proliferated. In a short span of time it had branches all over the United States with churches, missions, and hospitals—all dedicated to the idea that society's evils were caused by liquor. This particular group influenced the growth of the Women's Christian Temperance Union (WCTU) and the Anti-Saloon League. By 1869 it had become The National Prohibition Party, the spearhead of political action, which advocated complete suppression of liquor by law.

People who had no experience at all with drinking got involved in the crusade. In 1874 Frances Willard founded the WCTU in Cleveland. Women became interested in the movement, which simultaneously advocated social reform, prayer, prevention, education, and legislation in the field of alcohol. Mass meetings were organized to which thousands came. Journals were published; children's programs taught fear and hatred of alcohol; libraries developed. The WCTU was responsible for

Temperate temperance is best. Intemperate temperance injures the cause of temperance.

MARK TWAIN

All excess is ill, but drunkenness is of the worst sort.

WILLIAM PENN

Equal Suffrage. The probable influence of Woman Suffrage upon the temperance reform can be no better indicated than by the following words of the Brewer's Congress held in Chicago in 1881:

Resolved, That we oppose always and everywhere the ballot in the hands of woman, for woman's vote is the last hope of the prohibitionists.

SPOONER, WALTER W. *The Cyclopaedia of Temperance and Prohibition,* 1891.

the first laws requiring alcohol education in the schools, some of which remain on the books. All alcohol use—moderate, light, heavy, excessive—was condemned. All users were one and the same. Bacon, in describing the classic temperance movement, says there was "one word for the action—DRINK. One word for the category of people—DRINKER."

By 1895, many smaller local groups had joined the Anti-Saloon League, which had become the most influential of the temperance groups. It was nonpartisan politically and supported any prohibitionist candidate. It pressured Congress, state legislatures, and was backed by church groups in "action against the saloon." Political pressure mounted. The major thrust of all these activities was that the only real problem was alcohol, the only real solution, prohibition.

In 1919 Congress passed the Eighteenth Amendment, making it illegal to manufacture or sell alcoholic beverages. The Volstead Act had sixty provisions to implement Prohibition. The act was messy and complicated. There was no precedent to force the public cooperation required to make the act work. From 1920 to 1933 Prohibition remained in effect. Prohibition shaped much of our economic, social, and underground life. The repeal under the Twenty-first Amendment in 1933 did not remedy the situation. While there was a decline in alcoholism under Prohibition, as indicated by a decline in deaths from cirrhosis, nonetheless, Prohibition had failed. The real problems created by alcohol were obscured or ignored by the false wet–dry controversy. The quarrel raged between the manufacturers, retailers, and consumers on one side and the temperance people, many churches, and women on the other. Alcoholics and those with alcohol problems were ignored in the furor. When Prohibition was repealed the problem of abuse was still there, and the alcoholics were still there along with the stigma of alcoholism.

Another approach to alcohol problems is that of the "ostrich." The ostrich stance became popular after the failure of Prohibition and is still not totally out of fashion. Problems are often handled with euphemisms, humor, ridicule, and delegation of responsibility, arising from conflicting values and beliefs.

Our inconsistent attitudes toward alcohol are reinforced in subtle ways. For example, consider the hard-drinking movie heroes. There's the guy who drinks and drinks and then calls for more, never gets drunk, outdrinks the bad guys, kills off the rustlers, and gets the girl in the end. Then there's Humphrey Bogart, who is a drunken mess wallowing in the suffering of humankind until the pure and beautiful heroine appears, at which point he washes up, shaves, gets a new suit, and they live happily ever after.

Drunkenness versus alcoholism

It is important to see that alcoholism is not separate from alcohol. The alcoholic does not spring full-blown from someplace in outer space. In general it is a problem that develops over time. Alcohol is available everywhere. A person really has to make a choice *not* to drink in our society. In some sets of circumstances one could drink for the better part of a day and never seem out of place at all. Some brunches have wine punch, Bloody Marys, or café brulet as their accompaniment. Sherry, beer, or a mixed drink is quite appropriate at lunchtime. Helping a friend with an afternoon painting project or even raking your own lawn is a reasonable time to have a beer. Then, after a long day, comes the predinner cocktail, maybe some wine with the meal. Later, at cards with friends, drinks are offered. And surely, some romantic candlelight and a nightcap go hand in hand. For most people this combination of events would not be their daily or even weekend fare. The point is that none of the above would cause most people to raise an eyebrow. The accepted times for drinking can be all the time, anywhere. Given enough of the kind of days we described, the person who chooses to drink may develop problems. Alcohol is a drug and does have effects on the body.

Is alcoholism a purely modern phenomenon, a product of our times? There are no references to alcoholics as such in historical writing. The word itself is a modern one. But there are vague references as far back in time as the third century that distinguish between being merely intoxicated and being a drunkard. In a commentary on imperial law, a Roman jurist of that era suggests that inveterate drunkenness be considered a medical matter rather than a legal one. In the thirteenth century, James I of Aragon issued an edict providing for hospitalization of conspicuously active drunks. In 1655 a man named Younge, an English journalist, wrote a pamphlet in which he seemed to discern the difference between one who drinks and one who has a chronic condition related to alcohol. He says, "He that will be drawn to drink when he hath neither need of it nor mind to it is a drunkard."

History of alcohol treatment efforts

The first serious considerations of the problem of inebriety, as it was called, came in the eighteenth and nineteenth centuries.

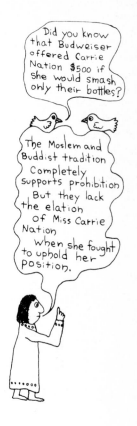

Did you know that Budweiser offered Carrie Nation $500 if she would smash only their bottles?

The Moslem and Buddist tradition completely supports prohibition But they lack the elation of Miss Carrie Nation when she fought to uphold her position.

The front door of the Boston Licensing Board was ripped down by the crush to get beer licenses the day Prohibition ended.

Two famous writings addressed the problem in what seemed to be a new light. Although their work on the physical aspects of alcohol became fodder for the temperance zealots, both Dr. Benjamin Rush and Dr. Thomas Trotter seriously considered the effects of alcohol in a scientific way. Rush, a signer of the Declaration of Independence and a surgeon general of the Army, wrote a lengthy treatise with an equally lengthy title, *"An Inquiry into the Effects of Ardent Spirits on the Human Body and Mind, with an Account of the Means of Preventing and the Remedies of Curing Them."* Rush's book is a compendium of the attitudes of the time, given weight by scholarly treatment. The more important of the two, and the first scientific formulation of drunkenness on record, is the classic work of Trotter, an Edinburgh physician. In 1804 he wrote "An Essay, Medical, Philosophical, and Chemical, on Drunkenness and Its Effects on the Human Body." He states: "In the writings of medicine, we find drunkenness only cursorily mentioned among the powers that injure health....The priesthood hath poured forth its anathemas from the pulpit; and the moralist, no less severe, hath declaimed against it as a vice degrading to our nature." He then gets down to the heart of the matter: "In medical language, I consider drunkenness, strictly speaking, to be a disease, produced by a remote cause, and giving birth to actions and movements in the living body that disorder the functions of health."

Trotter did not gain many adherents to his position, but small efforts were also being made in the United States at the time. Around the 1830s, in Massachusetts, Connecticut, and New York, small groups were forming to reform "intemperate persons" by hospitalizing them, instead of sending them to jail or the workhouse. The new groups, started by the medical superintendent of Worcester, Massachusetts, Dr. Samuel Woodward, and a Dr. Eli Todd, did not see inebriates in the same class with criminals, the indigent, or the insane. Between 1841 and 1874 eleven nonprofit hospitals and houses were set up. In 1876 the *Journal of Inebriety* started publication to advance their views and findings. These efforts were taking place against the background of the temperance movement. Naturally, there was tremendous popular opposition from both the church and the legislative halls. The *Journal* was not prestigious by the standards of the medical journals of that time, and before Prohibition the hospitals were closed and the *Journal* had folded.

Another group also briefly flourished. The Washington Temperance Society began in Chase's Tavern in Baltimore in 1840.

Six drinking buddies were the founders, and they each agreed to bring a friend to the next meeting. In a few months parades and public meetings were being held to spread the message: "Drunkard! Come up here! You can reform. We don't slight the drunkard. We love him!" At the peak of its success in 1844, the membership consisted of 100,000 "reformed common drunkards" and 300,000 "common tipplers." A women's auxiliary group, the Martha Washington Society, was dedicated to feeding and clothing the poor. Based on the promise of religious salvation, the Washington Temperance Society was organized in much the same way as the ordinary temperance groups, but with one difference. It was founded on the basis of one drunkard helping another, of drunks telling their story in public. The society prospered all over the East Coast as far north as New Hampshire. A hospital, the Home for the Fallen, was established in Boston and still exists under a different name. There are many similarities between the Washington Society and Alcoholics Anonymous (AA): alcoholics helping each other, regular meetings, sharing experiences, fellowship, reliance on a Higher Power, and total abstention from alcohol. The society was, however, caught up in the frenzies of the total temperance movement: the controversies, power struggles, religious fights, and ego trips of the leaders. By 1848, 8 short years after its founding, it was absorbed into the total prohibition movement. The treatment of the alcoholic became unimportant in the heat of the argument.

Recognition of the alcoholic as a sick person did not reemerge until comparatively recently. The gathering of a group of scientists at Yale's Laboratory of Applied Psychology (later the Laboratory of Applied Biodynamics) and the Fellowship of Alcoholics Anonymous, both begun in the 1930s, were instrumental in bringing this about. Also in the 1930s a recovered Bostonian alcoholic, Richard Peabody, first began to apply psychological methods to the cure of alcoholics. He replaced the terms "drunk" and "drunkenness" with the more scientific and less judgmental "alcoholic" and "alcoholism." At Yale, Yandell Henderson, Howard Haggard, Leon Greenberg, and later E. M. Jellinek founded the *Quarterly Journal of Studies on Alcohol (QJSA)*— since 1975 known as the *Journal of Studies on Alcohol.* Unlike the earlier *Journal of Inebriety,* the QJSA had a sound scientific footing and became the mouthpiece for alcohol information. Starting with Haggard's work on alcohol metabolism, these efforts marked the first attempt to put the study of alcohol and alcohol problems in a respectable up-to-date framework. Jellinek's masterwork, *The*

PORTRAIT OF A MAN WHO SWears He will never Have another drink

Wine is a bad thing.
It makes you quarrel with your neighbor.
It makes you shoot at your landlord,
It makes you—miss him.

Disease Concept of Alcoholism, was a product of the Yale experience. The Yale Center of Alcohol Studies and the Classified Abstract Archive of Alcohol Literature were established. The Yale Plan Clinic was also set up to diagnose and treat alcoholism. The Yale Summer School of Alcohol Studies, now the Rutgers School, educated professionals and laypeople from all walks of life. Yale's prestigious influence had far-reaching effects. The National Council on Alcoholism (NCA), a volunteer organization, also grew out of the Yale School. It was founded in 1944 by the joint efforts of Jellinek and Marty Mann, a recovered alcoholic and the NCA's first president, to provide public information and education about alcohol.

On the other side of the coin, Alcoholics Anonymous was having more success in treating alcoholics than any other group. AA grew, and in 1983 it estimated a membership of 1 million in both America and abroad. Its members became influential in removing the stigma that had been so long attached to the alcoholic. Lawyers, businesspeople, teachers, people from every sector of society began to recover. They could be seen leading useful, normal lives without alcohol. (More will be said later on the origins and program of AA itself.) The successful recoveries of its members have unquestionably influenced the course of recent developments.

New attitudes

The new attitudes toward alcoholism have become the foundation for public policy. Since 1960 alcoholism has been gaining recognition by the federal government as a major public health problem. At the center of the federal efforts is the National Institute of Alcohol Abuse and Alcoholism (NIAAA), established in 1971. The NIAAA sponsors research, training, public education, and treatment programs. The legislation creating NIAAA is a landmark in the history of society's responses to alcoholism. This bill, the Comprehensive Alcohol Abuse and Alcoholism Prevention, Treatment, and Rehabilitation Act of 1970, is known as the Hughes Act. Its sponsor was former Senator Harold Hughes, himself a recovering alcoholic. Beyond creating the NIAAA, it established what might be called a bill of rights for alcoholic individuals. It recognizes that they suffer from a "disease that requires treatment"; it provides protection against discrimination in hiring recovering alcoholics. In a similar vein, the Uniform Alcoholism and Intoxication Treatment Act, dealing with public intoxication, was recommended for enactment by the states. This act mandates treatment rather than punishment. These acts incorporate the new attitudes emerging toward alcoholics and alcohol abuse: it is a problem; it is treatable.

On the heels of this, there was a rapid increase during the 1970s in alcoholism treatment services, both public and private, both residential and outpatient. In addition, each state mandated alcohol (and drug abuse) services that focused on public information and education as well as treatment. Similarly, community mental health centers that received federal support were required to provide alcohol services. Though far from being totally transformed, health insurance coverage began to include rather than exclude alcoholism treatment services for its subscribers.

With this increase in alcohol services, there has emerged a new profession, the *alcohol counselor*. This group of professionals has formed the backbone of alcohol treatment. And too, alcohol education for all helping professionals is far more common, with a proliferation of workshops, special conferences, and courses. With the emergence of alcohol treatment as a new health care field, there have been efforts to develop standards for the treatment personnel and alcohol treatment agencies. In many states, alcohol counselors' associations have been formed. In some instances these groups certify alcohol counselors; in others, state licensure boards have been established. The concern with credentialing of alcoholism counselors began in the mid-'70s. Interestingly, a decade later, physicians in the field of substance abuse are beginning to look at the same questions. What qualifications should a physician have to work in the field? Is personal experience, the route by which many physicians initially entered, still sufficient? Tentative steps are being taken to consider establishing examinations or possibly a certification process similar to other medical specialties. These efforts have resulted from, and contributed to, our society's response to alcoholism as a major public health problem.

The attention that has been directed toward alcoholism over the past 15 years is just now broadening to the larger issue of alcohol problems and even alcohol use. Previously, the public's attitude could have been summarized as "the only *real* alcohol problem is alcoholism and that wouldn't happen to me." Now alcohol problems don't seem to be viewed as far removed from the average person. Drunken driving has captured public attention. This alcohol-related problem can potentially touch anyone. It has led to heated discussions as to the proper penalties/approaches to

those who receive DWIs, to responsibilities of hosts, to setting the legal drinking age. Citizen groups such as Mothers Against Drunk Driving (MADD) have to be given a large measure of credit for this. Furthermore, the concern about driving while intoxicated seems to have spilled over to attention to intoxication in general. It appears that intoxication is less acceptable and as likely to elicit disgust as to be considered funny or amusing. Other alcohol-related issues are beginning to hit the public policy agenda. Questions have been raised in some quarters about the advertisement of alcohol and how alcohol use is portrayed in the media. Some have called for the labeling of contents of alcoholic beverages, as is required for other foodstuffs or household products. There are also those lobbying for warning labels to be required on alcoholic beverages.

Alcohol use in relation to health and fitness is receiving greater attention. An ironic twist is the fact that the alcohol manufacturers are spending undisclosed amounts of the 1 billion plus dollar advertising budgets to sell lower alcohol content beverages! Alongside "lite" and near beers and wine coolers, there has been a dramatic growth in sales of sparkling waters and non-alcoholics wines and beers. Whether all this reflects a trend or a passing fad remains to be seen.

But it does appear that significant changes are underway in respect to our views on alcohol's problems and what constitutes appropriate alcohol use. A book published in late 1985, *How to control your social drinking*, is to our knowledge a first. It starts off by noting that it is not intended for alcoholics, for whom controlled drinking is not possible, but it is directed to the social drinker, who, in our drinking society, may find that it is easy to drink more than is intended. Basically it is a compilation of tips from hosts, party-goers, and top-level business executives on techniques to keep consumption down and the benefits of moderation. Its significance is not that it contains any startling new information, but that it was published, and presumably seen as a topic of sufficient general interest to generate book sales.

Another window on public attitudes is the way in which alcohol use is portrayed in the media, especially television programming. Within the past year, several network feature films aired in prime time with alcoholics as major characters. And on the soap operas, not only are several of the major characters alcoholics, some are recovering. Over all, from the soaps to cop shows, drinking behavior is portrayed less glamorously and far less frequently than in the past.

There were roughly 100 beer cans per man, woman, and child manufactured in the United States in 1972.

ALCOHOL COSTS: PAYING THE PIPER

In the United States, statistics on who drinks—what, where, and when—have been kept since 1850. However, making comparisons between different historical periods is difficult. One reason is that statistics have only been gathered methodically and impartially since 1950. Another reason is that there have been changes in the way the basic information is organized and reported. A century ago, reports included numbers of "inebriates" or "drunkards." In the 1940s through the 1960s, "alcoholics" were often a designated subgroup. Then came the 1970s and another change. "Heavy drinkers" or "heavy drinkers with a high problem index"(!) began to replace "alcoholics" as a category in reporting statistical information. Most recently, alcohol dependence syndrome has emerged as another category. So the task of identifying changes in drinking practices is not an easy one.

Who drinks what, when, and where

Nonetheless, out of the maze of statistics available on how much Americans drink, where they drink it, and with what consequences, some are important to note. It is estimated that over three fourths, or 77%, of men and 60% of women drink alcohol. They comprise 67% of the adult population. Per capita consumption during the 1960s rose 32%. In the 1970s, despite some ups and downs, consumption basically leveled off. However, since 1978, consumption has dropped by 5%. Whether this represents the beginning of a true downward trend or is just another momentary blip will become evident in several years. In 1984 the statistically average American consumed the equivalent of 2.69 gallons of pure ethanol. The average American drinks 2.34 gallons of liquor, 2.77 gallons of wine, and 30.4 gallons of beer. Because the alcohol content of each varies in terms of absolute alcohol, 36% of the alcohol comes from liquor, 14% from wine, and 50% from beer. Not only has there been a decline in total alcohol consumed, there has also been a shift in beverage preference. Since 1978, there has been a drop of about 10% in liquor consumption, with beer and wine becoming more popular.

How does alcohol use in the United States compare to that of other countries? In 1967, the United States had the second highest rate of alcoholism in the world: France was then ranked first. (More recent figures are not available for comparison, because "alcoholics" have given way to "problem drinkers.") Among industrial countries, the United States then ranked eighth in per

A Tale of 10 beers

3 drink nobe

5 Share 2

1 drinks 2

1 drinks 6

capita consumption for all categories of alcohol but was second in distilled spirits. Ten years later (1976) the U.S. position had dropped from eighth to fifteenth in a group of twenty-six industrial countries in total alcohol consumption, although it fell to only third for distilled spirits. That change did not reflect a decline in U. S. drinking but represented a more rapid increase in other countries. More recent figures are not available.

A word of caution: all of the above figures describe the statistically average American. However, it is important to realize that the average American is a myth. The typical American does not in fact drink his or her "statistical quota." First of all, recall that approximately one third do not use alcohol at all. Moreover, for the remaining two thirds there is wide variation in alcohol use. Thus 70% of the drinking population consumes only 20% of all the alcohol. The remaining 30% of the drinkers consumes 80% of the alcohol. Most significantly, one third of that heavy-drinking 30%, or less than 7% of the total population, consumes 50% of all alcohol. Picture what that means. Imagine having ten beers to serve to a group of ten people. If you served these to represent the actual consumption pattern described, you'd have the following. Three people would sit there empty handed. Five people would share two beers. That leaves two people to divide up eight beers. Of those two people, one person would take two and the other person would get a whole six-pack!

It is estimated that 10% of the total adult population are problem drinkers (This percentage is derived not from consumption figures but independently determined by the presence of problems attendent to alcohol use. The similarity though between proportion of very heavy drinkers and problem drinkers is striking!). Using 1985 census figures, and applying the usual proportions, 17.6 million persons, age 18 and over, are problem drinkers. It is also estimated that 1 out of 5 adolescents in the 14- to 17-year age range have a serious drinking problem; that is, 2.8 million teenagers. Thus in the United States an estimated 20.4 million people have drinking problems. For every person with an alcohol problem, it is estimated that four family members are directly affected. Thus approximately 81.6 million family members are touched by alcohol problems.

Over the past couple of decades, national public opinion polls have included questions about alcohol problems. An ever-increasing number of those interviewed have indicated an alcohol problem in their immediate family. In 1972, the figure was less than 1 out of every 10 people (12%). In 1978, 1 person in 4 (24%)

said that an alcohol problem had adversely affected his or her family life. In 1983, that figure rose to 1 out of every 3. And 1 year later in 1984, the figure reported by a Harris poll was that 38% of all households reported being beset by alcohol problems. Note that these figures do not distinguish among alcoholics and those who are nonalcoholic but abuse alcohol. These nonalcoholic problem drinkers might include the one-time drunken traffic offender who appears in court; or the person who, when drunk for the one and only time in his life, puts his foot through a window and ends up in a hospital emergency room. But we suspect that when reporting "troubles" people are not referring to those who miss work after a particularly festive New Year's Eve.

In the alcoholic population itself only 5% are on skid row. At least 95% of problem drinkers are employed or employable; they are estimated to make up 10% of the nation's work force. Most of them are living with their families. The vast majority live in respectable neighborhoods, are housewives, bankers, physicians, salespeople, farmers, teachers, clergy, and so forth. They try to raise decent children, go to football games, shop for their groceries, go to work, and rake the leaves. The Northeast, the Middle Atlantic, and the Pacific Coast states have the highest percentages of problem drinkers. They are predominantly males. However, the proportion of women with drinking problems is on the rise.

Economic costs

Although they are only a small portion of the drinking population, in combination alcohol abusers and alcoholics cost the United States a huge amount of time and money each year. Below is a breakdown of the economic costs of alcohol misuse and alcoholism for 1980. Though published in 1985, they report on 1980 data.

As an aside, typically, national statistics rely heavily upon the most recent census. Even when statistics are for a date after the census, they often are estimates derived from the most recent census. Though the census is conducted every 10 years, the quantity of information collected is such that it may take several years to analyze. When dealing with national counts of anything, from number of licensed drivers to the quantity of alcohol sold, gathering the necessary information from the various sources takes time. So always, the data available is an estimate. The most accurate figures will always be those for several years previous.

Costs of alcohol and alcoholism

	Billions of dollars
Direct	$17.9
Treatment	10.5
Crime	2.3
Motor-vehicle crashes (property damage, police and court costs)	2.2
Other (fire losses, highway safety, special education)	2.9
Indirect	71.7
Reduced productivity	54.7
Premature death	14.5
Incarceration	1.8
Motor-vehicle crashes	.5
Victims of crime (e.g., lost productivity)	.2
TOTAL	$89.6

How could you spend our grocery money on liquor again? How?

I'm economizing. Groceries are 42% more expensive and liquor is only up 12%.

The projected costs for 1983, based on the above data were $116.7 billion. Both the 1980 and 1983 totals represent a dramatic rise over the figure reported for 1977, which was $49.9 billion. The authors of the government-commissioned report point out that the major increase was due to inflation (38%) and a new formula for determining the effects of alcohol abuse in the workplace (47%); the rest of the change is attributable to the inclusion for the first time of the costs associated with fetal alcohol syndrome (8%), growth of the population (3%), and the remaining amount (4%) consisted of other minor changes.

The other side of the cost coin is economic revenues. The total tax revenues on alcohol raised by federal and state authorities amounts to approximately $12 billion. In 1985, the federal tax rates on distilled spirits saw their first increase since 1951. The tax on liquor was raised 20%. Nonetheless, alcohol, especially distilled spirits, is a true bargain. A report by a panel of the NRC observes that since 1967, because inflation has outstripped any federal and state tax increases, the real price of distilled spirits has been cut by nearly half. The real costs of beer dropped 20%, and the cost of wine dropped by almost 25%. Alcoholic beverages have become so inexpensive that their prices are now within the range of many nonalcoholic beverages. Whereas the costs of soda have tripled in that period, the costs of alcoholic beverages were not quite doubled, so both are now in the same price range.

The net effect of all this is that the typical American can drink more but spend less of the total family income to do it.

Personal costs

The personal cost of alcoholism is tremendous. In 1984, it was estimated that alcohol-related deaths may run as high as 10% of all deaths each year. The alcoholic's life expectancy is shortened by 15 years. Their mortality rate is two and a half times greater than that of nonalcoholics. They have a higher rate of violent deaths. Alcohol use figures prominently in accidental death and violent death for alcoholics and nonalcoholics.

Alcohol is the significant factor in motor-vehicle fatalities. Although on a bright note, the number of fatalities involving alcohol is on the decline. Between 1980 and 1984, there was a drop from 50% to 43%, which represents a 14% decline. Similarly, there has been a decline in deaths from cirrhosis. In fatal accidents involving pedestrians, 45% of those pedestrians had blood alcohol levels of 0.10%, the usual legal standard for intoxication. In fire-related deaths, alcohol is involved in a minimum of 50% of all cases. Alcohol is believed to be involved in approximately 50% of home accidents and about 70% of all drownings.

Alcohol plays a significant role in suicide. Studies indicate that in 4 out of 5 suicide attempts, the individual had been drinking, and that 35%–40% of all successful suicides are of non-alcoholics but alcohol related. Half of all successful suicides are alcoholics.

Alcohol use is a significant factor in cases of homicide and family violence. In as many as 67% of all homicides either the victim or the assailant, or both, had been drinking. Similarly,

I agree that raising the drinking age to 20 would cut down on motor vehicle fatalities but I think we could practically eliminate them if we raised the drinking age to 47.

How old is he?

48

drinking is seen as a precipitating factor in child abuse, wife beatings, and other family disruptions. Though the data on family violence remains limited, estimates of the role of intoxication vary from 30% to over 70%, depending on the particular population studied. A 1980 report of the Institute of Medicine, citing a figure at the higher range, indicated that in two thirds of incidents of family violence, alcohol was significantly implicated.

Crime and alcohol

Alcohol is also reflected in the national crime statistics. As noted already, drinking is implicated in over half of all homicides, and figures prominently in family violence. It is a significant factor in assaults in general, for 72% of the perpetrators and 79% of the victims alcohol was seen as playing a role. In attempted and completed rapes, alcohol again was involved: for 50% of the rapists and for 30% of the victims alcohol was a prominent feature. In cases of robbery, up to 22% of the offenders had been drinking. The current estimate of the total national bill for alcohol-related crimes and misdemeanors is $3 billion.

Health care and alcohol

Alcohol has an impact on the health care systems as well. Studies have consistently shown that a *minimum* of 20% of all hospitalized persons have a significant alcohol problem, whatever the presenting problem or admitting diagnosis. That is an absolute minimum. A recent study indicated that the figure is more likely to be one third of all hospitalized persons. For the Veterans Administration, estimates are higher— 50% of all VA hospital beds are filled by veterans with alcohol problems.

In terms of health care costs, alcohol figures prominently in our nation's annual medical bills to the tune of $14.9 billion. That $14.9 billion is equivalent to 12% of all adults' health expenditures. However, it appears that some people incur a disproportionate share of the costs. One large-scale study of hospital costs found that a small proportion of patients, only 13%, had hospital bills equal to the remaining 87%. The distinguishing characteristic of the high-cost group was not age, or sex, or economic status, or ethnicity. It was that those people were heavy drinkers and/or heavy smokers. Furthermore, a follow-up study found that high-cost users also had multiple hospitalizations. Those patients with a history of alcoholism had significantly more repeated hospitalizations than those without a history of alcoholism.

It is very unfortunate and ironic that of these health care costs, only a small proportion—13%— represents expenditures for rehabilitation or treatment of the primary alcohol problem. The bulk of the costs are for treatment of alcohol-induced illness and trauma. Equally disturbing is that the NIAAA estimates that approximately 85% of the nation's alcoholics and problem drinkers are not receiving any formal treatment. Even if one were to factor in the members of AA, who enter without involvement in formal treatment (i.e., approximately two thirds of the 1 million members of AA), that only reduces the "untreated" portion by another 5%!

Another recently recognized health care cost is that which accompanies fetal alcohol syndrome (FAS) and fetal alcohol effects (FAE). It is estimated that the current annual costs of treatment and the special education, training, and support services required add another $2.4 billion to the costs for our nation's health care. These infants grow to become children and eventually adults who will continue to require care.

If one considers the federal dollars spent on health research, alcohol is a health concern that is getting short shrift. For example, if one looks at the costs, both direct and indirect, associated with alcohol and heart disease, they are very similar—43 to 46 billion dollars, respectively. However, in terms of federal expenditures for research, 15 times more is spent on research on heart disease than alcoholism and alcohol abuse. And the amount spent on cancer research is 35 times greater, although the associated costs are only three quarters of those associated with alcohol abuse and alcoholism.

When it comes to health insurance, alcohol treatment and rehabilitation do not fare very well. Despite numerous studies that demonstrate that treating alcoholism is cost effective, and that any treatment is better than no treatment, alcoholism remains the only common major disease not routinely covered by health insurance. In 1982, 20 states had mandatory coverage of alcoholism for insurance sold in that state, 15 required alcoholism coverage as an option; and 15 had no requirements.

· · ·

Surveys of American attitudes toward alcohol use and alcohol problems have consistently indicated a growing public awareness of the dimensions of the problems related to alcohol use, an ever broadening acceptance of the view that alcoholism is a disease and belief that it should be treated as any other medical illness.

There is more awareness of the toll that alcoholism and alcohol abuse can take in our public and private lives. What people will individually and collectively do with this knowledge is the question. Statistics in future years will reflect the answer.

RESOURCES AND FURTHER READING

History and overview

Alcoholics Anonymous comes of age. New York: AA World Service, 1955.

Bacon, S.: The classical temperance movement in the U.S.A. *Br J Addict* 62:5-18, 1967.

Chafetz, M.: *Liquor, the servant of man.* Boston: Little, Brown & Co., 1965.

D.P. The Washingtonians. *AA Grapevine* 27(9):16-22, 1971.

Lender, M.E., and Kamchanappe, K.R.: Temperance tales; antiliquor fiction and American attitudes toward alcoholics in the late 19th and early 20th centuries. *J Stud Alcohol* 38(7):1347-1370, 1979.

Pittman, D.J., and Snyder, C.R. (Eds.): *Society, culture, and drinking patterns.* New York: John Wiley & Sons, 1962.

Rorabaugh, W.: *The alcohol republic: an American tradition.* New York: Oxford University Press, 1979.

Why people drink

Horton, D.: Primitive societies. In R. McCarthy (Ed.), *Drinking and intoxication.* New Haven, CT: College & University Press, 1959.

MacAndrew, C., and Edgerton, R.: *Drunken comportment.* Chicago: Aldine Publishing Co., 1969.

McClelland, D., et al: *The drinking man.* New York: The Free Press, 1972.

Weil, A.: Man's innate need: getting high. In *Dealing with drug abuse.* Ford Foundation Report, 1972.

Social costs

Fein, R.: *Alcohol in America: the price we pay.* Newport Beach, CA: Care Institute, 1984.

NIAAA, Department of Health, Education and Welfare: *1st special report to U.S. Congress on alcohol and health.* Washington, DC: U.S. Government Printing Office, 1971.

NIAAA, Department of Health, Education and Welfare: *2nd special report to U.S. Congress on alcohol and health, new knowledge.* Washington, DC: U.S. Government Printing Office, 1974.

NIAAA, Department of Health, Education and Welfare: *3rd special report to U.S. Congress on alcohol and health.* Washington, DC: U.S. Government Printing Office, 1978.

NIAAA, Department of Health and Human Services: *4th special report to Congress on alcohol and health.* Washington, DC: U.S. Government Printing Office, 1981.

NIAAA, Department of Health and Human Services: *5th special report to the U.S. Congress on alcohol and health.* Washington, DC: U.S. Government Printing Office, 1983.

Olson, S., and Gerstein, S.: *Alcohol in America: taking action to prevent abuse.* Washington, DC: National Academy Press, 1985.

Podolsky, D.M.: RTI report: economic costs of alcohol abuse and alcoholism. *Alcohol Health and Research World* 9(2):34-35, 1984/1985.

West, L.J. (Ed.): *Alcoholism and related problems.* Englewood Cliffs, NJ: Prentice-Hall, 1984.

Alcohol and the body

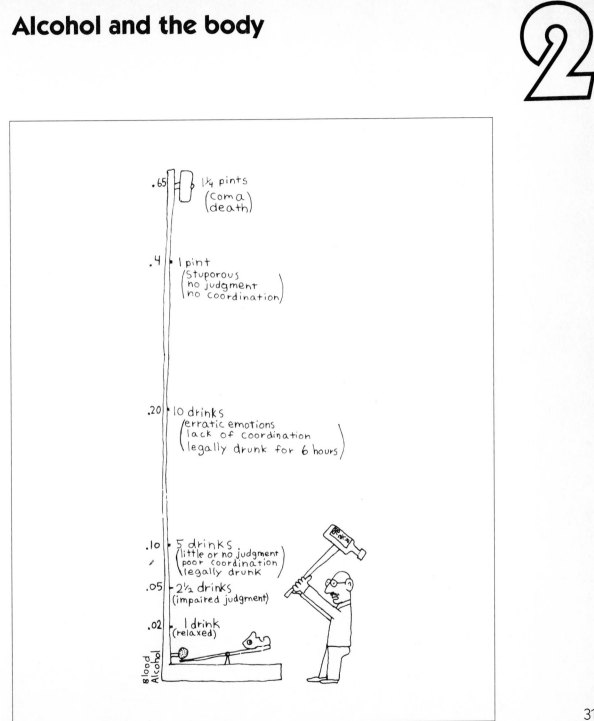

.65 — 1¼ pints
(coma
(death)

.4 — 1 pint
(stuporous
(no judgment
(no coordination)

.20 — 10 drinks
(erratic emotions
(lack of coordination
(legally drunk for 6 hours)

.10 — 5 drinks
(little or no judgment)
poor coordination
legally drunk

.05 — 2½ drinks
(impaired judgment)

.02 — 1 drink
(relaxed)

Blood Alcohol

✓✓ Alcohol is a drug. When it is ingested, there are specific and predictable physiological effects on the body. Any body. Every body. Alcoholic and nonalcoholic. This is all too often overlooked. Instead, attention is paid to the physical impact of chronic use or what happens with excessive use. What gets lost are the normal, routine effects on *anyone* who uses alcohol. Let us examine what happens to alcohol in the body, how it is taken up, broken down, and thereby alters the normal functions of the body.

DIGESTION

	Calories
Beer, 12-oz. can	173
Martini, 3 oz., 3:1	145
Olive, 1 large	20
Rum, 1 oz.	73
Sherry, sweet, 3 oz.	150
Fortified wines	120–160
Scotch, 1 oz.	73
Cola, 8 oz.	105
Pretzels, 5 small sticks	20

THE JOY OF COOKING

The human body is well engineered to take the foods ingested and change them into substances the organism needs to maintain life and to provide energy. Despite occasional upsets from too much spice or too much food, this process goes on without a hitch. The first part of this transformation is called digestion. A comparison might be made to the carpenter who dismantles an old building, salvages the materials, and later uses them in new construction. Digestion is the body's way of dismantling food to get the raw materials required by the body. Whether alcohol can be properly called a food was at one time a big point of controversy. Alcohol does have calories. One ounce of pure alcohol contains 210 calories. To translate that into drinks, there are 75 calories in an ounce of whiskey or 150 calories in a 12-ounce can of beer. Alcohol's usefulness as a food is limited, however. Sometimes alcohol is described as providing "empty calories." It does not contain vitamins, minerals, or other essential nutrients. Also when alcohol is present, it can interfere with the body's ability to use other sources of energy. As a food, alcohol is unique. It requires no digestion. Since alcohol is a liquid, no mechanical action by the teeth is required to break it down. No digestive juices need be added to transform it into a form that can be absorbed by the bloodstream and transported to all parts of the body.

ABSORPTION

So what happens to alcohol in the body? Surprisingly, absorption of alcohol begins almost immediately, with a very small amount being taken up into the bloodstream through the tiny capillaries in the mouth. But the majority goes the route of all food when swallowed: into the stomach. If other food is present in the stomach, the alcohol mixes with it. Here, too, some alcohol seeps into the bloodstream. Up to 20% can be absorbed directly from the stomach. The remainder passes into the small intestine to be absorbed. The amount of food in the stomach when drinking takes place has important ramifications. Alcohol is an irritant. It increases the flow of hydrochloric acid, a digestive juice secreted by cells of the stomach lining. Anyone who has an ulcer and takes a drink can readily confirm this. This phenomenon also explains the feeling of warmth in the tummy as the drink goes down. The presence of food acts to dilute the alcohol and therefore diminishes the irritant properties.

The amount of food in the stomach is a big factor in determining the speed with which the alcohol is absorbed by the bloodstream. The presence of food slows absorption. How quickly alcohol is absorbed depends on the total amount and the relative proportion of alcohol in the stomach contents. The significance of the rate of absorption is that it is largely responsible for the feelings of intoxication—thus, the basis for the advice to avoid drinking on an empty stomach. In addition to the impact of food in the stomach, the rate of absorption varies with the type of beverage. The higher the concentration of alcohol in a beverage (up to 50%, or 100 proof), the more quickly it is absorbed. This partially explains why distilled spirits have more apparent "kick" than wine or beer. In addition, beer contains some food substances that slow absorption. Carbon dioxide, which hastens the passage of alcohol from the stomach, has the effect of increasing the speed of absorption. Champagne, sparkling wines, or drinks mixed with carbonated soda give a sense of "bubbles in the head."

Meanwhile, on from the stomach to the pyloric valve. This valve controls the passage of the stomach's contents into the small intestine. It is sensitive to the presence of alcohol. With large concentrations of alcohol, it tends to get "stuck" in the closed position. When this pylorospasm happens, the alcohol trapped in the stomach may cause sufficient irritation and distress to induce vomiting. This phenomenon accounts for the nausea and vomiting that may accompany too much drinking. This "stuck" pylorus also may serve as a self-protective mechanism by preventing the passage into the small intestine of what might otherwise be life-threatening doses of alcohol.

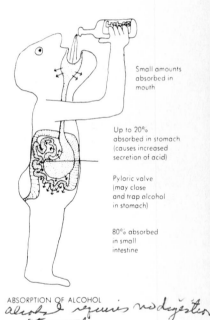

Small amounts absorbed in mouth

Up to 20% absorbed in stomach (causes increased secretion of acid)

Pyloric valve (may close and trap alcohol in stomach)

80% absorbed in small intestine

ABSORPTION OF ALCOHOL

BLOOD ALCOHOL CONCENTRATION

In considering the effects of alcohol, several questions come to mind. How much alcohol in how much person? How fast did the alcohol get there? Is the blood alcohol level rising or declining? Let us consider each of these in turn. The concentration of alcohol in the blood is our first concern. One tablespoon of sugar mixed in a cup of water yields a much sweeter solution than a tablespoon diluted in a gallon of water. Similarly, a drink with 1 ounce of alcohol will give a higher blood alcohol level in a 100-pound woman than in a 200-pound man. In fact, it will be virtually twice as high. Her body contains less water than his.

The second factor is rate of absorption, which depends on the amount and concentration of alcohol in the stomach and how rapidly it is ingested. So quickly drink a scotch on the rocks on an empty stomach, and you will probably be more giddy than if you drink more alcohol more slowly, say in the form of beer after a meal. Even with a given blood alcohol level, there is greater impairment the faster the level has been achieved. Impairment is based on both the amount absorbed and the rate of absorption. Finally, for any drinking occasion, there are different effects for a particular blood alcohol level, depending on whether the blood alcohol level is going up or coming down.

Once in the small intestine, the remainder of the alcohol (at least 80%) is very rapidly absorbed into the bloodstream. The bloodstream is the body's transportation system. It delivers nutrients the cells require for energy and picks up the wastes produced by cell metabolism. By this route, too, alcohol is carried to all parts of the body.

Although blood alcohol levels are almost universally used as the measure of alcohol in the body, this is not to imply that alcohol merely rides around in the bloodstream until the liver is able to break it down. Alcohol is both highly soluble in water and able to pass rapidly through cell walls. Therefore, it is distributed uniformly throughout the water content of all body tissues and cells. For a given blood alcohol level, the alcohol content in the tissues and cells varies in proportion to their amount of water. The alcohol content of liver tissue is 64% of that in the blood; of muscle, 84%; and that of the brain, 75%. It takes very little time for the tissues to absorb the alcohol circulating in the blood. For example, within 2 minutes, brain tissues reflect accurately the blood alcohol level.

Now that we have explained how alcohol is taken up by the body and distributed to the body tissues, what are the effects, and how is it broken down and removed?

BREAKDOWN AND REMOVAL

The removal of alcohol from the body begins as soon as the alcohol is absorbed by the bloodstream. Small amounts leave unmetabolized through sweat, urine, or the breath. The proportion of alcohol in exhaled air has a constant and predictable relationship to the blood alcohol concentration. This is the basis for the use of breathalyzers. At most, elimination by these routes accounts for only 5% of the alcohol consumed. The rest has to be changed chemically, metabolized.

The first step in the metabolism of alcohol is its change to acetaldehyde. A liver enzyme, alcohol dehydrogenase (ADH), accomplishes this. The acetaldehyde that is formed is then acted on by another liver enzyme, acetaldehyde hydrogenase. Then, very rapidly the acetaldehyde is metabolized into acetic acid. The acetic acid then leaves the liver and is dispersed throughout the body, where it is oxidized in cells and tissues to carbon dioxide and water. In summary, the chain of events is as follows:

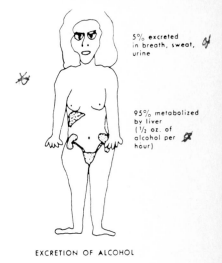

5% excreted in breath, sweat, urine

95% metabolized by liver (1/2 oz. of alcohol per hour)

EXCRETION OF ALCOHOL

alcohol → acetaldehyde* → acetic acid → carbon dioxide + water

As you can see, the liver occupies the key position in this process. Almost any cell or organ can break down the acetic acid, but only the liver can handle the first steps. The rate is set by the availability of a key substance (NAD^+), which is essential for the enzyme ADH to act. (When alcohol is oxidized to acetaldehyde, this cofactor NAD^+ is converted to NADH. As this happens the ratio, or proportion, of NADH to NAD^+ increases. The change in the relative amounts of these two substances has a number of important biochemical ramifications, which are discussed in Chapter 5.) Generally the rate at which food is metabolized depends on the energy requirements of the body. Experience will confirm this, especially for anyone who has taken a stab at dieting. Chopping wood burns up more calories than watching the

A drunken night makes a cloudy morning.
SIR WILLIAM CORNWALLIS

---

*It is at this point disulfiram (Antabuse), a drug used in alcoholism treatment, acts. Antabuse stops the breakdown of acetaldehyde by blocking acetaldehyde dehydrogenase. Thus acetaldehyde starts to accumulate in the system. It is very toxic, and its effects are those associated with an Antabuse reaction. A better term would be an acetaldehyde reaction. The toxicity of acetaldehyde usually isn't a problem. It breaks down faster than it was formed. But Antabuse does not allow this to take place so rapidly—thus the nausea, flushing, and heart palpitations. It has been observed that Orientals often have such symptoms when drinking. These are probably based on biochemical differences resulting from genetic differences. In effect, they have a kind of built-in Antabuse-like response.

tube. Too much food, and a storehouse of fat begins to accumulate around the middle. By balancing calories taken in our meals with exercise, we can avoid accumulating a fat roll. Again, as a food, alcohol is unique. It is metabolized at a constant rate. The liver does not have a "piece-rate" work-set when it comes to alcohol. The presence of large amounts does not prompt the liver to work faster. Despite alcohol's seeming potential as a fine source of calories, increased exercise (and hence raising the body's need for calories) does not increase the speed of metabolism. This is probably not news to anyone who has tried to sober up a drunk. It is simply a matter of time. Exercise may only mean you have a wide-awake drunk, rather than a sleeping one, to contend with. But he's still drunk. The rate at which alcohol is metabolized by the liver may vary a little between people. It will also increase somewhat after an extended drinking career. Yet the average rate is around 0.5 ounce of pure alcohol per hour. That is roughly equivalent to one mixed drink of 86-proof whiskey or one 12-ounce can of beer. The unmetabolized alcohol remains circulating in the bloodstream, "waiting in line." The presence of alcohol in the blood, and hence the brain, is responsible for its intoxicating effects.

ALCOHOL'S ACUTE EFFECTS ON THE BODY

What is the immediate effect of alcohol on the various body organs and functions?

Digestive system

As already noted, alcohol is an irritant, which explains the burning sensation as it goes down. Alcohol in the stomach promotes the flow of gastric juices. A glass of wine before dinner may thereby promote digestion by "priming" the stomach for food. But with intoxicating amounts, alcohol impedes or stops digestion.

Circulatory system

Wine prepares the heart for love, unless you take too much.
OVID

Alcohol has only minor effects on the circulatory system. Heartbeat and blood pressure are little affected. In moderate amounts, alcohol is a vasodilator of the surface blood vessels. These vessels expand near the skin surface, which accounts for the sensation of warmth and a flush to the skin that accompanies drinking. Despite the feeling of warmth, body heat is being lost. Thus whoever sends out the St. Bernard with a brandy cask to the aid of the snow-stranded traveler is misguided. Despite the illusion of warmth, a good belt of alcohol will likely further cool off the body.

Kidneys

Anyone who has had a couple of drinks may well spend some time traipsing back and forth to the WC. The increased urine output is not caused by alcohol's direct action on the kidneys and is not simply due to the amount of liquid consumed. This phenomenon is related to the effect of alcohol on the posterior portion of the pituitary gland, located at the base of the brain. The pituitary secretes a hormone regulating the amount of urine produced. As the pituitary is affected by alcohol, too little of the hormone is released, and the kidneys form a larger than normal amount of dilute urine. This effect is most pronounced when alcohol is being absorbed and the blood alcohol level is rising.

Liver

The liver is very sensitive to the acute effects of alcohol. (See Chapter 5 for more information about the long-term effects of alcohol on the liver.) It has been demonstrated that intake of even relatively small amounts of alcohol (1 to 2 ounces) by nonalcoholics can lead to accumulation of fat in liver cells.

The liver performs an incredible number of different functions—a very important one is its role in maintaining a proper blood sugar level. Sugar (the body's variety, called glucose) is the only source of energy that brain cells can use. Because the brain is the master control center of the body, an inadequate supply of food has far-reaching consequences. When alcohol is present in the system, the liver devotes all of its attention, so to speak, to metabolizing it. There is a stored form of glucose in the liver (glycogen), which is usually readily available. However, if it is not present because of an inadequate diet or fasting for a day or two, the liver will normally go through a more complicated biochemical process to transform other nutrients such as protein into glucose. However, this complicated maneuver is blocked by the presence of alcohol. In these cases hypoglycemia can result. In a hypoglycemic state there is a below-normal concentration of blood sugar. The brain is deprived of its proper nourishment. Symptoms include hunger, weakness, nervousness, sweating, headache, tremor. If the level is sufficiently depressed, coma can occur. Although hypoglycemia may be more likely and more severe in individuals who already have liver damage from chronic alcohol use, it can occur in otherwise normal people with healthy

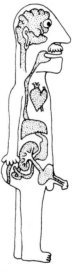

Interferes with brain activity, affecting first judgment, then muscular coordination, then sensory perception

Has few effects on heart or lungs except in high amounts, then may cause death

Interferes with liver's ability to maintain stable blood sugar

Leads to increased production of urine by kidneys

Irritates intestinal system; increases acid secretion by stomach

EFFECTS OF ALCOHOL

livers who have been drinking heavily and have not been eating properly for as little as 48 to 72 hours.

In individuals with adequate diets, other metabolic effects of alcohol may cause abnormally high levels of blood glucose, called hyperglycemia, a state similar to that which occurs in diabetics. In view of its potentially significant effects on blood sugar levels, the danger posed by alcohol for the diabetic is obvious.

The liver also plays an important role in the metabolism of other drugs. The presence of alcohol can interfere with this and in part be responsible for some alcohol–drug interactions. As mentioned before, the liver enzyme ADH is essential to the metabolism of alcohol. Quantitatively it is the liver's major means of metabolizing alcohol. The liver does have a "backup system," however. This secondary system is called MEOS (short for microsomal ethanol oxidizing system), and it is located in certain intracellular structures called microsomes. Probably only after long-term heavy drinking this secondary system begins to help out significantly in the metabolism of alcohol, yet it is mentioned here because it is a *major* system in metabolizing other drugs. Acutely the MEOS activity is inhibited dramatically by the presence of alcohol. Therefore, other drugs are not broken down at the usual rate. If other drugs in the system have a depressant effect similar to that of alcohol, this can be serious because the central nervous system will be subjected to both simultaneously. However, other problems can also result with other drugs. Suppose someone is taking a prescription drug, such as Dilantin or Coumadin, at set intervals and also drinks. The presence of alcohol acutely interferes with the metabolism of the medication, thus when the next scheduled dose is taken substantial amounts of the earlier dose remain, and cumulative toxic or side effects may occur.*

Central nervous system

The precise ways that alcohol affects the brain and thereby behavior are not fully understood. Recent research has indicated that it exerts major effects on the structure and function of nerve cell membranes. These changes may be transient with acute al-

---

*With chronic long-term alcohol use the activity of the MEOS is speeded up. In this instance the drugs are broken down faster, so higher doses must be administered to achieve a given therapeutic effect. (See Chapter 5, pp. 130-133 for more about alcohol–drug interactions.)

cohol intake or persist with chronic use. They probably play a major role in relation to the behavior associated with acute intoxication, and also account for the phenomena of tolerance and withdrawal.

In addition to its impact upon nerve cell membranes, alcohol also probably significantly affects the production and activity of a number of neurotransmitters, which convey messages from one nerve cell to another, as well as the receptors with which they interact. Possibly there may be inherited differences in the way alcohol is metabolized or influences the central nervous system (CNS). Such differences could be the biochemical basis for a genetic predisposition to alcoholism, which may be a significant factor in as many as 50% of all cases.

Without question, the CNS, particularly the brain, is the organ most sensitive to the presence of alcohol. This sensitivity is what being high, drunk, or intoxicated is all about. The intensity of the effect is directly related to the concentration of alcohol in the blood. The drug alcohol is a CNS depressant. It interferes with or lowers the activity of the brain. Not all parts of the brain are uniformly affected. If they were, the same amount required to release inhibitions would also be lethal by simultaneously hitting the parts controlling breathing.

Meanwhile, watch, or recall, someone becoming intoxicated and see the progression of effects. The following examples refer to typical CNS effects in men.

One drink. (The "drinks" here are a little under 1/2 ounce of pure alcohol, the equivalent of a 12-ounce beer or an ounce of 86-proof whiskey. Many generous hosts and hostesses mix drinks with more than 1 ounce of booze. So, as you read on, don't shrug off the "ten-drink" section as an impossibility. Five generous ones could easily have as much alcohol!) With one drink, the drinker will be a bit more relaxed, possibly loosened up a little. Unless he chugged it rapidly, thus getting a rapid rise in blood alcohol, his behavior will be little changed. Being of average height, weighing 160 pounds, by the end of an hour his blood alcohol level will be .02. (The actual measurement is grams %, or grams/100 milliliters. For example, 0.02 gr% = 200 mg%.) One hour later all traces of alcohol will be gone.

And this is our new antialcoholic whiskey bottle. Preliminary testing suggests that at a blood alcohol level of .03 people can no longer figure out how to pour themselves a drink.

Two and a half drinks. With two and a half drinks in an hour's time, your party-goer will have a .05 blood alcohol level. He's high. The "newer" parts of the brain, those controlling judgment, have been affected. That our friend has been drinking is apparent. He may be loud, boisterous, making passes. Disinhibited, he is saying and doing things he might usually censor. These are the effects that mistakenly cause people to think of alcohol as a stimulant. The system isn't really hyped up. Rather the inhibitions have been suspended, due to the depression by alcohol of the parts of the brain that normally give rise to them. At this time our friend is entering the danger zone for driving. With two and a half drinks in an hour, 2.5 hours will be required to completely metabolize the alcohol.

Five drinks. With five drinks in an hour, there is no question you have a drunk on your hands. The law would agree. A blood alcohol level of .10 is sufficient in most states to convict of DWI. By this time judgment is nil. "Off coursh I can drive!" In addition to the parts of the brain controlling judgment, the centers controlling muscle coordination are depressed. There's a stagger to the walk and a slur to the speech. Even though the loss of dexterity and reaction time can be measured, the drinker, now with altered perception and judgment, will claim he has never functioned better. Five hours will be required for all traces of alcohol to disappear from the system.

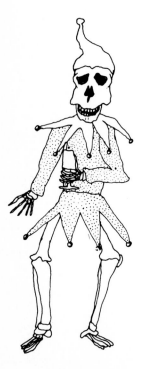

Ten drinks. This quantity of alcohol in the system yields a blood alcohol content of .20. More of the brain than just the judgment, perceptual and motor centers are affected. Emotions are probably very erratic—from laughter to tears to rage. Even if your guest could remember he had a coat—which he probably can't due to memory impairment—he'd never be able to put it on. Ten hours will be required for all the alcohol to be metabolized. Six hours, and he'll still be legally drunk.

One pint of whiskey. With this amount of booze, the drinker is stuporous. Though not passed out, nothing the senses take in actually registers. Judgment is gone, coordination wiped out, and sensory perception almost nil. With the liver handling 1 ounce of alcohol per hour, it will be 16 hours, well into tomorrow, before all the alcohol is gone.

One and one-fourth pints of whiskey. At this point, the person is in a coma and dangerously close to death. The vital brain centers, which send out instructions to the heart and breathing apparatus, are partially anesthetized. At a blood alcohol level of .4 to .5, a person is in a coma; at .6 to .7, death occurs.

Acute overdose/toxicity

As with many other drugs, acute overdoses with alcohol may be fatal. Usually this occurs when very large doses of alcohol are consumed over a very short period of time. Rapid absorption of the ingested alcohol leads to a rapid and steep rise in blood alcohol concentration (BAC) which may lead to loss of consciousness, coma, progressive respiratory depression, and death in a relatively short period of time.

In general, the acute lethal dose of alcohol is considered to be from 5 to 8 mg/kg of body weight. This amounts to between 350 and 560 ml of pure alcohol, which translates to 12 to 19 fluid ounces of pure alcohol, in the "average 155 pound" (70/kg) man. This is the equivalent of about a fifth to a fifth and a half of 86-proof liquor. Acute doses of this size of alcohol can be expected to result in BACs in the range of .35 to .7. BACs in this range have been consistently found in acute alcohol overdoses that have had fatal outcomes. This is not at all surprising, since it is known that a BAC in excess of .4 will severely, and very likely lethally, depress respiratory function.

Of course, the exact lethal dose and BAC in any individual will vary with age, sex, general physical health, and the degree of prior tolerance to alcohol. All things being equal, a very large, healthy, young adult male will tolerate a dose of alcohol that might well be fatal for a small, medically ill, elderly female. This is true, only more so, for the alcohol-tolerant alcoholic as compared to the alcohol-naive, novice drinker. Thus an alcoholic may tolerate an acute dose of alcohol that would kill an otherwise comparable nonalcoholic individual. However, although chronic tolerance to alcohol may provide the alcoholic with some margin of safety, this protection is finite. Thus, even the most severe alcoholic may do himself in by consuming acutely a sufficient amount of alcohol to raise the BAC to the upper end of the lethal range. Therefore it is probably fair to say that a BAC of .7 or more is virtually certain to be lethal in anyone. And the higher the level within the .35 and .7 range, the greater the risk of death.

Differences in women

Substitute a 120-pound woman in the foregoing examples, and the weight differential would certainly speed up the process. With one drink in 1 hour, she would have a BAC of .003; two and a half drinks, and she'd be up to .07. By five drinks, she'd have a .14 reading. Should she make it through a pint, she'd be in a coma with a level of .45. Tomorrow might not come as soon for her. Besides the differences in body weight, other factors can speed up or alter this process. Women and men differ in their relative amounts of body fat and water. Women have a higher proportion of fat and correspondingly lower amounts of water. Al-

cohol is not very fat soluble. Therefore, a woman and a man of the same body weight, both drinking the same amounts of alcohol, will have different blood alcohol levels. Hers will be higher. She has proportionately less water than he has in which to dilute her alcohol.

There is another critical difference between men and women in respect to how they handle alcohol. A woman's menstrual cycle significantly influences her rate of absorption and/or metabolism of alcohol. This difference presumably relates to the changing balances of sex hormones and appears to be the result of several interacting factors. During the premenstrual phase of her cycle, a woman absorbs alcohol more rapidly. The absorption rate is significantly faster than in other phases of the menstrual cycle. So premenstrually a woman will get a higher blood alcohol level than she would get from drinking an equivalent amount at other times. In practical terms, a woman may find herself getting drunk faster right before her period. There is also evidence that women taking birth-control pills also will absorb alcohol faster and thereby have higher blood alcohol levels.

Quite possibly other important biological differences may exist between men and women in terms of alcohol's effects. Virtually all the physiological research has been conducted on men, and researchers have then blithely assumed their findings to be equally true for women. Though the basic differences between absorption rates of men and women were reported as early as 1932, they were forgotten and/or ignored until the mid-1970s. Believe it or not, the impact of the menstrual cycle was first recognized and reported in 1976! With this failure to examine the effects of the primary and obvious difference between males and females, who knows what more subtle areas have not been considered. End of sermon!

Alcohol as anesthetic

Alcohol is an anesthetic, just as all the old western movies show. By modern standards, it is not a very good one: the dose required to produce anesthesia is very close to the lethal amount. When the vital centers have been depressed enough by alcohol to produce unconsciousness, it only takes a wee bit more to put someone permanently to sleep. Sadly, a couple of times a year almost any newspaper obituary column documents a death from alcohol. Usually it involves chugging a fifth of liquor on a dare, or as a prank, which very quickly yields a lethal dose of alcohol.

Despite biological differences between people, each and every human body reacts to alcohol in basically the same way, although for a given blood alcohol level a very heavy drinker who has developed tolerance to alcohol may show somewhat less impairment in function than would an inexperienced drinker. This uniform, well-documented response is what enables the law to set a specific blood alcohol level for defining drunkenness. This can be easily measured by blood samples or the breathalyzer. Carbon dioxide in the blood diffuses across small capillaries in the lungs to be eliminated in the exhaled air. The amount or concentration of it in the exhaled air is directly proportional to the amount or concentration dissolved in the blood. Exactly the same thing happens with alcohol. The breathalyzer measures the concentration of alcohol in the exhaled air; from this the exact concentration of alcohol in the blood can be determined.

CUMULATIVE EFFECTS

The immediate effects of the drug alcohol have been described. With continued drinking, changes take place. There are cumulative effects. Any drinker, not only the alcoholic, can testify to this. The first few times someone tries alcohol, with one drink they feel tipsy. With drinking experience, one drink no longer has that effect. In part this may reflect greater wisdom. The veteran drinker has learned "how to drink" to avoid feeling intoxicated, that is, by not chugging a drink or not drinking on an empty stomach. The other reason is that with repeated exposure, the CNS has adapted to the presence of alcohol. It can tolerate more alcohol and still maintain normal function. This is one of the properties that defines alcohol as an addictive drug. Over the long haul the body requires a larger dose to induce the effects earlier produced at smaller levels. Not only does this adaptation occur over long spans of time, there are also rapid adaptive changes in the CNS every time someone drinks. A drinker is more out of commission when the blood alcohol level is climbing than when it is falling. If someone is given alcohol to drink and then performs certain tasks, there are predictable results. Impairment is greater on the ascending limb, or absorption phase. As the blood alcohol level drops in the elimination phase, the individual will be able to function better with the same blood alcohol content. It is as if one learns to function better after "practice" with the presence of alcohol. In fact what probably has happened is that the brain has made some subtle adjustments in the way it functions. Here, too, there are differences between men and women. Both have more impairment as alcohol levels rise, but there are differences in the kinds of impairment. With intoxication, women appear to have greater impairment than men for tasks that require motor coordination. Yet, they are superior to men on tasks that require attention. Since driving requires both skills, neither appears the better bet on the highway.

OTHER ALCOHOLS

In this discussion of alcohol, it is clear that we have been referring to "booze," "suds," "the sauce," "hooch," or any of the other colloquial terms for beverage alcohol. To be scientifically accurate, "our kind" of alcohol is called ethanol, ethyl alcohol, or grain alcohol. Alcohol, if one is precise, is a term used to refer to a family of substances. What all alcohols have in common is that each has a particular grouping of carbon, hydrogen, and oxygen atoms, arranged in a similar fashion. They differ only in the number of carbons, and their associated hydrogens. Each alcohol is named according to the number of carbons aboard. Ethanol has two carbon atoms.

The other kinds of alcohol with which everyone is familiar are wood alcohol (methyl alcohol) with one carbon, and rubbing alcohol (isopropyl) with three carbons. With their different chemical makeup, they cause big problems if taken into the body. The difficulty lies in differences in rates of metabolism and the kinds of byproducts formed. For example, it takes nine times longer for methanol to be eliminated than ethanol. Although methanol itself is not especially toxic, when ADH acts on it, formaldehyde instead of acetaldehyde is formed. Formaldehyde is known to cause tissue damage, especially to the eyes. The formaldehyde then breaks down into formic acid, which is also not as innocent as the acetic acid produced by ethanol metabolism, and can cause severe states of acidosis. Ingestion of methyl alcohol can lead to blindness and can be fatal; thus it requires prompt medical attention.

As an interesting aside, the treatment of acute methanol poisoning is one of the handful of situations in clinical medicine where ethanol has a legitimate and important therapeutic role. In this situation giving ethanol will slow the rate of metabolism of methanol and reduce the level of toxic byproducts. This happens because the ethanol successfully competes with methanol for ADH. This effect, in conjunction with correction of acidosis, may ameliorate or entirely eliminate serious complications, if ethyl alcohol is administered rapidly enough.

Poisonings from nonbeverage alcohols don't just happen to alcoholics who in desperation will drink anything. Recently, there have been reports of an Italian wine scandal; table wines

"Medical Declarations" on the alcohol question. The third and final English medical declaration...written in 1871: "As it is believed that the inconsiderate prescription of large quantities of alcoholic liquids by medical men for their patients has given rise in many instances to the formation of intemperate habits, the undersigned are of the opinion that no medical practitioner should prescribe it without a sense of grave responsibility. They believe that alcohol, in whatever form, should be prescribed with as much care as any powerful drug...the directions for its use should be so framed as not to be interpreted as a sanction for use to excess, or necessarily for the continuance of its use when the occasion is past.
SPOONER, WALTER W. *The Cyclopaedia of Temperance and Prohibition*, 1891.

were laced with methanol resulting in upwards of 100 deaths. Far more common is the toddler who gets into the medicine cabinet, or maybe the teenager or adult who doesn't know that all alcohols are not the same and have different effects.

At present, it is becoming common knowledge that anything taken into the body (or breathed in for that matter) has effects on the body. All too often we are discovering these effects to be more harmful than had been previously thought. Chemical additives, fertilizers, and coloring agents are being found to be less benign than once supposed. Caution is urged in the use of all such agents, and the federal Food and Drug Administration (FDA) has outlawed some of them. Let us hope that this caution will begin to extend to the use of alcohol as well.

RESOURCES AND FURTHER READING

Kissin, B., and Beigleiter, H. (Eds.): *The biology of alcoholism.* New York: Plenum Press. (This seven volume series comprises *the* basic reference books on alcohol and alcoholism. See in particular Vol. 1 *Biochemistry*, Vol. 2 *Physiology and behavior*, and Vol. 3 *Clinical pathology.*)

NIAAA, Department of Health, Education, and Welfare: *1st special report to U.S. Congress on alcohol and health.* Washington, D.C.: U.S. Government Printing Office, 1971.

NIAAA, Department of Health, Education, and Welfare: *2nd special report to U.S. Congress on alcohol and health, new knowledge.* Washington, D.C.: U.S. Government Printing Office, 1974.

NIAAA, Department of Health, Education, and Welfare: *3rd special report to U.S. Congress on alcohol and health.* Washington, D.C.: U.S. Government Printing Office, 1978.

NIAAA, Department of Health and Human Services: *4th special report to Congress on alcohol and health.* Washington, D.C.: U.S. Government Printing Office, 1981.

NIAAA, Department of Health and Human Services: *5th special report to the U.S. Congress on alcohol and health.* Washington, D.C.: U.S. Government Printing Office, 1983.

Pattison, M.D., and Kauffman, E. (Eds.): *The encyclopedic handbook on alcoholism.* New York: Gardner Press, 1982.

Alcoholism

Drunkenness is nothing but voluntary madness.

SENECA

DEFINITIONS

The social problems associated with the use and misuse of alcohol have been described. Even if there were no such phenomenon as alcoholism, the mere presence of alcohol would lead to the disruption of the social order and considerable costs to society. Yet all statistics on dented fenders caused by inebriated drivers, or dollars lost by industry, or even percentage of alcohol-related hospital admissions have a limited gut-level impact. If seen as the product of many people's single uninformed encounter with alcohol, most of us would judge such statistics to be unfortunate or nuisances. But they would not strike us as a national tragedy. Our major concern and compassion usually flows toward people, not things. Not unexpectedly, the problem of alcohol that captures our attention is the person for whom alcohol is no longer servant, but master. The more than 10 million alcoholics and the approximately 50 million family members come immediately to mind when we consider the human dimensions of alcohol problems. The chances are very good that this concern is particularized with the faces of people we know or have known coming to mind.

What is alcoholism? Who is the alcoholic? These questions will confront the alcohol counselor daily. A physician may request assistance in determining if an alcohol problem exists. A client may ask, or a spouse may challenge, "Why, she can't be an alcoholic because...." Even in nonworking hours, the question may crop up during conversation with good friends or casual acquaintances. A number of definitions are available from a variety of sources. The word *alcoholic* itself can provide some clues. The suffix *-ic* has a special meaning. According to *Webster's New Collegiate Dictionary*:

> ic n suffix: One having the character or nature of; one belonging to or associated with: one exhibiting or affected by.

Attaching *ic* to alcohol, this word means a person whom those around him link with alcohol. Okay, that's a start. Clearly, not all drinkers are linked with alcohol, just as all baseball players are not linked with the Boston Red Sox. Why the link or association? The basis is probably frequency of use, pattern of use, quantity used, or frequency of signs that indicate the person has been tippling. "Belonging to" has several connotations, including an individual's being possessed by or under the control of. The Chinese have a saying that goes: "The man takes a drink, the drink takes a drink, and then the drink takes the man." This final step closely approximates what the word alcoholic means. Further, the progression itself provides a good picture of the progression of alcoholism.

Worth noting is that the discussion or debate on who is alcoholic and what is alcoholism is relatively recent. This doesn't mean society has never noticed the alcoholic before. Certainly, those in trouble with alcohol have been recognized for centuries, but their existence was accepted as a fact, without question. To the extent there was debate, it centered on why and how the alcoholic should be handled. Essentially two basic approaches prevailed. One was that "obviously" the alcoholic was morally inferior. The evidence cited was the vast majority of people who drank moderately, without presenting problems for themselves or the community. The other view has been that "obviously" the alcoholic was possessed, since no one in his right mind would drink like that of his own volition.

With increasing scientific study and knowledge of "the drink taking the man" phenomenon, the more complicated the task of definition became. In addition to the awareness that these people are distinctly different from the many who drink moderately, the other clear discovery was that all alcoholics are *not* alike. Not all develop DTs when withdrawn from alcohol. There are big differences in the quantity of alcohol consumed or the number of years of drinking before family problems arise. Many alcoholics develop cirrhosis, but more do not. The more time spent on study, the less is known with certainty. In some instances, what was previously seen as a single problem, alcoholism, is now discussed as alcoholisms.

As alcoholism was increasingly recognized as a disease, a number of attempts were made to define it. What follows is a sample and cross section of the definitions that were put forth:

E.M. Jellinek (1946), a pioneer in modern alcohol studies. "[Alcoholism is] any use of alcoholic beverages that causes any damage to the individual or to society or both."

One swallow doesn't make a summer but too many swallows make a fall.

G. D. PRENTICE

Marty Mann (1950s), a founding member of the NCA. "An alcoholic is a very sick person, victim of an insidious, progressive disease, which all too often ends fatally. An alcoholic can be recognized, diagnosed, and treated successfully."

Mark Keller (1960), former editor of the *Journal of Studies on Alcohol*. "[Alcoholism is] a chronic disease manifested by repeated implicative drinking so as to cause injury to the drinker's health or to his social or economic functioning."

Alcoholics Anonymous. AA has no official definition, but the concept of Dr. William Silkworth, one of AA's friends, is sometimes cited by AA members: an obsession of the mind and an allergy of the body. The obsession or compulsion guarantees that the sufferer will drink against his own will and interest. The allergy guarantees that the sufferer will either die or go insane. An operative definition in use in AA is that "an alcoholic is a person who cannot predict with accuracy what will happen when he takes a drink."

World Health Organization, WHO (1951). The alcoholism subcommittee defined alcoholism as "any form of drinking which in extent goes beyond the tradition and customary 'dietary' use, or the ordinary compliance with the social drinking customs of the community concerned, irrespective of etiological factors leading to such behavior, and irrespective also of the extent to which such etiological factors are dependent upon heredity, constitution, or acquired physiopathological and metabolic influences."

American Psychiatric Association, APA (1968). According to the Committee on Nomenclature and Statistics, "Alcoholism: this category is for patients whose alcohol intake is great enough to damage their physical health, or their personal or social functioning, or when it has become a prerequisite to normal functioning." Three types of alcoholism were further identified: episodic excessive drinking, habitual excessive drinking, and alcohol addiction.

American Medical Association, AMA (1977): "Alcoholism is an illness characterized by significant impairment that is directly associated with persistent and excessive use of alcohol. Impairment may involve physiological, psychological or social dysfunction." (From *Manual on Alcoholism*, edited by the AMA Panel on Alcoholism.)

Add to the above all the definitions casually used by each of us and our neighbors. Here we find considerable variation, from "alcoholism is an illness," to "it's the number one drug problem," to "when someone's drunk all the time." Although not necessarily conflicting, each of the expert definitions cited has a different focus or emphasis. Some are descriptive and others attempt to handle the origins of the problem. Several concentrate on the unfortunate consequences associated with alcohol use. Others zero in on hallmark signs or symptoms, especially loss of control or frequency of intoxication. This is true of both expert and lay definitions. Note that generally laypeople seem to have more permissive criteria!

The definitional situation was simplified—or confused, depending on your perspective—by actions taken by both the WHO (1977) and the APA (1980). Neither group was disputing the existence of the phenomenon of alcoholism. However, in large measure because of the multiple definitions that abounded, both groups, for medical–scientific purposes, substituted *alcohol dependence syndrome* for alcoholism. This new terminology has also introduced more consistency with other syndromes related to substance use. Thus the current APA *Diagnostic and Statistical Manual (DSM III)* distinguishes two separate alcohol-related syndromes: alcohol abuse and alcohol dependence. Both of these conditions include impairment in social or occupational functioning. The essential distinguishing feature is the presence of tolerance or withdrawal in the latter.

Criteria for choosing a definition

Before supplying another definition or examining further those just listed, a little digression is in order. That is, how does one know the "true" definition or select the best one? Guidelines used by physical scientists are worth examining. When faced with a choice between two possible explanations, they judge on the basis of two criteria. The first is called the Law of Parsimony. This means that the better explanation is the one that adequately explains the data with the fewest factors. An example will help to illustrate this.

A worker in a mental health clinic has a client who is feeling down, isn't getting along at work, reports his wife is nagging at him, and has liver problems. One explanation is that by chance his job is oppressive, his boss is obnoxious, by nature his wife has a nasty temperament, and furthermore, fate has conspired to give him a cirrhotic liver. Thus his feeling blue is a natural response to an unfortunate set of circumstances. An alternative explanation is that he is an alcoholic. The simplest explanation that fits the facts is the best.

The second criterion the scientist uses when choosing between competing theories is heuristic value. This means taking into account the theory or explanation's usefulness as a guide to action. A car mechanic has an understanding of what makes an automobile tick. When it goes on the blink, he therefore has some sense of how to go about correcting the situation. The same

I do Not drink
More Than
a Sponge. -Rabelais

is true for the counselor. Any definition of alcoholism should provide some clues about what should be done.

Applying these criteria to the many definitions available, which makes the most sense? This is going to depend on what the counselor is trying to do. The counselor will need to be acquainted with several, for use in different circumstances. For working with clients and family, the counselor should probably latch on to one all-purpose definition as a starting point. The one selected should be readily understood by most people. It should be faithful to the facts and, finally, it should be watertight. By watertight we mean inclusive, applicable to those in the early as well as the later stages of the disease. This is the major failing of most lay definitions. They are so specific and geared to the later stages that approximately 95%, or most alcoholics, cannot qualify.

For client education, a definition that seems to fit most of our purposes is a short one, closely following Jellinek and Keller: "Alcoholism is a disease in which the person's use of alcohol *continues* despite problems it causes in any area of life." Every definition has pluses and minuses. The utility of this one is its simplicity and its ability to cover people at various stages. The reference to disease suggests the potential for treatment and asserts that the sufferer is entitled (as are all sick people) to care, not punishment or ostracism. Its weakness is the failure to address the issue of causes. But inasmuch as this is likely to be a stumbling block for many clients—who would like to focus on the "whys"—this may not be a fatal flaw.

On the other hand, when it comes to clinical interactions with colleagues and other professionals, the day is past when each clinician has the luxury of defining the disease according to individual biases and preferences. Uniform terminology is essential. In this country, the APA's *Diagnostic and Statistical Manual* provides the approved lingo. Also it has the important advantage of providing explicit criteria for making the diagnosis. Although there is always room to quibble, and *DSM III* does have its critics, living with these imperfections is far preferable to the alternative.

The remainder of the chapter will be devoted to examining alcoholism as a disease, and then examining the major pieces of work that have led to our present understanding of what alcoholism is, its complexity, and how to recognize it. First of these is the work of E.M. Jellinek, who has been called the father of alcohol studies in the United States and the world. Next are the guidelines established by a committee of the NCA for diagnosing alcoholism, published in 1972. Following this, in 1980, there was the publication of the APA's diagnostic criteria for alcohol dependence. Then in 1983, a landmark study was published by George Vaillant, outlining the natural history of alcoholism and its recovery.

A DISEASE?

Anyone who is sufficiently interested in alcoholism to have read this far is probably well accustomed to hearing alcoholism referred to as an illness, disease, or sickness. This has not always been the case. As discussed earlier, alcoholism has not always been distinguished from drunkenness. Alternatively, it has been seen as a lot of drunkenness and categorized as a sin or character defect. The work of Jellinek was largely responsible for the shift to an illness model. In essence, through his research and writings, he said, "Hey, world, you guys mislabeled this thing. You put it in the sin bin, and it really belongs in the disease pile." How we label something is very important. It provides clues on how to feel and think, what to expect, and how to act. Whether a particular bulb is tagged as either a tulip or an onion is going to make a big difference (especially from the bulb's point of view). Depending on which I think it is, I'll either chop and sauté or plant and water. Very different behaviors are associated with each. An error may lead to strangely flavored spaghetti sauce and a less colorful flower bed next spring.

Implications of disease classification

Placing alcoholism in the category of disease has had a dramatic impact. Sick people are generally awarded sympathy. The accepted notion is that sick people do not choose to be sick, being sick is not pleasant, and care should be provided to restore health. During the period of sickness, people will not be expected to fill their usual roles or meet their responsibilities. A special designation is given to people in this situation: patient. Furthermore, sick people are not to be criticized for manifesting the symptoms of their illness. To tell a flu victim to stop "fevering" would be seen as pointless and unkind. With alcoholism an illness, the alcoholic is thought of as a sufferer and victim. Much of the bizarre behavior displayed is recognized as unwillful and a symptom of illness. No longer the object of scorn, the alcoholic is now seen to require care. The logical place to send the alcoholic is no longer jail, but a hospital, rehabilitation center, or other helping place. There has been a gradual shift in public attitudes since the 1940s. In a recent nationwide poll, over 80% of the respondents said they believed alcoholism to be an illness. Although Jellinek's efforts may have triggered this shift, a number of other events added impetus. The NCA put its efforts into lobbying and public education. The American Medical Association and American Hospital Association published various committee reports. State agencies developed programs for treating alcoholics. Various medical societies have begun to educate members on responsibilities toward alcoholics. Probably the biggest push has come from the presence of recovering alcoholics, especially through the work of AA. Virtually everyone today has personal knowledge of an apparently hopeless alcoholic who has gone off the sauce and seems a new, different person.

The formulation of alcoholism as a disease has opened up possibilities for treatment that were formerly nonexistent. It has brought into the helping arena the resources of medicine, nursing, social work, and others, who before had no mandate to help alcoholics. Also it is gradually removing the stigma associated with alcoholism. This improves the likelihood that individuals and families will seek help rather than cover up. Finally, the resources of the federal government have been focused on alcoholism as a major public health problem. A host of treatment and educational programs have been brought into being.

The early sales pitch for selling alcoholism as a disease was probably the slogan: "Alcoholism is an illness, just like any other." With a little imagination, you can picture folks going around the radio talk show circuit flashing this phrase. Now that the notion has gained acceptance, the time may be approaching for a new, or refined, formulation because there have been some disadvantages or limitations to the disease concept.

Refinement of disease classification

Some have been critical of the disease concept. Among the objections are that it possibly has put too much emphasis on the physician as the major helper. The doctor certainly has a role to play in diagnosis and physical treatment. However, medical training has not necessarily prepared physicians to do counseling. Even if it has, a physician, single handedly, couldn't provide all the time needed to offer counseling, support, and education. This requires a team of people. Yet the disease concept may imply that the doctor alone is qualified to provide or direct treat-

ment. Criticism has frequently been leveled at MDs for being un-
interested or unconcerned with the problems of alcoholism. Possibly the misuse of the disease concept may also foster unrealistic expectations and place undue burdens on them.

In a similar vein, the disease concept may create the false
idea that alcoholism can be treated with a pill and that the alcoholic does not have to do anything. This notion is a mistake
and an oversimplification of what the art of medicine is. Our age
has been an age of wonder drugs: penicillin, polio vaccines,
measles vaccines, and so on. Were a cancer vaccine to be developed, all would be delighted but few shocked. Television commercials constantly push "wonder drugs" to instantly relieve
headaches, insomnia, muscle pains, the blahs. We expect quick
results. The side of the picture we neglect, because it isn't so
spectacular, is the field of rehabilitative medicine. For instance,
with physical therapy, accident victims learn to walk again. In
these cases, patients are required to take active part in their recovery. To be successfully treated, an alcoholic must also take an
active part.

The other important distinction the layperson usually does
not make is between acute and chronic disease. *Acute disease*
means you get sick, are treated, become better, and that's the
end of it. *Chronic diseases* are different: once you have it, you
have it. Chronic diseases may be amenable to treatment and be
arrested. A person might be able to get along as well as before,
but there is always a possibility of relapse. Treatment is intended
to help you live around the illness, in spite of it. Diabetes falls
into this category as do some forms of bronchitis, arthritis, and
alcoholism.

In this book, considerable emphasis will be placed on alcoholism as a chronic disease. There are several general points to
be made at the outset. Medically speaking, one cannot cure a
chronic illness. By definition, given the current state of knowledge, chronic diseases are incurable. The medical approach to
chronic illness is summed up by the term *management*. Management may include specific medical treatments, but always there
is more to it. Consider the example of diabetes: insulin may be
prescribed, but that is not all that is done. A nutritionist will work
with the diabetic regarding diet, the patient will be taught to
check his urine, and in light of a diabetic's susceptibility to other
health problems, some modifications of daily routine may be introduced. The person with a chronic illness is not the passive recipient of a physician's doctoring. The chronically ill person be-

comes an active collaborator with the physician and assumes considerable responsibility for caring for and managing his own illness. Characteristically the management of chronic disease involves treatment of acute flare-ups; emotional support (after all, no one likes having a chronic illness); education, so that the individual can be informed about the illness and assist in self-care; rehabilitative measures that enable one to make the life changes that are necessary to live with the limitations imposed by the illness; and involvement of the family so they can be informed and supportive.

The other noteworthy characteristic of chronic illnesses is that they tend to develop slowly. Quite conceivably with an acute illness such as flu, one can go to bed feeling quite well and wake up the next morning sick. It literally happens overnight. However, one does *not* become diabetic, arthritic, or alcoholic overnight. The disease state develops slowly and there will be warning signs and symptoms prior to the point at which it is unequivocably present. For alcoholism, we have E. M. Jellinek to thank for sketching out this progression.

Another major criticism of the disease concept is that it can be used by alcoholics as a cop-out. "Don't look at me, I'm not responsible. I'm sick. Poor me (sigh, sigh)." Expect a drinking alcoholic to try shooting holes into any definition. Those who criticize the disease concept on this basis are possibly those who have been victims of the alcoholic's denial. Our sympathy goes out to them. Alcoholics do have a knack for immobilizing those around them, so that their drinking can continue undisturbed. As you acquire more information about alcoholism, you will be better able to see these ploys coming and effectively counter them. A one-liner that seems to handle the situation fairly well comes from a billboard on the Boston skyline. "There's nothing wrong with being an alcoholic, if you're doing something about it."

PHASES À LA JELLINEK

How did Jellinek arrive at his disease formulation of alcoholism? A biostatistician by training, he was logically fascinated by statistics, the pictures they portray, and the questions they raise. Much of his work was descriptive, defining the turf of alcoholism: who, when, where. One of his first studies, published in 1952, charted the signs and symptoms associated with alcohol addiction. This work was based on a survey of over 2,000 members of AA. Although differences certainly existed between persons, the similarities were more remarkable. There was a definite pattern to the appearance of the symptoms. Also, there was a progression of the disease in terms of increasing dysfunction. The symptoms and signs tended to go together in clusters. Thus Jellinek developed the idea of four different phases of alcohol addiction: the prealcoholic, prodromal, crucial, and chronic phases. These have been widely used in alcohol treatment circles. The four phases are often portrayed graphically.

In the *prealcoholic phase*, the individual's use of alcohol is socially motivated. However, the prospective alcoholic soon experiences psychological relief in the drinking situation. Possibly his tensions are greater than other persons', or possibly he has no other way of handling his tensions. It does not matter. Either way, he learns to seek out occasions where drinking will occur. At some point the connection becomes conscious. Drinking then becomes the standard means of handling stress. But the drinking behavior will not look different to the outsider. This phase can extend from several months to 2 years or more. An increase in tolerance gradually develops.

Suddenly the prealcoholic will enter the *prodromal phase*. (Prodromal means warning or signaling disease.) According to Jellinek, the behavior that heralds the change is the occurrence of "alcoholic palimpsests"—or blackouts. Blackouts are amnesia-like periods during drinking. The person seems to be functioning normally but later has no memory of what happened. Other behaviors emerge that give evidence that alcohol is no longer "just" a beverage, but a "need." Among these are sneaking extra drinks before or during parties, gulping the first drink or two, and guilt about the drinking behavior. Here consumption is heavy, yet not necessarily conspicuous. To look "okay" requires conscious effort by the drinker. This period can last from 6 months to 4 or 5 years, depending on the drinker's circumstances.

The third phase is the *crucial phase*. The key symptom that ushers in this phase is loss of control. Now taking a drink sets up a chain reaction. The drinker can no longer control the amount he will have once he takes a drink. Yet he can control whether or not he will take a drink, so it is possible to go on the wagon for a time. With loss of control, the drinker loses his cover-up. His drinking is now clearly different. This requires explanation, so rationalizations begin. Simultaneously, the alcoholic attempts a sequence of strategies to regain control. The thinking goes, "If I just———, then it will be okay." Common maneuvers attempted are periods of abstinence, changing drinking patterns,

geographical escapes, changing jobs. These are doomed to failure. The alcoholic responds to these failures. He is alternately resentful, remorseful, and aggressive. Life has become alcohol centered. Family life and friendships deteriorate. The first alcohol-related hospitalization is likely. Morning drinking may begin to creep in, foreshadowing the next stage.

The final stage in the process is the *chronic phase*. In the preceding crucial phase, the drinker may have been somewhat successful in maintaining a job and his social footing. Now, as drinking begins earlier in the day, intoxication is an almost daily, daylong phenomenon. Benders are more frequent. He may also go to dives and drink with persons outside his normal peergroup. Not unexpectedly the alcoholic finds himself on the fringes of society. When ethanol is unavailable, he'll drink poisonous substitutes. During this phase, marked physical changes occur. Tolerance for alcohol drops sharply. No longer able to hold his liquor, the alcoholic is stuporous after a few drinks. Tremors develop. Many simple tasks are impossible in the sober state. The alcoholic is beset by indefinable fears. Finally, the rationalization system fails. The long-used excuses are revealed as just that, excuses. The alcoholic is spontaneously open to treatment. Often, drinking is likely to continue because the alcoholic can imagine no way out of his dilemma. Jellinek did emphasize that alcoholics are not destined to go through all four stages before treatment can be successful.

SPECIES

The pattern on pp. 56–57 describes the stages of alcohol addiction. Jellinek continued his studies on alcoholics, focusing on alcohol problems in other countries. The differences he found could not be accounted for simply by the phases of alcohol addiction. These differences seemed more of kind than degree of addiction. This led to his formulation of species, or categories, of alcoholism. Each of these types he named with a Greek letter.

- **Alpha alcoholism**. A purely psychological dependence on alcohol. There is neither loss of control nor an inability to abstain. What is evident is the reliance on alcohol to weather any, or all, discomforts or problems in life. This use may lead to interpersonal, family, or work problems. A progression is not inevitable. Jellinek notes that other writers may term this species problem drinking.
- **Beta alcoholism**. Present when the various physical problems resulting from alcohol use develop, such as cirrhosis or gastritis, but the individual is not psychologically or physically dependent. This

species is likely to occur in persons from cultures where there is widespread heavy drinking and inadequate diet.

Gamma alcoholism. Marked by a change in tolerance, physiological changes leading to withdrawal symptoms, and a loss of control. In this species there is a progression from psychological to physical dependence. It is the most devastating species in terms of physical health and social disruption. This is the species Jellinek originally studied. It progresses in four phases: prealcoholic, prodromal, crucial, and chronic. The gamma alcoholic appears to be the most prominent type in the United States. This species is the most common among the members of AA. Characteristics of this species alone are often seen as synonymous with alcoholism.

Delta alcoholism. Very similar to the gamma variety. There is psychological and physical dependence, but there is no loss of control. On any particular occasion the drinker can control his intake. He cannot, however, go on the wagon for even a day without suffering withdrawal.

Epsilon alcoholism. Not studied in depth, but appeared to be significantly different from the others. Jellinek called this *periodic alcoholism*, marked by binge drinking. Though not elaborating, he felt this was a species by itself, not to be confused with slips by gamma alcoholics.

Having described these various species, Jellinek concluded in his book *The Disease Concept of Alcoholism* that possibly not all species are properly categorized as a disease. He speculated that maybe alpha and epsilon varieties are symptoms of other disorders. But there was no question in his mind that gamma and delta, each involving physiological changes and progression, are diseases. By more adequately classifying and categorizing the phenomena of alcoholism, he brought scientific order to a field that formerly had been dominated by beliefs. That was no modest contribution.

GUIDES FOR DIAGNOSIS

NCA Criteria

The next major step taken was in 1972 with a paper entitled "Criteria for the Diagnosis of Alcoholism," published in two major medical journals. This article was prepared by a special committee of the NCA. Its task was to establish guidelines to be used in diagnosing alcoholism. Physicians were thereby provided a firm set of standards to use in making a diagnosis.

The committee collected all the signs and symptoms of alcohol use that can be discovered through a physical examination, medical history, social history, laboratory tests, and clinical observations. These signs and symptoms were then organized into two categories, or tracks, of data. The first track consisted of the physiological and clinical data. Included were the things a physician can discover through a physical examination, laboratory tests, or medical history. The second track was termed the behavioral, psychological, and attitudinal; it included what the client or the family report about the patient's life situation, or the social history, or what the physician could directly observe about the patient's involvement with alcohol.

Within each of the two data tracks, the criteria were further divided into major and minor subgroups. That means exactly what you would expect. Major criteria are the "biggies"; only one must be present to diagnose alcoholism. However, several of the minor criteria from both tracks are required to make the diagnosis. Finally, each of the potential signposts is weighted as to whether it "definitely," "probably," or "possibly" indicates alcoholism.

Table 1 summarizes some of the key criteria set forth by the Criteria Committee.

There are many similarities between the symptoms of alcohol addiction developed by Jellinek in 1952 and the above criteria published 20 years later. However, Jellinek composed his list based on the self-reports of recovered alcoholics, so the signs are from their point of view. A good number of the symptoms Jellinek included involve deception and the alcoholic's attempts to appear normal. This provides little assistance to the physician or helper interviewing a drinking alcoholic. The physician is unable to rely on the usual instincts to believe the client. To further complicate diagnosis based on Jellinek's list, many of the behaviors included

Dirty Tom McAlear didn't bathe for 15 years and was drunk for seven years without once sobering up
    —Richard Erdoes
    1000 Facts about Booze

quick. I NEED A Drink. If I Sober up THE STENCH will Kill me.

TABLE 1

Criteria for diagnosis of alcoholism*

Physiological data	Diagnostic significance†	Behavioral data	Diagnostic significance†
Major criteria		**Major criteria**	
Physiological dependence, evidenced by withdrawal syndromes when alcohol is interrupted or decreased	1	Continued drinking, despite strong medical indications known to client	1
		Drinking despite serious social problems	1
Evidence of tolerance, by blood alcohol level of 0.15 without gross evidence of intoxication or consumption of equivalent of fifth of whiskey for more than one day by 180-lb man	1	Patient's complaint of loss of control	2
Alcoholic blackouts	2		
Major alcohol-related illnesses in person who drinks regularly			
Fatty liver	2		
Alcoholic hepatitis	1		
Cirrhosis	2		
Pancreatitis	2		
Chronic gastritis	3		
Minor criteria		**Minor criteria** (very similar to Jellinek's symptoms of phases of alcohol addiction)	
Laboratory tests			
Blood alcohol level of 0.3 or more at any time	1‡	Repeated attempts at abstinence	2
Blood alcohol level of 0.1 in routine examination	1‡	Unexplained changes in family, social, or business relationships	3
Odor of alcohol on breath at time of medical appointment	2	Spouse's complaints about drinking	2

*Modified from Criteria Committee, National Council on Alcoholism. Criteria for the diagnosis of alcoholism. American Journal of Psychiatry, August 1972, 129(2), 41-49.

†1, Must diagnose alcoholism; 2, probably indicates alcoholism; 3, possibly due to alcoholism.

‡There seems to be some discrepancy between 1, meaning must diagnose alcoholism, and the committee's statement that more than one of the minor criteria must be in evidence. We note this but have no explanation.

are not the kind of thing a physician can easily detect. So the NCA criteria were a marked improvement pinpointing objective measures for the physician, who, using readily available information, can cut through the alcoholic's alibis. For example, "odor of alcohol on the breath at the time of medical appointment" is designated as a "possible" sign. A person displaying this behavior "is under strong suspicion of alcoholism." The physician is directed to look for additional supporting evidence.

In the NCA Criteria, alcoholism is further described as a chronic progressive disease. Although incurable, it is very treatable. Because it is a chronic disease, the diagnosis once made can never be dropped. An individual successfully involved in a treatment program would have the diagnosis amended to "alcoholism: arrested" or "alcoholism: in remission." Suggested criteria are provided for determining when this change in diagnosis is appropriate. The panel recommended that factors other than the length of sobriety be taken into account. Among the factors listed as signs of recovery are full, active participation in AA, active use of other treatments, use of Antabuse-like preparations, no substitution of other drugs, and resumption of work. The paper is primarily interested in diagnosis, not treatment. Yet implicit in the standards suggested for diagnosing "alcoholism: arrested" is a view that alcoholism requires a variety of treatment and rehabilitative efforts.

DSM III Criteria

While definitely on the right track and more useful to the clinician, the NCA Criteria were nonetheless cumbersome. The publication of the APA's *Diagnostic and Statistical Manual* 3rd Ed. took the above criteria a step forward. That manual, known as *DSM III*, was a milestone not only for alcoholism, but other psychiatric conditions as well. It represented a major departure from previous diagnostic schemes. First, it set forth very specific diagnostic criteria, explicitly stating what signs and symptoms must be present to make a diagnosis. Also in some instances, it significantly revised, reorganized, and renamed the major groups of psychiatric problems. Thus, for the first time, *substance abuse disorders*, into which alcohol dependence/alcoholism falls, became a separate major category.

The checklist on page 63, derived from *DSM III*, indicates what is required to make the diagnosis.

DSM III is now undergoing revision. Following a process of review and comment, the *DSM III Revised* is scheduled for publication in 1987; a further "final revision," as *DSM IV*, is scheduled for publication in 1992. In the first drafts of the revision, several changes have been suggested. The major ones are dropping the diagnosis of alcohol abuse and the expansion of alcohol dependence to allow for cases in which there is psychological dependence and negative consequences but there is not evidence of physical dependence. In this proposed classification scheme a diagnosis of dependence could be made without evidence of tolerance or withdrawal. Whether these changes are eventually reflected in the final draft remains to be seen. In part this represents a response to those in the alcohol field who have noted that very serious problems can exist even if there is not marked phys-

Table 2

Diagnostic Checklist for *DSM III* Diagnoses of Alcohol Abuse and Alcohol Dependence (alcoholism)*

A. Has the client ever:

1. Needed to use alcohol on a daily basis to function adequately?	Yes___ No___ NA/NI___
2. Experienced difficulty cutting down or stopping drinking?	Yes___ No___ NA/NI___
3. Tried to control or reduce his drinking by restricting his drinking to certain times of the day or by temporarily stopping drinking completely?	Yes___ No___ NA/NI___
4. Remained intoxicated throughout the day for 2 or more days running?	Yes___ No___ NA/NI___
5. Consumed as much as a fifth of hard liquor, 1/2 gallon of wine, or two or more six-packs of beer at one time?	Yes___ No___ NA/NI___
6. Had periods during a time when she was intoxicated for which she had on memory?	Yes___ No___ NA/NI___
7. Continued to use alcohol despite physical disorder that could be exacerbated by such use?	Yes___ No___ NA/NI___
8. Consumed non-beverage alcohol?	Yes___ No___ NA/NI___

Yes to any of the above fulfills a "Yes" for A.   A. Yes___ No___

B. Has the client ever:

1. Been violent when intoxicated?	Yes___ No___ NA/NI___
2. Missed work as a result of drinking or its aftereffects?	Yes___ No___ NA/NI___
3. Lost a job due to drinking?	Yes___ No___ NA/NI___
4. Had a legal problem such as DWI, auto accidents while intoxicated, or other arrests for intoxicated behavior?	Yes___ No___ NA/NI___
5. Had arguments with family or friends because of excessive alcohol use?	Yes___ No___ NA/NI___

Yes to any of the above fulfills a "Yes" for B.   B. Yes___ No___

C. Have the items in A or B taken place over a period of greater than 1 month?   C. Yes___ No___

D. Has the client ever:

1. Noticed the need for markedly increased amounts of alcohol to achieve the desired effect?	Yes___ No___ NA/NI___
2. Noticed a diminished effect over time with regular use of the same amount of alcohol?	Yes___ No___ NA/NI___
3. Developed "shakes", "jittery nerves," or a generalized feeling of being ill occurring after stopping drinking or reducing the amount of alcohol intake, which were relieved by alcohol?	Yes___ No___ NA/NI___

Yes to any of the above fulfills a "Yes" for D.   D. Yes___ No___

1. A definite diagnosis for Alcohol Abuse is made when A, B and C are all "Yes".

2. A definite diagnosis for Alcohol Dependence (Alcoholism) is made when C, D and either A or B are "Yes".

*Developed by Trevor R. P. Price, M. D.

ical involvement, and that these warrant inclusion as dependence. The definition of dependence being proposed would be consistent with the definition of dependence used by the WHO, which does not require the presence of tolerance or withdrawal. To our minds an issue that is of greater concern would be the deletion of alcohol abuse as a diagnostic entity. (Here our chronic disease and health promotion bias is operative.) Presumably this is a group of people who can be identified as using alcohol in a high-risk fashion, for whom dependence, however it is defined, has not appeared. And presumably this is a group for whom some intervention is warranted to reduce likelihood of progression to alcoholism/dependence or to reduce the likelihood of negative consequences associated with drinking.

JELLINEK REVISITED

Natural history of alcoholism

In 1983, George Vaillant published *The Natural History of Alcoholism*. This book set forth the results of several studies that have been invaluable in confirming and in many instances amplifying our understanding of alcoholism as a disease. This work can be seen as representing an update on the work initiated more than 30 years earlier by Jellinek when he outlined the stages of alcohol addiction. Vaillant's work is based upon two groups of men who had been followed for approximately 40 years, from their adolescence into their 50s. One group, the College Sample, officially described as students from an eastern university, is comprised of Harvard students from the classes of 1942 to 1944. The other group, the Core City Sample, is comprised of men who were from high crime, inner city neighborhoods. They were selected to participate in the study when they were about 14 years old, primarily because they were not known to be seriously delinquent. In both instances at the beginning of study, the subjects were extensively interviewed and administered a variety of psychological tests; detailed family histories were obtained; many measures of the subjects' personal functioning were taken. These men were periodically recontacted to collect detailed information on the progress of their lives. The major reason for this research was to follow and study adult development through the life cycle. There was an interesting side benefit for the alcohol field. Not unexpectedly during the course of the study, members from both groups developed alcoholism. Thus for the first time, it became possible to begin to separate out "chicken from egg." The question could be asked: "What are the factors that distinguish those who develop alcoholism from those who do not?"

In brief, Vaillant determined that those who became alcoholic were *not* more likely to have had impoverished childhoods or to have had preexisting personality or psychological problems. Therefore, it was his conclusion that such problems, which are often cited as evidence of an "alcoholic personality" do not predate the emergence of the disease; rather, they are its symptoms or consequences. As for predictors of alcoholism, the significant determinants were a family history of alcoholism or having been raised in a culture with a higher rate of alcoholism.

Several other findings are also worth noting. Vaillant compared the various diagnostic classifications or diagnostic approaches. He discovered a very high overlap between those diagnosed as alcoholic (using *DSM III* criteria) and those identified as being "problem drinkers" with a high problem index, a sociological classification. The specific negative consequences seemed to be of little import. However, by the time the individual had experienced four or more negative consequences as the result of drinking, it was almost assured that a formal diagnosis of alcohol dependence could be made. Virtually no one had four or more alcohol-related problems through mere "bad luck."

Also, as alcoholism progressed over time, the number of problems tended to increase and the overall life situation— psychological adjustment, economic functioning, social and family relationships—deteriorated. Vaillant observed that studies which pointed to the contrary usually were reporting upon persons who went for treatment and were recontacted at a single point. He speculates that these studies simply have not followed the individuals for sufficient periods. While active alcoholism has a downward course, there will be, during the slide, both ups and downs. Presumably, people who present to treatment facilities are doing so at a low point. Therefore at follow-up, even if they continue as active alcoholics, it should not be surprising to find the situation somewhat improved. However, if follow-up were conducted at multiple points in time, the full ravages of untreated alcoholism would become apparent. As Vaillant notes, paraphrasing an AA saying, alcoholism is baffling, cunning, powerful,...*and* patient.

Vaillant concluded that there is indeed a progression to alcoholism, although there is not the orderliness of symptom appearance that Jellinek outlined. As a result of this progression, there are eventually only two likely outcomes. The men in the study either died or recovered through abstinence. The proportion who either returned to nonproblematic drinking or whose alcoholism stabilized was very small. And again, with more points of follow-up, this small middle ground continued to shrink.

Types of alcoholism

In respect to types of alcoholism, several possible subgroups are now being suggested. Those involved with the genetics research believe it is possible and useful to distinguish between *familial* and *nonfamilial* alcoholism. Familial alcoholism is marked by a positive family history of alcoholism, has an earlier age of onset, has no increased presence of other psychiatric disorders, and has more severe symptoms that necessitate early treatment. It appears that Jellinek recognized that this might be a possible subgroup of alcoholics. In 1940, he had proposed a diagnostic category termed "familial alcoholism."

Another set of distinctions sometimes made is between *primary* alcoholism and *secondary or reactive* alcoholism. The latter, secondary/reactive is seen as alcoholism that grows out of or is superimposed upon a psychological problem or psychiatric illness. This is not to imply that such researchers think that this alcoholism need not be treated in its own right. It does mean that in such cases the individual may require active treatment for more than alcoholism, i.e., treatment for the conditions that spawned or facilitated its development.

· · ·

In his book *The Disease Concept of Alcoholism*, Jellinek noted that a disease is "simply anything the medical profession agrees to call a disease." Thus alcoholism has been a disease for some time. It is interesting to note, however, it was 1985 before the American College of Physicians published a statement in the *Annals of Internal Medicine* outlining the physician's responsibilities in diagnosis and treatment of chemical dependency. Alcoholism is now officially also a medical disease. And with the advent of diagnostic criteria, we finally have some clear direction for determining who has it.

RESOURCES AND FURTHER READING

American College of Physicians: Chemical Dependence. *Ann Int Med* 102:405-408, 1985.

American Psychiatric Association: *Diagnostic and Statistical Manual*, ed. 3. Washington, DC: APA, 1980.

Criteria Committee, National Council on Alcoholism: Criteria for the diagnosis of alcoholism. *Am J Psychiatry* 129(2): 41-49, 1972.

Finn, R., and Clancy, J.: Alcoholism, dilemma or disease: a recurring problem for the physician. *Compr Psychiatry* 13(2):133-138, 1972.

Jellinek, E.M.: Phases of alcohol addiction. *Quarterly Journal of Studies on Alcohol* 13:673-684, 1952.

Jellinek, E.M.: *The disease concept of alcoholism*. New Haven, CT: Hill House Press, 1960.

Keller, M.: The disease concept of alcoholism revisited. *J Stud Alcohol* 37:1694-1717, 1976.

Vaillant, G.E.: *The natural history of alcoholism. Causes, patterns, and paths to recovery.* Cambridge, MA: Harvard University Press, 1983.

WHY?

What are the causes of alcoholism? As more knowledge is gained, the answers become more complex. It might be useful to make a comparison to the common cold. Once you have "it," there isn't much question. The sneezing, the runny nose, the stuffed-up feeling the cold tablet manufacturers describe so well leave little doubt—but why you? Because "it" was going around. Your resistance was down. Others in the family have "it." You became chilled when caught in the rain. You forgot your vitamin C. Everyone has a pet theory and usually chalks it up to a number of factors working in combination against one. Some chance factor does seem to be involved. There are times we do not catch colds that are going around. Explaining the phenomenon cannot be done with great precision. It is more a matter of figuring out the odds and probabilities, as the possible contributing factors are considered. The folks in the public health field have developed a systematic way of tackling this problem of disease, causes, and risks of contracting one. First, they look at the agent, the thing that causes the disease. Next, they take a look at the host, the person who has the illness, to find characteristics that may have made him a likely target. Finally, the environment is examined, the setting in which the agent and host come together. A thorough look at these three areas ensures that no major influences will be overlooked.

PUBLIC HEALTH MODEL

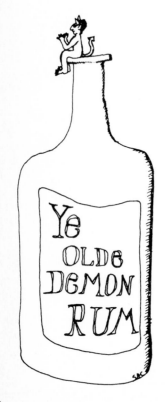

Alcoholism certainly qualifies as a public health problem. It is the third leading cause of death in the United States. It affects 1 out of every 10 adults. If alcoholism were an infectious disease such as polio, it would constitute an epidemic. People would be clamoring for a place in line to get vaccine. The response to alcoholism is pale in comparison.

From the public health viewpoint, the first item to be examined as a possible cause of alcoholism is the agent. For alcoholism, the agent is the substance, alcohol. This is such an obvious fact that it might seem silly to dwell on it. No one can be

Ye OLDe DeMON RUM

alcoholic without being exposed to alcohol. The substance must be used before the possibility of alcoholism exists. Alcohol is an addictive substance. With sufficient quantities over a long enough period, the organism will undergo physiological changes. When this has occurred and the substance is withdrawn, there is a physiological response, withdrawal. For alcohol there is a well-defined set of symptoms that may accompany cessation of alcohol use in an addicted person. An individual can be addicted to alcohol. To use this fact alone to explain alcoholism represents untidy thinking. That alcohol is addicting does not explain why anyone would drink enough to reach the point of addiction. Temperance literature tries to paint a picture of an evil demon in the bottle. Take a sip, and he's got you. This may appear humorous to those comfortable with drinking alcoholic beverages. It is obvious that drinking need not inevitably lead to a life of drunkenness. Let us look at the action of the drug itself. What invites its use and makes it a candidate for use sufficient to cause addition?

THE AGENT

We humans take any number of substances into our bodies—from meats to sweets, as solids or liquids. Although everyone overeats occasionally, considering habitual overeating as a form of "substance" abuse or the associated craving as powerful as that associated with drugs is a very recent concept. A physiological basis for this has not been identified. However, in the case of alcohol, the physiological effects themselves suggest some of the reasons it is such a likely candidate for abuse. First, alcohol is a depressant drug. One of its first effects is on the central nervous system, the "higher" centers related to judgment, inhibition, and the like. What is more important is what this feels like, how it is experienced. With mild intoxication comes relaxation, a more carefree feeling. It is generally experienced as a plus, a high. Preexisting tensions are relieved. A good mood can be accentuated. Alcohol is experienced as a mood changer, in a good direction. This capacity of alcohol is one factor to remember in trying to understand use sufficient for addiction.

A common expression is, "I sure could use a drink *now*." It may be said after a hard day at work, after a round of good physical exercise, or after a period of chaos and emotional stress, when the wobbly knees are setting in. This expression certainly includes the recognition that alcohol can be a mood changer. Equally as important is the word *now*. There is a recognition that

Candy is dandy
But liquor is quicker.
OGDEN NASH

the effects are immediate. Not only does alcohol make a difference, it does so very rapidly. If alcohol had a delayed reaction time, say 3 days, or 3 weeks, or even 3 hours, it wouldn't be a useful method for changing one's mood. Most people's lives are sufficiently unpredictable that drinking now for what may happen later would seem silly. So the speed of the mood change is another characteristic of the drug alcohol that enhances its likelihood of abuse.

Alcohol has another characteristic common to all depressant drugs. With mild inebriation, behavior is less inhibited; there are feelings of relaxation. However, at the same time there is a gradual increase of psychomotor activity. The drinker is unaware of this while feeling the initial glow. As the warm glow subsides, the increased psychomotor activity will become apparent. He may feel wound up, edgy, very similar to the feelings caused by too much coffee, especially in combination with cigarettes. The increase in psychomotor activity builds up gradually and extends beyond the feeling of well-being. Because it is delayed and its onset masked, the drinker is not very likely to recognize it as a product of the alcohol use. Instead, he thinks the edginess is his "normal" self. In fact, it is more probable that the drinker is feeling less serene or calm than when he began. What would be the rational thing to do? Have another drink! It is quite possible that many people, including nonalcoholics, have a second or third drink to get rid of the very feelings created by earlier drinks. There is one nasty catch to this approach. The agitation phase that accompanies alcohol consumption extends considerably beyond the relaxed initial experience. A second drink will only temporarily cover the edginess of the first drink. The second drink, with its own edge coming on behind, will combine with the edge left over from the first. Were this to continue, a point

would be reached when the accumulated tensions and increased psychomotor activity could no longer be masked by adding more alcohol. Normally, people are wholly unaware of this phenomenon because it is interrupted after two or three drinks. They have set their limit. They have dinner and go on to other activities. They go to bed.

These particular characteristics of alcohol do not alone account for the phenomena of alcoholism, but they are certainly responsible for the *possibility* of alcoholism. As other factors are examined, we can see how an interaction may work.

THE HOST—GENETIC FACTORS

The belief that alcoholism runs in families has long been a part of the folk wisdom. In your childhood, possibly, a great aunt explained away the town drunk with "He's his father's son." No further comment was necessary. The obvious truth was so clear: that many of life's misfortunes are the result of "bad" genes. Just such an inadequate understanding of genetics, supported by warped theological views, led to statutes that authorized the sterilization of the feebleminded, hopelessly insane, and chronically drunk. In the face of new knowledge, such an approach has fallen into disrepute. It is now clear that heredity is not as simple as it seemed. Each individual, at the point of conception, receives a unique set of genetic material. This material is like a set of internal "instructions" that guide the individual's growth. In some respects, the genetic endowment simply sets down limits, or predispositions. The final outcome will depend on the life situation and environment in which the person finds (or places) himself. Thus some people tend to be slim and some tend to put on weight easily. Such a *tendency* is probably genetic. Whether the person is fat, thin, or just right depends on him.

Nature versus nurture

What are the facts about heredity in alcoholism? Actually, alcoholism does run in families. The child of an alcoholic parent is more likely to become alcoholic. One study tracing family trees found that 50% of the descendents of alcoholics were also alcoholics. Though that figure is a bit higher than other similar studies, it is simply a more dramatic example of the typical finding that suggests that the offspring of alcoholics have a four times greater risk of developing the disease.

Yet something's running in families is not proof that it is inherited. After all, speaking French runs in families—in France.

The peculiar charm of alcohol lies in the sense of careless well-being and bodily comfort which it creates. It unburdens the individual of his cares and fears.... Under such conditions it is easy to laugh or to weep, to love or to hate, not wisely but too well.

DR. HAVEN EMERSON, *Alcohol and Man*

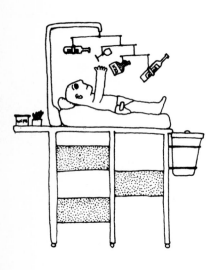

Drunkards beget drunkards.

PLUTARCH

Recognizing the role of psychological factors influencing behavior, separating nature from nurture, becomes a complex, but necessary, job. Certainly, an alcoholic parent would be expected to have an impact on a growing child. It is not unreasonable to expect that inherent in the family lies the soil of addiction. Yet again, the simple fact that this sounds reasonable does not make it true.

The most current hypothesis is that heredity does play a significant role in the development of alcoholism in some people. Research to determine which people and by which mechanisms, is virtually exploding and much has been learned since the early 1970s. If heredity is a factor, there must be some basic biochemical differences between those who are prone to alcoholism and those who are not.

The observations of people working in the area of alcohol rehabilitation and treatment would tend to support a constitutional vulnerability. Certain individuals develop alcoholism very early in life, and it progresses very rapidly in the absence of any unique identifiable psychological stress. At AA meetings the remark may be heard, "I was an alcoholic from my first drink." Usually this means that for seemingly idiosyncratic reasons the speaker never drank "normally" as did his peers, but used, and was affected by, alcohol differently. Interestingly, back in 1940, Jellinek, recognizing a possible hereditary factor, had suggested a distinguishable "familial" type of alcoholism.

Twin and adoption studies

Heredity. The heredity of form and the heredity of mental traits and character are unquestioned . . . Inebriety belongs to the same class, and has been recognized as hereditary for ages. On one of the monuments of Egypt there is a drawing of a drunkard father and several drunken children, and the grouping conveys the idea that the inebriety of the parent was the direct cause of the children's disgrace.

SPOONER, WALTER W. *The Cyclopaedia of Temperance and Prohibition*, 1891.

Scientific investigational methods using an experimental model are not possible in the task of separating nature and nurture. Human research requires locating individuals with particular life experiences or characteristics and then comparing them to those with other backgrounds. Twin studies and adoption studies are the two classical methods for doing this. Donald Goodwin is an alcoholism researcher who has worked extensively on the topic of alcoholism and heredity. Many of his (and others') studies have used data from Scandinavia, because these countries keep very complete records of marriages, births, and other data, making it easier to trace families. One early study was based on a large sample of twins. In each set, *one* twin was alcoholic. The researchers determined whether the twins were identical or fraternal. They then interviewed the twin of the known alcoholic. The prediction: if alcoholism has a hereditary basis, the other twin of identical sets would then be more likely to also be alcoholic than if he were fraternal. The assumption was made because identical twins share the same genetic material. That proved to be the case. However, the hereditary endowment does not act to totally dictate the development of alcoholism because not all the identical twins were both alcoholic. It was further discovered that there exists an apparent predisposition toward having, or being spared, the social deterioration associated with alcoholism. If both twins were alcoholic, the best predictor of the other twin's life situation was not how much or how long he had been drinking. The life situation of the first twin was more reliable. So there appears to be a hereditary predisposition both to alcoholism and the social problems associated with it.

An adoption study conducted by Goodwin using Danish subjects further supports the influence of heredity. He traced children born of alcoholic parents. These children had been adopted by age 6 weeks. He then compared them to adopted children of nonalcoholic biological parents. The adoptive families of both groups were essentially the same. He discovered that those whose natural parents were alcoholic were in adulthood themselves more likely to be alcoholics. Thus the alcoholism cannot be attributed simply to the home environment.

The subjects of the above studies were men. Some initial work has been conducted with female adoptees. The results have been less conclusive, perhaps because the sample sizes were smaller. Also, given the strong cultural prohibitions against women drinking heavily, this may have served as a cultural "protection" against the development of alcoholism.

Further studies based on half-siblings (again males) have helped separate the relative influence of genetic makeup versus home environment. Of the half-siblings, one had an alcoholic parent, the other did not. Thus, one of the children had a biological predisposition the other did not. The children were raised together. In a portion of the cases both were raised in a nonalcoholic family. In other cases, both grew up in an alcoholic home. As expected, those with genetic background positive for alcoholism were themselves more likely to develop alcoholism. Of equal significance, being reared in an alcoholic home did *not* further increase the likelihood of developing alcoholism for either the biologically at-risk children or those without a biological predisposition. This has been confirmed by other studies; being reared in a home with the alcoholic parent does not further increase the probability of alcoholism. Such findings provide strong ~~support~~ for the importance of the genetic predisposition in some cases of alcoholism.

Genetic marker studies

Another group of studies are known by the shorthand title of "genetic marker" studies. In such investigations, attempts are made to link alcoholism to any traits that are known to be inherited. This would establish a genetic basis for alcoholism. Some of the possibilities that have been studied include blood types. It is known that blood type is inherited; the genes controlling this may also be responsible for other characteristics. Other leads that have been followed include other blood substances; ability to taste or not taste phenylthiocarbamide; and blue-yellow color blindness. While no one link has yet turned up, research is proceeding at a rapid pace on several promising fronts.

Studies of nonalcoholic blood relatives

These studies are sometimes referred to as studies of persons at high risk, and are similar to the genetic marker studies. Any genetic difference between those who are biologically prone to alcoholism and those who are not will, as noted, be manifested in some biochemical differences. Efforts are underway to see what factors may distinguish between these two groups. The major hypotheses are that there may be differences in the way our bodies handle alcohol and our brains experience its effects. The differences could conceivably be differences of metabolism, or differences in response to chronic exposure to ethanol, or possibly a unique response to a single dose (e.g., those at high risk having greater pleasure and those at low risk more discomfort).

What does the research to date show? There does seem to be a difference in metabolism. In one study, a group of presently nonalcoholic young men with an alcoholic father or brother showed greater acetaldehyde levels during alcohol metabolism than another similar group who did not have an alcoholic family member. Much higher levels of acetaldehyde often accompanies drinking in Orientals. At these higher levels it produces an Antabuse-like reaction, which discourages alcohol consumption and thereby provides protection against the development of alcoholism. Paradoxically though, with a modest increase of acetaldehyde, the addiction process may be facilitated. Another preliminary study has looked at how alcohol's effects are experienced, again using young men who exhibit no symptoms of alcoholism but have an alcoholic blood relative. Those having an alcoholic family member describe a lesser response to a single dose of alcohol than those with no alcoholic blood relative. To translate this, those with a family history of alcoholism didn't feel as "high" as did those without alcoholism in the family. Other researchers have determined that those with a family history of alcoholism have greater muscle relaxation with a single dose of alcohol than those without a family background. After drinking, those at "high risk" also have been reported to have more brain alpha wave activity, as measured by electroencephalogram (EEG). And among the more interesting findings, "high-risk" subjects perform more poorly on portions of standard neuro-psychological tests that measure brain function. This finding is interesting because it has long been recognized that alcoholics do poorly on such tests. This diminished performance had always been presumed to be the result of brain damage from heavy drinking. Now the question has to be asked whether this condition predates the alcoholism.

Most research initially discussed the differences described above as deficiencies, as something "missing" or "lacking." It is now being recognized that what is inherited may not necessarily be a deficiency but might, paradoxically, be viewed as a "strength." In other words, some people might inherit an ability to handle alcohol "too well." They may be more immune to negative physical consequences of drinking such as nausea and hangovers, or be able to function better than the average person when alcohol is ingested. This perspective may be useful in client education.

Familial alcoholism

Given the strong evidence for the role of a genetic factor in some cases of alcoholism, researchers are suggesting that we begin to think in terms of two types of alcoholism, familial and nonfamilial. Goodwin suggests that familial alcoholism is characterized by a positive family history of alcoholism, earlier age of onset, more "destructive" symptoms that necessitate treatment at a relatively young age, and no increased likelihood of other psychiatric illness.

Animal studies

A very different avenue of investigation involves animal studies. These studies cannot be directly generalized to humans. However, work with chimps, baboons, or rats can shed light on the promising areas for human investigation and provide clues.

Some of the more curious studies involve rats. Different strains of rats were given a choice of water or water spiked with alcohol of differing concentrations. Inevitably, they sampled each and usually opted for plain water. If the only liquid available had alcohol added, they would drink it. Several strains of rats were important exceptions. They preferred alcohol and water solutions of around 5%. These "drinking rats" could be inbred and produce offspring that preferred even higher alcohol concentrations. The tentative conclusion is that biochemically they are different from their water-drinking counterparts. Interestingly, even "drinking rats" very rarely choose to drink to intoxication. Although a taste for alcohol may exist, they do not go on to become alcoholic. Dogs are apparently different, in that they will drink to intoxication more frequently. They will even indulge in several days of "heavy" drinking, but they stop spontaneously. Despite the fact that the dogs seem to experience what the experimenters interpret as a hangover or mild withdrawal, the animals abstain. Unless the dogs were binge drinkers, it would appear that alcoholism is a human problem.

THE HOST—PSYCHOLOGICAL FACTORS

It is important to note at the outset of this section that although in the past psychological factors were seen as precursors and/or predictors of future alcoholism, this has been disproven by recent research conducted by Vaillant. This fact has not yet been sufficiently publicized to have become part of the fund of general knowledge. Many people, both health professionals and members of the general public, would, if asked, still assume some psychological explanation of alcoholism. To understand this widely held viewpoint, it is necessary to look at how this perspective developed.

Research stopped during prohibition, no alcohol = no problem was the short-lived attitude. Much of what we now take for "fact" was only recently established. Until 1953, the DTs were thought to be caused by malnutrition, not by alcohol withdrawal. The fetal alcohol syndrome was only reported in the United States in 1973. Cirrhosis was still thought to be exclusively the result of malnutrition until 1976. It is not surprising that the theories to explain alcoholism had centered upon psychological predispositions. The theorists were using all the facts available to them at the time. Furthermore, to look at behavior "psychologically" was to be quite up to date in the late 1930s and into the 1940s and 1950s.

Our present almost unthinking acceptance of psychological factors as the significant determinants of behavior represents a revolution in approaching human behavior that began little more than 100 years ago. The credit for this revolution goes to Dr. Sigmund Freud. A testimony to his influence is our common daily use of words such as unconscious, neurotic, repressed, anxious, and Freudian slip to describe behavior. Although Freud might not consider our usage proper, nonetheless these words have been added to our vocabularies.

Psychological needs

It is now generally recognized that our behavior is at least partially determined by factors of which we are unaware. What are these factors? Our grade school geography classes usually focused on food, clothing, and shelter as the three basic human needs. But there are emotional needs, just as real and important, if people are to survive healthy and happy. What do we need in this realm? Baruch, in her book *New Ways of Discipline: You and Your Child Today*, puts it this way:

> What are the emotional foods that every human being must have regardless of age? What are the basic emotional requirements that must come to every small infant, to every growing child, to every adult?
>
> In the first place, there must be affection and a lot of it. Real down-to-earth, sincere loving. The kind that carries the conviction through body warmth, through touch, through the good mellow ring of the voice, through the fond look that says as clearly as words, "I love you because you are you."
>
> Closely allied with being loved should come the sure knowledge of belonging, of being wanted, the glow of knowing oneself to be a part of some bigger whole. Our town, our school, our work, our family—all bring the sound of togetherness, of being united with others, not isolated or alone.
>
> Every human being needs also to have the nourishment of pleasure that comes through the senses. Color, balanced form and beauty to meet the eye, harmonious sounds to meet the ear. The heady enjoyment of touch and taste and smell. And finally, the realization that the pleasurable sensations of sex can be right and fine and a part of the spirit as well as the body.
>
> Everyone must feel that he is capable of achievement. He needs to develop the ultimate conviction, strong within him, that he can do things, that he is adequate to meet life's demands He needs also the satisfaction of knowing that he can gain from others recognition for what he does.
>
> And most important, each and every one of us must have acceptance and understanding. We need desperately to be able to share our thoughts and feelings with some other person, or several, who

If it weren't for gin and tonics and "The Guiding Light," I wouldn't be able to rely on anything.

really understand....We yearn for the deep relief of knowing that we can be ourselves with honest freedom, secure in the knowledge that says, "This person is with me. He accepts how I feel!"[1]

If these needs are not satisfactorily met, the adult is not whole. A useful notion to assess what has happened is to think of the unmet needs as "holes." Everybody has some holes. They can vary in number, size, and pattern. What is true for all is that holes are painful. Attempts are made to cover up, patch over, or camouflage our holes. Thus we feel more whole, less vulnerable, and more presentable.

Psychological approaches to alcoholism

The various psychological approaches that emerged essentially were all attempts to categorize the nature of the "holes," their origins, and why alcohol is used to cover them up. Although seemingly logical enough at the time, there was a major flaw. The people being studied were already alcoholics, and the concept that an "alcoholic personality" might be a result of the disorder rather than an underlying cause was unheard of. One of the strengths of Vaillant's work was that he began, not with alcoholics, but individuals *prior* to the development of alcoholism. In effect, he studied large samples of people over time, beginning in late adolescence. Some of these people later developed alcoholism, and others did not. Thus he was able to see what the predictors of alcoholism were.

Theories of personality

Among the theories of personality that earlier shaped our thinking, the first was the psychoanalytical, based on the work of Freud. Freud himself never devoted attention to alcoholism. However, his followers did apply aspects of his theory to this disease. It is impossible to briefly present the whole of Freud's work. He recognized that psychological development is related to physical growth. He identified stages of development, each with its particular, peculiar hurdles that a child must overcome on the way to being a healthy adult. Tripping over one of the hurdles, he felt, led to difficulties in adulthood. Some of the events of childhood are especially painful, difficult, and anxiety producing. The situation may persist unrelieved by the environment. This makes the child feel incompetent, resulting in a hole. The child would seek unique ways to patch over the holes. However, the existence of the hole shapes future behavior. It may grow larger, requiring more patchwork. The hole may render the child more vulnerable to future stress and lead to new ones.

The concept of oral fixation was used in applying *psychoanalytic theory* to alcoholism. This meant the holes began in earliest childhood. Observe infants and see how very pleasurable and satisfying nursing and sucking are. Almost any "disease" or discomfort can be soothed this way. An individual whose most secure life experiences are associated with this period will tend to resort to similar behaviors in times of stress. These people will also, as adults, tend to have the psychological characteristics of that life period. The major psychological characteristics of the oral period are the infant's egocentricity and inability to delay having his needs met. He's hungry when he's hungry, be it a convenient time from mother's viewpoint or not. And he's oblivious to other people except as they fit into his world. Thus the alcoholic, according to this theory, was likely to be an individual who never fully matured beyond infancy. He was stuck with childlike views of the world and childlike ways of dealing with it. He was easily frustrated, impatient, demanding, wanted what he wanted when he wanted it. He had little trust that people could help him meet his needs. He was anxious and felt very vulnerable to the world. Nursing a drink seemed an appropriate way of handling discomforts. Alcohol was doubly attractive because it worked quickly: bottled magic.

Another psychoanalytic concept applied to male alcoholics was that of latent homosexuality. The origins of alcoholism were seen to be rooted in the oedipal period, which corresponds to the preschool, kindergarten age. According to Freud, an inevitable part of every little boy's growing up is a fantasy love affair with his mother. There is an accompanying desire to get Dad out of the picture. Given the reality of Dad's size, he has a clear advantage in the situation. The little boy eventually gives up and settles on being like Dad, rather than taking his place. Through this identification process, the little boy assumes a male role. Several possible hitches can occur. Maybe the father is absent, or the father is not a very attractive model. In such instances, the child will not grow to manhood with a sense of himself as a healthy, whole male. As an adult he may turn to alcohol to instill a sense of masculinity. Or he may like drinking because it provides a socially acceptable format for male companionship.

Other personality theorists focused on different characteristics. Adler latched onto the *feelings of dependency*. He saw the roots of alcoholism being planted in the first 5 years of life. He thought firstborn children were most likely to become either alcoholic or suicidal. In this view the dynamics of both are essentially the same. The firstborn is displaced or dethroned by the next child. He loses a position in which both parents pampered him, and thus feels less important. If the parents are unable to reassure him, he has increased feelings of inferiority and pessimism. The feelings of inferiority or the longing for a sense of power require strong proofs of superiority for satisfaction. When new problems arise, arousing anxiety, the person seeks a sense of *feeling* superior rather than really overcoming difficulties. Theoretically, then, drinking as a solution is, to the alcoholic, intelligent. Alcohol does temporarily reduce the awareness of anxiety and gives relief from the inferiority feelings. Without the relief of alcohol, the inferiority feelings and anxiety could build up and lead to the ultimate escape of suicide.

Another psychological approach to alcoholism attempted to define the *alcoholic personality*. The hope was to identify common characteristics by looking at groups of alcoholics. At this point such attempts have largely been abandoned. Because active alcoholics were studied, what appeared to be the "alcoholic personality" was in fact a set of symptoms for alcoholism. Thus the behavior being studied was either drugged or behavior essential to continue the drugged state. Although an alcoholic personality exists, it is unrelated to the *pre*alcoholic personality.

In 1960, William and Joan McCord published their *Origins of Alcoholism*. Their studies used extensive data collected on 255 boys throughout their childhoods. What they found negated many of the psychoanalytic theories. In brief, oral tendencies, latent homosexuality, and strong maternal encouragement of dependency were not, in fact, predictors of alcoholism. From their analysis, a consistent, statistically significant picture emerged. The typical alcoholic, as a child, underwent a variety of experiences that heightened inner stress. This stress produced the paradoxical effect of intensifying both his need for love and his strong desire to repress this need. The conflict produced a distorted self-image. McCord and McCord examined "the personality of alcoholics, both in childhood and in adulthood. In childhood, the alcoholics appeared to be highly masculine, extroverted, aggressive, 'lone-wolfish'—all manifestations...of their denial of the need to be loved. An analysis of the personality of adult alcoholics leads to the conclusions that the disorder itself

'Tis pity wine should be so deleterious, For tea and coffee leave us much more serious.
—Byron

When he's drunk he recites Swinburne.

produces some rather striking behavioral changes." Their contribution highlighted the complexity of the social and psychological interactions.

. . .

On the heels of the above was the emergence of what has been called the *human potential*, or *growth movement*. In essence it was devoted, not to "curing" mental illness, but to applying the expertise of psychology and psychiatry to assisting "normal" people to function better (whatever that means to them). Tied in with this was the emergence of new psychological or personality theories. The primary question became "What is going on now, and how can the individual/client change?" The previously important question "Why, or how, did the sickness or screwed-up-ness originate?" was less important. Transactional analysis, popularly known as TA, and reality therapy were two of these arrivals. Both made a big splash in lay circles as well as in the professional community. Both were used to address the problem of alcoholism.

Games Alcoholics Play by Claude Steiner applied TA to alcoholism and the alcoholic. According to his thesis, the origins of alcoholism lay in the alcoholics' childhood conditions and their responses to them. For example, the child found himself in a predicament with his parents. When he behaved in a way that felt good or made sense to him, he ran into problems. He discovered the real him wasn't okay. To overcome this and become okay, he adopted a life-style or script for himself. In the script, he attempted to respond so as to counterbalance the message that said, "You're not okay." For the alcoholic, the dominant script theme according to Steiner, was "Don't think." This originated in a home where there were clear disparities between what was going on and what the parents said was happening. An observant child picks this up. If he pointed it out, he got a "You just do what I say," or "You just mind your own business," or "Don't get sassy." To survive, he is seen as needing to find mechanisms for tuning out, turning off. As an adult, being an alcoholic is a fine way to continue the "Don't think" script.

William Glasser developed *reality therapy*. He believed that besides the obvious and inborn biological needs, all humans have two basic needs: to love and be loved, and to feel that we are worthwhile to ourselves and others. Failure to fill these needs

leads to pain. A possible solution is the route to addiction; use of some substance or behavior that, while it continues, completely removes the pain.

• • •

Learning theories

The other major class of psychological theories used to explain alcoholism comes from a different branch of psychology. These are the learning theories, which look at behavior quite differently. They see behavior as a result of learning motivated by an individual's attempt to minimize unpleasantness and maximize pleasure. What is pleasant is a very individual thing. A child might misbehave and be "punished," but the punishment, for that child, might be a reward and more pleasant than being ignored.

In applying learning theories to alcoholism, the idea is that alcoholic drinking has a reward system. Either alcohol, or its effects, are sufficiently reinforcing to cause continuation of drinking by the individual. Behavior most easily learned is that with immediate, positive results. The warm glow and feeling of well-being associated with the first sips are more reinforcing than the negative morning-after hangover. This theory would hold that anyone could become alcoholic if the drinking were sufficiently reinforced. Vernon Johnson, founder of a highly successful treatment program and author of a book, *I'll Quit Tomorrow*, gave great emphasis to the importance of learning in explaining drinking. He noted that users of alcohol learn from their first drink that alcohol is exceedingly trustworthy (it works every time) and that it does good things. This learning is highly successful, sufficient to set up a lifetime relationship with alcohol. The relationship may alter gradually over time, finally becoming a destructive one, but the original positive reinforcement keeps the person seeking the "good old days" and minimizing the destructive elements. Seen in this light, alcoholism is not so far distant from people who remain in what are now unsatisfactory marriages, jobs, or living situations out of habit or some hope that the original zest will return.

The aforementioned theories were formulated in the "salad days" of psychology and alcohol studies. The first modern efforts to understand the causes of alcoholism focused exclusively on psychological factors. These early efforts assumed that physiological factors or environmental factors were irrelevant. Growing understanding of alcohol as a drug and mounting evidence of biological influence has led knowledgeable people to seriously question psychological factors as a single, definitive explanation of alcoholism.

However, with the publication in 1983 of *The Natural History of Alcoholism* the debate was finally settled. In that work Vaillant, in effect, showed that psychological factors were at most of minimal consequence as a cause of alcoholism. His research reported on the follow-up of two very different groups: members of Harvard University's Grant Study, and an inner city sample. In both groups, those who developed alcoholism were not distinguishable from their colleagues along psychological lines. Again it was a family history of alcoholism which was a predictor, in combination with an individual's cultural background and the norms associated with alcohol use.

Current thinking

Psychology is the study of behavior. Within the field of psychology, it is currently recognized that a number of different influences must be considered in explaining behavior. This general approach is now being applied to alcoholism as a behavior. For lack of a better phrase, this may be termed the "slot-machine theory." To be alcoholic requires getting three cherries. An individual may be born with a physiological cherry. The environment and culture he is raised in may provide a second, or sociological, cherry. Finally, an individual's personality makeup, with its unique set of holes, may be the third cherry. On the other hand, there could be some variation: say two-thirds physiological and one-third sociological. The point is, one lone cherry does not seem to be an accurate predictor of who becomes alcoholic.

At this point, a comment on the relationship of alcoholism to mental illness is in order. By way of preface, it must be noted that the modern approach to mental illness is identical to the one being presented for alcoholism. Psychiatrists and psychologists are also looking at biological predispositions to mental illness. It would probably be fair to say that increasingly behavior is being seen as a result of the interaction of biological and psychological factors, in the context of an individual's environment. Hence the old body *or* mind approach is out of date. Is there a special relationship of alcoholism to mental illness? No. Alcoholics do not have a substantially greater incidence of mental illness than the general population. To put it crassly, being "crazy" does not cause alcoholism; nor, on the other hand, is being alcoholic a protection against having other psychiatric disorders.

THE ENVIRONMENT—SOCIOLOGICAL FACTORS

Cultural orientation's effects on alcoholism rates.

Several distinctive drinking patterns and attitudes toward alcohol's use have been identified. Which orientation predominates in a culture or a cultural subgroup was, and in certain cases still is, thought to be influential in determining that group's rate of alcoholism. One such attitude toward drinking is total *abstinence*, as with the Muslims or Mormons. With drinking forbidden, the chances of alcoholism are exceedingly slim. Expectedly, the group as a whole has a very low rate of alcoholism. There is an interesting twist we'll get to later about what happens when members leave the group.

Another cultural attitude toward alcohol promotes *ritual use*. The drinking is primarily connected to religious practice, ceremonies, and special occasions. Any heavy drinking in other contexts would be frowned on. When drinking is tied to social occasions, with the emphasis on social solidarity and camaraderie, this is termed *convivial use*. Finally, there is *utilitarian use*. The society "allows" people to drink for their own personal reasons, to meet their own needs, for example, to relax, to forget, or to chase a hangover. Rates of alcoholism are highest where utilitarian use is dominant.

Differences among nations are growing less marked with such developments as television, jet planes, increased travel. Italy has adopted the cocktail party; America is on France's wine kick. Nonetheless, a look at some of the differences between the traditional French and Italian drinking habits shows that cultural attitudes toward the use of alcohol can influence the rate of alcoholism. Both France and Italy are wine-producing countries—France first in the world, Italy second. Both earn a substantial part of their revenue from the production and distribution of wine. Yet the incidence of alcohol addiction in Italy in 1952 was less than one fifth that of France.

In France there were no controls on excessive drinking. Indeed there was no such thing as excessive drinking. Wine was publicly advertised as good for the health, creating gaiety, optimism, and self-assurance. It was seen as a useful or indispensable part of daily life. Drinking in France was a matter of social obligation; a refusal to drink was met with ridicule, suspicion,

and contempt. It was not uncommon for a Frenchman to have a little wine with breakfast, to drink small amounts all morning, to have half a bottle with lunch, to sip all afternoon, to have another half bottle with dinner, and to nip until bedtime, consuming 2 liters or more a day. Frenchmen do get drunk. On this schedule, drunkenness does not always show up in drunken behavior. The body, however, is never entirely free of alcohol. Even people who have never shown open drunkenness have withdrawal symptoms and even DTs when they abstain. The "habit," and the social atmosphere that permits it, seemed to be facilitating factors in the high rate of alcoholism in France.

Italy, on the other hand, which had the second highest wine consumption in the world, consumed only half of what was consumed in France. Italy had a low rate of alcoholism on a world scale. The average Italian didn't drink all day but only with noon and evening meals. One liter a day was the accepted amount, and anything over that was considered excessive. There was no social pressure for drinking as in France. As Jellinek said, "In France, drinking is a must. In Italy it is a matter of choice." Drunkenness, even mild intoxication, was considered a terrible thing, unacceptable even on holidays or festive occasions. A guy with a reputation for boozing would have had a hard time getting along in Italy. He would have had trouble finding a wife. Both she and her parents would have hesitated to consent to a marriage with such a man. His social life would have been hindered, his business put in jeopardy; he would have been cut off from the social interaction necessary for advancement.

Jews have historically had a low rate of alcoholism. Jewish drinking patterns were similar to the Italians', bolstered by the additional restraint of religion. The Irish were more like the French and had a high incidence of alcoholism for many of the

same reasons. The Irish had many ambivalent feelings toward alcohol and drunkenness which tend to produce tension and uneasiness. Drinking among the Irish (and other groups with high rates) was largely convivial on the surface; yet purely utilitarian drinking—often lonely, quick, and sneaky—was a tolerated pattern.

What, then, are the specific factors that account for the differences? These are obviously not based on abstinence. Among the Italians and Jews, many used alcohol abundantly and yet they had a low incidence of alcoholism. While the attitudes in these cultures may have changed over the years, some factors still seem to be found in certain groups that do affect the rates of alcoholism. Low rates of alcoholism are found in groups where the children are gradually introduced to alcohol in diluted small amounts, on special occasions, within a strong, well-integrated family group. Parents who drink a small or moderate amount with meals, who are consistent in their behavior and their attitudes, set a healthy example. There is strong disapproval of intoxication. It is neither socially acceptable, stylish, funny, nor tolerated. A positive acceptance of moderate, nondisruptive drinking and a well-established consensus on when, where, and how to drink create freedom from anxiety. Drinking is not viewed as a sign of manhood and virility, and abstinence is socially acceptable. It is no more rude to say no to liquor than to coffee. Liquor is viewed as an ordinary thing. No moral importance is attached to drinking or not drinking; it is neither a virtue nor a sin. In addition, alcohol is not seen as the primary focus for an activity; it accompanies rather than dominates or controls.

High rates of alcoholism tend to be associated with the reverse of the above patterns. Wherever there has been little agreement on *how* to drink and *how not to drink*, alcoholism rates go up. In the absence of clear, widely agreed-upon rules, whether one is behaving or misbehaving is uncertain. Ambivalence, confusion, and guilt can easily be associated with drinking. Those feelings further compound the problem. Individuals who move from one culture to another are especially vulnerable. Their guidelines may be conflicting, and they are caught without standards to follow. Thus individuals who belong to groups that promote abstinence similarly run a very high risk of alcoholism if they do drink.

A recent review of the literature reinforces the above observations. The following norms and drinking practices have been identified as predictive of alcohol problems: (1) solitary drinking; (2) overpermissive norms of drinking; (3) lack of specific drink-

Portrait
of a woman
who has never
Tasted alcohol.

Portrait of
a man who never
has more than
one drink.

ing norms; (4) tolerance of drunkenness; (5) adverse social behavior tolerated when drinking; (6) utilitarian use of alcohol to reduce tension and anxiety; (7) lack of ritualized and/or ceremonial use of alcohol; (8) alcohol use apart from family and social affiliative functions; (9) alcohol use separated from overall eating patterns; (10) lack of child socialization into drinking patterns; (11) drinking with strangers, which increases violence; (12) drinking pursued as a recreation per se "sui generis"; (13) drinking concentrated in young males; and (14) a cultural milieu that stresses individualism, self-reliance, and high achievement.

Such studies have provided insights into what the broad determinants are for differing rates of alcoholism. In many cases they describe traditional practices of specific groups that have changed in the intervening years. For example, a report by the French National Institute of Agriculture Reform and the National Office of Table Wines shows that French drinking patterns have changed dramatically. Drinking is no longer seen as a part of everyday nourishment but has become a source of pleasure. These changes are being attributed to automation and television. The workers in a Renault factory are not going to be sipping wine throughout the day as was the custom of their grandfathers who were manual laborers. The bistro no longer serves as the hub of social life, and the practice of stopping by after work has declined with television. The French, just like their American counterparts, head home to an evening by the tube—the news, the Monday-night soccer match, the late movies. A word of caution to clinicians: just as cultural differences between groups are becoming less marked, so too it cannot be assumed that every member of the specific group follows the group norms. Thus being Jewish is no protection against alcoholism. The historically low rates of alcoholism among Jews may lead to underdiagnosis of those who are.

Beyond the influence of broad-based cultural factors, there has been recent interest in the relative influence of cultural subgroups, such as family or peers, as well as the characteristics of the immediate drinking situation. Not surprisingly, much of this research has focused upon adolescents and the factors that promote or protect against alcohol use and abuse. Some of these studies have come up with some interesting findings. For example, in a group of people drinking, the heaviest drinker sets the pace for the others. Thus, how much an individual drinks on a particular occasion is likely to be influenced by the amount consumed by others in the group. Another is that adolescent alcohol use increases with perceived access to alcohol and the perceived

No nation is drunken where wine is cheap; and none sober where the dearness of wine substitutes ardent spirits as the common beverage.

THOMAS JEFFERSON

"Man comes from dust and ends in dust" (Holy Day Musaf prayer)—and in between, let's have a drink.

YIDDISH PROVERB

lack of degree of adult supervision. However, such pieces of research have not as yet been integrated into an overall theoretical approach about the influences of the smaller social subsystems in which we all live.

Effect of legal sanctions and approaches

The focus thus far has been on the unwritten rules that govern drinking behavior and influence the rates of alcoholism. How about the rules incorporated into law, which govern use and availability? What impact do they have on the rates of alcoholism? Though their impact is less than the factors just discussed, which permeate all of daily life, they do make a difference. Think back to this nation's experience of Prohibition. On one level it can only be described as a fiasco. It did not abolish all problems associated with alcohol use. Moreover, research on alcohol problems was abandoned and those who were alcoholics were further ostracized. On the other hand, with the lowering of consumption there was a reduction in the rate of alcoholism. Death from cirrhosis during Prohibition did decline. Few would maintain that Prohibition was a successful experiment. What is clear is that laws, if they are to work, must to a large degree reflect how people want people to behave.

Short of Prohibition, there are still significant ways society can influence the use of alcohol. Among these are cost of alcoholic beverages, regulations on advertising, and when and where alcohol may be sold. Evidence from other countries strongly suggests that the rate of alcoholism is related to per capita consumption. So banning advertising, increasing taxes, as well as other measures calculated to reduce sales can be expected to achieve a lower rate of alcoholism. Discussion is hot and heavy on these issues. Many states are now busy raising the legal drinking age as a way of handling at least some alcohol problems. Several years ago the governor of Alaska, in what he acknowledged was a drastic and probably unpopular move, proposed a legislative package to "combat the grim statistics" of alcohol abuse in the state: among the proposals were allowing bush villages to establish possession limits on alcohol, adopt unlimited sales taxes on alcohol, and impose a 2-week lag time between purchase and pickup.

It must be noted here that in the United States, the laws in reference to alcohol use are set by the states for the most part. The blood alcohol level used to define legal intoxication is not even universally the same in the United States. States may vary

as well on when, where, and what a citizen may drink within its borders. And some states even vary from county to county— Texas, for example. And these laws go from dry, to beer only, to anything at all but only in private clubs, to sitting down but not walking with drink in hand, ad infinitum.

Beyond laws governing consumption, sales and pricing, the legal arena influences alcohol use in other ways. This has to do with the issue of liability and suits that can be filed for compensation when death or injury occurs as a result of drinking. There have long been Dram Shop laws, which hold a tavern owner or bar keeper liable as the result of serving an obviously intoxicated customer. Until several years ago these were rarely invoked. This is no longer the case. Liability has also been extended to hosts or to those who might allow an intoxicated person to use their car. In large part it has been the issue of liability, particularly in light of higher legal drinking ages, which has prompted college campuses to pay attention to issues of alcohol use.

An alternative cultural view

One approach has not received the attention we believe it deserves. It fits neatly into neither the sociological nor the psychological approach to the etiology of alcoholism. It was advanced in a provocative paper by the late Gregory Bateson, a maverick anthropologist–sociologist. One of his many concerns was how people process information, drawing on their culture and their own style of thinking. An essay published in 1972, "The Cybernetics of 'Self': A Theory of Alcoholism," offers some intriguing ideas as to why alcoholism may be reaching epidemic proportions in Western cultures. It certainly provides an interesting hypothesis on why abandoning alcohol is so difficult for the alcoholic.

Bateson points out that Western and Eastern cultures differ significantly in the way they view the world. Western societies focus on the individual. The tendency of Eastern cultures is to consider the individual in terms of the group or in terms of one's relationships. To point out this difference, consider how you might respond to the question "Who is that?" The "Western" way to answer is to respond with the person's name, "That's Joe Schmoe." The "Eastern" response might be "That's my neighbor's oldest son." This latter answer highlights the relationship of several persons.

One of the results of Westerners' zeroing in on the individual is an inflation of the sense of "I." We think of ourselves as wholly

The Last Straw
New Hampshire's budget woes have not yet set the masses marching in the streets.
Warnings that our schoolchildren will be deprived have not done it.
Warnings that a student's costs for attending the University of New Hampshire will rise have not done it.
Warnings that there will be less treatment for the mentally ill have not done it.
Warnings that there will be reduced counseling services for the troubled have not done it.
Warnings that there will not be enough manpower to ensure pure water supplies have not done it.
Warnings that law enforcement officials may not be able to hold down the crime rate have not done it.
But now you better batten down the hatches and keep your riot shields handy.
This week there was a headline that said, "LIQUOR STORES THREATENED BY BUDGET."
That'll do it.

Editorial in *The Valley News*, Lebanon, New Hampshire, in September 1977, as the New Hampshire legislature and governor had failed to adopt a budget for the state.

separable and independent. Also we may not recognize the relationships of ourselves to other persons and things and the effects of our interactions. According to Bateson, this can lead to problems. One example he cites is our relationship to the physical environment. If nothing else, the ecology movement has taught us that the old rallying cry of "man against nature" does not make sense. We cannot beat nature. We only win—that is, survive—if we allow nature to win some rounds too. To put it differently, we are now starting to see ourselves as a part of nature.

How does this fit in with alcohol? The same kind of thinking is evident. The individual who drinks expects, and is expected, to be the master of alcohol. If problems develop, you can count on hearing "control your drinking," "use willpower." The person is supposed to fight the booze and win. Now there's a challenge. Who can stand losing to a "thing?" So the person tries different tactics to gain the upper hand. Even if he quits drinking for a while, the competition is on: me versus it. To prove that he is in charge, sooner or later, he will have "just one." If disaster doesn't strike then, the challenge continues to "just one more." Sooner, or later....

Bateson asserted that successful recovery requires a change of world views by the person in trouble with alcohol. The Western tendency to see the self (the I) as separate and distinct from, and often in combat with, alcohol (or anything else) has to be abandoned. The alcoholic has to learn the paradox of winning through losing, the limitations of the I and its interdependence with the rest of the world. He continues with examples of the numerous ways in which AA fosters just this change of orientation.

A truism seems to be that the more we learn about a given topic, the more we know we don't know. As research methods become increasingly more sophisticated, the flaws in older studies come to light. Cultural and subcultural differences are at best difficult to tease out. With television, jet travel, and so forth, differences are less clear cut than was once the case. However, historically the differences in rates of alcoholism from culture to culture were substantial enough to provoke study and research. As with genetic and psychological approaches, they, too, fall short of fully explaining the phenomenon of alcoholism. But a review of the various ideas brought to light by past studies is useful in learning to look at the ways in which cultural attitudes might contribute to high rates of alcoholism, or conversely, to identify those attitudes that promote moderate use.

Statistically, the odds on becoming an alcoholic have in the past varied significantly from country to country. Studies in epidemiology once showed that the Irish, French, Chileans, and Americans had a high incidence of alcoholism. The Italians, Jews, Chinese, and Portugese had substantially lower rates. The difference seemed to lie with the country's habits and customs. Indeed whether someone drinks at all depends as much on culture as it does on individual characteristics.

Culture includes the unwritten rules and beliefs by which a group of people live. Social customs set the ground rules for behavior. The rules are learned from earliest childhood and are followed later, often without a thought. Many times it is such social customs that account for the things we do "just because...." The specific expectations for behavior differ from nation to nation, and between separate groups within a nation. Differences can be tied to religion, sex, age, or social class. The ground rules apply to drinking habits as much as to other customs. Cultures vary in attitudes toward alcohol use just as they differ in the sports they like or what they eat for breakfast.

Change our culture, change our drinking attitudes?

The one area in which we are beginning to come to some agreement is the area of drinking and driving laws. This is in large part because of the pressure exerted by organizations such as MADD and SADD combined with the threat of loss of federal aid to highways. In most states the drinking age is again being raised to 21 in the face of statistics that showed death tolls from drinking and driving accidents went up when the age limit was lowered and down when it was raised. No responsible adult could vote otherwise in the face of such statistics. Lobbying for stricter penalties for drinking and driving offenses has for the most part been successful. Advertising campaigns to combat drinking and driving are now commonplace, at least at holiday times—the beginnings of one small step.

But as a society we have been attempting to "have our booze and drink it too." We want alcohol without the associated problems. Because that is not possible, the question is what compromises are we willing to make? What inconveniences and costs is society willing to assume? Will we accept a ban on package sales after 10 PM on the assumption that folks who want to buy alcohol at that hour don't need it? Will we allocate a reasonable share of the alcohol tax dollar to help the inevitable percentage who get into trouble with the drug?

America in the 1980s is moving toward, but has not yet achieved, a consensus on how, when, and where to drink. Convivial and utilitarian drinking have largely replaced ritual use of alcohol. In some quarters, it remains manly and sophisticated to drink. In others, drinking is felt to be unnecessary, if not outright decadent. The attitudes toward alcohol embodied in our liquor laws testify to this contradiction. The law implies minors should not drink, yet on the magical twenty-first (maybe eighteenth) birthday, they are treated as if they suddenly know how to handle alcohol appropriately.

With alcohol everywhere, until agreement emerges on appropriate and inappropriate use, American society will continue to be a fertile breeding ground for alcoholism.

RESOURCES AND FURTHER READING

Bales, R.: Cultural differences in rates of alcoholism. *QJSA* 6:480–499, 1946.

Bateson, G.: The cybernetics of "self": a theory of alcoholism. *Am J Psychiatry* 34:1–18, 1971.

Goodwin, D.: Alcoholism and genetics. *Arch Gen Psychiatry* 42:171–174, 1985.

Goodwin, D.: Studies of familial alcoholism: a review. *J Clin Psychiatry* 45(12):14–17, 1984.

Johnson, V.: *I'll quit tomorrow.* Rev. ed. New York: Harper & Row, 1980.

Keller, M.: The disease concept of alcoholism revisited. *J Stud Alcohol* 37:1694–1717, 1976.

McCord, W., and McCord, J.: A longitudinal study of the personality of alcoholics. In D.J. Pittman and C.R. Snyder (Eds.), *Society, culture, and drinking patterns.* New York: John Wiley & Sons, Inc. 1962.

Pattison E.M.: Cultural level interventions in the arena of alcoholism. *Alcoholism Clinical and Experimental Research* 8(2):160–164, 1984.

Vaillant, G.: *The natural history of alcoholism.* Cambridge, MA: Harvard University Press, 1983.

Medical complications

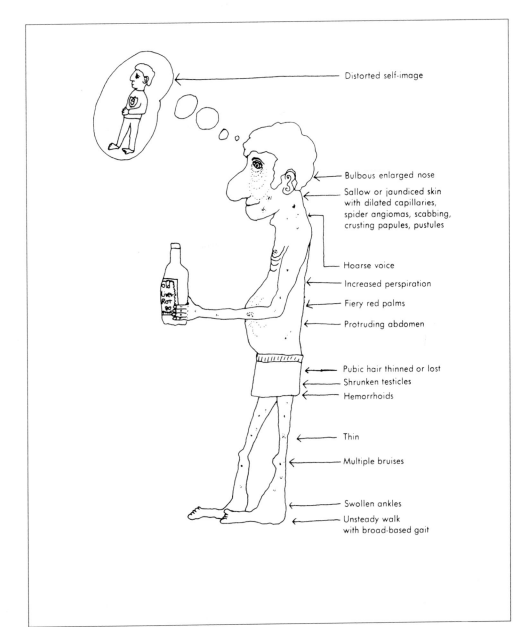

5

Distorted self-image

Bulbous enlarged nose

Sallow or jaundiced skin with dilated capillaries, spider angiomas, scabbing, crusting papules, pustules

Hoarse voice

Increased perspiration

Fiery red palms

Protruding abdomen

Pubic hair thinned or lost

Shrunken testicles

Hemorrhoids

Thin

Multiple bruises

Swollen ankles

Unsteady walk with broad-based gait

Alcoholism is one of the most common chronic diseases in all of medicine. The prevalence is 7% in the population at large. Untreated, its natural history is a predictable, gradually progressive downhill course. The observable early symptoms and manifestations of the primary disease alcoholism are for the most part behavioral and nonphysical. Later in its course alcoholism causes a wide variety of medical complications, in a multitude of different organ systems. These are associated with a host of different physical signs and symptoms.

It is important to emphasize the distinction between the primary disease alcoholism and its late secondary medical complications. Alcoholism, the disease, is one of the most highly treatable of chronic illnesses. If recognized and treated early—that means *before* major medical complications have occurred—it may be entirely arrested. Successfully treated clients can function quite normally, with the only long-term disability being that they cannot use alcohol. On the other hand, if unrecognized or untreated, its complications are likely to be irreversible and eventually fatal.

Other chapters in this book focus on the primary disease alcoholism, particularly as it appears at an early and highly treatable stage. This chapter focuses on the late secondary medical complications of alcoholism. It also touches on common medical problems that may be aggravated by moderate alcohol use. An acquaintance with the medical complications of chronic alcoholism is equivalent to familiarity with an exceedingly broad cross section of medical disease, because nearly every organ system is affected. In the past, in view of the protean and multisystem manifestations of both tuberculosis and syphilis, it was said "to know TB or syphilis is to know medicine." The same can now be said of alcoholism: to know alcoholism is to know medicine.

In this section we will touch briefly, in a systems-oriented fashion, on most of the major alcohol-related problems. First, however, let us examine a composite picture of a person afflicted with the visible stigmata of chronic alcoholism.

VISIBLE SIGNS AND STIGMATA OF CHRONIC ALCOHOLISM

Statistically, the typical alcoholic is male; thus we will say he. However, women alcoholics can and do show virtually all the same signs of chronic heavy alcohol use, except those involving the reproductive organs. Bearing in mind that any given alcoholic may have many or only a few of these visible manifestations, let us examine a hypothetical chronic drinker who has them all.

He is a typically thin, but occasionally somewhat bloated-appearing, middle-aged individual. Hyperpigmented, sallow, or jaundiced skin accentuates his wasted, chronically fatigued, and weakened overall appearance. He walks haltingly and unsteadily with a broad-based gait (ataxia); multiple bruises are evident. He perspires heavily. His voice is hoarse and croaking, punctuated by occasional hiccups, and he carries an odor of alcohol on his breath.

The abdomen protrudes. Closer examination of it reveals the *caput medusae*—a prominent superficial abdominal vein pattern, so called because of the resemblance of these distended vessels to the snakes that the mythological Medusa had on her head in place of hair. There is marked ankle swelling, and he has hemorrhoids. His breasts may be enlarged, his testicles shrunken, and his chest, axillary, and/or pubic hair entirely lost or thinned. Inspection of the skin reveals dilated capillaries, acnelike lesions, and maybe a bulbous enlarged nose. There is scabbing and crusting secondary to generalized itching. He has spider angiomas on the upper half of the body. These are small red skin lesions that blanch with light pressure applied to their centers and spread into a spidery pattern with release of pressure. His palms, especially the lateral portions, are fiery red (liver palms). He may have "paper money" skin, so called because tiny capillaries are distinctly visible, much like the tiny red-colored fibers in a new dollar bill. In colder climates, there may be evidence of repeated frostbite. The fingernails are likely to be affected. They may have either transverse white-colored bands (Muehrcke's lines) or transverse furrows, or may be totally opaque without moons showing at the base of the nail. He may well have difficulty fully extending the third, fourth, and fifth fingers due to a flexion deformity called Dupuytren's contracture. A swelling of the parotid glands in the cheeks, giving him the appearance of having the mumps, is known as "chipmunk facies." Finally, a close look at the whites of the eyes reveals small blood vessels with a corkscrew shape.

There are more old drunkards than old physicians.

RABELAIS

Now, with these externally visible characteristics in mind, let us look inside the body at the underlying diseased organ systems and see how they may account for them.

GASTROINTESTINAL SYSTEM

Many a man keeps on drinking till he hasn't a coat to either his back or his stomach.

GEORGE D. PRENTICE

Alcohol effects the gastrointestinal (GI) system in a variety of ways. This is the route by which alcohol enters the body and is absorbed. It is where the first steps of metabolism take place. Moderate amounts of alcohol can disturb and alter the normal functioning of this system. Moreover, chronic heavy use of alcohol can raise havoc. Alcohol can have both direct and indirect effects. Direct effects are any changes that occur in response to the presence of alcohol. Indirect effects would be whatever occurs next, as a consequence of the initial, direct impact.

Irritation, bleeding, and malabsorption

Chronic use of alcohol, as does any alcohol use, stimulates the stomach lining's secretion of hydrochloric acid and irritates the gut's lining. It also inhibits the muscular contractions called peristalsis that pass food along the intestines. In combination, these effects can lead to a generalized irritation of the mucous membrane lining the gut, especially in the stomach. Chronic heavy drinkers may also complain of frequent belching, loss of appetite, alternating diarrhea and constipation, morning nausea, and vomiting.

Irritation, rather than being found throughout the GI system, is more often localized to particular portions. If the esophagus is irritated, esophagitis results. This is experienced as midchest pain and pain on swallowing. Acute and chronic stomach irritation by alcohol results in gastritis, which involves inflammation, abdominal pain, and maybe even bleeding. Chronic alcohol use, if not indeed causing, can certainly aggravate ulcers of the stomach or duodenum (the first section of the small intestine). Bleeding can occur at any of the irritated sites. This represents a potentially serious medical problem. Bleeding from the GI tract can be either slow or massive. Either way, it is serious. Frequently, for reasons to be discussed later, the alcoholic's blood clots less rapidly. So the body's built-in defenses to reduce bleeding are weakened. Surgery may be required to stop the bleeding in some cases.

In addition to the causes of GI bleeding just mentioned, there are several other causes. The irritation of the stomach lining, not unexpectedly, upsets the stomach. With that can come prolonged violent nausea, vomiting, and retching. This may be so severe as to cause mechanical tears in the esophageal lining and bring on massive bleeding. Another cause of massive and often fatal upper GI bleeding is ruptured, dilated veins along the esophagus (esophageal varices). The distention and dilation of these veins occurs as a result of chronic liver disease and cirrhosis, as we shall see shortly.

Chronic irritation of the esophagus by a combination of long-standing heavy alcohol consumption and cigarette smoking significantly increases the risk of developing cancer there. The result of chronic excessive use of alcohol on small intestinal function can lead to abnormal absorption of a variety of foodstuffs, vitamins, and other nutrients. Although no specific diseases of the large intestine are caused by alcohol use, diarrhea frequently occurs. Hemorrhoids, also a byproduct of chronic liver disease and cirrhosis, are common in chronic alcoholics.

Pancreatitis

Alcohol is frequently the culprit in causing acute inflammation of the pancreas, known as *acute pancreatitis*. The pancreas is a gland tucked away behind the stomach and small intestine. It makes digestive juices, which are needed to break down starches, fats, and proteins. These juices are secreted into the duodenum through the pancreatic duct, in response to alcohol as well as other foodstuffs. They are alkaline and thus are important in neutralizing the acid contents of the stomach, thereby helping to protect the intestinal lining. The pancreas also houses the islets of Langerhans, which secrete the hormone insulin, needed to regulate sugar levels in the blood.

Currently there are two major theories as to how alcohol causes acute pancreatitis. The first, which is currently less favored, suggests that the pancreatic duct opening into the duodenum can become swollen if the small intestine is irritated by alcohol. As it swells, pancreatic digestive juices cannot pass through it freely; they are obstructed or "stopped up." In addition it has been suggested that bile from the bile duct, which opens into the pancreatic duct, may "back-up" into the pancreatic duct and enter the pancreas itself. The pancreas then becomes inflamed. Because the bile and digestive juices cannot freely escape, in effect, autodigestion occurs.

The second theory holds that some of the excess fats in the bloodstream caused by excessive drinking are deposited in the pancreas. These fats are then digested by pancreatic enzymes

Pouring to achieve a large "head" on the beer enhances the bouquet and allows less carbonation to reach the stomach.

A drunkard is like a whiskey bottle, all neck and belly and no head.

AUSTIN O'MALLEY

whose usual task is breaking down dietary fats. In turn, the products of this process, free fatty acids, cause cell injury in the pancreas, which results in further release of fat-digesting enzymes. Thus a vicious cycle is set up. The symptoms of acute pancreatitis include nausea, vomiting, occasional diarrhea, and severe upper abdominal pain radiating straight through to the back. Chronic inflammation of the pancreas can lead to calcification, visible on abdominal x-ray films. This is a relapsing illness almost always associated with long-standing alcohol use as a result of chronic cell damage. In chronic pancreatitis, diabetes can result from the decreased capacity of the pancreas to produce and release insulin.

Liver disease

The liver is a most fascinating organ. You recall that it is the liver enzyme, alcohol dehydrogenase (ADH), that begins the breakdown process of alcohol. The liver is also responsible for a host of other tasks. It breaks down wastes and toxic substances. It manufactures essential blood components, including clotting factors. It stores certain vitamins, such as B_{12} which is essential for red blood cells. It helps regulate the blood-sugar level, a very critical task, because that is the only food the brain can use. Liver disease occurs because the presence of alcohol disturbs the metabolic machinery of the liver. Metabolizing alcohol is always a very high-priority liver function. Therefore, whenever alcohol is present, the liver is "distracted" from other normal and necessary functions. For the alcoholic, this can be a good part of the time.

As you may know, liver disease is one of the physical illnesses most commonly associated with alcoholism. Three major forms of liver disease are associated with alcohol abuse. The first is *acute fatty liver*. This condition may develop in anyone who has been drinking heavily, even for relatively brief periods of time. Fatty liver gets its name from the deposits of fat that build up in normal liver cells. This occurs because of a decrease in breakdown of fatty acids and an increase in the synthesis of fats by the liver. The latter is a result of the "distracting" metabolic effects of alcohol (see Chapter 2.) Acute fatty liver occurs whenever 30% to 50% or more of the dietary calories are in the form of alcohol. This is true even if the diet is otherwise adequate. Acute fatty liver is a reversible condition if alcohol use is stopped.

Alcoholic hepatitis is a more serious form of liver disease that often follows a severe or prolonged bout of heavy drinking. Although more commonly seen in alcoholics, hepatitis, like acute fatty liver, may occur in nonalcoholics as well. In hepatitis there is actual inflammation of the liver and variable damage to liver cells. One may also find associated evidence of acute fatty liver changes. Frequently liver metabolism is seriously disturbed. Jaundice is a usual sign of hepatitis. Jaundice refers to the yellowish cast of the skin and the whites of the eyes. The yellow color comes from the pigment found in bile, a digestive juice made by the liver. The bile is being handled improperly and is therefore circulating in the bloodstream in excessive amounts. Other symptoms of alcoholic hepatitis may include weakness, easy fatigability, loss of appetite, occasional nausea and vomiting, low-grade fever, mild weight loss, increasing ascites, dark urine, and light stools.

Although in some patients hepatitis is completely reversible with abstinence from alcohol, in others it may be fatal or go on to become a smoldering chronic disease. Among patients who stop drinking, only 1 in 5 will go on to develop alcoholic cirrhosis. But 50% to 80% of those who continue drinking will develop cirrhosis. Alcoholic hepatitis is in many cases clearly a forerunner of *alcoholic cirrhosis*, but it is thought that alcoholic cirrhosis can also appear without the prior occurrence of alcoholic hepatitis.

Cirrhosis of the liver is a condition in which there is widespread destruction of liver cells. These are replaced by nonfunctioning scar tissue. In fact, the word *cirrhosis* simply means scarring. There are many different types and causes of cirrhosis, but long-term heavy alcohol use is the cause in the vast majority (80%) of cases. It is estimated that about 1 in 10 long-term heavy drinkers will eventually develop alcoholic cirrhosis. Given the nature of the disease, it is accompanied by very serious and often relatively irreversible metabolic and physiological abnormalities. That is very bad news. In fact, more than half of the patients who continue to drink after the diagnosis of alcoholic cirrhosis has been made are dead within 5 years.

In alcoholic cirrhosis the liver is simply unable to perform its work properly. Toxic substances, normally removed by the liver, circulate in the bloodstream, creating problems elsewhere in the body. This is particularly true of the brain, as we shall see later. The liver normally handles the majority of the blood from the gut or intestinal tract as it returns to the heart. The cirrhotic liver, now a mass of scar tissue, is unable to handle the usual blood flow. The blood, unable to move through the portal vein (the route from the blood vessels around the intestines to the liver), is forced to seek alternative return routes to the heart. This leads to pressure and "backup" in these alternative vessels. It is this pressure that causes the veins in the esophagus to become distended, producing esophageal varices and inviting hemorrhaging. The same pressure accounts for hemorrhoids and the caput medusae mentioned above.

Another phenomenon associated with cirrhosis is ascites. Here the liver "weeps" tissue fluid directly into the abdominal cavity. Again, this is caused by the back pressure. This fluid would normally be taken up and transported back to the heart by the hepatic veins and lymphatic system. Large amounts of fluid can collect and distend the abdomen; a woman, for example, can look very pregnant. If you were to gently tap the side of a person with ascites, you would see a wavelike motion in response, as fluid sloshes around. Another result of alcoholic liver disease is diminished ability of the liver to store glycogen, the body's storage form of sugar. There is also less ability to produce glucose from other nutrients such as proteins. This can lead to low blood-sugar levels (see also Chapter 2). This is an important fact when it comes to treating an alcoholic diabetic: insulin also lowers the blood sugar.

Another situation in which this is important is in treating apparent coma in any alcoholic. Insufficient amounts of blood sugar may cause coma, essentially because the brain is without enough of a fuel supply to function. Intravenous glucose may be necessary to prevent irreversible brain damage. On the other hand, alcohol and alcoholic liver damage may lead to states of diabetes-like, higher than normal blood-glucose levels. This occurs in large part because of the effects of alcohol and alcoholic liver disease on certain other glucose-regulating hormones in the body besides insulin.

Hepatic coma (hepatic encephalopathy) can be one result of cirrhosis. In this case, the damage comes from toxins circulating in the bloodstream. In essence, the brain is "poisoned" by these wastes and its ability to function seriously impaired, leading to coma. Cancer of the liver is another complication of long-standing cirrhosis. Another source of bad news is that, of people who get cirrhosis, as many as 50% will also have pancreatitis. So these persons have two serious medical conditions. Still other complications may include GI bleeding, salt and water retention, and renal failure. The main elements of treatment for cirrhosis are abstinence from alcohol, multivitamins, a nutritionally balanced adequate diet, and bed rest. Even with such treatment, the prognosis of cirrhosis is not good and many of the complications just described may occur.

The different forms of alcohol-related liver disease result from specific changes in liver cells. Unfortunately, there is no neat and consistent relationship between a specific liver abnormality and the particular constellation of symptoms that develops. Although laboratory tests indicate liver damage, they cannot pinpoint the kind of alcohol-related liver disease. Therefore, some authorities believe a liver biopsy, which involves direct examination of a liver tissue sample, is essential to evaluate the situation properly.

Until the early 1970s it was believed that liver damage common to alcoholism was *not* a direct effect of the alcohol. Rather, it was believed that the damage was caused by poor nutrition. It has since been learned that alcohol itself plays a major direct role. Liver damage can occur even in the presence of adequate nutrition when excessive amounts of alcohol are consumed.

HEMATOLOGICAL SYSTEM

The blood, known as the hematological system, is the body's major transportation network. The blood carries oxygen to the tissues. It takes up waste products of cell metabolism and carts them off to the lungs and kidneys for removal. It carries nutrients, minerals, and hormones to the cells. The blood also protects the body through the anti-infection agents it carries. Although the blood looks like a liquid, it contains formed elements (solid components). These formed elements include red blood cells, white blood cells, and platelets. They are all suspended in the serum, the fluid or liquid part of the blood. Each of the formed elements of the blood is profoundly affected by alcohol abuse. Whenever there is a disturbance of these essential blood ingredients, problems arise.

Red cells

Let us begin with the red blood cells. The most common problem here is anemia, too few red blood cells. Anemia is a general term like fever. It simply means insufficient function or amounts. Logically, one can imagine this result coming about in a number of ways. Too few can be manufactured if there is a shortage of nutrients to produce them. If they are produced, they

can be defective. They can be lost, for example, through bleeding. They can actually be destroyed. In fact, alcohol contributes to anemia in each of these ways.

How does alcohol abuse relate to the first situation, inadequate production? The most likely culprit here is inadequate nutrition. Red blood cells cannot be manufactured if the bone marrow does not have the necessary ingredients. Iron is a key ingredient. Alcohol or some of its metabolic products, like acetaldehyde, are thought to interfere with the bone marrow's ability to use iron in making hemoglobin, which is the oxygen-carrying part of the blood. Even if there is enough iron in the system, it "just passes on by." On the other hand, a poor diet, not uncommon among alcoholics, may mean an insufficient iron intake. Chronic GI bleeding may also result from chronic alcohol abuse. If so, the iron in the red blood cells is lost and not available for recycling. This type of anemia is called *iron-deficiency anemia*. Another variety, *sideroblastic anemia*, is also related to nutritional deficiencies. This comes from too little pyridoxal phosphate (a substance that facilitates the production of vitamin B_6 related cofactor). This substance is also needed by the bone marrow cells to produce hemoglobin.

These first two varieties of anemia account for the inadequate production of red blood cells. Another variety, *megaloblastic anemia*, is also related to nutritional deficiencies: too little folate. This happens because folate is not in the diet in sufficient quantities, and/or the small intestine is unable to absorb it properly because of other effects of chronic alcohol abuse. What results then is defective red blood cell production. Without this vitamin, red blood cells cannot mature. They are released from the bone marrow in primitive, less functional forms that are larger than normal.

Chronic loss of blood from the gut, GI bleeding, can result in anemia. Here the bone marrow simply cannot make enough new cells to keep up with those that are lost. The body normally destroys and "recycles" old red blood cells through a process called *hemolysis*. Abnormally rapid hemolysis may occur in alcoholics. The life span of red cells can be shortened by up to 50%. One abnormal cause of hemolysis is hypersplenism, which results from chronic liver disease. The spleen, enlarged and not working properly, destroys perfectly good red blood cells as well as the old worn-out ones. Toxic factors in the serum of the blood are also thought to be responsible for three other varieties of hemolysis. *Stomatocytosis* is a transient, relatively benign form of anemia related to binge drinking and unrelated to severe alcoholic liver disease. *Spur cell anemia*, on the other hand, is associated with severe, often end-stage, chronic alcoholic liver disease. The name comes from the shape of the red cell, which, when seen under the microscope, has jagged protrusions. *Zieve's syndrome* is the co-occurrence in an alcoholic patient of jaundice, transient hemolytic anemia, elevated cholesterol levels, and acute fatty liver disease without enlargement of the spleen.

In France, and maybe elsewhere, other changes in red blood cells have been reported in those who drink at least 2 to 3 quarts of wine each day. These are changes typically seen with lead poisoning. (Lead, even in low concentrations, can mean trouble.) Excessive intake of wine in France is thought to be a significant source of dietary lead. In the United States, there are periodically reports of lead poisoning connected with alcohol use. However, the circumstances are different; the beverage has not been wine, but moonshine! In these cases, old car radiators were used in the distilling process.

White cells

We now move on to the effects of alcohol on white blood cells. These cells are one of the body's main defenses against infection. The chronic use of alcohol affects white cells. This contributes to the increased susceptibility to and frequency of severe infections, especially respiratory tract infections in alcoholics. Alcohol has a direct toxic effect on the white blood cell reserves. This leads to a reduced number of two types of white cells to fight infection (both granulocytes and T-lymphocytes). *Chemotaxis*, or white cell mobilization, is diminished by alcohol. In other words, although the white cells' ability to kill the bacteria is not affected, they have difficulty reaching the site of infection in adequate numbers. Alcohol also interferes with white cell adherence to bacteria, which is one of the body's defensive inflammatory reactions. Possibly this occurs because under the influence of alcohol, white cells may have a diminished ability to ingest bacteria.

Platelets

Alcoholics are frequently subject to bleeding disorders. They bruise easily. Bleeding can occur in the GI tract, the nose, and the gums. This is largely explained by the effect of alcohol in decreasing the number of platelets. Platelets are a major component of the body's clotting system and act like a patch on a leak.

Alcohol has a direct toxic effect on bone marrow production of platelets. Thus, 1 out of every 4 alcoholic patients will have abnormally low platelet counts. Within 1 to 3 days of stopping drinking, these begin to rise toward normal. Recall that severe liver disease can cause hypersplenism. This can cause abnormally rapid destruction of platelets and thereby contribute to the low platelet counts seen in alcoholics.

Clotting factors and DIC

When the liver's metabolic processes are disrupted by the effects of chronic alcohol use, there is often a decrease in the production of some of the necessary serum-clotting factors. One thing to bear in mind is that there are thirteen to fifteen such substances needed to make a clot. Of these, five are liver produced; ergo, liver disease may in this way frequently lead to bleeding problems in alcoholics.

Severe liver damage can also contribute to the occurrence of *disseminated intravascular coagulation* (DIC). This is a life-threatening state of diffuse, abnormally accelerated coagulation. This consumes large quantities of clotting factors, as well as platelets. This leads to dangerously lowered amounts of both which can, in turn, result in excessive and uncontrolled bleeding.

Alcohol and the immune system

Another area of current research is examining ways the immune system may be altered by alcohol. Actually, there are two different immune systems. One is associated with *circulating immune factors*, such as complement and immunoglobulins, in the blood system. The other is associated with *antibodies attached to individual cells*. Changes in both systems can occur with chronic alcohol use. The ability of serum (the unformed elements of the blood) to kill gram-negative bacteria is impaired by alcohol. This may be related to the diseased liver's lowered ability to produce complement, an important agent in the body's inflammatory response. Many immune and defensive responses depend on its presence. Although not clearly established, the effects of alcohol on B-lymphocytes may lead to decreased production of circulating antibodies, which normally fight bacterial infections. Alcohol has also been shown to decrease the numbers of T-lymphocytes, which mediate *cellular immunity* . It also inhibits their responsiveness to stimuli that activate their functioning. These changes probably account in large part for the alcoholic's increased susceptibility to infection.

Recent research has suggested that alcohol-induced changes in some white cells together with changes in the cell-based immune system may lead to an increased production of certain types of fibrous tissues. It is just such fibrous tissues that are characteristic of cirrhosis. A current $64 question is whether the scar tissue of cirrhosis can at least in part be attributed to white cell changes and alterations in the cells' immune response that are induced by chronic alcohol use.

Even though the hematological complications of chronic heavy alcohol use are many and potentially quite serious, they are in general totally reversible following abstinence. But the liver disease that caused them may be so severe as to preclude this. The speed with which they reverse is often dependent upon improvement in the underlying liver disease. But the reversal can be enhanced in many instances by administering the deficient substances, such as folate, pyridoxine, and iron, in addition to restoring a fully adequate diet.

CARDIOVASCULAR SYSTEM

Long-term heavy alcohol use is thought to be directly responsible for a specific form of heart muscle disease, known in the past as *alcoholic cardiomyopathy*, but now referred to as *alcoholic heart muscle disease (AHMD)*. This occurs in 2% of alcoholics in a clinically apparent form. However, it is estimated that 80% have similar though less severe and thereby subclinical forms of alcohol-related heart muscle disease. When clinically apparent, AHMD is a severe condition with low-output heart failure, shortness of breath with the least exertion, and dramatic enlargement of the heart. (Low-output failure occurs when the pumping action of the heart cannot maintain a sufficient output of blood to meet the body's usual, normal demands. This results from abnormal function of the heart muscle as a primary cause.) AHMD occurs most commonly in middle-aged males who have been drinking heavily for 10 or more years. It often responds well to discontinuing alcohol, plus long-term bed rest. (As some have noted, "Abstinence makes the heart grow stronger.") Other standard medical treatment for congestive heart failure is also helpful as adjuncts in the treatment of AHMD. Another form of heart disease with high-output congestive heart failure known as *beriberi heart disease* may be seen in alcoholism. (High-output heart failure, a form of secondary heart failure, occurs when an otherwise normal heart fails, because it can't keep up with the abnormally high rate of output being demanded by the body.) In this case this results, for reasons that are unclear, from a deficiency

Absinthe makes the heart grow fonder.
ADDISON MIZNER

of vitamin B$_1$, thiamine. It may respond dramatically to correction of the thiamine deficiency and replacement of thiamine in the diet.

As an aside, a rather unusual and specific type of severe cardiac disease was noted to occur a few years ago among drinkers of a particular type of Canadian beer. It was found to be due not to alcohol per se, but rather to the noxious effects of small amounts of cobalt. The cobalt had been added to the beer to maintain its "head." These cases occurred in the mid to late 1960s and had a mortality rate of 50% to 60%. Fortunately, the cause was identified, and presumably cobalt-induced heart disease will no longer occur. An earlier similar epidemic of congestive heart failure due to arsenic-contaminated beer occurred around the turn of the century in England.

A variety of *abnormalities in cardiac rhythm* have been associated with alcohol. In fact, nearly the entire spectrum of such abnormalities may be caused by acute and chronic alcohol intake. Such arrhythmias, as they are called, may affect either the upper (atrial) or lower (ventricular) portions of the heart. The upper (atrial) chambers of the heart are like the primers to the lower (ventricular) part that acts as the pump. Thus ventricular rhythm irregularities tend to be more serious. Atrial fibrillation and atrial flutter occur in the upper heart muscles and produce an ineffective atrial beat that diminishes the priming of the ventricular beat to follow. Paroxymal atrial tachycardia is another alcohol-induced irregular rhythm in the upper part of the heart. It produces a different and more rapid than usual beat. Alcohol also causes an increase in the frequency of premature ventricular contractions. These along with atrial flutter and fibrillation are the most common alcohol-induced arrhythmias. There are also irregular or in-between contractions of the lower part of the heart. They can create a very dangerous condition. If the irregular contractions occur in a particular pattern, which may be induced by alcohol, they can cause sudden death. In fact, studies have shown an increased incidence of sudden death in alcoholic populations. Another effect is sinus tachycardia with palpitations. This is thought to occur because of the effects of alcohol and its metabolite, acetaldehyde, in releasing norepinephrine. The sinus node is the normal pacemaker of the heart. Its rate of firing can be greatly increased by the amount of circulating epinephrine and norepinephrine.

Recently there have been reports of a new alcohol-induced, arrhythmia-related syndrome. It goes by the name *holiday heart*

syndrome. As you might expect with that name, arrhythmias occur after heavy alcohol intake, around holidays and on Mondays after weekend binges. The syndrome involves palpitations and arrhythmias, but no evidence of cardiomyopathy or congestive heart failure. The signs and symptoms clear completely after a few days of abstinence.

Alcohol, even in moderate amounts, exacerbates certain abnormalities of blood fats in individuals with *Type IV hyperlipoproteinemia*, but not in normal persons who don't have this condition. Alcohol elevates fat levels of a particular kind believed to increase the rate of development of arteriosclerosis (hardening of the arteries). The coronary arteries thus become increasingly occluded or blocked, making premature heart attacks more likely. Even small amounts of alcohol can significantly affect this disorder in individuals at risk.

Alcohol is well known to cause dilation of peripheral superficial blood vessels and capillaries. It does not seem to have a similarly predictable effect on the coronary arterial blood vessels and the blood flow through them. Therefore, despite its use in treating angina in the past, currently this is not considered helpful. Recent studies indicate that in persons with angina, alcohol decreases exercise tolerance. Thus alcohol use may be dangerous especially in conjunction with vigorous exercise or physical activity.

On the other hand, perhaps somewhat surprisingly, findings of recent research suggest that moderate amounts of alcohol (two or fewer drinks per day) may provide a protective effect against the occurrence of heart attacks in people without blood fat abnormalities. Such reports suggest that one cocktail per day has roughly the same effect on serum cholesterol as the average lipid-lowering diet or regular vigorous exercise. It leads to increased level of HDL cholesterol and decreased levels of LDL cholesterol. Higher and lower levels of these substances, respectively, are associated with lower risks of heart attacks. So moderate daily use of alcohol may be desirable from your heart's point of view.

In work recently reported, a definite link was shown between heavy drinking and *hypertension.* Heavy drinkers had both elevated systolic and diastolic blood pressures. This was true even when weight, age, serum cholesterol, and smoking were controlled for. Although this relationship seems well established, the specific role alcohol plays in the development of atherosclerosis is much less clear, especially in view of the multiple and complex interaction of factors causing this condition.

Wine is at the head of all medicines.
TALMUD: BABA BATHRA, 58b

GENITOURINARY SYSTEM

Urinary tract

Almost uniquely, the kidneys are not commonly directly affected by alcohol in major ways. What happens in the kidneys generally is the result of disordered function elsewhere in the body. For example, alcohol promotes the production of urine through its ability to inhibit the production and output of antidiuretic hormone by the hypothalamic–pituitary region of the brain. The blood goes to the kidney for filtering, and water and wastes are separated from it and excreted through the bladder. Normally, in this process, antidiuretic hormone allows water to be reabsorbed by the kidney to maintain the body's fluid balance. When the hormone levels are suppressed, the kidney's capacity to reabsorb water is diminished. Instead, it is excreted from the body. Alcohol only inhibits this hormone's production when the blood alcohol level is rising. This is so after as little as 2 ounces of pure alcohol. When the blood alcohol level is steady, or falling, there is no such effect. In fact, the opposite may be true. There may be a retention of fluids by the body. This makes the use of intravenous fluids as a standard practice in treating alcoholics in withdrawal not only often useless, but possibly even hazardous.

Alcohol can lead to acute urinary retention and recurrence and exacerbation of urinary tract infections and/or prostatitis. This is due to its ability to cause spasm and congestion in diseased prostate glands as well as in the tissues around previously existing urethral strictures. It has recently been found that patients with alcoholic cirrhosis occasionally have abnormalities involving the glomeruli in their kidneys. These are tiny, round, encapsulated capillary structures that constitute the extreme upstream end of the kidneys' major functional unit, the nephron. The glomeruli function a bit like a sieve or a filter. As blood passes through the capillary network, wastes as well as some essential fluids and electrolytes are filtered out. The resultant ultrafiltrate is passed on into the tubular portion of the nephron. Cells, serum proteins, and other components of the filtered blood that remain behind are returned to the general circulation. While proceeding downstream through the nephron (the renal tubules), the ultrafiltrate undergoes much further processing and modification. Other wastes and excess water are added; while essential minerals and electrolytes are reabsorbed and conserved. What emerges from the tubule is urine, eventually to be excreted without further modification.

With this as a background, let's look at the two main types of glomerular abnormality. The first, a form of *glomerulosclerosis* that is much more common, rarely causes significant problems. The second, which is fortunately far less common, results in inflammatory damage to the glomeruli that can interfere with the filtration process and elimination of the wastes produced by the kidney. This condition is sometimes called *cirrhotic glomerulonephritis*.

Cirrhosis may cause a number of troubles further on down the nephron. It can cause (1) increased reabsorption of sodium, which may play a significant role in the ascites and edema of cirrhosis; (2) abnormal handling of H^{+1}, HCO_3^-, and other ions by the renal tubule; and (3) an inability to excrete excess water normally, which may cause serious electrolyte disturbances such as a decreased serum sodium level. The causes of all these functional renal abnormalities, not fully understood, are complex and very likely caused by a number of factors in combination.

A nearly uniformly fatal, but fortunately uncommon, consequence of chronic alcohol use is the *hepatorenal syndrome*. This is thought to be caused by a toxic serum factor, or factors, secondary to severe liver disease. These factors cause shifts in kidney blood flow and diminish effective perfusion (filtering through) of the kidney. Unless the underlying liver disease is somehow reversed, irreversible kidney failure can occur. One reason *for not* giving diuretics to relieve ascites in alcoholics with liver disease is that they can precipitate this disorder. Interestingly, there appears to be nothing intrinsically wrong with the kidneys themselves. They can be transplanted into a patient without underlying liver disease and perform normally. Likewise, liver transplantation in such patients will restore normal kidney function. Thus the kidney failure is thought to be due to some circulating toxic factor(s) presumably resulting from the associated liver disease.

Reproductive system

Chronic heavy alcohol use affects the reproductive system in both men and women. In women there may be skipped menstrual periods; in men, diminished libido, impotence, and on occasion, sterility. In addition to its many other functions, the liver plays an important role in the balance of sex hormones. So when the liver is impaired, an imbalance of sex hormones results. Both male and female sex hormones are normally present in both sexes, only in different proportions. The increased levels of female hormones in alcoholic men, due to the decreased liver metabolism of these hormones can lead to "feminization" of features. Breasts can enlarge, testicles shrink, and a loss or thin-

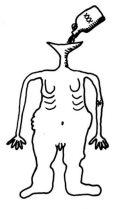

ning of body hair can occur. Sex-hormone alterations in males also result from alcohol's direct inhibitory action on the testes, which decreases the production of testosterone, a male sex hormone. Also ingestion of alcohol may speed up the liver's metabolism of testosterone, thereby decreasing its levels. Testosterone levels may be lowered as well by alcohol's direct inhibiting effect on various brain centers, such as the hypothalamus and pituitary gland. These are involved in the production and release of luteinizing hormone (LH), which in turn prompts the release of testosterone. Thus, when alcohol diminishes LH levels, the net effect is decreased testosterone levels. This brain-mediated hormonal effect of alcohol is a direct one, independent of any liver or nutritional problems. Alcohol also probably reduces the number of LH receptors in the testes with a similar result

The situation in women in terms of sex-hormone alterations is not as completely understood. In part this is because the female reproductive system, located within the body, is less accessible to study and research. However, it is also because the effects of the use of alcohol by women as a distinct area of inquiry is a fairly recent development. Nonetheless there is some evidence that alcohol may have direct toxic effects on both the ovaries and the pituitary. These are likely to play a role in the menstrual and fertility changes in female alcoholics.

Finally, although sexual interests and pursuits may be heightened by alcohol's release of inhibitions, ability to perform sexually can be impaired. For example, in men there may be either relative or absolute impotency, despite alcohol-fueled increased desire. Centuries ago Shakespeare in *Macbeth* (Act 2; Scene 1) described these paradoxical effects of alcohol:

MACDUFF: What three things does drink especially provoke?
PORTER: Merry, sir, nose-painting, sleep, and urine. Lechery, sir, it provokes, and unprovokes; it provokes the desire, but it takes away the performance.

Abstinence from alcohol, improvement in liver disease, and an adequate diet will, in part, though often not completely, reverse the alcohol-induced changes in sexual and reproductive functions. Some males may also benefit from testosterone replacement.

ALCOHOL AND PREGNANCY

Fetal alcohol syndrome

Since 1971, considerable attention has been directed toward the effects of chronic alcohol use during pregnancy. At that time, a researcher reported his observations of infants born to alcoholic mothers. The constellation of features observed have since been termed the fetal alcohol syndrome. Alcohol can pass through the placenta to the developing fetus and interfere with prenatal development. At birth, infants with fetal alcohol syndrome are smaller than normal both in weight and length. The head size is smaller, probably related to arrested brain growth. These infants also have a "dysmorphic facial appearance"; that is, they are strange looking, just appear "different." Although the difference is not easily described, changes include: an overall small head, flat checks, small eyes, and a thin upper lip, among others. At birth the infants are jittery and tremulous. Whether this jitteriness is the result of nervous system impairment from the long-term exposure to alcohol and/or miniwithdrawal is unclear. There have been reports of newborn infants having the scent of alcohol on their breath. Cardiac problems and retardation are also associated with the fetal alcohol syndrome in almost half of the cases (46%). This syndrome is now being seen as the third leading and major preventable cause of mental retardation. (See Chapter 6 for further discussion of the effects of maternal alcoholism on children.)

Fetal alcohol effects

It is now well established that a mother does not have to be an alcoholic to expose her unborn baby to the risks of alcohol during pregnancy. Nor do alcohol's effects on the fetus have to occur as the full-blown fetal alcohol syndrome. They can occur with variable degrees of severity. When less severe, they are referred to as fetal alcohol effects. Perhaps even more worrisome than the classic fetal alcohol syndrome in offspring of alcoholic mothers are reports documenting the adverse effects on the unborn baby of the mother's drinking more than two drinks (1 ounce of pure alcohol) on even a single occasion. As little as two drinks a day may lead to an increased risk of abnormalities. This two-drink figure is not a numerical average but refers to the amount of alcohol consumed on any 1 day. As the amount of alcohol consumed on any given day rises, the risk also increases.

Less than two drinks	Very little risk
Two to four drinks	10% risk of abnormalities
Ten drinks	50% risk of abnormalities
Over ten drinks	75% risk of abnormalities

Not surprisingly given similar findings with other drugs, the teratogenic effects of alcohol are greater in the first 3 months of pregnancy, as compared to the fourth through ninth months. Based on this information, in the summer of 1977 the NIAAA issued a health warning, advising expectant mothers not to have more than two drinks a day. In 1981, a much stronger warning was issued. The U.S. Surgeon General (the nation's highest public health official) advised that women wishing to become pregnant as well as women who are pregnant consume *no* alcohol.

How alcohol interferes with normal prenatal growth is not fully understood. Research with animals suggests that alcohol crosses the placenta freely and diffuses throughout fetal tissues in much the same fashion as it does in adults. As a toxin alcohol disrupts the normal growth sequence; the developing fetus cannot later "make up" for these disruptions. The particular abnormalities seen are directly related to the critical development that was occurring when alcohol was present.

Preliminary research suggests too that the alcohol level of some of the fetal tissues may be higher than that of the mother. If this is in fact the case, the reason has not been clearly identified. One would predict that the alcohol, because it can pass freely through the placenta to the fetus, should be able to exit just as easily. Therefore, both mother and fetus would be expected to have equivalent blood alcohol levels. However, case reports of women who drank alcohol during labor and in whom blood alcohol level studies were done, indicate that the newborn baby's blood alcohol and tissue alcohol levels do not drop as fast as the mother's. The reason presumably is that the infant has an immature liver. Newborns do not have the fully developed enzyme systems (alcohol dehydrogenase) necessary to metabolize and eliminate alcohol as rapidly as their mothers do. Thus for a given maternal blood alcohol level, the fetus may have a somewhat higher blood and tissue alcohol concentration for a longer period of time than might be expected.

RESPIRATORY SYSTEM

Alcohol affects the respiratory rate. Low to moderate doses of alcohol increase the respiration rate, presumably by direct action on the medullary respiration center in the brain. In larger, anesthetic, and/or toxic doses the respiration rate is decreased. This latter effect may contribute to respiratory insufficiency in persons with chronic pulmonary disease. In the past it was thought that alcohol for the most part spared the lungs as far as the direct harmful effects were concerned. This is apparently not the case. Recently such effects have been increasingly recog-

Heredity. There are on record many instances of inebriety in children conceived soon after marriage (when the parents drank wine), although children born to the same parents later in life (when the parents abstained) were temperate. If the parent is intoxicated at the time of conception, the child is likely to be a victim to insanity, inebriety and idiosy. Mothers who indulge in intoxicants freely before the birth and during the lactation of their children impart to them impulses toward inebriety....

SPOONER, WALTER W. *The Cyclopaedia of Temperance and Prohibition,* 1891.

nized and investigated. These include interference with a variety of important pulmonary cellular defenses, both mechanical and metabolic. There is interference also with oxygen transport, thereby contributing to chronic airflow obstruction, and possibly producing bronchospasm in some individuals. All these direct effects of alcohol on the lung may have significant negative consequences for clients with emphysema, chronic obstructive pulmonary disease, chronic bronchitis, and asthma.

A variety of noxious effects occur in an indirect fashion. The combination of stuporousness or unconsciousness, and vomiting, as a result of alcohol use, can lead to aspiration of mouth and nose secretions or gastric contents. The mouth and nose contents can lead to bacterial infection. With an alcoholic's diminished defenses against infection, pulmonary infections, especially with pneumococci and gram-negative bacteria, seem to occur more frequently and severely than in nonalcoholics. Also, with decreases in defenses the incidence of tuberculosis is higher in alcoholics. Thus any alcoholic with a newly positive skin test for tuberculosis should be considered for treatment to prevent possible active infection with the tuberculosis bacteria. However, the drug commonly used to treat TB (INH) carries a two times greater risk of hepatotoxicity in alcoholics. Therefore, for those with a long-standing positive skin test this risk would probably suggest that INH not routinely be given as a preventative measure.

Normal cilia pushing dust out bronchial tree

drunk cilia with hangovers

ENDOCRINE SYSTEM

The endocrine system is composed of the glands of the body and their secretions, the hormones. Hormones can be thought of as chemical messengers, released by the glands into the bloodstream. They are vital in regulating countless body processes. There is a very complex and involved interaction between hormonal activity and body functioning.

Alcohol can affect the endocrine system in three major ways. Although there are many glands, the pituitary gland, located in the brain, can be thought of as the "master gland." Many of its hormonal secretions are involved in regulating other glands. So one way that alcohol can affect the endocrine system is by altering the function of the pituitary. If this happens, then other glands are unable to function properly because they are not receiving the proper hormonal instructions. Alcohol can also affect other glands directly. Despite their receiving the correct instructions from the pituitary, alcohol can impede their ability to re-

spond. Finally, interference with the endocrine system can develop as a result of liver damage. One of the functions of the liver is to break down and metabolize hormones, thereby removing them from the system. With liver disease, this capacity is diminished and hormonal imbalances can result.

Several hormonal changes have already been mentioned. As previously described, the level of testosterone, the male sex hormone, is lowered by alcohol in a number of different ways. First is the direct inhibiting action of alcohol on the testes. Next is inhibition of the portion of the pituitary gland that secretes LH, the hormone that stimulates the testes' secretion of testosterone. Another factor is that the liver's clearance of testosterone may be increased in the alcoholic. Finally, malnutrition, which frequently occurs in alcoholics, may inhibit the hypothalamic-pituitary-testicular axis at all levels.

Serious liver disease reduces the liver's ability to break down another of the pituitary's hormones, melanocyte-stimulating hormone (MSH). This may result in increased levels of MSH, which leads to a general deepening of skin pigmentation and frequently a "dirty tan" skin color.

The adrenal glands are also affected by alcohol. The adrenals produce several hormones and thus serve multiple functions. One function known to us all comes from the release of adrenaline (epinephrine) when we are frightened or fearful. The effects of this charge of adrenaline, rapid heart-beat and sweating, comprise "the fight-or-flight response." Heavy intake or withdrawal of alcohol prompts increased discharge of catecholamines by the adrenals. This may be partly responsible for the rapid heartbeat and hypertension during withdrawal. Another adrenal hormone, aldosterone, which plays a major role in regulating the body's salt and water levels, is increased with both heavy use and withdrawal. This often leads to significant and potentially serious salt and water imbalances visible clinically as swelling (edema). An increased aldosterone level is also frequently seen in cirrhosis with ascites. This is thought to be, in part, the cause of the peripheral edema that is often seen with this condition. In some alcoholics the adrenals secrete excess cortisol. This causes a condition clinically indistinguishable from Cushing's disease, which is characterized by increased secretion of corticosteroids. What distinguishes it from true Cushing's disease and identifies it as pseudo-Cushing's is that with hospitalization and abstinence from alcohol it clears rapidly and normal cortico-steroid levels are restored.

Animal research is raising several interesting questions about alcohol's effects on the endocrine system. In animals, heavy drinking increases the levels of norepinephrine in the heart. So the question is being asked whether this may contribute to the development of alcoholic heart muscle disease (alcoholic cardiomyopathy.)

As earlier alluded to in Chapter 2, carbohydrate metabolism, which is ordinarily regulated by the hormone insulin, can be adversely affected by chronic alcohol intake. Heavy drinking may lead to abnormally high levels of glucose similar to those seen in diabetics. This condition is referred to as hyperglycemia. Usually all that is needed to correct this is abstinence from alcohol and an improved, well-balanced diet.

Long-term excessive alcohol intake as well as short-term heavy drinking binges can, on the other hand, lead to low blood sugar levels, known as hypoglycemia. This disturbance in endocronic function is caused by two factors. First, due to poor diet and liver dysfunction there are decreased liver stores of glycogen, the body's stored form of glucose that is usually available for conversion into circulating glucose. Second, there is a diminished ability by the liver to produce glucose on its own by converting amino acids into glucose, a process known as glucogenesis. (This results from the increased ratio of NADH to NAD^+ mentioned in Chapter 2, which occurs when the liver is faced with metabolizing large quantities of alcohol.) Hypoglycemia can cause coma. If prolonged, irreversible brain damage can result. This is a medical emergency and must be treated as rapidly as possible with intravenous 50% dextrose solution.

The increased NADH to NAD^+ ratio is also a major factor in causing two dangerous forms of metabolic acidosis frequently seen in alcoholics. The first is known as alcoholic ketoacidosis. It occurs when the altered ratio leads to the production not of carbon dioxide and water, as alcohol is metabolized, but instead produces ketones that are organic acids. The second, lactic acidosis, also occurs because of the altered ratio of NADH to NAD^+. In this case there is an increased production of lactate. Both types of acidosis are dangerous and must be treated with intravenous fluids and sodium bicarbonate.

Another area of research is whether alcohol's effect on the endocrine system might contribute to the development of different types of cancer. Heavy drinkers are known to have a higher incidence of skin, thyroid, and breast cancers. Recall that the pituitary gland is the master control gland. It influences the activity of various other gland tissues through the hormones it secretes. Alcohol inhibits the breakdown of pituitary MSH. It may also play a role in the release of hormones that promote thyroid activity and milk production by the breast. These three hormones have one thing in common: they affect their target tissues, the skin, thyroid gland, and breast, by causing these tissues to increase their metabolic activity. So, the pieces may be falling into place. Cancer, simply put, occurs when there is uncontrolled or abnormal cellular metabolic activity and growth. Is it possible that alcohol's presence over long periods of time produces so many hormonal messages to the skin, thyroid, and breast tissues that in certain patients in some as yet undetermined fashion, tumors may be produced? Maybe.

SKIN

Chronic alcohol use affects the skin in a variety of ways both directly and indirectly. Its most pronounced direct effect is dilation of the vessels of the skin. A variety of pathological effects on other systems are mirrored indirectly by the condition of the skin. Some examples will be instructive. A chronic flushed appearance, itching, jaundice, thinning of the skin, changes in hair distribution, the presence of spider angiomas, a grayish cast to the skin, and fingernail changes all reflect significant liver dysfunction. Bruising, paleness, and skin infections may reflect major abnormalities in the hematological system.

Skin changes may be helpful in suggesting the presence of a variety of nutritional deficiencies in alcoholism. These include: vitamin B, especially niacin (pellagra), vitamin C, and zinc deficiencies. Skin manifestations often may reflect as well the chaotic life circumstances of many alcoholics. There may be evidence of accidents, such as bruises, abrasions, lacerations, and multiple old scars. There may be evidence of frostbite in colder climates. Nicotine stains and/or cigarette burns may be present. And there may be signs of poor personal hygiene, including body lice or scabies.

Heavy and chronic alcohol use, among other causes, will precipitate or aggravate a condition called *rosacea* in predisposed persons. This condition includes flushing and inflammation especially of the nose and middle portion of the face. Particularly striking is the excessive growth of the subcutaneous tissue of the nose, a condition called *rhinophyma* or "rum nose."

Another skin condition associated with chronic alcoholism and alcoholic liver disease is *porphyria cutanea tarda*, which includes increased pigmentation, hair growth, and blistering in sun-exposed areas.

Some have thought that there may be a causal link between alcoholism and major primary skin diseases such as psoriasis, eczema, and scleroderma. Others feel that it is more likely that these conditions are simply much harder to manage and therefore seem to be more severe in alcoholics because of the multitude of other medical problems, nutritional inadequacy, and poor treatment compliance often seen.

MUSCULOSKELETAL SYSTEM

Chronic alcohol use affects the skeletal system in three major ways. It may play a causal or contributing role in a number of different types of arthritis, generalized osteoporosis, and asceptic necrosis of various bones.

Chronic heavy alcohol use is associated with at least four different types of arthritis. *Gouty arthritis* results from increased uric acid levels. These can be increased in two ways. One is as a result of the increased levels of organic acids that accompany the altered ratio of NADH to NAD$^+$. In this instance the kidneys try unsuccessfully to secrete both uric acid as well as these acids and excess amounts of uric acid accumulate. Another comes from lead-contaminated "moonshine." Here the lead damages the kidneys and leads to increased uric acid levels. In both cases abstinence and specific treatment for gouty arthritis may prove beneficial. In conjunction with *alcoholic pancreatitis*, arthritis occurs that is believed to be due to the direct or indirect damage to joints by the enzymes that are circulating in the bloodstream as the result of damage to the pancreas. *Degenerative arthritis*, also known as osteoarthritis, occurs more frequently with chronic heavy alcohol use. This is probably due to the higher frequency of falls, injuries, and fractures in alcoholics. *Septic arthritis* (infection in the joint space) is also seen more frequently in those who use alcohol heavily over long periods. This is probably a result of at least three factors. First, osteoarthritis causes a roughened joint surface where blood-borne infectious agents may be more likely to settle, and as just noted osteoarthritis is more frequent in alcoholics. Second, for a number of reasons, for example, more frequent infection of all types, more frequent injuries, and less attention to hygiene, alcoholics are likely to have a higher incidence of blood-borne bacterial infections. Third, in general the body's defenses against such infections are diminished in alcoholics.

Osteoporosis, a generalized thinning or demineralization of the bones occurring especially in the elderly, is accelerated by heavy alcohol use. This condition, which can lead to a 25% decrease in bone mass, in turn frequently leads to fractures. Fractures of the hip, especially the neck of the femur, the wrist, the upper arm bone or humerus, and the vertebral bodies in the spinal column are most common. Rib fractures are also quite common in heavy drinkers, but they are probably due to an increased frequency of falls and trauma rather than to osteoporosis per se. The possible causes of osteoporosis in alcoholics are many. These include alcohol-induced loss of calcium and/or magnesium through the kidneys, decreased absorption of calcium and/or vitamin D by the small intestine due to the effects of chronic alcohol use, and the demineralizing effects of adrenal corticosteroid hormones, the release of which is stimulated by alcohol.

Aseptic necrosis or bone death, especially of the head of the femur, due to inadequate blood supply to that region is another condition especially frequent in alcoholic men. In fact, as many as 50% of clients with this condition (of whom two thirds are men) will have a history of heavy alcohol use. Deformity of the hip joint often results and can lead to severe arthritis, which can be disabling and may eventually require total hip joint replacement. The cause is unknown but postulated to be fat deposits, which are thought to be caused by pancreatitis or due to alcohol-induced abnormalities in the liver's metabolism of fats (see Chapter 2). These deposits lodge in the small arterial vessels supplying the femoral head and cut off necessary nutrition and oxygen supplies to that area. This leads to bone death. In addition to the hip, aseptic necrosis can affect other joints, such as the shoulder, wrist, knee or ankle.

NERVOUS SYSTEM

The central nervous system (CNS) is perhaps the major organ system most widely and profoundly affected by the effects of both acute and chronic alcohol use. The major acute effect of alcohol on the CNS is that of a depressant. The common misconception that alcohol is a stimulant comes from the fact that its depressant action disinhibits many higher cortical functions. It does this in a somewhat paradoxical fashion. Through the depressant effects of alcohol, parts of the brain are released from their normal inhibitory restraints. Thus abnormal behaviors that would ordinarily be "censured" can occur. Acute alcohol intoxication, in fact, induces a mild delirium. Thinking becomes fuzzy, and orientation, recent memory, and other higher mental functions are altered. An electroencephalogram (EEG) done when someone is high would show a diffuse slowing of normal brain waves, associated with this mild state of delirium. These acute effects are, of course, completely reversible.

Physical dependence

Chronic alcohol use can lead not only to psychological dependence, but to physical dependence (the preferred phrase for addiction). This is a state marked by the development of tolerance and withdrawal symptoms. What is tolerance? This refers to changes that occur as a result of repeated exposure to alcohol. There are changes in how the body handles the alcohol (metabolic tolerance) and changes in alcohol's impact on the nervous system (functional or behavioral tolerance). With the development of tolerance there is both an increased rate of metabolism of alcohol and a decrease in behavioral impairment for a particular blood-alcohol level. The nontolerant individual will have a relatively constant and predictable amount of impairment for a given dose of alcohol. As tolerance develops, the person requires increasing amounts of alcohol to get the effects previously had at lower doses. Tolerance represents the nervous system's ability to adapt and function more or less normally despite the presence of alcohol. This adaptation occurs rapidly. For example, if the blood alcohol levels are raised slowly, virtually no signs of intoxication may be seen. The reason(s) are unclear. The best guess is subtle shifts or adjustments in nerve metabolism. Furthermore, if the dose of alcohol leading initially to high blood alcohol levels is held constant, nonetheless the blood alcohol level may fall somewhat and clinical evidence of intoxication may decrease. The basis for this metabolic tolerance has not been established. Chronic heavy drinkers well along in their drinking careers often experience a sharp drop in tolerance. Rather than being able to drink more, with only a drink or two they become intoxicated. This phenomenon is referred to as *reverse tolerance*. The reason for this drop in tolerance is thought to be related, in part, to the decreased ability of a diseased liver to metabolize alcohol.

Withdrawal

In chronic alcohol users, the most dramatic effects on the central nervous system are those associated with an acute lack of alcohol. An individual who has regularly abused alcohol— that

is, developed tolerance—will have withdrawal symptoms whenever there is a relative absence of alcohol. This means that the person may still be drinking, but the amount being consumed is less and the usual blood alcohol level is therefore lowered. The symptoms can include intention tremors (the shakes when he tries to do something), which are rapid and coarse, involving the head, tongue, and limbs. Most likely these will be worse in the morning, assuming that the last drink was the night before and the blood alcohol level has dropped since then. Another manifestation of alcohol withdrawal in the early stages is the all too familiar "hangover headache." This is most likely related to vascular change and probably has nothing to do with the brain. The brain itself has no pain receptors. So any headache pain must be from the nerves of the surrounding lining, skin, vessels, muscles or bones.

If the chronic alcohol drinker does not take more alcohol, he is likely to develop other symptoms of withdrawal. The withdrawal syndrome is the nervous system's response to the lack of alcohol. It is thought to be a sort of rebound effect. In the absence of alcohol and its chronic suppressant effects, certain regions of the brain become overactive. The severity of the symptoms of withdrawal can vary widely, depending on the length of time of heavy drinking and the amount of alcohol consumed, plus individual differences in people. Symptoms of withdrawal can include tremulousness, agitation, seizures, and hallucinations. This will be discussed later in detail.

Alcohol idiosyncratic intoxication (pathological intoxication)

Aside from withdrawal symptoms, other important CNS disorders are related to alcohol use. A relatively unusual manifestation is a condition previously called pathological intoxication, now classified as alcohol idiosyncratic intoxication. Some susceptible persons, for reasons unknown, have a dramatic change of personality when they drink even small amounts of alcohol. It is a transient psychotic state, with a very rapid onset. The individual becomes confused and disoriented, may have visual hallucinations and be very aggressive, anxious, impulsive, and enraged. In this state the person may carry out senseless, violent acts against others or himself. This can last for only a few minutes or several hours. Then the person lapses into a profound sleep and has amnesia for the episode. If you were to interview this person later, the individual would be unlikely to display any

A boxcar filled with beer derailed near White River Junction, Vermont, a few winters ago. It was successfully attacked by looters on bobsleds and snowmobiles.

BOSTON GLOBE

of the madness that reigned during the episode. Most likely he would report: "I don't know what happened, I just went bananas." The relationship of this syndrome to other organic impulse disorders is unclear.

Organic brain disease

Chronic alcohol use can also lead to varying degrees of dementia and organic brain disease. The particular type of brain disease, its name and associated impairment, is determined by the portion of the brain that is involved. *Wernicke's syndrome* and *Korsakoff's psychosis* are two such syndromes closely tied to alcoholism. Sometimes they are discussed as two separate disorders. Other times people lump them together as the Wernicke–Korsakoff syndrome. Both are caused by nutritional deficiencies, especially thiamine, a B vitamin, in combination with whatever toxic effects alcohol has on nerve tissue. In addition, recent evidence suggests a genetic factor in the form of an inherited lack of an enzyme (transketolase) may play an important role in the development of Wernicke–Korsakoff's. The difference, pathologically, is that Wernicke's syndrome involves injury to the midbrain, cerebellum, and areas near the third and fourth ventricles of the brain; whereas Korsakoff's psychosis results from damage to areas of the brain important to memory function (the diencephalon, hypothalamus, and hippocampal formation), and is often associated with damage to peripheral nerve tissue as well. Prognostically, Wernicke's syndrome has a brighter picture. Often when recognized and treated early it responds very rapidly to thiamine therapy. Korsakoff's psychosis is much slower and less likely to improve. Someone with Korsakoff's psychosis will probably require nursing home or custodial care.

Clinically, a person with Wernicke's syndrome is apt to be confused, delirious, and apprehensive. There is a characteristic dysfunction called nystagmus and/or paralysis of the eye muscles that control eye movements. Nystagmus and other eye signs are often one of the first symptoms to appear and to disappear with treatment. Ataxia, difficulty in walking, and difficulty with balance due to peripheral nerve and/or cerebellar damage are a typical part of Wernicke's.

Korsakoff's psychosis presents a somewhat different picture. There is severe memory loss and confabulation, which is the hallmark sign. It occurs in an individual who is otherwise alert, responsive, and able to attend to and comprehend the written

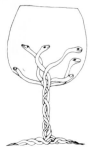

and spoken word. In other words, the memory impairment is greatly out of proportion to other cognitive dysfunctions. Because of the severe damage to areas of the brain crucial to memory, the person simply cannot process and store new information. Thus in order to fill in the memory gaps, he makes up stories. These are not deliberate lies: trickery would require more memory and intent than someone with Korsakoff's psychosis could muster. For example, were you to ask someone with this disorder if he had met you before, his response might be a long, involved story about the last time the two of you had been together. It would be pure fantasy. This is the phenomenon of confabulation. Memory both for things that happened recently as well as long ago is variably but often severely impaired. However, recent memory is more likely to be impaired in the early stages. Both retrograde amnesia and an inability to learn new information occur. Things simply are not stored for recall, and the person cannot remember things even 5 minutes later. With Korsakoff's psychosis, ataxia may also be present. There is a characteristic awkward gait, with feet spread apart to assist in walking. Korsakoff's and Wernicke's diseases can both have a sudden, rapid onset. However, it is not infrequently the case that Korsakoff's psychosis follows a bout of delirium tremens (the DTs).

Cerebral atrophy (generalized loss of brain tissue) often can occur in chronic alcoholic persons. Most typically this is seen in people in their 50s and 60s. Another name for this disorder is *alcoholic dementia*. A variety of factors common in alcoholics most likely combine to cause this condition.

Treatment of these diseases includes administration of thiamine, a well-balanced diet, and discontinuation of alcohol. This treatment is more successful in reversing the signs and symptoms of Wernicke's syndrome. Only about 20% of persons with Korsakoff's psychosis recover completely. The recovery process is slow, taking perhaps from 6 months to a year. The mortality rate of the combined disorder is around 15%. The dementia associated with cerebral atrophy is irreversible, but probably nonprogressive with abstinence and adequate nutrition.

Alcoholic cerebellar degeneration is a late complication of chronic alcohol use and nutritional deficiencies. It is more likely to occur in men, usually only after 10 to 20 years of heavy drinking. In such cases patients gradually develop a slow, broad-based, lurching gait, as if they were about to fall over. This results from the fact that the cerebellum, the area of the brain that is damaged, is what coordinates complex motor activity. There is no associated cognitive or mental dysfunction because the portions of the brain governing such activities are not affected. But signs of peripheral neuropathy and malnutrition may be present.

Two forms of organic brain dysfunction are a direct result of severe alcoholic liver disease. They are known as acute and chronic *portosystemic encephalopathy* (PSE). They are caused by the diseased liver's diminished ability to prevent naturally occurring toxic substances from getting into the general body circulation (e.g., ammonia or glutamine, which are normally confined to the portal circulation). This raises havoc with the CNS. In both acute and chronic forms of PSE, there may be cognitive and memory disturbances, changes in levels of consciousness (to the extreme of so-called hepatic coma), a flaplike tremor, and a foul, musty odor to the breath. In the acute form, which is much less frequent, there is no evidence of chronic liver disease that is typically present in the chronic form. Along with abstinence from alcohol, to enable the liver to normalize as much as possible, aggressive, multipronged medical management is aimed at reducing the body's production of toxic nitrogen-containing substances.

A particularly severe variant of chronic PSE is known as *chronic hepatocerebral disease*. This is a complication of longstanding liver disease, where the brain is adversely affected by toxins chronically circulating in the bloodstream. As a result there is a proliferation of scarlike CNS cells as well as areas of cell death in regions of the brain. As a consequence, there is a corresponding loss of function, with dementia, ataxia, impairment of speech (dysarthria), and sometimes bizarre movements. Scarred or damaged brain tissue cannot be repaired; thus, any such losses are permanent. Patients with this condition often require chronic care facilities.

Two final organic brain diseases, which are quite obscure but serious, are also related to alcohol abuse and nutritional deficiencies. First, *central pontine myelinosis* involves a part of the brainstem known as the pons. For reasons that are unclear, this tends to occur in conjunction with markedly lowered serum sodium levels. This disease can vary in intensity from being inapparent to rapidly progressing to death over a 2- to 3-week period. The pons among other things controls respiration. As it degenerates, coma and finally death occur from respiratory paralysis. Second, *Marchiafava–Bignami disease*, also exceedingly uncommon, involves the nerve tracts connecting the frontal areas on the two sides of the brain. Their degeneration leads to diminished language and motor skills, gait disorders, incontinence, seizures, dementia, hallucinations, and frequently eventual death.

A term one is likely to hear in discussion of alcoholism and the effects of alcohol on the CNS is "wet brain." A physician would most likely look blank if you were to use this term in a discussion, because there is *no* specific medical condition that goes by this name. Probably it developed colloquially among nonmedical alcohol workers to encompass nonreversible organic brain syndromes other than Korsakoff's psychosis. The confabulation of Korsakoff's psychosis is so distinctive that it probably is recognized as different. From our experience, wet brain seems to be used to describe clients who have significant mental impairment and diminished physical capacity due to long-standing alcoholism and who require nursing home care.

Nerve and muscle tissue damage

Nerve tissue other than the brain can also be damaged by chronic alcohol use. The most common disturbance is *alcoholic polyneuropathy* from nutritional deficiencies. This has a gradual onset and progresses slowly. Recovery is equally slow, and generally incomplete, taking weeks to months with discontinuation of alcohol, plus appropriate vitamins. Most commonly the distal nerves (those farthest from the body trunk) are affected first. The damage to these nerves seems to be caused primarily by nutritional deficiencies, though direct toxic effects of alcohol may be involved. Typically, someone with polyneuropathy will have a painful burning of the soles of the feet, yet an absence of normal sensation. Because there is sensory impairment, the individual isn't getting feedback to the brain to tell him how his body is positioned. This loss of position sense may lead to a slapping style of walk because he's unsure of where his feet and legs are in relation to the ground.

Muscle damage often accompanies nerve damage. There is often a wasting of muscle tissue in the areas affected by nerve damage, because in some fashion muscles are improperly nourished if there is surrounding nerve damage. Other forms of muscle damage and degeneration have been reported even in the absence of neuropathy. One form involves acute muscle pain, swelling, and destruction of muscle tissue in the aftermath of acute binges and is referred to as acute *alcoholic myopathy*.

Another form seen in chronic heavy drinkers is chronic alcoholic myopathy and involves the proximal muscles (those nearer the body trunk). Yet another type of muscle damage may result when a person is intoxicated, passes out, and lies in the same position for a long time. With constant pressure of body weight on the same muscles, pressure necrosis can result, leading to muscle degeneration, which like any other myopathy means that muscle proteins (myoglobins) are released into the bloodstream. If these myoglobin levels are too high, kidney failure can occur. Potassium is also a byproduct of such muscle breakdown. An increase in the level of potassium can be quite dangerous. Also, for reasons that are currently unclear, alcoholics are known to be very prone to muscle cramps.

An entity known as *alcohol–tobacco amblyopia* (dimness of vision) is another CNS disorder. As the name implies, it is associated with chronic, excessive drinking and smoking. It is due to bilateral and often only partially reversible degeneration of the optic nerves. It is characterized by slow onset of blurred, dim vision with pain behind the eye. There is difficulty reading, intolerance of bright light, and loss of central color vision. Although eventually blind spots can occur, total blindness is uncommon. The cause is thought to be a vitamin deficiency coupled with the toxic effects of alcohol. Treatment includes B-complex vitamins, plus abstinence, and is usually effective in reversing the eye symptoms. Typically recovery is slow and only partial.

Subdural hematoma

An indirect result of chronic alcoholism is the increased frequency of subdural hematomas, which occur as the result of falling down and striking the head. A blow on the head can cause bleeding of the vessels of the brain lining, the dura. The skull is a rigid box, so any bleeding inside this closed space exerts pressure on the brain. This can be very serious and is very often overlooked. Presenting signs and symptoms can vary widely, although fluctuating states of consciousness (i.e., drifting in and out of consciousness) are often associated with this. Treatment involves removal of the blood clot.

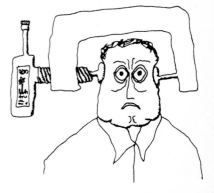

Other miscellaneous CNS disturbances

Other neurologic conditions occur with increased frequency in alcoholics. These include bacterial menengitis, post head trauma seizures, and concussive syndrome. Strokes (cerebrovascular accidents) and brain hemorrhages seem to occur with increased frequency during acute alcohol intoxication. Whether this is also true in cases of chronic alcoholism is as yet unproven.

NEUROPSYCHOLOGICAL IMPAIRMENT

Personality change has long been regarded as an aspect of chronic alcohol use. Historically this was chalked up to serious underlying psychological problems. Then the emphasis shifted to viewing the "alcoholic personality" as a life-style the alcoholic developed to rationalize his alcoholic problems and/or to protect his right to drink. There was little systematic research to explore a physiological basis, if any, and to correlate it to personality changes. This is now changing. Neuropsychological research, using psychometric tests, has uncovered specific impairments associated with alcohol abuse.

Overall intellectual deterioration is not seen until very late in the course of alcoholism. The IQ of most alcoholics, especially verbal IQ, remains relatively intact and normal. Nonetheless, there are other specific deficits, including decreased ability to solve problems, a lessened ability to perform complex psycho-motor tasks, a decreased ability to use abstract concepts, and memory impairment. Drinking history is the major factor determining severity of impairments. How much alcohol, for how long are the questions to be asked. These deficits tend to improve with abstinence. The first 2 to 3 weeks bring the most dramatic improvement. After that, improvement is gradual for the next 6 months to a year. It is important to realize that the improvement, though considerable, is not necessarily complete.

The areas of the brain that seem to be the most affected are the frontal lobes and the right hemisphere. This may help to explain the profound personality changes associated with chronic alcohol use. In fact, some of the behaviors accompanying alcoholism, such as inability to abstain and loss of control, may partially be a product of organic brain dysfunctions. Most of the impaired functioning being discussed is subtle. It is not readily apparent. In fact, many of those in the clinical studies documenting neuropsychological impairment seemed "normal." They often were described as "young, intelligent, and looking much like any other citizen." That should alert us to the possibility that such alcohol-related brain damage may be more widespread than previously thought.

OTHER MISCELLANEOUS EFFECTS

Alcohol is also related to a variety of other signs, symptoms, and conditions that do not fit neatly into a discussion of a particular organ system.

Hodgkin's disease is a form of lymphatic cancer that, although certainly very serious, is becoming more and more treatable. Many persons with Hodgkin's disease who drink alcohol may experience pain in the regions involved with the disease. In some clients this may be the first indicator of the illness, leading to early diagnosis, treatment, and thereby probably improving the prognosis.

Alcohol abuse may also be associated with *Dercum's disease*, which is characterized by symmetrical and painful deposits of fat around the body and limbs.

An interesting property of alcohol is its ability to alleviate dramatically the tremor in persons with *familial tremor*. As suggested by the name, this condition runs in families. It may occur in relatively young persons though more typically in the elderly. The cause is unknown. To account for the heavier than expected drinking seen in many patients with this condition, it has been hypothesized that they might be medicating themselves by drinking and thereby be inviting alcoholism. Fortunately, other drugs are as effective as alcohol with this condition, and much safer.

Alcohol abuse is associated with a variety of *metabolic disorders*, such as the following:

- Hyperuricemia, that is, elevated uric acid levels in blood, which, as described earlier, may cause a number of medical complications.
- Diminished potassium levels (hypokalemia) because of excess mineral-regulating hormone (aldosterone), associated with cirrhosis and ascites.
- Decreased magnesium levels in the blood, which probably result from the combined direct effect of alcohol on the kidneys' handling of magnesium along with decreased oral intake and increased loss through the GI system.
- Metabolic acidosis, an increase of hydrogen ion concentration in the blood with a lowered pH resulting from alterations in the liver's metabolic functioning, may be seen. This can be a life-threatening occurrence and requires prompt and vigorous treatment, as previously described.
- Decreased levels of calcium and phosphate are seen not infrequently in alcoholics. Neither the cause nor clinical significance of these is well understood.

In closing, what have been described here are the many medical complications frequently associated with chronic heavy

Teetot'lers seem
To die the
Same as
others,
So what's the
use of
Knocking
off the
beer?
-A.P.Herbert

drinking and/or alcoholism. It is, however, important to realize that health problems can arise from any alcohol use. One does not have to be an alcoholic or problem drinker first. We predict it will become increasingly popular to discuss alcohol use as a risk factor for the development of a variety of illnesses, rather than to limit the focus to alcoholism and major disease states. The current general notion is that alcohol poses a health hazard "only if you really drink a lot." Evidence indicates this is not so. A recent study of mortality from all causes over a 10-year period in nondrinkers and people with varying degrees of alcohol use revealed that those who took up to two drinks per day had the lowest mortality rate of any of the groups. Nondrinkers and those who took from three to five drinks per day both had a 50% higher mortality rate, whereas those who took six or more drinks per day had a 100% higher rate. Among nondrinkers, the mortality rate from coronary artery disease was significantly higher than in the groups using zero to two drinks per day. Cancer, cirrhosis of the liver, accidents, and a variety of pulmonary conditions were major factors in the increased mortality among heavy drinkers.

ADVICE FOR THE MODERATE DRINKER

It probably comes as no great surprise to most people that excessive use of alcohol over a long period of time can lead to serious problems. What is unfortunately less recognized and appreciated is that, even in moderate amounts, alcohol use can present medical risks.

For some people, in some circumstances, what is usually considered a moderate amount of alcohol is too much. The most striking example is the caution against alcohol use during pregnancy. Among the other conditions, many not uncommon, in which even relatively modest alcohol use can create problems are hypertension, coronary artery disease and/or congestive heart failure, idiopathic epilepsy, particular kinds of hyperlipoproteinemias, diabetes mellitus, gout, osteoporosis, various skin conditions including psoriasis, and gastric and duodenal ulcers. Although none of these conditions may constitute an absolute contraindication, all fall into the category of *relative* contraindications. A glass of wine with meals once or twice a week may present no problem, but several drinks before dinner, plus wine, or an evening on the town may be ill-advised. As a general rule, those being treated for any medical condition ought to inquire about the need to modify temporarily what may be very moderate drinking. In addition to the possibility of alcohol complicating a

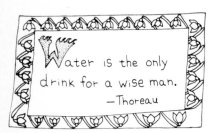

Water is the only drink for a wise man.
—Thoreau

medical condition, there is the issue of possible interactions with medications prescribed to treat them.

ALCOHOL-DRUG INTERACTIONS

Alcohol is a drug. Thus, not unexpectedly, when taken in combination with other medications, there can be undesirable and quite possibly dangerous alcohol–drug interactions. These interactions can vary from individual to individual, but they are largely dependent on the amount of alcohol and type of other medication consumed, as well as the person's drinking history. The nonalcoholic drinker, who has not developed tolerance, will have a very different response than the habitual drinker. In fact, the consequences may be far more serious.

Two basic mechanisms can explain virtually all alcohol–drug interactions. One is that the acute presence of alcohol affects the liver's ability to metabolize other drugs. Acutely in the nonalcoholic, the MEOS system, which metabolizes a variety of other drugs as well as alcohol (see Chapter 2), may be significantly inhibited in the presence of alcohol. Therefore, drugs ordinarily metabolized by the MEOS system will not be removed as rapidly or completely as usual. Thus they will be present in higher than expected levels. Obviously, this can result in unexpected toxic effects. On the other hand, for those with a long history of heavy drinking, alcohol has the opposite effect on the MEOS system. The MEOS action is enhanced or speeded up through a process known as enzyme induction. Thus, certain drugs will be removed (i.e., metabolized) more quickly. The result of this is that the individual will very likely *not* be receiving the intended therapeutic effects of a given dose of the drug. Because the medication is being removed more rapidly, its levels in the body will be lower than expected. To compensate for this, it may be necessary to increase the dose of the drug administered in order to achieve the desired therapeutic effect.

The other major source of difficulty results from so-called additive effects. Alcohol is a CNS depressant. Other medications may also depress CNS functions. When two depressant drugs are present simultaneously their effects are combined and may often be far greater than would be expected with the sum of the two. It is also important to be aware that drugs and alcohol are not metabolized instantaneously. Recall that it takes the body approximately an hour to handle one drink (whether the drink is a 12 ounce bottle of beer or one mixed drink with a shot of 80-proof liquor). Therefore, if someone has had several drinks, an hour or

two later alcohol will still be in the system and will still have the potential for significant additive effects with other depressant drugs taken at that point, or vice versa.

Table 2 outlines many of the potential interactions of alcohol with several commonly prescribed medications. These include the general types of interactions just described as well as a variety of other types not specifically discussed. Note that this chart is *not* all-inclusive. Because a drug is not listed don't assume that there is no interaction with alcohol. Anyone who uses alcohol and is taking other medications is well advised to ask his or her physician or pharmacist specifically about potential interactions in every instance.

SLEEP AND SLEEP DISTURBANCES IN ALCOHOLICS

Many people say they can't sleep unless they have a drink or two before bedtime, "to relax." On the other hand, alcohol actually interferes with sound sleep. To understand this paradox, we will take a look at how people sleep, how alcohol affects normal sleep, and what can be done for clients who cannot sleep after they have stopped drinking.

Scientists have studied sleep by recording brain waves of sleeping subjects on the EEG. Everyone sleeps in basically the same way. There are four stages of sleep: stage 1, stage 2, delta, and REM. Each stage has characteristic brain-wave patterns. These stages occur in a fairly predictable sequence throughout the night.

Sleep patterns

Before we can fall asleep, we need to relax. This is a fairly individualized affair—one person's relaxant is another person's tension! Some relax best in a dark, quiet bedroom; others need a loudspeaker blasting rock music before they can let go. In either case, as soon as one can become drowsy, the brain will show alpha waves.

Next comes the transition period, a time when one is half asleep and half awake. This is called *stage 1*. One still feels awake but does not attend to input from the environment. Little dreamlets or pictures may appear in front of the mind's eye. Stage 1 sleep lasts anywhere from 2 to 10 minutes in normal sleepers, but it can last all night in some recovering alcoholics.

Finally, there comes the real thing—sleep! The average, nondreaming sleep is called *stage 2*, and we spend about 60% to

Text continued on page 134.

TABLE 2

The interaction effects of alcohol with other drugs

Type of drug	Generic name	Trade name	Interaction effect with alcohol
Analgesics Nonnarcotic	Salicylates	(Products containing aspirin) Bayer Aspirin Bufferin Alka-Seltzer	Heavy concurrent use of alcohol with analgesics can increase the potential for GI bleeding. Special caution should be exercised by individuals with ulcers. Buffering of salicylates reduces possibility of this interaction.
Narcotic	Codeine Morphine Opium Oxycodone Propoxyphene Pentazocine Meperidine	 Pantopon Parepectolin (paregoric) Percodan Darvon Darvon-N Talwin Demerol Tylox	The combination of narcotic analgesics and alcohol interact to reduce functioning of the CNS and can lead to loss of effective breathing function and respiratory arrest: death may result.
Antianginal	Nitroglycerin Isosorbide dinitrate	Nitrosat Isordil, Sorbitrate	Alcohol in combination with antianginal drugs may cause the blood pressure to lower—creating a potentially dangerous situation.
Antibiotics Antiinfective agents	Furazolidone Metronidazole Nitrofurantoin	Furoxone Flagyl Cyantin Macrodantin	Certain antibiotics, especially those taken for urinary tract infections and trichomonas infections, have been known to produce disulfiram-like reactions (nausea, vomiting, headaches, hypotension) when combined with alcohol.
Anticoagulants	Warfarin sodium Acenocoumarol Coumarin derivatives	Coumadin, Panwarfin Sintrom Dicumarol	With chronic alcohol use, the anticoagulant effect of these drugs is inhibited. With acute alcohol use the anticoagulant effect is enhanced: hemorrhaging could result.
Anticonvulsants	Phenytoin Carbamazepine Primidone Phenobarbitol*	Dilantin Tegretol Mysoline Luminal*	Chronic heavy drinking can reduce the effectiveness of anticonvulsant drugs to the extent that seizures previously controlled by these drugs can occur if the dosage is not adjusted appropriately. *Enhanced CNS depression may occur with concurrent use of alcohol.
Antidiabetic agents Hypoglycemics	Chloropamide Acetohexamide Tolbutamide Tolazamide Insulin	Diabinese Dymelor Orinase Tolinase Iletin	The interaction of alcohol and either insulin or oral antidiabetic agents may be severe and unpredictable. The interaction may induce hypoglycemia or hyperglycemia; also disulfiram-like reactions may occur.

*See also CNS depressants.

References: Lipman, A. G. Drug interactions with alcohol. Modern Medicine, Feb. 15, 1976, pp. 67–69. Fact sheet—drug interactons with alcohol. National Clearinghouse for Alcohol Information, February 1976. It's dangerous to mix alcohol and drugs. National Clearinghouse for Alcohol Information. The whole college catalog about drinking. U.S. Department of Health, Education, and Welfare, NIAAA. Courtesy of Nebraska Division on Alcoholism, DPI, P.O. Box 94728, Lincoln, NE

Continued.

TABLE 2

The interaction effects of alcohol with other drugs—cont'd

Type of drug	Generic name	Trade name	Interaction effect with alcohol
Antidepressants Tricyclics	Nortriptyline Amitriptyline Desipramine Doxepin Imipramine	Aventyl Elavil, Endep Pertofrane Sinequan Tofranil	Enhanced CNS depression may occur with concurrent use of alcohol and antidepressant drugs. Alcohol itself can cause or exacerbate clinical states of depression.
Monoamine oxidase inhibitors (MAOI)	Pargyline Isocarboxazid Phenelzine Tranylcypromine	Eutonyl Marplan Nardil Parnate	Alcoholic beverages (such as beer and wines) contan tyramine, which will interact with an MAOI to produce a hypertensive hyperpyrexic crisis. Concomitant use of alcohol with MAOIs may result in enhanced CNS depression.
Antihistamines	(For example) Chlorpheniramine Diphenhydramine	(Many cold & allergy remedies) Coricidin Allerest Benadryl	The interaction of alcohol and these drugs enhances CNS depression.
Antihypertensive agents	Rauwolfia preparations Reserpine Guanethidine Hydralazine Pargyline Methyldopa	Rauwiloid Serpasil Ismelin Apresoline Eutonyl Aldomet	Alcohol, in moderate dosage, will increase the blood pressure-lowering effects of these drugs, and can produce postural hypotension. Additionally, an increased CNS-depressant effect may be seen with the rauwolfia alkaloids and methyldopa. Alcohol itself causes hypertension and may counteract the therapeutic effect of antihypertensive agents.
Antimalarials	Quinacrine	Atabrine	A disulfiram-like reaction and severe CNS toxicity may result if antimalarial drugs are combined with alcohol.
CNS depressants Barbiturate sedative hypnotics	Phenobarbital Pentobarbital Secobarbital Butabarbital Amobarbital	Luminal Nembutal Seconal Butisol Amytal	Since alcohol is a depressant, the combination of alcohol and other depressants interact to further reduce CNS functioning. It is extremely dangerous to mix barbiturates and alcohol. What would be a nondangerous dosage of either drug by itself can interact in the body to the point of coma or fatal respiratory arrest. Many accidental deaths of this nature have been reported. A similar danger exists in mixing the nonbarbiturate hypnotics with alcohol.
Nonbarbiturate sedative hypnotics	Methaqualone Glutethimide Bromides Flurazepam Chloral hydrate	Quaalude Doriden Neurosine Dalmane Noctec	Disulfiram-like reactions have been reported with alcohol use in the presence of chloral hydrates.

TABLE 2
The interaction effects of alcohol with other drugs—cont'd

Type of drug	Generic name	Trade name	Interaction effect with alcohol
Tranquilizers (major)	Thioridazine Chlorpromazine Trifluoperazine Haloperidol	Mellaril Thorazine Stelazine Haldol	The major tranquilizers interact with alcohol to enhance CNS depression, resulting in impairment of voluntary movement such as walking or hand coordination; larger doses can be fatal. Increases incidence and severity of extrapyramidal side effects of theses drugs.
Tranquilizers (minor)	Diazepam Meprobamate Chlordiaze- poxide Oxazepam Lorazepam Alprazolam	Valium Equanil Miltown Librium Serax Ativan Xanax	The minor tranquilizers depress CNS functioning. Serious interactions can occur when using these drugs and alcohol.

CNS stimulants	Caffeine
	Amphetamines
	
	Methlyphenidate
	Dextroamphet-
	   amine
	Methamphet-
	   amine
		(In coffee and cola)
		Vanquish
		Benzedrine
		Ritalin
		Dexedrine
		Desoxyn
		Ritalin
			The stimulant effect of these drugs can reverse the depressant effect of alcohol drugs on the CNS, resulting in a false sense of security. They do not help the intoxicated person gain control over coordination or psychomotor activity.

Disulfiram (anti-alcohol preparation)	Disulfiram	Antabuse	Severe CNS toxicity follows ingestion of even small amounts of alcohol. Effects can include headache, nausea, vomiting, convulsions, rapid fall in blood pressure, unconsciousness, and—with sufficiently high doses—death.
Diuretics (also antihypertensive)	Hydrochlothiazide Chlorothiazide Furosemide Quinethazone	Hydrodiuril, Esidrix Diuril Lastix Hydromox	Interaction of diuretics and alcohol enhances the blood pressure—lowering the effects of the diuretic; could possibly precipitate hypotension.

80% of our sleep in this stage. Stage 2 is a medium deep and restful sleep, and the first episode of it will last about 20 to 45 minutes.

Gradually, sleep deepens until we are in the soundest sleep of the night: delta sleep. The length of time one spends in *delta sleep* depends on age. This type of sleep lasts only a few minutes for older people, but up to 2 hours for children. Delta sleep is mainly concentrated in the early part of the night, there is rarely any left after approximately the first 3 hours of sleep.

After delta, we return to stage 2 sleep for awhile. Then, about 60 to 90 minutes after falling asleep, the most exciting sleep begins. This is rapid eye movement (*REM*) *sleep*. The brain waves now resemble a waking pattern. The eyes are moving rapidly under closed eyelids, but the body is completely relaxed and asleep. During REM sleep we dream. The first dream of the night lasts about 5 minutes. Following it, there is a return to stage 2 and then, possibly, some delta sleep again, but it is not quite as deep as the first time. After the few minutes more delta, we return again to stage 2. The second dream of the night occurs about 3 hours after sleep onset and lasts about 10 minutes.

The cycle of alternating nondreaming (stage 2) and dreaming (REM) sleep then continues throughout the night. Dreams occur about every 90 minutes. As the night goes on, nondreaming sleep becomes shorter, and dreaming (REM) sleep becomes longer.

From the above, you can see that you are guaranteed about four dreams in 6 hours of sleep. In fact, you dream for about 20% of an average night. During dreaming, part of the brain is awake, part is not. For example, the long-range memory part of the brain does not function during dreaming. So, in order to remember a dream, you have to wake up from it and think about the dream immediately after you awaken. (Because dreaming is a light state of sleep, one often wakes up from it.) Someone who reports dreaming a lot either is not sleeping very well, and therefore wakes up a lot, or thinks about the dreams a lot just after awakening. Someone who claims never to dream is probably a reasonably sound sleeper, with few awakenings. That person probably also jumps right out of bed upon waking and therefore forgets the dreams. Someone who claims to be dreaming "more" lately has either become more interested in himself and thinks more about his dreams, or is waking up more because he has developed poorer sleep.

Sleep seems to be good for both body and mind. Stage 2 and delta are thought to be mainly body-recovery sleep. When this sleep functions well, the body feels refreshed on awakening in the morning. Delta sleep appears to be more efficient than stage 2 in refreshing the body. Dreaming sleep, on the other hand, has something to do with our psychological recovery. People do not go crazy if they are deprived of dreams, as was originally believed, but they lose some psychological stability. Someone who is usually very reliable, stable, and punctual may become irresponsible, irritable, and impulsive if deprived of REM sleep. As to the amount of sleep someone needs, the old 7 to 8 hours rule is useless. It depends on the individual. Some of us do perfectly well with only 2 or 3 hours; 12 hours are necessary for others.

Sleep disturbances

Why do we need sleep? Take it away and see what happens! Despite what most of us think, an occasional sleepless night is not all that devastating. Although you might feel awful and irritable, total loss of sleep for 1 or 2 nights has surprisingly little effect on normal performance and functioning. Two exceptions are very boring tasks, such as watching radar blips or driving long distances, or very creative tasks, such as writing an essay; these are affected by even 1 night of very little sleep. On the other hand, for most jobs of average interest and difficulty, one can draw on one's reserves and "rally" to the task even after 2 to 4 totally sleepless nights if one really tries to do so.

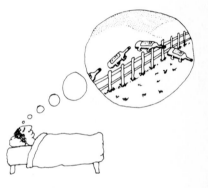

Three brain systems regulate the state of our existence: the awake or arousal system (the reticular activating system), the sleep system, and the REM (dreaming) system. There is a continual struggle among the three, each trying to dominate the other two. The three different systems have different anatomical bases in the brain and apparently run on different neurochemicals. If you influence these neurochemicals, then you disturb the balance among the three systems. Alcohol does disturb these neurochemicals.

It is not too difficult to disturb the balance between the waking and the sleeping systems for a few days. Stress and stimulants (coffee, Dexedrine) will strengthen the waking system; sleeping pills will help the sleeping system. However, after just a few days or weeks, the brain chemistry compensates for the imbalance, and the chemicals become ineffective. Therefore, after just 1 month on sleeping pills, an insomniac's sleep will be as poor as ever. There is even some evidence that the continued use of sleeping pills in itself causes poor sleep. Furthermore, when the sleeping pill is withdrawn, sleep will become extremely poor for a few days or weeks because the brain's chemical balance is now disturbed in the opposite direction. Many people stay on sleeping pills for decades even though the pills do not really help them because of this "rebound insomnia" when they try to sleep without drugs.

Because one sleeps so poorly for awhile when withdrawing from the chronic use of sleeping pills, caution should be used. Go slowly, cutting down on the use of sleeping pills in very gradual doses over a period of weeks. Abrupt withdrawal from some sleeping pills can be dangerous and even cause seizures. In addition, practically all sleeping pills, contrary to advertising, suppress dreaming sleep. After stopping the pills, the dreaming sleep increases in proportion to its former suppression. It can then occupy from 40% to 50% of the night. Dreaming sleep, too, takes 10 days or so to get back to normal. During these days there is very little time for deep sleep, as dreaming takes up most of the night.

You feel exhausted in the morning because you had very little time for body recovery. Nonetheless, people who have taken heavy doses of sleeping pills for a long time often sleep better after being withdrawn than they did while taking them. It is all right to take a sleeping pill on rare occasions, say before an important interview, or after 3 to 4 nights of very poor sleep. However, it does not make any sense to take sleeping pills regularly for more than a week.

Insomnia

Insomnia can be based on either an overly active waking system or a weak sleeping system. On rare occasions, this can have an organic or genetic basis. Some people have a defective sleep system from birth. However, most insomnias are based on psychological factors. Any stress, depression, or tension will naturally arouse the waking system. If that is the problem, the cure obviously involves helping the person deal with the psychological stress.

Surprisingly, poor sleep is often little more than a bad habit! Say a person went through a stressful life situation a few years back and, quite naturally, couldn't sleep for a few nights because of it. Being very tired during the day after a few poor nights, he then needed sleep more and more. So the person tried harder and harder to get to sleep; but the harder one tries, the less one can fall asleep. Soon a vicious cycle develops. Everything surrounding sleep becomes emotionally charged with immense frustration, and the frustration alone keeps you awake.

How do you break this habit? The rules for its treatment are simple, and treatment is effective, provided the individual sticks with it. The first step is for the person to recognize that he or she is misusing the bed by lying in it awake and frustrated! The specific rules for treatment are as follows: (1) Whenever you can't fall asleep relatively quickly, get up because you are misusing the bed. You can do your "frustrating" somewhere else, but not in the bedroom! (2) As soon as you are tired enough and think you might fall asleep quickly, you are to go to bed. If you can't fall asleep quickly, you are to get up again. This step is to be repeated as often as necessary, until you fall asleep quickly. (3) No matter how little sleep you get on a given night, you have to get up in the morning at the usual time. (4) No daytime naps! If the individual with a counselor's help and support sticks to this regimen for a few weeks, the body again becomes used to falling asleep quickly.

Shortening the time spent in bed is also crucial to many insomniacs. Because they haven't slept during the night, many insomniacs stay in bed for half the morning. They want to catch a few daytime naps, or they feel too tired and sick after not sleeping to get up. Pretty soon they lie in bed routinely for 12, 14, even 20 hours. They sleep their days away while complaining of insomnia. It is important that one maintain a regular day/night rhythm, with at least 14 to 16 hours out of bed, even if the nights are marred by insomnia.

Alcohol's effects on sleep

What does alcohol do to all this? Many find that a nightcap "fogs up" an overly active waking system. No question, some people can fall asleep faster with a drink. However, alcohol depresses REM (dreaming) sleep, and it causes more awakenings later at night. The drinker frequently awakens many times throughout the night, leading to a lack of recovery during sleep. These effects continue in chronic drinkers. In addition, the pressure to dream becomes stronger the longer it is suppressed. The dreaming sleep system will finally demand its due. Thus after a binge there is a tremendous recovery need for dreaming. It is thought that part of the DTs and the hallucinations of alcohol withdrawal can be explained by a lack of sleep (many awakenings) and a pressure to dream (lack of REM).

The great fragmentation of sleep and a lack of delta and REM sleeps in chronic alcoholics is a serious problem. Even though they think they sleep well, there is little or no recovery value in it. This very poor sleep makes people want to sleep longer in the morning and during the day, which adds to the usual problems of coping.

What happens to sleep when the booze is taken away from a chronic alcoholic? First, there is the rebound of dreaming. Increased dreaming can last up to 10 days before subsiding. Often there are nightmares because dreaming is so intensive. The sleep fragmentation lasts longer. A loss of delta sleep can go on for as long as 2 years after drinking ceases. In sober alcoholics as a group, there are still more sleep disturbances than in nonalcoholics. We don't know why. It could be due to some chronic damage to the nervous system during the binges, as has been produced in alcoholic rats, or it could be that some alcoholics were poor sleepers to start with. In any case, it appears that the longer one can stay on the wagon, the more sleep will improve.

Sweet dreams !

BLACKOUTS

Having covered a multitude of physical disorders associated with alcohol abuse, it would seem that there is nothing left to go wrong! Yet there remains one more phenomenon associated with alcohol use. It is highly distinctive: the blackout. Contrary to what the name may imply, it does not mean passing out or losing consciousness. Nor does it mean psychological blocking out of events, or repression. A blackout is an amnesia-like period that is often associated with heavy drinking. Someone who is or has been drinking may appear to be perfectly normal. He or she seems to function quite normally with the task at hand. Yet later, the person has no memory of what transpired. A better term might be *blank-out*. The blank spaces in the memory may be total or partial. A person who has been drinking and who experiences a blank-out will not be able to recall how he got home, how the party ended, how he landed the 747, how she did open-heart surgery, or how the important decisions were made at a business lunch. As you can imagine, this spotty memory can cause severe distress and anxiety, to say nothing of being dangerous in certain circumstances.

What causes blackouts? The exact mechanisms are not fully understood. But apparently during a blackout, memory function is severely and selectively impaired by alcohol while virtually all other spheres of affect, cognition, behavior, and brain function remain relatively in tact. Up to one third of alcoholics report never having had a blackout at all. Some alcoholics have blackouts frequently, and still others only have them on occasion.

Recent research indicates that blackouts occur in nonalcoholics who have drunk more heavily than they usually do, and to the point of intoxication. However, blackouts have usually been associated with alcoholism that is at a fairly advanced stage. And thus, they are thought to be generally, although nonspecifically, dose dependent and dose related. As a general rule, the greater the severity of the alcoholism (the heavier the drinking and the greater the number of years over which it has occurred), the more likely the occurrence of blackouts. There is also a positive relationship between the extent and duration of alcohol consumption during any given drinking episode and the occurrence of blackouts. Several other factors correlate with the occurrence of blackouts in alcoholics: poor diet, high tolerance, a history of a prior head injury, and the tendency to gulp drinks.

The current research findings on blackouts differ in significant respects from the oft-quoted work of Jellinek done in the 1950s. Recall that in describing the phases of alcohol addiction (Chapter 3), Jellinek focused on blackouts as heralding the onset of the prodromal phase. Thus he suggested that they were an early manifestation of the disease or denoted those persons who had a high risk of later developing it. He felt that blackouts had a high degree of specificity in predicting eventual alcoholism. Other studies done recently have found that from 30% to 40% of young to middle-aged, light to moderate (social) drinkers have had an alcohol-induced blackout, at least once. Typically, these had occurred on one of the few occasions in their lives when they had gotten truly inebriated. In fact, among these individuals, blackouts seem to be more frequent among those who generally are light drinkers.

How does one reconcile the disparities between these old and new research findings? One possibility is that individuals vary in their "susceptibility" to blackouts. Accordingly, those people who experience the blackout-producing effects of alcohol may find it so frightening and unpleasant that they will be strongly motivated to drink in moderation. Others, possibly with a genetic predisposition to alcoholism, may have a natural high "tolerance" to this effect. Consequently, they will not experience blackouts until relatively late in their drinking careers, after the disease of alcoholism has been established. In effect, those who become alcoholics, not having experienced blackouts earlier, may have been deprived of an important, physiological warning signal.

What is evident, despite the still limited research, is that for some reason, in some people, alcohol selectively interferes with the mechanisms of memory. Memory is one of the many functions of the brain, a complex process that in general is still poorly understood. We can recall and report what happened to us 5 minutes ago. Similarly, many events of yesterday or a week ago can be recalled. In some cases our memories can extend back many years or even decades. Psychological and neuropsychological research has identified different types of memory, categorizing them into immediate, short-term or recent, and long-term memory. Memory of whatever type involves the brain's capacity to receive, process, and store information. According to one popular theory of memory function, the brain has at least two different kinds of "filing systems" for information. Immediate memory is stored for very short periods electrochemically. Long-term memory involves a biochemical storage system that is relatively stable over long periods. Short-term or recent memory is a way station somewhere between these two that is thought to involve the process of conversion of electrochemical brain activity into stable neuronal, probably protein macromolecules. This is the point at which, it is hypothesized, alcohol exerts its influence to impair memory function. It is suspected that this occurs because alcohol interferes with the metabolic production of proteins by certain neuronal cells. This in turn is what inhibits the brain's ability to move short-term memory into longer-term storage. Although alcohol interferes with the "conversion process," it does not seem to interfere directly with the electrochemical basis of immediate memory (events occurring during the blackout itself) or for events from before the blackout (those already stored in long-term memory banks as stable protein macromolecules). This could account for the seemingly normal appearance and function, even with respect to relatively complicated tasks, of the person in a blackout. The amnesia that occurs during a blackout is typically one of two types. It may be sudden in onset, complete and permanent; or it can lack a definite onset and be something that the person is unaware of until he is reminded about or spontaneously recalls the forgotten event. In the latter instance the recall is usually dim and incomplete. Interestingly, in such cases, recall may be enhanced by the use of alcohol. This facilitation of recall by alcohol is thought to reflect the phenomenon of state-dependent learning, in which theory has it that whatever has been learned is best recalled when the person is in the same state or condition as existed at the time of the original learning.

In conclusion, it might be noted that there has been discussion of blackouts being employed as a defense in criminal proceedings. Although a novel approach, it would appear that there is no evidence to support the contention that a blackout alters judgment or behavior at the time of its occurrence. The only deficiency appears to be in later recalling what occurred during the blackout. Of course, having no memory of an event would make it difficult to prepare a case or decide from one's own knowledge whether to plead guilty or innocent!

It is hoped that more can be learned of blackouts in the future. Research is difficult, because it depends almost entirely on anecdotal self-report. Thus far no one has found a predictable way to produce blackouts experimentally. Nor can one know for sure when a spontaneous blackout is occurring. Thus, to date it has not been possible to use new, highly sophisticated neurological diagnostic techniques, which might help us understand the neurophysiological basis of blackouts.

WITHDRAWAL

Alcohol is an addictive drug; when it is taken in sufficient quantities, the body, particularly the CNS, becomes adapted or accustomed to its presence. Drinking as much as a quart of liquor daily for 1 week can create a state of physical dependence. After physical dependence has been established, if consumption is curtailed, there will be symptoms. Taken together, these symptoms constitute the so-called abstinence or withdrawal syndrome. One sure way to terminate an abstinence syndrome is to administer more of the addictive drug. Another aspect of physical dependence, a term that is replacing addiction, is that tolerance develops. Over the long haul, increasing amounts of the drug, for which tolerance has been established, are necessary to achieve the same effect and to continue to ward off withdrawal symptoms. The withdrawal symptoms for any drug are generally the mirror images of the effects induced by the drug itself. Alcohol is a depressant. Therefore the alcohol abstinence syndrome is characterized by symptoms that are indicative of an activated state. A hangover, a kind of miniwithdrawal, testifies to this. Being jumpy, edgy, irritable, hyped up—these well-known symptoms are the exact opposite of alcohol's depressant qualities.

The physiological basis of withdrawal is hypothesized to be related to alcohol's depressant effects on the CNS. With regular chronic use of alcohol, the activity of the CNS is being chronically depressed. With abstinence, this chronic depressant effect is removed. There follows a "rebound" hyperactivity. An area of the CNS particularly affected is the reticular activating system, which modulates or "oversees" the general level of CNS arousal and activity. The duration of the withdrawal syndrome is determined by the time required for this "rebound" overactivity to be played out and a normal baseline level of neurophysiological functioning to be reestablished. Studies of CNS activity with EEGs during heavy drinking, abstinence, and withdrawal support this view.

Not everyone physically dependent on alcohol who stops drinking has the same set of symptoms. In part, the severity of the withdrawal state will be a function of how long someone has been drinking and how much. Another big factor is going to be the person's physical health plus his unique physiological characteristics. Therefore, accurately predicting the difficulties with withdrawal is impossible. Despite the phrase abstinence syndrome, withdrawal can occur even while someone continues to drink. The key factor is a *relative lowering* of the blood alcohol level. Thus *relative abstinence* is the condition that triggers withdrawal. This phenomenon often prompts the alcoholic's morning drink. He is treating his withdrawal symptoms.

Withdrawal syndromes

Four different major withdrawal syndromes have been described in conjunction with alcohol. Although they can be distinguished for the purposes of discussion, clinically the distinctions are not so neat. In real life, these different syndromes blend together.

The earliest and most common sign of alcohol withdrawal is a generalized state of *hyperarousal*. This can include anxiety, irritability, insomnia, loss of appetite, rapid heart beat (tachycardia), and tremulousness. Avoiding this state often is what motivates the actively drinking alcoholic to have a morning or midday drink. Recall that with increasing tolerance, increasing amounts of an addictive drug are necessary to ward off withdrawal symptoms and only a relatively lowered blood alcohol level (BAC) is necessary to induce withdrawal. An alcoholic who is used to drinking heavily in the evenings is eventually going to find himself feeling shaky the next morning. The blood alcohol level will have fallen from the level of the night before. A drink, by raising the BAC, will take this discomfort and edginess away. With time, further boosts of booze during the course of the day may be necessary to maintain a BAC sufficient to prevent the shakes. As tends to be the case with all addicting drugs, progressively increasing amounts of alcohol will be consumed, not for their positive effects, but as a means to avoid withdrawal symptoms.

If the physically dependent person abstains completely, there will be a marked increase of symptoms. The appearance is one of stimulation. The alcoholic will startle easily, feel irritable, and in general be "revved up" in a very unpleasant way. There's a fast pulse, increased temperature, elevated blood pressure, sweating, dilated pupils, and a flushed face. Sleeping will be difficult. Usually these symptoms subside over 2 or 3 days. The shakes will go away, and the vital signs return to normal. However, feeling awful, being irritable, and having difficulty sleeping can persist for 2 to 3 weeks or even longer. Although the judicious use of medication (benzodiazepines) may make the withdrawal process more tolerable by lessening the severity of symptoms, this acute withdrawal syndrome by itself often does not require medical treatment. But it is important that the person not be left alone and be carefully observed for signs of incipient DTs. When the acute stage passes, the probability of developing DTs is greatly lowered. However, if the acute symptoms do not resolve or if they should worsen, beware. Be sure the person is evaluated by a physician, as this indicates that the progression to DTs is likely.

Another syndrome of alcoholic withdrawal is *alcoholic hallucinosis*. This condition occurs in some 25% of those withdrawing from alcohol. It is usually seen early, within the first 24 hours of withdrawal. It includes true hallucinations, both auditory and visual. It also includes illusions, the misperception or misinterpretation of real environmental stimuli. The individual with hallucinosis is oriented, knows who he is, where he is, and the time. Very bad nightmares often accompany this withdrawal syndrome. It is believed that the nightmares may be due to REM rebound following the release from alcohol's long suppression of dreaming sleep. This rebound effect usually clears by the end of the first week of withdrawal. In a small number of cases, however, a chronic and persistent form of the syndrome may develop and continue for weeks to months. Acute alcoholic hallucinosis is not dangerous in itself and does not necessarily require specific medical treatment. It is important, however, to recognize it as a common withdrawal phenomenon, and not be misled into thinking that the hallucinations are necessarily indicative of an underlying, primary psychiatric disorder.

The chronic form of alcoholic hallucinosis accompanying alcohol withdrawal is often thought of as a separate syndrome. It is characterized primarily by persistent, frightening auditory hallucinations. Usually the hallucinations have a distinctly paranoid flavor and are of voices familiar to the patient, often of relatives or acquaintances. In the early stages they are threatening, demeaning, or arouse guilt. Because they are true hallucinations, the person believes they are real and acts on them as if they were. This can lead to the person doing harm to himself or others. When the hallucinations persist over time they become less frightening and may be tolerated with greater equanimity by clients. (Some patients with chronic hallucinosis may develop a schizophrenia-like condition and require treatment with antipsychotic medications.) However, in most instances alcoholic hallucinosis does not indicate an underlying psychiatric problem but simply represents the CNS's response to the absence of alcohol. Appropriate treatment entails observing someone in an environment in which he will be safe, plus possible use of mild sedation. Alcoholic hallucinosis, unless very severe, probably should not be treated with antipsychotic medications during the first 2 to 4 days of withdrawal. During that period there is an increased risk for seizures, and such drugs are known to also lower the seizure threshold.

Epilepsy. This fearful disease is one of the maladies to which the excessive drinker is subject. It is most frequent among absinthe drinkers....In its early stages alcoholic epilepsy is comparatively easy of cure. It is cured spontaneously sometimes by simple total abstinence from alcohol.

SPOONER, WALTER W. *The Cyclopaedia of Temperance and Prohibition,* 1891.

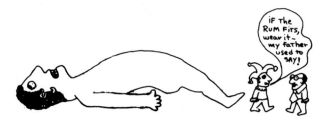

Convulsive seizures, sometimes referred to as "rum fits," also occur in association with acute alcohol withdrawal. These seizures are almost always generalized, grand mal, major motor seizures, in which the eyes roll back in the head, the body muscles contract and relax and extend rhythmically and violently, and there is loss of consciousness. In fact, they are so typical that the occurence of any other type of seizure should raise concern about causes other than simply alcohol withdrawal. After the seizure, which lasts a minute or two, the person may be stuporous and groggy for as long as 6 to 8 hours. Although very frightening to watch, convulsive seizures in and of themselves are not dangerous. Any treatment during a seizure is limited to protecting the person's airway and to preventing injury, by placing a pillow under the head or inserting a gag in the client's mouth to avoid biting the tongue. A serious complication of a single, isolated seizure is the development of *status epilepticus*, in which seizures follow one another with virtually no intervening seizure-free periods. Usually only one or two seizures occur with acute alcohol withdrawal. Status epilepticus is very uncommon and, if present, also suggests causes other than alcohol withdrawal. The only long-term treatment of alcohol withdrawal seizures is to prevent them through abstinence. Unless a person in withdrawal has a history of prior seizures, anticonvulsant drugs are not routinely prescribed. If they are used for seizures clearly attributable to acute alcohol withdrawal, they should be discontinued prior to discharge because further seizures would not be expected after withdrawal. It is critical, though, to rule out any other possible cause of the seizures and not merely to assume that alcohol withdrawal is responsible. Infections, electrolyte disturbances, or falls with associated head trauma, or subdural hematoma, to which the alcoholic is prone, can be causes. Seizures are most likely to occur between 12 and 48 hours after stopping alcohol, but they can occur up to 1 week after the last drink. Alcohol withdrawal seizures indicate a moderate to severe withdrawal problem. One third of all persons who have seizures are said to go on to develop DTs, which is serious business.

Withdrawal seizures are also thought to be caused by "rebound" CNS hyperexcitability. Alcohol has an anticonvulsant effect acutely, in that it raises the seizure threshold. With abstinence, however, the seizure threshold is correspondingly lowered. (This has been postulated as the basis for the increased seizures in epileptics who drink, because these seizures tend to occur the morning after, when the blood alcohol level has fallen.)

Delirium tremens (DTs) is the most serious form of alcohol withdrawal syndrome. In the past, mortality rates as high as 15% to 20% were reported. As many as 1 of every 5 persons who went into DTs died. Even now with modern treatment, there is a 1% to 2% mortality rate. The name indicates the two major components of this withdrawal state. Either of these components can predominate. Delirium refers to hallucinations, confusion, and disorientation. Tremens refers to the heightened autonomic ner-

vous activity, marked tremulousness and agitation, fast pulse, elevated blood pressure, and fever. Someone who eventually goes on to develop the DTs will initially have all the symptoms first described with early withdrawal. However, instead of clearing by the second or third day, the symptoms continue and, in fact, get worse. In addition to increased shakiness, profuse sweating, fast pulse, hypertension, and fever, there are mounting periods of confusion and attacks of anxiety. In full-blown DTs there are delusions and hallucinations, generally visual and tactile. The terrifying nature of the hallucinations and delusions is captured by the slang phrase for DTs, "the horrors." Seeing bugs on the walls and feeling insects crawling all over the body naturally heighten the anxiety and emotional responses. In this physical and emotional state of heightened agitation, infections, respiratory problems, fluid loss, and physical exhaustion create further difficulties. These complications contribute substantially to the mortality rate. The acute phase of DTs can last from 1 day to a week. In 15% of cases it is over in 25 hours; in 80% within 3 days. The person will then often fall into a profound sleep and, on awakening, feel better though still weak. Usually he or she will have little memory of what has happened.

Since there is no specific cure for it, treatment of DTs is aimed at providing supportive medical care while it runs its course. Vital signs are monitored closely to spot any developing problems. Efforts are made to reduce the agitation, conserve energy, and prevent exhaustion. This involves administering medication to achieve some degree of sedation. Despite arguments to the contrary, there simply is no clear-cut single regimen obviously superior to all others. Amounts and type of medication will be determined by the patient's physical condition. One of the concerns will be liver function. The liver, possibly damaged by alcohol, is the organ that is needed to metabolize virtually any drug given. If the liver is not up to the task, drugs will not be as speedily removed from the body, a situation that can lead to further problems. The benzodiazepines (Ativan, Librium, Valium, Serax) are often the first choice. They seem at least as effective as other agents; they have a wider margin of safety and less toxicity than some of the alternative drugs; and they contribute a significant anticonvulsant effect as well. The specific benzodiazepine chosen will depend upon a number of pharmacological considerations. Their dose is decreased gradually over time as symptoms abate in order to avoid cumulative unwanted sedation. Paraldehyde, an old, time-tested, and effective agent, has in recent years become less popular. It is metabolized by the liver and consequently must be used with care when there is significant liver disease. It must also be carefully stored in sealed brown bottles to prevent its breakdown into acetaldehyde. Last, it imparts an objectionable odor to the breath that is unavoidable, because it is extensively excreted by the lungs. The major tranquilizers, or antipsychotic agents, are also somewhat less desirable. Although they have sedative properties, they also lower the seizure threshold, which is already a problem for withdrawing alcoholics as mentioned above. Whatever medication is used, the purpose is to diminish the severity of the acute symptoms accompanying the DTs, not to introduce long-term drug treatment for the alcoholism.

Although predictions cannot be made about who will go into DTs, those who fit the following description are the most likely candidates. A daily drinker who has consumed over a fifth a day or more for at least a week prior to abstinence, and who has been a heavy drinker for 10 years or more is statistically very susceptible. The occurrence of withdrawal seizures, or the persistence and worsening rather than improvement over time of the acute early withdrawal symptoms, should be indicators that the DTs are more likely to occur. If with a prior period of acute abstinence the person had convulsions, extreme agitation, marked confusion, disorientation, or DTs, they are also more likely to have them again. Another ominous sign is recent abuse of other sedatives, especially barbiturates, which also have potentially very serious withdrawal syndromes, much like that seen with alcohol. Abuse of multiple drugs complicates withdrawal management. If there is evidence of physical dependence on more than one drug, generally simultaneous withdrawal will not be attempted. Serial withdrawal of each drug in turn is the preferred approach.

Late withdrawal phenomena

In those who have received high doses of benzodiazepines as treatment for the symptoms of acute alcohol withdrawal, the very same symptoms, including seizures, may reappear 2 to 3 weeks after withdrawal from alcohol when the benzodiazepines are discontinued. This is more likely to occur if high doses were required acutely and if they were stopped abruptly. Probably this represents a separate sedative–hypnotic withdrawal syndrome caused by discontinuing the benzodiazepines and is not a delayed or reemergence of alcohol withdrawal. It can be treated by reintroducing the benzodiazepines and then more gradually dis-

Delirium Tremens. Delirium tremens, or mania a potu, *is a nervous disorder caused by the habitual use of alcoholic stimulants, and in regard to its pathological tendency may be defined as nature's ultimate protest against the continuance of the alcohol vice. The first remonstrance comes in the form of nausea, langor and sick headache—symptoms familiar in the experience of every incipient toper. Loss of appetite and general disinclination to active exercise are the penalties of intemperance in its more advanced stages of development, and those injunctions remaining unheeded, nature's ultimatum is expressed in the incomparable distress of nervous delirium. Insomnia, or chronic sleeplessness is superadded to a chronic loss of appetite; headaches and dizziness alternate with fits of frantic restlessness; the pulse becomes feeble and rapid, the breath feverish, and twitchings of the motor muscles keep the hands and tongue in a trembling motion; the patient raves or talks incessantly and is terrified by ghastly visions. Continued sleeplessness aggravates these symptoms to an appalling degree and at last results in utter exhaustion of the nervous system.*

SPOONER, WALTER W. *The Cyclopaedia of Temperance and Prohibition,* 1891.

continuing them. Another late withdrawal phenomenon is known as *protracted abstinence* syndrome. This is characterized by the persistence over a variable but prolonged time period (several weeks to months) of symptoms suggestive of the acute stages of alcohol withdrawal. These can include variable cognitive and memory disturbances, anxiety and irritability, insomnia, tremulousness, depressive symptoms, and an intense desire to drink. Unfortunately alcohol provides prompt relief for this persistent and often intensely uncomfortable state. This may account in part for relapse among some treated alcoholics.

Some cautions

Not all those who experience withdrawal symptoms intend to! Withdrawal will occur by itself in a physically dependent person whenever a drug is reduced or terminated. So circumstances may play their part and catch some people unaware. Thus addicted individuals who enter hospitals for surgery, thereby having to curtail their usual consumption, may, to their surgeon's (and even their own) amazement, develop acute withdrawal symptoms. Another possibility is the family vacation, when the secretly drinking housewife, who has been denying a problem, intends to just sweat it out. She can wind up with more than she bargained for.

Any counselor working with active alcoholics is going to work with people who do want to loosen their grip. Giving up alcohol can be tough on the body as well as the emotions. In making any assessment, the counselor will have to be concerned about the real possibility of physical dependence. Planning has to include arrangements for care during the process of physical withdrawal. No person should be alone. Family members need to know what to be alert to so that needed medical treatment can be provided. A simple rule of thumb is that if there is any significant likelihood of DTs, seek hospitalization. Virtually every alcoholic has stopped drinking for a day or so, so he has some sense of what happened then. If you see a client who wishes to enter treatment and there has been any kind of difficulty previously during withdrawal, seek medical evaluation around management of withdrawal. Even when there is not a history of prior difficulty around withdrawal, if current symptoms are worse, seek medical treatment immediately. At every step along the way it is imperative that the alcoholic receive lots of TLC. He needs repeated reassurance and support. He needs his questions answered and all procedures explained. Anything that can be done to reduce anxiety and fear is vitally important. Such supportive steps may surprisingly often help clients through alcohol withdrawal without the use of sedative–hypnotic medications.

RESOURCES AND FURTHER READING

Kissin, B., and Beigleiter, H. (Eds.): *The biology of alcoholism.* New York: Plenum Press. (This seven volume series comprises *the* basic reference collection on alcohol and alcoholism. See in particular Vol. 1 *Biochemistry,* Vol. 2 *Physiology and behavior,* Vol. 3 *Clinical pathology,* and Vol. 7 *The pathogenesis of alcoholism.*)

Pattison, M.E., and Kauffman, E. (Eds.): *The encyclopedic handbook on alcoholism.* New York: Gardner Press, 1982.

West, L.J. (Ed.): *Alcoholism and related problems: issues for the American public.* Englewood Cliffs, NJ: Prentice-Hall, Inc., 1984.

Behavior of the alcoholic

6

There are some striking similarities in the behavioral "look" of alcoholics. This is true be the alcoholic male or female, age 17 or 70. From these, a general profile can be drawn. Although not applying totally to all alcoholics, this profile would cause signal bells to ring when seen by someone familiar with the disease. Indeed, it was this fact that in part prompted the futile pursuit for "the alcoholic personality."

THE COMPOSITE ALCOHOLIC

Our composite alcoholic would be most confusing to be around. The active alcoholic is always sending mixed messages. "Come closer, understand/Don't you dare question me!" Jubilant, expansive/secretive, angry, suspicious, laughing/ crying. Tense, worried, confused/relaxed, "Everything's fine." Uptight over bills/financially irresponsible. (Buying expensive toys for the kids, while the rent goes unpaid.) Easygoing/fighting like a caged tiger over a "slight." Telling unnecessary lies and having them come to light is not uncommon behavior. He might also spend considerable, if not most, of his time justifying and explaining why he does things. He is hard to keep on the track. He always has a list of complaints about a number of people, places, and things. (If only....) He considers himself the victim of fate and of a large number of people who are "out to get" him. He has thousands of reasons why he really needs/deserves a drink. He will come in exuberant over a minor success and decline rapidly into an "I'm a failure because of..." routine. He's elusive. Almost never where he said he'd be when he said he'd be there, or he's absolutely rigid about his schedule, especially his drinking times.

The mood swings are phenomenal! The circular arguments never quite make sense to a sober person, and a lot of hand-throwing-up results. The thought that he might be crazy is not at all unusual from either side because of the terrible communication problems. Perfectionistic at some times and a slob at others. Though occasionally cooperative, he's often a stone wall. His life is full of broken commitments, promises, and dates that he often doesn't remember making. Most of all, the behavior denotes guilt. The active alcoholic is extremely defensive. This seems to be one of the key behaviors that is picked up early and seen, but not understood, by others. "Wonder why Andy's so touchy? What a short fuse!" Certainly, at times a drunken slob is much in evidence, but often the really heavy drinking is secretive and carefully hidden. It would be easier to pin down the alcoholism if the behaviors described only occurred with a drink in hand. This is often not the case. The behaviors are sometimes more pronounced when the alcoholic is going through an "on the wagon," or controlled drinking, phase. The confusion, anger, frustration, and depression are omnipresent unless a radical change in attitude toward the drinking takes place.

HOW, IF NOT WHY

The preceding profile is a fair description of alcoholic behavior. This kind of behavior is part of the disease syndrome. Unfortunately, this behavior pattern develops slowly, and the many changes of personality occur gradually, making them less discernable to the alcoholic and the family. So the slow, insidious change of personality is almost immune to recognition as it is happening. Despite the fact that the alcoholic is vulnerable to a host of physical problems, neither current neurological nor physiological data can yet adequately explain this behavioral phenomenon. Despite the inability to provide a simple answer, however, one can describe how the transformation occurs. Vernon Johnson, in *I'll Quit Tomorrow*, has developed a four-step process that neatly sets forth the personality changes that occur in the alcohol-dependent person. His explanation really describes what alcoholism feels like from "the inside out." Becoming familiar with these stages will be helpful in dealing with alcoholics and problem drinkers.

Alcohol dependence requires the use of alcohol, an obvious fact. Another obvious fact: for whatever reasons, drinking becomes an important activity in the life of the problem drinker or alcoholic. The alcoholic develops a relationship with alcohol. The relationship, with all that word implies, is as real and important a bond as with friends, a spouse, or a faithful dog. Accordingly, energy is expended to maintain the relationship. The bond with the bottle may be thought of as an illicit love affair. Long after the thrill, pleasure, and fun are gone, all kinds of mental gymnastics are gone through to pretend it's still great.

The first step Johnson describes is quite simple. The alcoholic starts out like everyone else. Every drinker first *learns the mood*

Woe unto them that rise up early in the morning, that they may follow strong drink.

ISAIAH 5:11

swing. This learning has a physiological basis. Alcohol is a drug; it has acute effects. It makes us feel good. Someone's mood could be plotted at any time on a graph, on which one end represents pain and the other end euphoria. If someone is feeling "normal" and then has a drink, his mood shifts toward the euphoric end. Then after the effects of the alcohol wear off, it's back to the starting position.

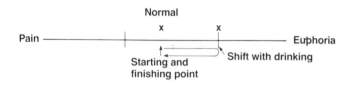

Anyone who drinks learns this pharmacological effect of alcohol and learns that it happens consistently. Alcohol can be depended upon. What's more if you'll reflect back on Chapter 2 and alcohol's effects, a number of things make this learning potent. One doesn't have to wait very long to experience what alcohol does. Its effects can be felt almost immediately, especially for the new drinker described here.

The second stage in the developmental process is *seeking the mood swing.* This happens after someone learns that alcohol can be counted on to enhance or improve mood. This stage, too, is one that applies to most social drinkers. Drinking now can have a particular purpose. Anyone who drinks occasionally does so to make things better. Whatever the occasion—an especially hard day at work, a family reunion, celebrating a promotion, or recovery from a trying day of hassling kids—the expectation is that alcohol will help. In essence, the person is entering into a contract with alcohol. True to its promise, alcohol keeps its side of the bargain. By altering the dose, the person can control the mood swing. Still there are no problems. Nothing up to this point would suggest that alcohol use can be anything but pleasurable.

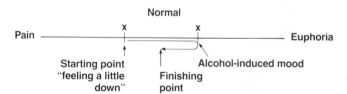

Somewhere along the line, most drinkers will have a negative drinking experience. It may happen early on in someone's drinking career. This unpleasant event can be the hangover of the morning after. Or it can be the sensation of closing one's eyes and feeling the world begin to spin. Or it may not be the physical aftermath of intoxication but behavior that occurred while drunk, making the person squirm at its recollection. At any rate, most people are quite clear that alcohol was the culprit. They tell themselves, never again, and that's that.

For a significant minority of drinkers, it doesn't happen that way. These are the people bound for trouble with alcohol. According to Johnson, these people have crossed a thin line separating the second and third phases. The third phase is *harmful dependence*, in which alcohol suddenly demonstrates a boomerang effect. Alcohol, which previously had only a beneficial, positive effect, now has some negative consequences. To continue drinking in the same fashion is going to exact *emotional costs*. Unwilling to discontinue their use of alcohol to alter their moods, they are willing to pay the price. In a sense, they remain "loyal" to their relationship with booze. This decision to pay the price isn't a conscious decision, logically thought out. It's based on how the person is feeling. In the pain–euphoria chart, the mood shift initially heads in the right direction, achieves the drinker's purpose, but in swinging back, drops the person off in a less comfortable place than the original position.

Wine in excess keeps neither secrets nor promises.

CERVANTES, *Don Quixote*

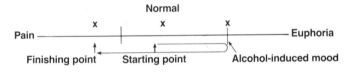

The costs are psychological. Drinking behavior and its consequences are inconsistent with values and self-image. To continue drinking requires revamping the personality. The normal psychological devices will be used to twist reality just enough to explain away the costs. Every person does this every day to some degree. If I'm walking down the street, say hello to a friend and get no response, my feelings are momentarily hurt. Almost automatically I tell myself, "He must not have seen or heard me." So I shut off the hurt feelings with an explanation that may or may not be true. I pick the "reality" that makes me comfortable. Another time, if I'm particularly ill-tempered and nasty, acting in a way I don't really like, I become uncomfortable with myself. I could say to myself: "Yep, I sure have been a grouch." More likely it will come out: "I've not been myself. It must be the pressure of work that has gotten to me." In this fashion, each of us attempts to control our discomfort and maintain psychic harmony. The budding problem drinker does this to keep harmony in the relationship with alcohol. One way to twist reality to explain away the costs is to suppress emotions. When feeling some

One of the disadvantages of wine is that it makes a man mistake words for thoughts.

SAMUEL JOHNSON

negative emotions arising, the alcoholic tries to push this away. "I just won't think about it." So, the fellow who made an ass of himself at last night's party tries to ignore the whole thing. "Heavens, these things happen sometimes. There's no sense in worrying about it." However, pretending your emotions aren't there doesn't make them disappear. They simply crop up somewhere else. Because suppression doesn't work totally, other psychological gymnastics are used. Rationalization is a favorite device—coming up with a reason that inevitably stays clear of alcohol itself. "I really got bombed last night because Harry was mixing such stiff ones." Here we see projection at work as well. The reason for getting bombed was that the drinks were *stiff*, and it's *Harry's* fault! No responsibility is laid on the drinker or on alcohol.

Several other factors allow these distortions to go unchallenged. Again, one is attributable to the action of the drug. Alcohol warps perceptions. The only firsthand memory anyone will have of a drinking event is the one that was laid down in a drugged state. So if someone under a haze of alcohol perceives herself as being clever and witty, sobering up in the morning is not going to be sufficient to make her realize that she was loud, coarse, and vulgar. This "rosy memory" is termed by Johnson "euphoric recall." Until very recently, it was quite unlikely that other people would take it upon themselves to let the drinker know what the scene really was.

Now, there might not be any problems if these instances of distortion were only occasional—but they aren't. And what is worse, with continued heavy drinking, the discrepancy between what is expected to happen and what does happen becomes larger and larger. Proportionately, so does the need for further distortion to explain it. Drinking is supposed to improve the mood, but the budding alcoholic keeps being dropped off further down on the pain side.

A vicious cycle is developing. The mental gymnastics used to minimize the discomfort are also preventing the alcoholic from discovering what is really happening. None of the defenses, even in combination, are completely foolproof. At times, the alcoholic feels real remorse about his behavior. At those times it doesn't matter where the blame lies—on Harry, on himself, on alcohol— any way you cut it, the drinker regrets what's happening. So a negative self-image is developing.

For the most part, the drinker truly believes the reality of the projections and rationalizations. Understandably, this begins to erode relationships with others. There are continual hassles over whose version of reality is accurate. This introduces additional tensions as problems arise with friends, family, coworkers. The alcoholic's self-esteem keeps shrinking. The load of negative feelings expands. Ironically, the alcoholic relies more and more heavily on the old relationship with alcohol. Drinking is deliberately structured into life patterns. Drinking is anticipated. The possibilities of drinking may well determine which invitations are accepted, where business lunches are held, and other life activities. Gradually, *all* leisure time is set up to include drinking.

The stage is now set for the last developmental phase in the emergence of alcoholism. The alcoholic now *drinks to feel normal.* By now the alcoholic is in chronic pain, beset by a load of negative feelings, constantly at the negative end of the mood scale. If you also factor in a growing physical dependence, alcohol is required to avoid withdrawal. This is often wholly unappreciated by those for whom drinking is not a problem. It is assumed erroneously that the alcoholic is drinking to feel "good" and have "fun." By this point the idea of drinking to feel euphoria has long since gone. Alcohol has become essential just to achieve a normal feeling state.

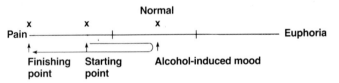

In addition to achieving this normal feeling state, alcohol may assist "normal" functioning in other respects. Psychologists have documented the phenomenon of "state-dependent learning." Things learned in a particular context are most readily recalled under similar circumstances. Thus things learned when sober are best recalled later when sober. Similarly, information learned while intoxicated will also be more available for recall later when the person is again (or still) intoxicated. Thus the heavy drinker may have a repertoire of behavior, coping mechanisms, social skills, even information that, if learned during drinking, is less accessible when sober. In fact, drinking may be necessary to tap a reservoir of knowledge. This fact is what sometimes explains the alcoholic's inability to find liquor stashes that were hidden when drunk. Another way in which alcohol may be essential to "normalize" function is to ward off withdrawal symptoms if the drinker has become physically dependent.

Boundless intemperance
In nature is a tyranny; it hath been
Th'untimely emptying of the happy throne
And fall of many kings.

SHAKESPEARE, *Macbeth*

Other memory distortions are not uncommon at this point. Blackouts may mean the absence of memory for some events. Repression is a psychological mechanism that also blocks out memory. Further havoc continues to be raised by the alcoholic's "euphoric recall." The alcoholic remembers only the good times, and the sense of relief associated with drinking. The problems and difficulties seemingly don't penetrate.

DETERIORATING FUNCTIONING

Given the transformation of thinking, the distorted view of reality, and the ebbing self-esteem, the alcoholic's functioning deteriorates. Each of us is expected to fulfill various roles in life. For each slot we find ourselves in, an accompanying set of expectations defines appropriate behavior. Some of the typical roles are parent, spouse, employee, citizen, friend. Other roles may be more transient, such as scout leader, committee chairman, patient, or Sunday school teacher. No matter what the role, the alcoholic's performance suffers. There are expectations that others have of someone in a position. The alcoholic does not meet them. Behavior is inconsistent. The active alcoholic is undependable. Sometimes doing what is expected, and doing it beautifully, the next time he may fail completely, offering later the flimsiest excuse. To add insult to injury, he gets furious at you for being disappointed, or annoyed, or not understanding. This has a profound impact on the people around the alcoholic. Being filled with the normal insecurities of all humans, those around the alcoholic think it might/must be their fault. Unwittingly others accept the alcoholic's rationalizations and projections. People around the alcoholic are confused. Often they feel left out. They sense and fear the loss of an important relationship, one that has been nourishing to them. In turn, their usual behavior is kinked out of shape. Now, in addition to whatever problems the alcoholic has directly with alcohol, interpersonal relationships are impaired. This adds more tension.

FAMILY AND FRIENDS

Let us focus on the family and friends of the alcoholic next. Applying behavioral learning terms, the alcoholic has those around him on a variable-interval reinforcement schedule. There they are, busily trying to accommodate the alcoholic. Everyone feels that somehow if they behave differently, do the "right thing," the alcoholic will respond. One time they're harsh, the next time they try an "understanding" tack. Then another time

they might try to ignore the situation. But nothing works. The alcoholic's behavior does not respond in any predictable way to their behavior. If he happens to be a "good boy" or she's been a "perfect lady" on occasion, it really has no connection to what the family has or has not done. The others, in fact, are accommodating themselves to the alcoholic. Never sure why some times go better, they persist in trying—and trying some more. Meanwhile, the alcoholic stays inconsistent and unpredictable.

Eventually the family as well as close friends give up and try to live around the alcoholic. Alternately the drinker is ignored or driving them crazy. Yet out of love and loyalty, all too long the alcoholic is protected from the consequences of the drinking. In the marital relationship, if one spouse is alcoholic, the other gradually assumes the accustomed functions of the drinking partner. If the wife is alcoholic, the husband may develop contingency plans for supper in case it isn't ready that night. If the husband is alcoholic, the wife may be the one who definitely plans to attend Little League games. If the husband is up to it, fine; if not, a ready excuse is hauled out. This leads to resentments on both parts. The spouse carrying the load feels burdened; the alcoholic feels deprived and ashamed.

MARITAL RELATIONSHIPS

In the marital relationship, if one partner is alcoholic, you can count on sexual problems. In American society, concern over sexual performance seems to be the national pastime. Sexual functioning is not merely a physical activity but has strong psychological components. How someone feels about herself and her partner is bound to show up in the bedroom. Any alcohol use can disturb physiological capacity for sex. Shakespeare said it most succinctly: alcohol provokes the desire but takes away the performance. In the male, alcohol interferes with erection, popularly referred to as "brewer's droop." The psychological realm has as strong an impact. Satisfying sexual relationships require a relationship, a bond of love and affection. In the alcoholic marriage, neither partner is able to trust that bond. There are doubts on both sides. Problems result in many ways. A slobbering drunk invites revulsion and rejection. By definition he is an unattractive, inconsiderate lover. Any qualities of love have, for the moment, been washed away by booze. Intercourse can also become a weapon. Wives or husbands can use the old Lysistrata tactic of emotional blackmail: refusing sex unless the partner changes behavior. On the other hand, both partners can approach inter-

Wine makes a man better pleased with himself; I do not say that it makes him more pleasing to others.
SAMUEL JOHNSON

course as the magic panacea. If they can still make love, that can make up for everything else lacking in the relationship. Sexual fears and anxiety, which are rampant in the total population, are compounded in the alcoholic marriage.

AT WORK

Often, although the alcoholic is deeply mired in the symptoms of deterioration in the social, family, and physical areas, the job may remain intact. The job area seems to be the last part of the alcoholic's life to show the signs of illness. The job is often the status symbol for both the alcoholic and the spouse. He might think or say: "There's nothing wrong with me. I'm still bringing in a good paycheck!" She is likely to make excuses to his boss on his behalf to protect the family livelihood—and vice versa.

Intervention is, of course, possible at even the earliest signs. This is often not the case, but that picture is gradually changing. Much effort is being made to alert employers to the early signs of alcoholism and to acquaint them with the rehabilitation possibilities. The employer is in a unique position to exert some pressure on the alcoholic at a relatively early stage. Recommending that someone go for treatment may well be a precipitating factor in a recovery. The fact that the boss sees the problem and calls a spade a spade can go far in breaking down the denial system. Keeping a job may be important enough to get the alcoholic to begin to see the problem more realistically. Employee assistance programs and their impact on earlier intervention and treatment will be discussed at length in a later chapter.

Alcoholics often believe that their cover-up, or diversionary, tactics are successful. Most people are unwilling to confront someone with a drinking problem until it is no longer possible to ignore it. A study conducted almost 15 years ago found that some person other than a family member had noticed a drinking problem on an average of 7 years prior to an alcoholic's seeking help. Vaillant's work confirmed this, too. While 4 or more alcohol-related problems were virtually sufficient to guarantee a diagnosis of alcoholism, it wasn't in fact until 11 separate such incidents had occurred that someone entered treatment. Often the alcoholic has no idea how obvious the difficulties are to so many other people. When an alcoholic is finally confronted, it can be a great shock to find out how much of the telltale behavior was, in fact, observed. The rationalization and denial systems actually

Who hath woe? who hath sorrow? who hath contentions? who hath babbling? who hath wounds without cause? who hath redness of eyes? They that tarry long at the wine.

PROVERBS 28:31–32

convinced the active alcoholic that no one on the job or in the community knew about the drinking problem.

All of this disruption causes pain and confusion for alcoholics and those around them, and unfortunately, most of the attempts that all of these people make to alter the situation don't work. Regardless of good will, alcoholism rarely responds to the more common maneuvers of concerned people. It takes special knowledge of the dynamics of the disease, of its effects on others, and of the various treatments that do work to begin to break these destructive patterns.*

RESOURCES AND FURTHER READINGS

Johnson V.: *I'll Quit Tomorrow*, rev. ed. New York: Harper & Row, 1980.

---

*An autobiography or biography of an alcoholic would be informative in understanding the alcoholic's behavior.

Effects of alcohol problems on the family

7

Alcoholism is often called the *family illness*, referring to the tremendous impact active alcoholics have on those around them. There is no way the family members can escape or ignore the alcoholic. The majority of the alcoholic's impairments are behavioral. So in the day-to-day interactions of family life, the family members are confronted with alcoholic behavior, which initially may appear to have little connection to the drinking. The family is confused, bewildered, angry, and afraid. Because they act accordingly, their responses characteristically become as impaired as those of the alcoholic.

Were we to single out the major development in the alcohol field during the last decade, it would be the vastly increased attention to the plight of the alcoholic's family. This is evidenced particularly with involvement of families in alcohol treatment. In the early 1980s a review of two books purporting to be comprehensive tomes on alcoholism noted the scanty attention paid to the impact of active alcoholism on the family. The reviewer plaintively asked, "Why is so much written about the effects of alcoholism upon a patient's liver enzymes and so little written about the effects of parental alcoholism on the children?" Although formal research remains limited, it is gaining increased attention.

Certainly, no family member ever caused alcoholism. Yet the family may, despite its best intentions, behave in a way that allows the alcoholic to continue drinking. They may protect the alcoholic, make excuses, buy into the alibis, cover up. They might call the employer, pretending the alcoholic has "the flu." Other facilitating behavior can include covering a bad check or retaining a good lawyer to beat a DWI charge. The alcoholic's actions are bound to increase the family's anxiety level. The alcoholic drinks more to relieve his own anxiety, which in turn ups the family's even higher. The higher the anxiety, the more the family members react by anxiously doing *more* of what they were already doing and then the alcoholic drinks more because of the higher anxiety, ad infinitum. The thing can become a spiraling squirrel cage or a collapse. The family is no better able to cope with the alcoholism than is the alcoholic.

THE FAMILY'S RESPONSE

Joan Jackson, in a classic monograph on "Alcoholism and the Family," published in 1954, was the first to describe the stages that occur as a family comes to grips with an alcoholic in its midst. Her stages were initially intended to describe the family in which the husband and father is the alcoholic. With modification, they probably describe any alcoholic family. These stages are sketched out here in order of appearance.

What do you mean, I was drunk? I may have been drinking, but you were the one who was drunk.

Denial

Early in the development of alcoholism, occasional episodes of excessive drinking are explained away by both marriage partners. Drinking because of tiredness, worry, nervousness, or a bad day is not unbelievable. The assumption is that the episode is an isolated instance and therefore no problem. If the couple is part of a group where heavy drinking is acceptable, this provides a handy cover for the developing dependency. A cocktail before dinner easily becomes two or three, and wine with the meal and brandy afterward also pass without much notice.

Attempts to eliminate the problem

Here the spouse recognizes that the drinking is not normal and tries to pressure the alcoholic to quit, be more careful, or cut down. "If you only pulled yourself together and used a little willpower," or "If you really love me, you won't do this any more." Simultaneously, the spouse tries to hide the problem from the outside and keep up a good front. At the same time the alcoholic probably sneaks drinks or drinks outside the home in an attempt to hide the amount from the spouse. Children in the family may well start having problems in response to the family stress.

Vernon Johnson many years later in *I'll Quit Tomorrow* pointed out that these early attempts to eliminate the problem may be successful. In such cases, formal alcohol treatment or AA involvement is unlikely. Indeed, it may not be needed. The danger for families at this point, however, would be to enter some general counseling, whether with clergy, psychiatrist, or social worker, that fails to address the problem drinking head on. In such cases, therapy unfortunately can become a part of the denial. It can be a way both to continue drinking and to pretend to be doing something about it.

Disorganization and chaos

The family equilibrium has now broken down. The spouse can no longer pretend everything is okay and spends most of the time going from crisis to crisis. Financial troubles are common. Under real stress, possibly questioning his or her own sanity, the spouse is likely to seek outside help. Unfortunately, spouses often ask help from friends who know no more than they do about what to do. Similarly, they may seek out a member of the clergy who has no training in dealing with alcoholism. (If they do seek trained help at this point or become involved with Al-Anon, the process will take a different course altogether.)

Reorganization in spite of the problem

The spouse's coping abilities have strengthened. He or she gradually assumes the larger share of responsibility for the family unit. This may mean getting a job or taking over the finances. The major focus of energy is no longer directed toward getting the alcoholic partner to shape up. Instead, the spouse takes charge and fosters family life, despite the alcoholism.

Efforts to escape

Separation or divorce may be attempted. If the family unit remains intact, the family continues living around the alcoholic.

Family reorganization

In the case of separation, family reorganization occurs without the alcoholic member. If the alcoholic achieves sobriety, a reconciliation may take place. Either path will require both partners to realign roles and make new adjustments.

As mentioned, Jackson's formulations are focused on the family in which the husband is alcoholic. Families with an alcoholic wife and mother exist, too. An interesting difference is found in marriage outcomes, depending on which partner has the alcohol problem. Male alcoholics have a significantly higher divorce rate than nonalcoholic men. But among alcoholics, the female alcoholic is much more likely to be divorced than is the male alcoholic. In the past, those trying to account for this difference speculated that women who marry alcoholics have unconscious, neurotic needs to be married to weak, inadequate males. The implication was that because of this need, they will stay married to a drunk. That view was replaced by the idea that the difficulties seen in the alcoholic's wife come simply from the stress of living with him. With more research other factors have

Portrait of a woman who can't understand why her husbands were all alcoholics.

Somebody PUT TOO MUCH ice iN MY DRiNK!!

been identified as possibly playing a role. For all persons, it is recognized that one's true love and the choice of a marriage partner
is not a random event. People tend to select marriage partners
with similarities to their parents. Many women who marry alcoholic men are daughters of alcoholics. For them, a situation
that appears to us stressful and painful may be what they saw
and expect in a marriage. Those involved in alcohol treatment
are struck by the fact that some women marry or live with a succession of alcoholics.

Given economic realities, it is not unlikely that the nonalcoholic wife stays in her marriage longer than the nonalcoholic
husband because she feels the need of the husband's financial
support to maintain the family. Indeed, following a divorce the
economic situation does decline for the majority of women and
their children. On the other side, men in general are less likely to
seek outside help for any kind of problem. Therefore, the husband of a female alcoholic may see no option other than divorce
to save himself as well as the children.

Of course, not all families experience these stages in an identical textbook fashion. Different families seem to get stuck in different stages. Some never move beyond denial. Some seem
trapped in an endless cycle of chaos and crisis. And some go
through painful successions of attempts to escape from the situation, reconciliations, and later attempts again to escape. Our understanding of the factors that account for these differences is
limited. One factor that may make a difference is when the problem drinking emerged. Paolino and McCrady, who have studied
alcoholic marriages, suggest that the wives who are most able to
help themselves and their families are those who were married
before their husbands became problem drinkers.

THE FAMILY SYSTEM

The most common approach to the alcoholic family considers
the family a system. Central to this view is the belief that
changes in any part of the system (any family member) of necessity affect all of the others. The other members, in response, also
make changes in an attempt to maintain the family equilibrium.
An example might be a circus family specializing in a high-wire
balancing act. All six members of the act climb up to the top of
the tent. In turn they step out upon the thin wire to begin an in-
tricate set of maneuvers to build a human pyramid high above
the audience. Timing and balance are critical; the interdependence is obvious. Each member is sensitive to even the tiniest

If I were a college student, I would dedicate myself, without fanaticism, but with firm courage and flaming enthusiasm, to the noble cause of Total Abstinence, in order to stop the use of Drink, which has been the great curse to the human family.

JOSEPH HENRY CROOKER, 1914

we have no idea why little Ebenezer might be having Trouble at School. Everything at home is fine!

movements of the rest in order to keep making the adjustments of balance necessary to maintain the routine. If only one of the six members fails to do what is expected, or is not exactly where he is supposed to be, the entire routine fails.

In essence, families with an impaired member do the same thing. The alcoholic's behavior begins to invade the family routine. Everyone else is put off balance. Doing the same things over again doesn't work, so each member scrambles around to find some place, or role, that will restore the equilibrium. In fact, most families do achieve a precarious, though unhealthy, new balance based on the drinking behavior. If the alcoholic starts to get well and returns to more normal behavior, or leaves the family system, the balance is again thrown off. Either way, outside help is strongly recommended to short-circuit the probability of continuing an unhealthy balance in the family. Because each family member has come to relate to the others on the basis of the inappropriate roles, it is virtually impossible to make corrections from inside the system. To return to the circus family, were one member to leave, those remaining would have to regroup as a new act. Conversely, having adjusted over a period of time to altered performance by an impaired member, should that person return in an unimpaired role again, yet another adjustment would be necessary. They would, in either case, stop performing for the moment and call another aerialist to help them develop new routines and supervise their practice. The old relationships, timing, and patterns would be set aside as they learned to work in new ways.

In terms of the kinds of accommodations that alcoholic families make, there can be a range of responses; there is no single routine. At one extreme the drinking alcoholic is almost like a boarder in the family's household. The family isolates and walls off the alcoholic, expects little, gives little. In this way the nonalcoholic family members maintain some stability and continuity. At the other extreme the entire family life is alcohol centered, responding to the crises of the moment. In addition, families can vacillate between patterns of accommodating the alcoholic, depending on whether the alcoholic is drinking or on the wagon.

One of the very common, though unintended, consequences of the family's accommodations is what has been described as "enabling." In attempting to live with and around the alcoholism and keep the pain level down for themselves, the family's behavior may well allow the drinking to continue. This can range from the excuses made to others to "overlooking" and not commenting upon the most outrageous behavior.

CHILDREN OF ALCOHOLICS

In 1984, the Children of Alcoholics Foundation estimated that in America, there are 7 million children under the age of 18 growing up in an alcoholic family. These children deserve special attention. In an atmosphere of conflict, tension, and uncertainty, their needs for warmth, security, and even physical care may be inadequately met. In a family where adult roles are inconsistently and inadequately filled, children lack good models to form their own identities. It is likely that such children will have a hard time as they enter into relationships outside the home, at school, or with playmates. A troubled child may be the signal of an alcohol problem in a family. Although alcoholics comprise only 7% of the American population, their children account for approximately 20% of all referrals to child guidance clinics.

It cannot be emphasized too strongly how much remains unknown in respect to the impact of alcoholism on children. In 1984, for this very reason, one of the first acts of the newly established Children of Alcoholics Foundation was hosting an invitational conference of national alcohol experts to address the needs and opportunities for research. In the discussion below of coping styles of children and the impact that continues into adulthood, it must be emphasized that this is not based on unbiased, scientific research. Much of what is now being attributed to children of alcoholics has originated out of self-help groups of adults who grew up in alcoholic homes. Although their wounds are real, one must ask how far one can safely generalize from their experiences. They may represent a minority of children of alcoholics. Or they may be speaking primarily for another generation, when alcoholism treatment was less common, when family treatment was unheard of, and when alcoholism was more of a stigma.

Without question, growing up with an alcoholic parent is far from ideal. At the same time, the experiences of children in alcoholic families vary greatly. There are different patterns of drinking and different behaviors associated with drinking. Children are of various ages as are the parents when the drinking problem becomes apparent, or when loss of control occurs. All of these will influence how the drinking affects the child. The specific problems of particular children will vary. Furthermore, a child's own natural resilience may be buttressed by the nurturance of extended family, scout leaders, teachers and neighbors, or par-

ents of peers. Thus, the experience of a child may be less impoverished than it might appear. Also, many of the problems encountered are not reserved exclusively for the alcoholic home.

Nonetheless, in thinking of children it is hard not to think in terms of the dramatic. Put the book down for a moment. Take five minutes to imagine what life *might* be like for a child with an alcoholic parent.

- *As a preschooler.* What is it like to lie in bed listening to your parents fight? Or to have Daddy disappear for periods of time unexpectedly? Or to be spanked *really* hard and sent away from dinner just because your milk spilled? Or to have a succession of sitters because Mommy works two jobs? Or to get lots of attention sometimes and be in the way the next moment?

- *As an elementary-school child.* What is it like when your mom forgets to pack a lunch? Or you wait and wait after scout meeting for a ride, long after the other kids have been picked up? Or your dad cancels out on the cub scout hike because he is sick? Or you're not allowed to bring friends home to play? Or your friends' moms wouldn't let them ride in your car? Or you're scared to tell your mom you need a white shirt to be a pilgrim in the class Thanksgiving play?

- *As an adolescent.* What is it like if you can't participate in school functions because you must get home to care for your younger brothers and sisters? Or the money you made mowing lawns is missing from your room? Or your dad's name is regularly featured in the court column? Or your mother asks you to telephone her boss, because she has a black eye from falling down. Or there's no one from your family to come to the athletic awards banquet...or...

The problems may begin before birth. As discussed in Chapter 5, maternal alcohol use can influence fetal development. At its most extreme, this is expressed as fetal alcohol syndrome. In addition to the direct impact of the drug, behaviors associated with alcoholism may have direct effects on fetal development. Physical trauma, falls, malnutrition, or abnormalities of glucose metabolism are not uncommon in alcoholics. Any of these could have an impact on the developing baby.

The emotional state of the expectant mother probably influences fetal development. It certainly has an influence on the course of labor and delivery. The emotional state of the alcoholic expectant mother might differ dramatically from that of a normal, healthy, nonalcoholic expectant mother, and may be a source of problems. An alcoholic expectant father may exert some indirect prenatal influences. If he is abusive or provides little emotional and financial support, this could cause anxiety in the mother. Lack of support and consequent anxiety during pregnancy is associated with more difficult deliveries. In a similar vein, stress at certain times during pregnancy increases fetal activity. This, in turn, is linked to colicky babies. No specific data are available on labor and delivery for either female alcoholics or wives of male alcoholics. Increased maternal anxiety may precipitate problems of labor and delivery. Furthermore, these difficulties are related to developmental disorders in the children.

Another crucial time in any infant's life comes shortly after delivery. The very early interactions between mother and infant are important influences in the mother–child relationship. Medications that may be required for a difficult delivery may make the bonding more difficult. Both mother and infant, under the effects of the drug, are less able to respond to each other.

A new mother needs emotional and physical support to help her deal with the presence of the baby in her life. At a minimum, the baby requires food, warmth, physical comfort, and consistency of response from the mother. In the case of a family with an active alcoholic, one cannot automatically assume everything is going smoothly. Any worker in contact with the family ought to question whether the infant is getting adequate care and should also check for any evidence of child abuse.

Children's coping styles

Some children of alcoholics may be having quite apparent and obvious problems. Yet, given the potential for a chaotic environment in the alcoholic family, again it is sometimes more striking how well the children do cope with alcoholism. Drawing on a family systems approach to the alcoholic family, counselors have identified several distinctive coping styles that children adopt.

One of these coping styles is to be the *responsible* one. This role usually falls to the only child or the oldest child, especially the oldest daughter. The child may assume considerable responsibility not only for him- or herself, but also for younger brothers and sisters—taking over chores, keeping track of what needs to be done. In general, this child compensates as much as possible for the instability and inconsistency introduced by the parental alcoholism.

Another coping response is that of the *adjuster.* This child doesn't take on the responsibilities of managing; instead the child follows directions and easily accommodates to whatever comes along. This child is remarkable for how much he takes in stride.

The third style is to be the *placater*. This role involves managing not the physical affairs, as the responsible one does, but the emotional affairs. This child is ever attuned to being concerned and sensitive to others. It may include being sympathetic to the alcoholic, and alternately the nonalcoholic parent, always trying to soothe ruffled feathers.

What each of these roles has in common is that each in its own way is a model for survival, a coping strategy. These roles can also provide the child with support and approval from persons outside the home. For example, the responsible one probably is a good student, Mommy's little helper, and gets praise for both. The danger for the child is that the child becomes frozen in these roles, that the roles become the lifetime pattern. What is helpful in childhood can become a deficiency for an adult. The responsible one can become an adult who always needs to be on top of things, in control, destined to the stress of attempting to be a lifetime superachiever. The flexible one (the adjuster) may be so tentative, so unable to trust, as to be unable to make the long-term commitments that are required to succeed in a career or intimate adult personal relationships as a spouse or parent. Likely as not, the adjuster adults are so attuned to accommodating others that they allow themselves to be manipulated. An ever-present option for the adult adjuster is to marry someone with a problem, such as an alcoholic, which allows the continuation of the adjuster role. The adult placaters are continually caring for others, often at the price of being unaware of their own needs or being unable to meet them. This can lead to large measures of guilt and anger, neither of which a placater can easily handle. On the other hand, in adulthood, these coping styles can be translated into skills. The sensitivity and ability of the placater to be sympathetic and understanding may be assets in helping professions such as social work, psychiatry, counseling. So too, the responsible ones may have acquired skills that can serve them in good stead. The challenge for both is to appreciate the origins and be attuned to the pitfalls.

A different but similar typology set forth of the roles that children adopt in response to parental alcoholism includes the *family hero, the lost child, the family mascot,* and *the scapegoat.* The first three have much in common with the three styles just discussed: the responsible one, the adapter, and the placater. The specific labels are less important than the fact that children do

THe family
Scapegoat

develop coping styles in response to the family stress of alcoholism. For the majority of children, the coping style may not
elicit external attention or invite intervention. The exception is
the scapegoat, who is likely to be acting out. This is the one most
likely to be in trouble in school, or in trouble with the authorities.
This is the one who, usually acting angry and deviant, may be
the only child clearly seen as having a problem. If the child is a
teenager, the trouble may take the form of drug or alcohol abuse.
(This is discussed in the section on adolescents in Chapter 10.)
Frequently through the attention focused on this child by outsid-
ers or the family, the family alcohol problem may first surface. Of
course, initially the family will see the child as the central problem. The scapegoat's behavior takes the focus off the parent's alcohol problem. Also by providing the parents a common problem
to tackle, it may help keep a fragile marriage intact. Often the
family may develop the myth that the drinking is the parent's
coping response to the child's behavior. Alternately, the child
may be held responsible for aggravating the parent's drinking.

Adult children of alcoholics

Insights into the effects of parental alcoholism are becoming
available from the recent emergence of self-help groups for adult
children of alcoholics. Presumably because attention and help
for the alcoholic is such a recent phenomenon, they, as children,
received no help in confronting these issues, no matter what the
fate of the alcoholic parent. Whether the alcoholic parent died
from the disease, left the home, or recovered, the grown children
are experiencing difficulties that developed from their experiences in the alcoholic family.

Several common themes, or "holes," are worth commenting
on. An extreme fear of abandonment is one. Because the alcoholic parent may have been so often absent, late picking them
up, or indeed "left them" due to death, divorce, or true abandonment, no amount of assurance from other loved ones is ever
enough to dispel this anxiety. "I know you *say* you love me, but
someday you'll leave me, too," is the underlying motive for a lot
of clutching, dependent behavior that often does push people
away, fulfilling the terrible prophecy. On the other hand, the fear
may be so great that they remain unable to form any deep attach-
ment, "knowing" it will only cause them pain.

Some may have spent a lot of time trying by various behaviors
to control or change the drinking pattern of their parent, and inevitably failing, they often come to feel as though they are "fail-

ures" ahead of time. Life seems overwhelming, especially because the behaviors developed in an attempt to cope with the alcoholic aren't usually effective elsewhere. They feel caught in a "no win" situation and very often choose to live out their lives considerably below the level of their abilities and talents. An easy job, in an easy place, with surface relationships is another way to avoid pain.

Others may have received so little approval at home that they work intensely for outside approval. They may become obsessive overachievers, courting success at any cost to relationships of any kind. They may become *workaholics*, competitive and defensive. Unfortunately, this choice often achieves high rewards and regard in this work ethic–oriented society, and no one attends to the personal destruction around them. Their expectations of themselves, and consequently of others, often destroy their relationships with those around them much as alcoholism does.

One deeply buried and usually unacknowledged theme is intense guilt feelings. A young child suffering from neglect or outright abuse from an alcoholic parent feels anger and hatred in response to such treatment. A perfectly natural momentary "I wish she were dead!" can become an habitual thought, and added to it, the horror of thinking such a thing. The cruelty of other children who know about the "drunk" at home may have left deep scars; the inevitable feeling is that if only the parent hadn't been around, life would have been better. No matter what the outcome of the problem, such feelings were and are felt to be abnormal, "sinful," not allowed, and therefore never discussed. Couple this with guilt over the failure to have changed the situation by being a "better" or "different" child! The anger at the parent can spill over throughout life, long after the parent is dead, creating even more buried guilt. These are only examples of some of the far-reaching effects that can be encountered by adults of any age who lived with an active alcoholic when growing up.

From the literature of adult children of alcoholic groups has come a set of characteristics seen as common to adult children. These include fear of losing control, fear of feelings, fear of conflict, an overdeveloped sense of responsibility, feelings of guilt when standing up for oneself, an inability to relax or let go or have fun, harsh self-criticism, living in a world of denial, difficulties with intimate relationships, living life from the stance of a victim, the tendency to be more comfortable with chaos than security, the tendency to confuse love and pity, the tendency under pressure to assume a black and white perspective, suffering under a backlog of delayed grief, a tendency to react rather than to act, and an ability to survive.

These characteristics, though not generated by researchers, have the ring of truth for those who are still coming to grips with a childhood in an alcoholic family. They are felt to offer a useful framework for addressing this legacy. Some active in the self-help movement of adult children have suggested that this adult behavior pattern should be considered as a psychiatric disorder similar to posttraumatic stress syndrome, which has been identified in Vietnam veterans.

It cannot be assumed that all children who grew up or are now growing up in an alcoholic home have these personality characteristics. Nor can it be assumed that all problems encountered in adult life can be laid to being a child of an alcoholic. But the adult-children-of-alcoholics framework may well be useful to those suffering from problems, of whatever origins, who need in adulthood to find some way out of the impasse and make needed changes.

Genetic vulnerability

Another way in which the child of an alcoholic is vulnerable is in terms of genetic endowment. Children of alcoholics are considered people at risk for development of the disease in an approximate 4:1 ratio to those without an alcoholic parent. Research has suggested that children of alcoholics are also more likely to suffer from attention deficit disorders with hyperactivity than children of nonalcoholic parents.

ALCOHOLISM IN OTHER FAMILY MEMBERS

Alcoholism is obviously not limited only to the parental generation. It may occur in adolescents. Or it may occur in grandparents. The effects on the family are still powerful, though possibly less dramatic. Both adolescent alcohol problems and alcoholism among the elderly are discussed in Chapter 10. However, it is important to realize that despite the family member affected, the response of the family will resemble the stages described by Jackson.

• • •

The effects of alcoholism are not limited to the alcoholic alone. The problems discussed here are now being seen as requiring intervention. Increasingly, issues of the family are a central part of alcohol treatment. Treatment approaches to the alcoholic family are discussed in Chapter 9.

RESOURCES AND FURTHER READING

Black C.: *Children of alcoholics. Alcohol Health and Research World* 4(1), 23–27, 1979.

Conference Report on Research Needs and Opportunities for Children of Alcoholics, 1984. Available from Children of Alcoholics Foundation, Inc., 540 Madison Avenue, New York, NY 10022.

Cork R.M.: *The forgotten children.* Toronto: Addictions Research Foundation, 1969.

Elkin M.: *Families under the influence.* New York: W.W. Norton & Company, 1984.

Jackson J.: The adjustment of the family to the crisis of alcoholism. *Quarterly Journal of Studies on Alcohol* 15(4):562–586, 1954.

Johnson V.: *I'll quit tomorrow,* rev. ed., New York: Harper & Row, 1980.

Jones C.L., and Battje R.J.: *Etiology of drug abuse: implications for prevention,* Washington, DC: National Institute on Drug Abuse, 1985.

Paolino T.J., McCrady B.S. *The Alcoholic Marriage: Alternative Prospectives.* New York: Grune & Stratton, 1977.

Treatment

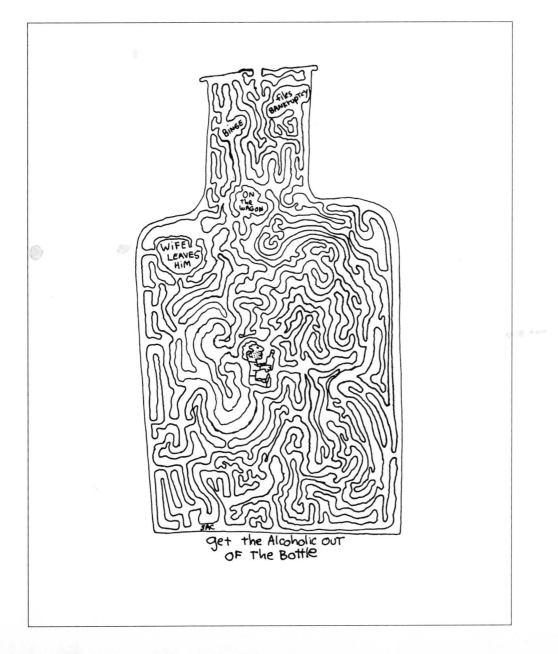

8

OVERVIEW

When one is acutely aware of alcohol problems and alcoholism, the question arises: "How do you treat them?" Perhaps your question is more personal: "How can I help?" As a prelude to this, it is essential to consider how people get better and what treatment or intervention is about. An understanding of what happens in treatment is important to anyone who cares about someone in trouble with alcohol and who wants to be supportive.

At this juncture in earlier editions, we (1) made a principled plea for early intervention, (2) backed that up with the reminder that this approach is indicated for any chronic disease process, then (3) acknowledged that this represented an ideal, which unfortunately was infrequently reflected in actual practice, and (4) proceeded to zero in on alcoholism treatment. There was virtually no mention of evaluation, diagnostic assessment, or treatment approaches to other problems associated with alcohol use. Indeed, 5 to 10 years ago the alcohol clinician had very little need for, or opportunity to use, those skills. The diagnosis of alcoholism for all practical purposes had occurred prior to the client's arrival in the alcohol worker's office. Very few individuals came into contact with alcohol facilities in error. The chief practical use for an alcohol professional to be informed of diagnostic criteria was for client education. This information was also helpful in educating other workers, thereby facilitating referrals of clear-cut alcoholics who were going undetected. Similarly, the major role of the alcohol use history was in developing treatment plans, rather than its being a prerequisite for diagnosis.

In days past, those who by today's classification are alcohol abusers, if they became clients in alcohol services, were treated as "early stage alcoholics." Accordingly, they were provided the standard alcoholism treatment. Their life situations often were reminiscent of the typical alcoholism client's circumstances 10 to 20 years prior to treatment. Remember, an average of 7 years elapsed from the point of alcoholism's being clearly present prior to the point of entering treatment. That fact was used to "sell" the diagnosis and attempt to lead the client to accept it, hopefully with gratitude! Alcohol treatment professionals obviously recog-

As muse or creative companion, alcohol can be devastating. In Memoriam: To those who did battle with this two-faced spirit.

John Barrymore
John Berryman
Lillian Roth
U. S. Grant
O. Henry (William Sydney Porter)
Eugene O'Neill
Stephen Crane
Hart Crane
F. Scott Fitzgerald
Edna St. Vincent Millay
Jack London
Ernest Hemingway
Dylan Thomas
Diana Barrymore
Isadora Duncan
Sinclair Lewis
Kenneth Roberts
Judy Garland
Joseph McCarthy
Robert Benchley
Edgar Allen Poe
Jim Thorpe
Charles Jackson
Dame May Whitty
Sarah Churchill
Jackson Pollock
W. C. Fields
Audie Murphy
Henri de Toulouse-Lautrec
Baudelaire
Brendan Behan
Ring Lardner
Robert Lowell

nized that such individuals were different from the usual client. It was re ognized that providing full-blown alcoholism treatment might be a bit drastic. However, it was viewed as the prudent, cautious approach. Even if the alcoholism diagnosis were incorrect, initiating treatment seemed preferable to the alternative, which would be allowing alcoholism to go unaddressed. The two choices were then perceived to be either loss of drinking "privileges" or potential loss of life. And equally important was the fact that, at the time, the clinician could offer the problem drinker no other treatment choices.

The situation now is dramatically different. Alcoholics continue to be the majority of those seen by alcohol facilities. At the same time there is an ever increasing proportion of referrals for other alcohol-related problems. One can no longer assume that arrival at an alcohol treatment program is a clear indicator of alcoholism. The problem may be alcohol abuse. The referral may have followed on the heels of an incident caused by alcohol use. There are self-referrals of individuals who are concerned about a family member, a friend, or their own alcohol use. Similarly, alcohol treatment personnel are called upon more and more by other helping professionals—school counselors, social workers, physicians, clergy—to provide consultation.

With clients now reflecting the spectrum of alcohol problems, there is increasing demand upon alcohol counselors to provide a thoughtful assessment and to match clients to the appropriate treatment. Other pressures come into play and demand assessment and treatment planning skills. A significant one is tied to economics. Insurance companies, state regulatory agencies, as well as clients, their families and employers no longer automatically accept without question 28-day residential or inpatient care as *the* treatment of choice. The realization that there are options has become apparent. Alcohol treatment programs advertise on TV. There has been a mushrooming of programs, a wider variety of services to choose from in almost every community. Also, a growing number of treated and recovering people have opinions on the strengths and weakness of various programs. In this climate, assessment, evaluation, and diagnostic skills become more central.

Theoretical perspectives

It may have been far simpler when the major and exclusive concern of the alcohol counselor was alcoholism. The difficulty for the alcohol counselor was rarely in knowing how to treat the person sitting in the office. The real challenge and major frustration was in getting those who needed care across the threshold. As the clinical concerns broaden to encompass a range of alcohol problems, life is more complicated for the clinician. The remarks presented here are intended to provide a framework and offer orientation.

If oriented primarily toward alcoholism, ironically that orientation serves as a set of blinders preventing recognition of other alcohol problems. In thinking of alcoholism, we naturally think in terms of its progression—from alcohol use, to alcohol problems, to alcohol abuse, to alcoholism. In this framework, severity depends upon where the client falls on that continuum. This contains some pitfalls. The necessity for action or intervention is understandably associated with what is perceived as the seriousness of the situation. Thus, the person with the alcohol problem may be seen as in less danger. True, there may be less danger in respect to the alcohol*ism*. But that is only half of the picture.

Problems of alcohol use. Alcohol problems are not restricted to alcoholism. Nor are they restricted to use at intoxicating levels. The danger of alcohol use by the individual who is depressed is not alcoholism--it's suicidal thoughts being "loosened" by the impaired state and diminished capacity. Therefore, those who are in treatment for depression should be counseled to abstain from alcohol. Of course, adolescents provide some of the most dramatic examples. For teenagers, the primary danger isn't alcoholism, although it certainly does occur. The leading causes of death in this age group are accidents and suicide, both of which are clearly linked to alcohol use. Alcohol use may have more subtle dangers for adolescents, such as impeding emotional and social maturation.

Any drinker is at some risk for alcohol problems. Alcohol is a potent pharmacological agent. Negative consequences can follow on the heels of a single drinking episode. These would represent problems of acute use. Or negative consequences can result from the pattern of use. This represents a chronic problem. Evaluation and assessment needs to consider both possibilities.

What is a "safe" dose of alcohol or a low-risk pattern of alcohol use? This varies from individual to individual. What is judicious use varies for a single individual throughout his life span. Alcohol use is a health issue in the broadest sense. The alcohol counselor is unlikely to see an individual until some problem becomes evident. Therefore, much of the burden of prevention and identifying individuals at risk falls to those outside the alcohol field.

Another pitfall can occur from thinking of all alcohol problems in terms of the progression of alcoholism. It is a temptation to treat all alcohol problems as emerging alcoholism. That means offering alcoholism treatment. This can cause clients to balk and to bolt. At the same time it sets up barriers when dealing with other professionals. It can give the impression of alcohol clinicians being "technicians," not therapists, always ready to apply their treatment formula indiscriminately.

Chronic disease framework. In approaching the spectrum of alcohol problems, the model for managing chronic disease is very useful. It offers an approach that assures that acute problems are effectively addressed. At the same time, it assures that alcoholism will not develop unnoticed. All acute problems are seen as requiring attention in their own right *and* as potential warnings of a possible long-term problem. The following example may help.

In respect to general medical management of chronic disease processes, among the most significant actions are those taken *prior* to the clear onset of the full-blown disease process. An example may be illustrative…heart disease. A young male comes into his physician's office. He is overweight, both smokes and drinks, consumes a cholesterol-laden diet, never exercises, and has a family history of males who keel over prior to age 50 of coronary disease. From his physician's perspective, he is a walking time-bomb. The physician does not have to be convinced that this individual will be true to his genes to be comfortable intervening. It is sufficient to know that statistically this individual is at risk. Even if wholly asymptomatic, that is, having no elevation of blood pressure, the physician will feel perfectly comfortable urging rather drastic changes to reduce risk. (These changes for our hypothetical young man are equivalent to the changes associated with abstinence.) If the physician in question were really on top of it, he would refer this client to several groups, load him down with pamphlets, and through continuing contacts monitor compliance, and provide encouragement and support. We would hold up *this* model with respect to the optimal management of alcohol problems. In this framework, the most relevant question is no longer: "Is this person alcoholic?" The central question instead becomes: "If this person continues with the current alcohol use pattern is he or she at risk for *developing* alcoholism or alcohol-related problems?"

Using the framework of chronic disease, many of the questions that now plague caregivers are circumvented. In the discussion that follows, we are going to act as if alcohol problems/ abuse/alcoholism is a condition very like heart disease. Specifically, how does this apply to alcohol problems and alcoholism? As a chronic disease, alcoholism has well-demonstrated warning signs. It develops slowly over time. For this reason, it would probably be impossible ever to pinpoint an exact time at which a nonalcoholic "turns" alcoholic. No one wakes up in the morning having come down with a case of alcoholism overnight! Remember, the time when it is most critical to act is before the disease process is firmly established, when the individual is in that "gray" area, not a clear-cut yes or no. So a useful frame of reference is to think in terms of whether someone is *developing* alcoholism. If so, then intervention is appropriate.

Another benefit is that it makes clear that any alcohol problem is sufficently serious to warrant continuing attention. It has become widely recognized that alcoholism isn't "cured" and that ongoing efforts will be needed to maintain sobriety. Similarly, alcohol problems shouldn't be assumed to be "fixed" by a brief single encounter with a clinician, or participation in an alcohol education class. An ongoing relationship is appropriately established to monitor the client's status. Over time, there needs to be the opportunity to assess the efforts to moderate risks and alter dangerous drinking. If these efforts prove to be unsuccessful, then further intervention is going to be required.

For those who have doubts that this has any likelihood of becoming the dominant model for alcohol problems, we would suggest that you consider the changes that have occurred over the last 25 years with respect to smoking. They have been nothing short of dramatic. We may well be on the brink of a similar revolution with respect to alcohol use. Questions about smoking are now a standard part of any medical history. Probably very few smokers are unaware that smoking may cause or aggravate medical problems. A smoker who sees a physician expects to be asked questions about smoking and awaits the associated comments that smoking is ill-advised. Beyond that there is the increasing likelihood that a referral will be made to a smoking cessation program. Also the attitudes of the general public have changed. There is now a vocal antismoking lobby who do not wish to put up with secondhand smoke; there are also the concerned family members and friends of smokers, who are more frequently expressing their concerns directly to the smoker.

If one reflects upon what has occurred in just the last 5 years with respect to alcohol use, one cannot help but notice some significant changes. The general public's attitudes toward use of alcohol have shifted significantly. Alcohol is more commonly thought of as a drug. It appears that drunkenness is tolerated far less and has become socially less acceptable. The possibility that an intoxicated person puts others in jeopardy is now an issue of public concern. Reinforcing this is a heightened interest in the general population in a variety of efforts to promote health—be it around diet, exercise, or other self-care measures. This has provided a moderating influence around alcohol use. So along with less red meat, fewer animal fats, jogging, and Jane Fonda's workout, there's more Perrier water. Coupled with all this are the improvements that have taken place in the professional training of physicians, clergy, nurses, social workers, and teachers with respect to alcohol, alcohol problems, and alcoholism, compared to the previous generation.

There are, at the same time, some obstacles to this becoming the norm. In the abstract, a person can be well informed about alcohol problems, but when they pop up in real life it can be a different matter. And all too often, along with the realization that there is a possible alcohol problem comes a lot of hand-wringing and waiting. The family, friends, physician, clergy— all those involved—can be immobilized. They can too often wait until the possible problem has progressed to the point where it is unequivocally and unquestionably the real thing, alcoholism.

Another obstacle is the absence of agreement within the alcohol field itself as to what constitutes appropriate treatment for those who are seen prior to clear-cut alcoholism. This should not be a surprise. The alcohol field has not had the similar collective experience with alcohol problems that it has had with alcoholism. The legacy of the nontraditional approaches to alcoholism treatment of several years ago may make clinicians squeamish. We refer to the efforts to teach controlled drinking to alcoholics, an approach that has since been thoroughly disproven and discredited. Efforts to assist problem drinkers to drink in a fashion that reduces risks and does not invite problems may appear to be reminiscent of controlled drinking. However, groups exist outside of the formal alcohol treatment field who have had experience dealing specifically with alcohol problems, particularly the drinking–driving programs and efforts on the college campuses. This experience may prove a useful guide in the future.

SCREENING AND EVALUATION

The ability to intervene in an alcohol problem depends upon two obvious factors. First, it requires the problem to be identified. Second, it requires an adequate evaluation to determine what the problem is. Alcohol problems can present in many guises. They are also quite common. Consequently, screening for alcohol problems should be routine in any counseling or medical setting.

Screening instruments

Several very easily administered screening tests have been shown to be very effective in identifying those with alcoholism or alcohol problems. They do not provide sufficient information to allow a counselor or others to formulate a treatment plan. But if routinely administered, they can assist in identifying those whose alcohol use warrants closer scrutiny. In assuring that those who don't "look" like people with alcohol problems don't go undetected, these tests may have less utility in a setting that deals exclusively with alcohol and/or drug problems. But they are still worth having in your repertoire, if only to teach to others who may be less comfortable in discussing, and less experienced in dealing with, alcohol issues. Several are described below.

CAGE. Since its introduction in 1970, the CAGE developed by Ewing and Rouse has become recognized as one of the most efficient and effective screening devices. It consists of four questions, which are as follows:

- "Have you ever felt you should *Cut* down on your drinking?"
- "Have people *Annoyed* you by criticizing your drinking?"
- "Have you ever felt bad or *Guilty* about your drinking?"
- "Have you ever had a drink first thing in the morning to steady nerves or get rid of a hangover?" (*Eye-Opener*)

Two or three affirmative answers should create a high index of suspicion. Four positive responses indicate alcoholism. The CAGE is both easy to administer and reliable in distinguishing alcoholics, as well as being less intimidating than some of the other instruments.

Michigan Alcohol Screening Test (MAST). The MAST has become the other most widely used screening instrument. The original MAST, first published in 1971 by Selzer and associates, was a 25-item yes or no questionnaire. It was designed for use either within a structured interview or for self-administration. The questions touch on medical, interpersonal, and legal problems resulting from alcohol use. (There is a weighted scoring system, and one question (#7) is not scored.) Since its introduction, the reliability and validity of the MAST have been established in multiple populations.

MAST (Michigan Alcoholism Screening Test)

Points		
2	(*1.)	Do you feel you are a normal drinker?
2	2.	Have you ever awakened the morning after some drinking the night before and found that you could not remember part of the evening before?
1	3.	Does your wife (or parents) ever worry or complain about your drinking?
2	*4.	Can you stop drinking without a struggle after one or two drinks?
1	5.	Do you ever feel bad about your drinking?
2	(*6.)	Do friends or relatives think you are a normal drinker?
0	7.	Do you ever try to limit your drinking to certain times of the day or to certain places?
2	*8.	Are you always able to stop drinking when you want to?
5	(9.)	Have you ever attended a meeting of Alcoholics Anonymous (AA)?
1	10.	Have you gotten into fights when drinking?
2	11.	Has drinking ever created problems with you and your wife?
2	12.	Has your wife (or other family member) ever gone to anyone for help about your drinking?
2	(13.)	Have you ever lost friends or girlfriends/boyfriends because of your drinking?
2	(14.)	Have you ever gotten into trouble at work because of drinking?
2	15.	Have you ever lost a job because of drinking?
2	(16.)	Have you ever neglected your obligations, your family, or your work for 2 or more days in a row because you were drinking?
1	17.	Do you ever drink before noon?
2	18.	Have you ever been told you have liver trouble? Cirrhosis?
2	(19.)	Have you ever had delirium tremens (DTs), severe shaking, heard voices or seen things that weren't really there after heavy drinking?
5	(20.)	Have you ever gone to anyone for help about your drinking?
5	(21.)	Have you ever been in a hospital because of your drinking?
2	22.	Have you ever been a patient in a psychiatric hospital or on a psychiatric ward of a general hospital where drinking was part of the problem?
2	23.	Have you ever been seen at a psychiatric or mental health clinic, or gone to a doctor, social worker, or clergyman for help with an emotional problem in which drinking has played a part?
2	24.	Have you ever been arrested, even for a few hours, because of drunk behavior?
2	(25.)	Have you ever been arrested for drunk driving or driving after drinking?

*   Negative responses are alcoholic responses.
( )   Indicates questions included in the Brief MAST.
—   Indicates questions included in the SMAST.
Scoring: A score of three points or less is considered nonalcoholic; four points is suggestive of alcoholism; a score of five points or more indicates alcoholism.

Several variations have since been developed. The *Brief MAST* uses ten of the MAST items. The *Short MAST* (SMAST) was specifically created to be self-administered and uses 13 items found to be as effective as the entire MAST for screening.

Trauma Index. Recognizing how commonly trauma is associated with excessive alcohol use, a five-question scale was developed by several Canadian researchers to identify early-stage problem drinkers, among both men and women, in an outpatient setting. The questions are as follows:
"Since your 18th birthday, have you..."
1. had any fractures or dislocations to bones or joints?
2. been injured in a traffic accident?
3. had a head injury?

4. been injured in an assault or fight?
5. been injured after drinking?

Two or more positive responses are indicative of excessive drinking or alcohol abuse. Though not as sensitive as the CAGE or the MAST, it will identify slightly over two thirds of problem drinkers.

For those with doubts. A word to those who are suspicious of screening instruments and their ability to detect a problem, especially given that denial is a prominent symptom of alcoholism. The CAGE and the MAST have both been used extensively. The Trauma Index is a newer instrument. As part of the creation, development and early testing, the client's responses to the questions were compared to the judgments of trained alcohol clinicians. Indeed, those who answered the indicated number of questions positively were those whom the clinicians agreed had alcoholism.

If you remain leery, reflect back to the description of the active alcoholic in Chapter 6. This candor is possibly not so unexpected. What the alcoholic may often strongly disagree with is not the "facts," but their interpretation. Thus, the alcoholic might very readily acknowledge that a family member has expressed concern about drinking. What the alcoholic would be likely to dispute is whether the concern is justified. The client may provide the interviewer a very lengthy and unsolicited rebuttal of the family's need for concern and a justification for the drinking. In such situations, the interviewer needs to note the initial response to the question despite the justification.

In using these screening instruments, a modicum of common sense is in order. The purpose is to be able to rapidly and easily obtain a rough assessment of an alcohol problem. Err on the conservative side. One should be cautious in disregarding a score that is positive for the presence of an alcohol problem. But even when the score does not indicate alcoholism, if something does not ring true, follow up.

Follow-up questions. William Clark of Harvard Medical School has authored some of the best material on alcoholism diagnosis directed to physicians. Although his comments are concerned with the medical interview, they would be useful in any counseling situation. He has three basic rules: (1) Ask about the person, not about the alcohol. He is a firm believer in routinely using the CAGE questions. (2) Use the lab sparingly. (That's easy for non-physicians to follow!) (3) Be prepared ahead of time with some follow-up questions for use when the CAGE is positive. He suggests a series of follow-up questions to get at preoccupation with alcohol. To help remember them he has two mnemonics, HALT and BUMP.

- Do you usually drink to get *High?*
- Do you sometimes drink *Alone?*
- Have you found yourself *Looking* forward to drinking?
- Have you noticed an increased *Tolerance* for alcohol?
- Do you have *Blackouts?*
- Have you found yourself using alcohol in an *Unplanned* way?
- Do you drink for *Medicinal* reasons?
- Do you work at *Protecting* your supply of alcohol?

Then to get at the common problems associated with alcohol use, he has a last series of questions:

- *Family* history of alcohol problems
- *Alcoholics* Anonymous attendance
- *Thoughts* of having alcoholism
- *Attempts* or thoughts of suicide
- *Legal* problems
- *Driving* while intoxicated
- *Tranquilizer* or disulfiram use

The device for remembering this is FATAL DTs.

Alcohol use history

When routine screening provides evidence of an alcohol problem, then a more detailed alcohol use history is always indicated. Similarly, an alcohol use history should be an integral part of an interview with any troubled person, whether the person has come to a physician or hospital with a physical problem, or to a social worker, psychiatrist, psychologist, or clergy member concerning an emotional or life adjustment problem. The reasons for this should now be clear. As we have previously noted, this is a drinking society; most people drink at least some alcohol. We have also noted that alcohol is a chemical and not as benign a one as previously thought. It simply cannot be ignored as a possible factor in whatever brings a person to a caregiver of any kind. Again, do not limit your attention to alcoholism alone. The purpose of the alcohol use history is simply to get as clear a picture of alcohol use as you would of other medical aspects, family situation, job difficulties, feelings, or whatever. It is part of the information-gathering process, which is later added up to give you an

idea of what is going on in the person's life and how best to proceed.

Many sample drinking history forms are floating around— for physicians, for nurses, and others. Our bias is that the attitude of the questioner is as important, if not more important, than the actual list of questions. If asking about drinking strikes you as an invasion of privacy, a waste of time, or of little use because the presenting problem is clearly not alcohol related, then you are going to be uncomfortable asking and will probably get unreliable answers from a now uncomfortable client. If your bias is the opposite, and you see alcohol lurking in the corner of every problem, again discomfort and unreliable answers will probably be your lot. Somehow you need to begin with a more objective stance. Alcohol might or might not be a factor, just as any other aspect of the client's life might or might not be of concern.

When to ask. It takes practice to take a reliable alcohol history. It also takes recognition of timing and a good look at what is in front of you. It may seem redundant to say, but an intoxicated or withdrawing client cannot give you good information. You wouldn't expect accurate information from someone going under anesthesia or coming out of it. Unfortunately, some of the forms we have seen are designed to be filled out on admission or intake with no recognition of this factor. Again, use your common sense. Try to ask the questions you need to at a time when the person is at least relatively comfortable both emotionally and physically. Ask them matter-of-factly, remembering that *your own drinking pattern is no yardstick for others.* For example, when someone responds to the question "How much do you usually drink?" with "About four or five drinks or so," don't stare open mouthed.

What to ask. Basically, the information needed is what does the client drink, how much, how often, when, where, and is it or, has it been, a problem in any area of his life, including physical problems. These questions can be phrased in different ways. In general, however, we lean to a more informal approach than sitting there filling out a form as you ask the questions in order. Another issue that we consider to be as important as the above information, but that is not included on most forms, is the question of what the drinking does for the client. Questions such as "How do you feel when you drink?," "What does alcohol do for you?," and "When do you most often want a drink?" can supply a lot of information.

How to ask. If the questions are asked conversationally along with other questions regarding general health, social aspects, and other use of drugs or medications, most people will answer them. The less threatened you are by the process, the more comfortable the individual being questioned will be.

Recording the data in the record

Alcohol use should be adequately described in the agency chart or medical record so that changes in drinking practices can be detected over time. If there is no evidence of alcohol being a problem, that too should be noted. Notes in the chart should include sufficient objective detail to provide meaningful data to other clinicians. Avoid one-word descriptions such as "socially" or "occasionally." If the agency does not have a prescribed format, it is suggested that the following be included for all clients: the drinking pattern, problems related to alcohol use, expression of concern by family or friends, and the MAST or CAGE score.

WHAT NEXT?

Making a referral

Having identified an alcohol problem, the clinician who isn't primarily an alcohol counselor is faced with referring the client to an alcohol facility. This may be either for further evaluation or for treatment. To accomplish this means keeping several things in mind. First, you cannot enthusiastically recommend the unfamiliar. Therefore, you need to know about various facilities, what they are like, their programs and personnel. Second, in making any referral, there's always a danger of clients falling through the cracks. This is especially true of alcoholics. They have a knack for finding cracks. Therefore, you need to be actively involved in the referral. Don't just give an agency name and phone number with instructions for the client to call. You make the appointment with a specific individual, at a specific time and inform/involve the family. Third, if you've had an ongoing relationship with the client, a referral may feel like abandonment. As appropriate, continue the contact and let the client know that you are in this together.

In large measure, the ability to affect a successful referral lies in your conveying a sense of concern and hopefulness. It also depends upon assisting the client to see the difficulties in a new light, that there may be a disease causing these difficulties, that it's not a question of who is at fault. In presenting the need for referral, remember that someone can absorb only so much information at one time. Consider for a moment the woman whose physician discovers a lump in her breast. The physician's next step is making a referral to a surgeon for a biopsy and possibly to an oncologist. This is not the time to discuss the relative merits of radical mastectomy and/or chemotherapy in terms of 5-year survival. Nor is it the time to talk of side effects from chemotherapy. Such presentations would be likely to cause the woman to run, because she abandons hope, or to retreat into denial. The important messages to convey initially are (1) the situation is serious enough to warrant further investigation, (2) I'm referring you to someone I/we can trust, and (3) I'm in this with you. That same concern is what one is attempting to convey when making a referral for alcohol problems.

In an alcohol setting

For those working in a designated alcohol treatment program, the situation is a bit different. Here, the person may be referred or come in with a good idea that alcohol is a problem. The person may, however, want to prove that it isn't. Because of the alcohol treatment designation, the questions about alcohol can be more forthright and in depth. But the responses may be more guarded—particularly responses to how much and how often. Indeed, some suggest never asking these questions, at least in an initial encounter. The reason is because they are the questions most likely to trigger the client's defenses. It is probably *the* topic that has caused the most friction with family. If asked, the responses can range all the way from a gruff "a few and just socially" to a bragging "a whole case of beer whenever I feel like it." The grain of salt theory can be applied here and so noted in your record keeping. It is not, however, an occasion for an "Aw, come on!" response from you. Simply record the answer and reserve your comment for the appropriate place in the records. A clearer picture will emerge as therapy begins (if it does). Remember, the client will usually need to feel somewhat comfortable with you before total candor can occur. And there is always the real possibility that the client doesn't *know* exactly how much or how often. The key thing for the counselor is to get as much reasonably reliable information as possible in order to proceed with appropriate treatment or referral. Information about quantity and frequency is not necessary to diagnose alcoholism. It can be useful in gauging the level of physical dependence and assessing possible withdrawal problems. However tolerance can be gleaned indirectly by other means, such as "How many drinks does it take to feel the effect?"

Another point to consider is that you do not always have to get all the history at one sitting. If a client comes to a treatment facility smelling of alcohol, clearly uncomfortable, and somewhat shaky, you need to know immediately how much alcohol has been consumed, for how long, and when the last drink was taken. You also need to know about other physical problems and what happened on other occasions when drinking was stopped. These questions are necessary to determine if the client needs immediate attention from a physician. Or if the client is not in crisis, the evaluation may occur over several outpatient visits.

One method of gathering information when a client is not in immediate physical difficulty is used regularly at a treatment facility in our area. Clients are asked to review their drinking beginning with the first drinking experience they remember. This chronological review gives the counselor a complete picture of the drinking pattern and also serves to give clients the opportunity of looking at the developing drinking habits for the first time. It often helps them to see the shifts and changes that signaled/led to an emerging problem and can thus be used as a therapeutic lever.

Initial interview. The initial interview is intended to get a sense of the general picture. As a result of the initial interview, the alcohol counselor will want to be able to answer the following questions:

1. What is the problem the client sees?
2. What does he want?
3. What brings him for help now?
4. What is going on in his life (the "facts" of the family situation, social problems, medical problems, alcohol use—how much, how long)?
5. Is there a medical or psychiatric emergency?
6. What are the recommendations?

Certainly, much other information could be elicited. But the answers to the foregoing questions make up the essential core for making decisions about how to proceed.

Counseling is an art, not a science. No series of rules can be mechanically followed. However, one guideline is in order for an initial interview. It is especially apt in situations in which someone is first reaching out for help. *Don't let the interview end without adopting a definite plan for the next step.* Why? People with alcohol problems are ambivalent. They run hot and cold.

They approach and back off from help. The person who comes in saying "I'm an alcoholic and want help" is very, very rare. You are more likely to meet the following: "I think I may have a problem with alcohol, sort of, but it's really my ———— that's bugging me." The concrete plan adopted at the close of the interview may be very simple. The plan may be nothing more than agreeing to meet a couple of times more, so that you, the counselor, can get a better idea of what's going on. Set a definite time. Leaving future meetings up in the air is like waving good-bye. It is not uncommon for the alcoholic to try to get off the hook by flattering the counselor. "Gee…you've really helped me. Why don't I call you if things don't improve? Why, I feel better already, just talking to you."

Despite the title of alcohol counselor, a client first coming to an agency is not coming to you to have you "do your treatment routine" on him. It is more likely that he wants a clean bill of health. He wants to figure out why his drinking isn't "working" anymore. The only thing that may be clear is the presence of drinking. The client is often unaware of the relationship of his drinking to the problems in his life. As he paints a picture of what is going on in his life, the counselor will certainly see things the client is missing or ignoring.

Client's view
of world

Counselor's view
of client's world

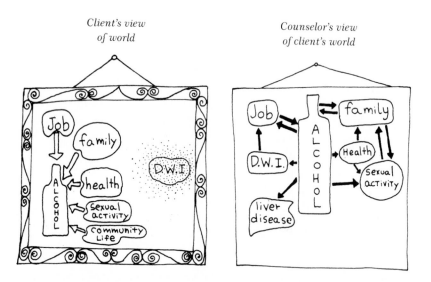

You can see that the client is alcoholic. In your opinion, the client may need a rehabilitation facility. However, at the moment, the client is unable to use the treatment. First, it is necessary for him to make some connections—that is, get his arrows pointed in the right direction.

Family involvement. Participation of family in the evaluation is very desirable and becoming the norm. So much so that it's hard to imagine why family involvement was not always the case. In some instances family members may be the more reliable historians. Even if not, their perspective on the problem is essential. By including family members, the counselor can assess firsthand their needs and their ability to provide support, as well as engage them as partners in treatment.

Treatment planning. An evaluation may take one or more sessions. The goal of the evaluation is to develop a "recipe" or plan that will offer the client the optimal chance of getting those arrows pointed in the proper direction. The essential tasks of treatment will be discussed shortly. The treatment plan may use many of the treatment techniques to be discussed in Chapter 9. If the diagnosis is alcoholism, this can be provided on either an inpatient or outpatient basis. In deciding which of these to recommend, the following items should be considered.

Indications for in-patient care
- history of unsuccessful out-patient treatment
- potential withdrawal problems
- medical problems
- few social supports
- a family that needs "time out"
- ambivalence about need for treatment

Indications for out-patient care
- first treatment attempt
- intact and supportive family
- able to use available supports
- no medical complications
- recognizes need for treatment
- little risk of withdrawal

Treatment planning for the veteran. A few comments are warranted in respect to treatment planning for the client who has been in treatment previously. A portion of the evaluation needs to focus on prior treatment. What was the treatment? Did the client have a period of stable sobriety? If so, what contributed to its maintenance? To what does the family or client attribute the resumption of drinking? These perceptions may be insightful or way off base. However, they are important beliefs that will either need to be supported or challenged. If a stable sobriety was never achieved, what are their hypotheses as to what went wrong? Is there evidence to suggest a psychiatric disorder that has gone undiagnosed?

The client who has been through treatment a number of times and has not gained sobriety is often termed a "treatment failure." That is obviously a very loaded label for the client, the family (if they still are on the scene), as well as the treatment staff. It is never possible to predict when treatment will "take." Nonetheless simply one more exposure to the same treatment may not be the best clinical decision. The comparison might be made to someone with an infection that does not respond to a particular drug. Simply increasing the dosage probably won't work. One of the things treatment veterans do have going for them is a knowledge of what doesn't work. To the extent possible, the client should be actively engaged in treatment planning and making a commitment to it, for example, agreeing ahead of time to attend more AA meetings, seeking an AA sponsor, entering a halfway house after inpatient care, continuing in aftercare.

One of the difficulties commonly encountered with these clients is that they show up in the midst of serious crises, for example, a medical illness requiring hospitalization or family turmoil or legal problems. This can lead to a situation in which the person, willing to comply or at least not to resist, in essence finds himself entered into a program. Although one may need to respond to the crisis, it is imperative to engage the client as soon as possible in planning treatment after the crisis is stabilized.

If someone comes to an agency with a history of multiple unsuccessful treatment attempts in that agency's program, the question needs to be asked if a referral to another facility might now be indicated. It is important this not be done as "punishment." Instead it should be a clinical decision based on the possibility that entry into treatment elsewhere may increase the odds in favor of a different outcome because that staff will not have been involved in the previous efforts and see the client as a "failure."

TREATMENT OF ALCOHOL PROBLEMS

We expect that in the future alcohol treatment will not be so exclusively directed toward treatment of alcoholism. Nonetheless, we have not yet reached that point. So the major portion of this chapter will soon turn to alcoholism. However, first, even though there are not yet universally accepted standards of treatment for other alcohol problems, we do have some suggestions. These we think can serve as a conservative stance until the time when a body of clinical experience with alcohol problems exists, similar to that which has been acquired around alcoholism.

Alcohol incidents

By alcohol incidents, we refer to the individual who has experienced some negative consequences as the result of drinking. It may be an accident, an altercation, whatever. However, a thorough evaluation indicates no pattern of recurring problems to indicate abuse. Nor is there alcoholism.

First, the "thou shall nots." Don't presume that the incident has been enough to teach someone a lesson and guarantee that there will be no future difficulties. It's easy to assume that the embarrassment, guilt, discomfort, or anxiety that resulted was sufficient. It may even seem almost cruel to discuss it further. Others may mistakenly think the polite, kind thing to do is "just not mention it." Especially with younger people, who may be those most likely to experience an alcohol-related problem, the incident may be treated by peers as a joke. What is required? All those who may have contact, be it emergency room personnel, or school counselor, or police, or family, all need to acknowledge the role of alcohol in what occurred. The actual or potential seriousness needs to be made clear. If you recall the progression of alcoholism in the framework set forth by Johnson and described in Chapter 6, the absence of feedback by others in the face of alcohol-related incidents is, in part, what allows a chronic alcohol problem to blossom.

In the face of an incident involving alcohol, alcohol education is essential. This should not be cursory and superficial, but detailed. Alcohol as a drug has to be explained to the individual in light of what has occurred. What does BAC mean?…How is it that alcohol can induce poor choices? What happens when someone chugs drinks?…or what are the mechanisms for alcohol–drug interactions?

The underlying message is that if people are going to use the drug alcohol, they need to be fully informed about it. Don't assume that people, however bright and sophisticated, are sufficiently knowledgeable about alcohol and its actions to figure out what the risks are. So the evaluation should also include an inventory of drinking practices, a review of settings in which drinking takes place, behaviors associated with drinking, plus family history of alcoholism or medical conditions that may be adversely

If it is a small sacrifice to discontinue the use of wine, do it for the sake of others; if it is a great sacrifice, do it for your own sake.

S.J. MAY

influenced by alcohol use. The question to be answered is this: "Are there circumstances that are likely to place the individual at risk?" If so, specific steps should be discussed to address these. What might the person do who is faced with being a passenger in a car with an intoxicated driver? For the person who takes allergy medications, what are the implications for drinking? Identify potential problems and help the client think through—ahead of time—what should be done. Research undertaken about techniques for prevention of drug abuse came up with an interesting finding. One of the most successful techniques in reducing teen-age drug use was to literally have the kids practice how to say no. Adequate information alone wasn't enough. What was needed were tips for applying it. What is being suggested here is an extension of that. This is very important, too, in the event that future problems with alcohol use occur. If a problem were handled in the fashion suggested here, later it could be safely assumed that the individual, from that point on, was fully informed! A subsequent problem would indicate that a serious ongoing problem with alcohol was emerging and alcoholism may be budding.

It is important that an alcohol incident not be treated as a "secret." It is suggested that the client's consent be secured to bring the situation to the attention of the client's family, friends, or spouse, and also the family needs to be informed in order to be aware and supportive of what is recommended. Although in an ideal world at least one follow-up visit might be scheduled just to check in with the individual, it is more likely that this will not happen. The family physician, often an untapped ally, *is* in a position to monitor how things are going in the future. The family physician is in a position to routinely inquire about alcohol use, and therefore may be in the best position to spot any future difficulties. Because one of the most useful factors in spotting an alcohol problem early is detecting changes that occur over a period of time, getting the occurrence of an alcohol problem into the individual's medical record is important. A brief communication with the physician will accomplish that. For the person at risk for developing alcoholism, the signs and symptoms that should trigger a need for further evaluation should be understood by all.

Alcohol Abuse

Alcohol abuse is similar to alcohol dependence (alcoholism) except for the absence of physical dependence, that is withdrawal and/or tolerance (see Chapter 3). Practically speaking, alcohol abuse can be considered to be present when there is a pattern of alcohol problems and the sense that alcoholism is "just around the corner." Alcohol abuse may be present in an individual even if loss of control is unclear because there may have been no efforts to control or moderate alcohol use. If physical dependence and loss of control have not occurred, then moderation of drinking practices from a physiological standpoint is possible. However, depending upon the person's social situation and life circumstances, this may still represent a monumental feat. Consider the college student who is heavily into the partying and drinking set. Changing drinking patterns will require marked changes in the student's circle of friends, daily routine, and choices of recreational activities. To achieve this magnitude of change will require the client be engaged in more than a Dutch uncle talk!

To do this, to our minds, requires that the individual be engaged in some formal alcohol treatment, which involves alcohol education, individual counseling, and participation in a group with others in the same situation. Monitoring the individual's efforts to moderate alcohol use and avoid future problems is imperative. Through this process, in a number of cases, evidence may mount that there is loss of control, or preoccupation with drinking. Therefore abstinence and alcoholism treatment is now needed. In essence, if efforts to address alcohol abuse are unsuccessful, the diagnosis of alcoholism can now be made.

ALCOHOLISM TREATMENT

Alcoholism treatment is nothing more (or less) than the interventions designed to short-circuit the alcoholic process and provide an introduction to a sober, drug-free existence. Alcoholism is the third leading cause of death in the United States. It shouldn't be. In comparison to other chronic disease, it is significantly more treatable. Virtually any alcoholic who seeks assistance and is willing to actively participate in rehabilitation efforts can realistically expect to lead a happy, productive life. Sadly, the same is not true for a victim of cancer, heart disease, or emphysema. The realization that alcoholism is treatable is becoming more widespread. The public efforts of prominent individuals who are recovering has contributed to this acceptance. Both professional treatment programs and AA are discovering that alcoholics today are often younger and in the early or middle stages of alcoholism when they seek help. It is imperative for the helping professions to keep firmly in mind the hopefulness that surrounds treatment.

Just as people initially become involved with alcohol for a variety of reasons, there is similar variety in what prompts treatment. For every person who wends his way into alcoholism, there is also an exit route. This exit is most easily accomplished with professional help. The role of the counselor or therapist is to serve as a guide, to share knowledge of the terrain, to be a support as the alcoholic regains his footing, and to provide encouragement. The counselor cannot make the trip for the alcoholic but can only point the way. The counselor's goal for treatment, the destination of the journey, is to assist the alcoholic in becoming comfortable and at ease in the world, able to handle his life situation. This will require the alcoholic to stop drinking. In our experience, a drinking alcoholic cannot be happy, healthy, at peace with himself, or alive in any way that makes sense to him, not to us. The question for the counselor is never "How can I make him stop?" The only productive focus for the counselor is "How can I create an atmosphere in which he is better able to choose sobriety for himself?"

In this discussion, abstinence is presumed to be required for alcoholism treatment. There was a time when researchers were actively exploring controlled drinking as an alternative (see Behavioral Approaches, Chapter 9). The optimism that was initially reported was met with scepticism by veteran alcoholism clinicians. When the fates of those treated by controlled drinking were examined, the sceptics were proven right. In virtually all cases, there was serious relapse and further alcohol problems. Vaillant, when questioned as to an alcoholic's ability to resume social drinking, uses the example of a motorist who decides to remove the spare tire from the car trunk. Disaster may not strike the next day, or the next week, or even within the month. But sooner or later... And the seriousness of the consequences cannot be predicted ahead of time. It may be only a flat tire in one's driveway, or it may be on a very busy freeway during rush hour.

Abstinence as a requisite for a solid recovery appears to have a physiological basis. Tolerance once established is maintained, even in the absence of further alcohol use. Were someone who has been abstinent for a considerable period to resume drinking, the person would very quickly be physically capable of drinking amounts consistent with the highest levels previously consumed. Drinking isn't resumed with a physiologically "clean slate." It

may have taken ten or more years for an alcoholic to reach a consumption level of a fifth a day, though that level can be reinstated
within literally days, even after a decade of sobriety.

Obstacles to treatment

If alcoholism is so highly treatable, what has been going
wrong? Why aren't more people receiving help? The obstacles do
require examination. Historically, one big handicap has been society's attitude toward alcohol and its use. Unfortunately, the alcoholic's chances of being treated for alcoholism have long been
slim. Oh, he will receive treatment: for depression, gastritis, cirrhosis—but less often for the alcoholism. Despite all the public
education and information, the notion remains lurking that talking about someone's drinking is in bad taste. It seems too private, somehow, none of anyone's business. Most of us have a
good feel for the taboo topics— sexual behavior, people's way of
handling their children. The way someone drinks has been a
strong taboo. Of course, an alcoholic has a stake in keeping the
drinking and its associated problems off limits. Should the drinking behavior be discussed, the alcoholic's rationalization combined with the tendency to "psychologize," analyze, and get to
the reason would spring another trap. The notion that someone
drinks alcoholically only *because* he is an alcoholic sounds circular and simpleminded. Thus, everyone scurries around to find
the "real" cause. Alcoholism as a phenomenon, a fact of life, gets
pushed aside and forgotten in the uproar.

Another obstacle is the confusion introduced for alcoholics
and their families by the behavioral symptoms of alcoholism.
One common characteristic of alcoholic behavior is the extreme
variation, the lack of consistency, sometimes good mood, sometimes foul mood, sometimes sloshed, sometimes sober. This inconsistency invites a host of explanations. Further, this very inconsistency allows the alcoholic, family, and friends to hope
things will get better if left alone. It permits them to delay seeking assistance. It almost seems to be human nature to want—
and wait—for things to improve on their own. Consider for a moment the simple toothache. If the toothache comes and goes, you
probably will delay a trip to the dentist. After all, maybe it was
something hot you ate? Maybe it was caused by something cold?
Maybe, or maybe…? On the other hand, if the pain is constant,
if it is clearly getting worse, if you can remember wicked tooth-
aches in the past, you'll probably call immediately for an
emergency appointment with your dentist. The total time you are

actually in pain in the latter case may be much less than what you would have put up with in the former example, but you are spurred into action because it doesn't look like it will improve by itself.

Unfortunately, even when alcoholism treatment is instituted, it can be seriously unbalanced, zeroing in on only a part of the symptomatology. When this happens, alcoholism treatment can end up resembling treatment for depression, or cirrhosis, or just a "rest cure." These one-sided approaches are major sources of recidivism and failure, and not infrequently they have given the impression that alcoholism treatment doesn't work.

Factors in successful treatment

Having alluded to failure and some sense of what to avoid, let us proceed to success. The likelihood of success is greatly enhanced if treatment is tailored to the characteristics of the disease being treated. The following factors, always present in the alcoholic, should guide both the planning and process of treatment.

1. *Dysfunctional life-style.* The alcoholic's life-style has been centered on alcohol. If this is not immediately evident, it is because the particular alcoholic has done a better-than-average job of disguising the fact. Thus, the counselor cannot expect a large repertoire of healthy behaviors that come automatically. Treatment will help build these, as well as dust off and rediscover behaviors from the past to replace the warped "alcoholic" responses. This fact is what makes residential treatment desirable. Besides cutting down the number of easy drinking opportunities, it provides some room to make a new, fresh beginning.

2. *Few experiences of handling stress without alcohol.* Alcohol has been the alcoholic's constant companion. It is used to anticipate, get through, and then get over stressful times. Alcoholics, to their knowledge, are without any effective tools for handling problems. In planning treatment, be alert to what may be stressful for a particular client and provide supports. In the process, the counselor can tap skills within the alcoholic to be turned to rather than the bottle.

3. *Psychological wounds.* Alcohol is the alcoholic's best friend and worst enemy. The prospect of a life without alcohol seems either impossible or so unattractive as to be unworthwhile. The alcoholic feels lost, fragile, vulnerable, fearful. No matter how well put together the client can appear, or how much

strength or potential the counselor can see, the client, by and large, is unable to get beyond those feelings of impotence, nakedness, nothingness. Even when being firm and directive, the counselor has to have a gentle awareness of this.

4. *Physical dysfunctions.* Chronic alcohol use takes its toll on the body. Even if spared the more obvious physical illnesses, the alcoholic must contend with other subtle disturbances of physical functioning. Sleep disturbance can last up to 2 years. Similarly, a thought impairment would not be unusual on cessation of drinking. The alcoholic in the initial stage of recovery will have trouble maintaining attention. There will be diminution of adaptive abilities. During treatment, education about alcohol and its effects can help allay fears.

5. *Chronic nature of alcoholism.* A chronic disease requires continuing treatment and vigilance regarding the conditions that can prompt a relapse. This continued self-monitoring is essential to success in treatment.

6. *Deterioration in family function.* As described in Chapter 7, the family needs as much help as the alcoholic. Better outcomes result when they have a treatment program of their own in conjunction with the alcoholic's treatment.

Recovery process

Recall how the progression of alcoholism can be sketched out. Similarly, recovery is a process that does not happen all at once. Gradually, in steps, the alcoholic becomes better able to manage his or her life. For the purpose of discussion, there are three distinguishable stages of recovery: the introductory phase, the active treatment phase, and the continuing maintenance of recovery. There is no clear-cut beginning or end point. Yet each phase has its observable hallmarks.

Preliminary or introductory phase. The preliminary or introductory phase begins when the problem of alcoholism comes to the foreground. This happens when the alcoholic lets those nagging suspicions surface that there is something wrong with the drinking. On personal initiative, he might make some initial inquiries, which may be directed to friends and associates.

"You know, Jane was really mad at me for getting a bit tipsy when we went out last Friday night. You were there. I don't see anything wrong with letting go after a long hard week, do you? She's always on my back about something these days."

Often others may not recognize these queries as a disguised or tentative "cry for help."

Do you really think I drink like a fish?

Ideally the friend, coworker, or colleague who is the recipient of these initial queries listens carefully and avoids the trap of offering false reassurance or reinforcing denial with a comment like "Oh, you're just imagining it." Ideally they will share the information that people can get in trouble with alcohol, that alcohol use can be a significant health problem; they will then urge the seeking of a professional opinion, and do whatever they can to see that the person gets there. The first overture may instead be made to the alcoholic by a member of the clergy, family member, friend, or perceptive physician—someone who is sufficiently concerned to speak up and take the risk of being accused of meddling. Suspecting an alcohol problem, any one of them might request that the alcoholic seek an alcohol expert to explore the possibility. On the other hand, a court may "sentence" an individual convicted of DWI to alcohol treatment. Increasingly common also is that the spouse of the alcoholic may seek counseling as a result of the chaos of living with an alcoholic; or the employer may notice developing problems and attempt to intervene.

At this point the alcoholic is a fish nibbling at the bait. He moves close and backs off. He wants to know, but he doesn't. Of course his drinking causes him problems, but he doesn't want (is scared) to stop. What he really wants to learn is how to drink well. He wants to drink without the accompanying problems. In getting in touch with a counselor, the chances are pretty good he wants the counselor to teach him how. (This represents an impossible request, so the counselor must avoid getting sucked into trying.)

What *can* the counselor do? First, the counselor must make a careful evaluation of the problem in order to assess its nature and severity. Following that, a tentative treatment plan will be devised, possibly using outside expert opinions. These treatment recommendations will then be discussed with the client. This discussion will explain the recommendations, including any possible "risks" of treatment contrasted with the dangers of not initiating treatment.

The assessment process for an alcohol problem or alcoholism, just like any other evaluation process, is intended initially to collect data. The counselor in a very general way will be endeavoring simply to get a clear picture of what is going on in the client's life.

In terms of the specifics, keep in mind that it is of the utmost importance to avoid getting into a defensive position. You need not be defensive as to the reason you can't be helpful in teaching the alcoholic how to drink successfully. That is guaranteed to push the alcoholic's seesaw and drive him away. There is, however, a mutual goal "to have things be okay." The counselor can buy into this without accepting the client's means of achieving it. The task of the therapy will be to assist the alcoholic to see his behavior and its consequences accurately. As this occurs, the client will be confronted with the impossible nature of his request. The counselor will be most successful by being open, honest, patient. The counseling is doomed if you are seduced into playing the "patsy," or if you try to seduce the client by being the "good guy, rescuer." Having a coworker with whom to discuss cases and their frustrations can help keep the objectives in sight.

Alcoholism is a disease that requires the client to make a "self-diagnosis" for successful treatment to occur. Treatment, full steam ahead, cannot begin until the alcoholic, inside himself, attaches that label to cover all that is going on with him. A head, or intellectual, understanding does not suffice. It must come from the heart. In fact, the whole thing can be confusing. He certainly doesn't have to be happy. He simply needs to know it's true. Then without hope of his own, he borrows the counselor's belief that things can change.

Active treatment phase. At this point of acknowledgment, seeing alcohol as the culprit, and with a desire to change, the alcoholic by himself is at a dead end. If he knew what to do, he would have done it. Thus he, in essence, turns the steering of his life over to the counselor or therapist. The counselor, in turn, must respond by providing clear, concrete, simple stage directions. The alcoholic needs to have a rehabilitative regimen set forth for him. He needs his environment simplified. The number of decisions he is confronted with must be pared down. He is able to deal with little more than "How am I going to get through this day (or hour) without a drink?" Effort needs to be centered on doing whatever is necessary to buy sober time. To quote the old maxim: "Nothing succeeds like success." A day sober turns on the light a little. It has become something that is possible. For the alcoholic, this is an achievement. It does not guarantee continued sobriety, but it demonstrates the possibility. In the sober time, the alcoholic is gaining skills. He discovers behavior that can be of assistance in handling those events that previously would have prompted drinking.

Although we are not attempting to discuss specific techniques of treatment here, a mention of AA is nonetheless in order. Anyone in the alcoholism treatment field will acknowledge that clients who take up AA have a much better chance of recovery. This is not accidental. AA has combined the key ingredients essential for recovery. It provides support; it embodies hope. It provides concrete suggestions without cajoling. Its slogans are the simple guideposts needed to reorder a life. And its purpose is never lost.

The necessity for a direct and uncluttered approach to the alcoholic cannot be overstressed. He is not capable of handling anything else. This is one of several reasons for the belief that alcoholism has to be the priority item on any treatment agenda. The only exceptions are life-threatening or serious medical problems. For the alcoholic to work actively and successfully on a list of difficulties is overwhelming. Interestingly enough, when alcoholism treatment is undertaken, the other problems often fade. Furthermore, waiting to treat the alcoholism until some other matter is settled invites the alcoholic's ambivalence to surface. This waiting feeds the part of him that says, "Well, maybe it isn't so bad after all," or "I'll wait and see how it goes." Generally the matters are unsolvable because an actively drinking alcoholic has no inner resources to tackle anything. He is drugged.

Focusing on alcoholism as a priority, the alcoholic's acceptance of this, and providing room and skills to experience sobriety make up the meat of therapy. As this takes place, the alcoholic is able to assume responsibility for managing his life, using the tools he has acquired. With this, the working relationship between counselor and client shifts. They collaborate in a different way. The counselor may be alert to potential problematic situations, but the client increasingly takes responsibility for identifying them and selecting ways to deal with them. Rather than being a guide, the counselor is a resource, someone with whom the client can check things out. At this point, the alcoholic's continuing treatment has begun.

Continuing treatment phase. The alcoholic learns, as do others with a chronic disease, the importance of being able to identify situations, and their responses to them, that may signal a flare-up. For the alcoholic, this entails maintaining a continuing awareness of the alcoholic status, if sobriety is to continue. The alcoholic certainly will not continue to see the counselor for a lifetime as a reminder of the need to be vigilant. However, each one will need to develop other alternatives to succeed in staying sober.

"Why do I drink?" This is the recurrent theme of many active alcoholics and those beginning active treatment. In our experience, focusing on this question, even when it seems most pressing to the client, is of little value. It takes the client off the hot seat. It looks to the past and to causes "out there." The more important question is the nitty-gritty of the present moment: "What can be done now?" If there is a time to deal with the "whys," it comes during the continuing treatment phase. Don't misunderstand. Long hours spent studying what went wrong, way back, are *never* helpful. Rather, the reason can be discerned from the present, daily-life events, on those occasions when taking a drink is most tempting. Dealing with these can provide the alcoholic with a wealth of practical information about himself for his immediate use. Dealing with the present is of vital importance. The alcoholic, who has spent his recent life in a drugged state, has had less experience than most of us (which isn't much) in attending to the present. His automatic tendency is to analyze the past and/or worry about the future. The only part of life that he can hope to handle effectively is the present.

A client's hope for change often must be sparked by the counselor's belief in that possibility. Your attitudes about your clients and their potential for health exerts a powerful influence. This doesn't mean you cannot and will not become frustrated, impatient, or angry at times. Whether therapy can proceed depends on what you do with these feelings. You can only carry them so long before the discomfort becomes unbearable. Then you will either pretend they aren't there or unload them on the client. Either way your thinking can become "she can never change," "this guy is hopeless," or "she's just not ready." When that happens, counseling is not possible even if the people continue meeting. A better approach is to have a coworker with whom you can discuss these feelings of impotence and frustration. Doing this makes it easier to say "I know he can change, even if I can't imagine how it will happen. Certainly, stranger things have happened in the history of the world." At this point therapy can proceed. However, if an impasse in working with a particular client isn't broken through, the client should be referred to a coworker.

Treatment is a process involving people. People have their ups and downs, good days, bad days. Some that you think will make it, won't. Some that you are sure don't have a chance will surprise you. There will be days when you will wonder why you ever got into this. On others it will seem a pretty good thing to be

doing. Remembering that it is an unpredictable process may help you keep your balance.

Common themes in alcoholism treatment

Early in the recovery process, many alcoholics have a tendency to become quite upset over very small matters. They look well, feel well, and sound well—but they really aren't quite there yet. This can be very trying for both counselor and client and the family, too. Remembering and reminding them of how sick they have recently been makes this less threatening. The steps after any major illness seem slow and tedious. There are occasional setbacks; yet eventually all is well. It works that way with alcoholism, too. It is simply harder to accept because there are no bandages to remove, scars to point to, or clear signs of healing to check on. It cannot be emphasized enough that it *takes time*.

During this early phase of treatment, one point often overlooked is the alcoholic's inability to function on a simple daily basis. It is almost inconceivable to therapists (or anyone else for that matter) that a person who seems reasonably intelligent, looks fairly healthy after detoxification, and is over 21 can have problems with when to get up in the morning or what to do when he is up! Along with family, work, and social deterioration caused by the alcoholic life-style, the simple things have gotten messed up, too. Alcoholics may have gargled, brushed their teeth, and chewed mints continually while drinking in an effort to cover up. They may, on the other hand, have skipped most mealtimes and eaten only sporadically with no thought to their nutritional needs. They may have thrown up with some regularity. Also, as we have seen in Chapter 5, their sleep is not likely to be normal. Getting dressed without trying to choke down some booze to quell the shakes may be a novel experience. It may have been years since the person has performed the standard daily tasks in a totally drug-free state.

Alcoholics are rather like Rip Van Winkles during the early weeks of their recovery. Everything they do is likely to feel strange. The face looking back at them from the mirror may even seem like a stranger's. They became used to the blurred perceptions they had experienced while drinking. It is terribly disconcerting to find virtually every task one faces a whole new thing. Whereas it used to take 2 very careful days to prepare Thanksgiving dinner, it now requires only a few hours. The accompanying wine for the cook, trips back to the store for forgotten items (and by the way, a little more booze), the self-pity over *having* to do it, the naps necessary to combat the fatigue of the ordeal, the incredible energy devoted to controlling the drinking enough to get everything done—all these steps are eliminated.

The newly sober alcoholic is continually being faced with the novelty of time—either time left over, or the experience of not enough time, or near panic over what to do next. Many clients will need help in setting up schedules. After years of getting by on the bottle, they have to regain a sense of the "real" time it takes to accomplish some tasks. He may plan to paint the entire house in 2 days or, conversely, decide that he can't possibly fit a dentist appointment, a luncheon engagement, and a sales call into one. She may believe that it is all she can manage to stop by the bank on the way to work, and pick up a loaf of bread and the dry cleaning on the way home. Tomorrow she intends to make new living room drapes in time for that evening's dinner party! The perception of time is as distorted as other areas of perception. Reassurance that this is a common state of affairs, along with assistance in setting realistic daily goals, is greatly needed. This is one reason newcomers to AA find the slogans "Keep it simple" and "First things first" so helpful.

The alcoholic may not mention the dilemmas over time and schedules to you. There may be a sense of shame over such helplessness in the face of simple things. However, a gentle question from you may open the floodgates. This provides the opportunity to help bring order out of chaos. You can offer the alcoholic some much-needed guidance in remastering the details of daily living. All too often the wail is heard, "I don't know! The house was a mess.…The kids were a mess.…I was a mess.…I just couldn't handle it, so I drank!"

Another area in which the counselor has to reorient the alcoholic to reality involves the misperception of events. The faulty memories caused by the drugged state will have to be reexamined. One cannot always wait for some sudden insight to clear things up. For example, he is talking to you about difficulties he has had with his wife. He remembers her as a nagging bitch on his back about a "few little drinks." You might remind him that on the occasion in question, he was picked up for driving while intoxicated with a blood alcohol content of 0.20—clearly not a few. Then go on to point out that because he has misperceived the amount he was drinking to such an extent, he may have misperceived his wife's behavior. The opportunity is there, if indicated, to educate the client briefly on the distortions produced by the drug, alcohol, and to suggest that sober observations of his wife's behavior are more valid. You might instead suggest a couple's meeting, but keep clearly in front the issue of the alcohol use.

Different strokes for different folks.   Another easy trap to fall into is to expect the same course of recovery to occur for most clients. Alcoholics don't get sick at the same rate, and they don't get well at the same rate. One will be up and at 'em and lookin' good in very short order; another will seem to be stuck, barely hanging on, forever. And there are all the degrees in between. What is a hang-up for one is a breeze for another. Don't assume that you know what is going to be a problem for any one particular alcoholic. We have tried to point out some of the most common, but there are lots of surprises around still. There are just no formulas or easy prescriptions that will work every time. There is no substitute for knowing a particular alcoholic and dealing with the one sitting before you.

Still later. At a point, after about 3 months, when the sober alcoholic reaches some level of comfort with the new state of affairs, the focus can shift. The attention has been virtually at the level of the mechanics of daily living. With that out of the way, or reasonably under control, the focus can move on to sorting out the alcoholic's stance in the world, feelings, and relationships. Though 3 months is a somewhat arbitrary designation, it is not wholly so. Recall the subacute withdrawal syndrome (Chapter 5). The alcoholic may pass through the acute withdrawal period within 5 days, but a longer period is required to regain the ability to concentrate, for example. Thus, there is a physical basis for what the alcoholic can focus on productively. This does not mean that all the problems previously discussed are totally overcome, or that work is not proceeding along some of the above paths. It simply means that other problems may now be surfacing. It is also at this point that some assessment should be made as to whether to refer the client to other professionals if the present caregiver is not equipped to handle this next phase. Some problems are fairly common and counselors must be alert to them. Most of these basically require finding a balance point between two extremes of behavior that are equally dangerous. John Wallace, a psychologist who has had long experience working with alcoholics, has neatly described his observations. He compares these extremes to rocks and whirlpools that must be avoided in the recovery "voyage."

Denial. One of the first difficulties is the denial problem. The tendency, when faced with the alcoholic's massive rejection of reality, is to want to force him to face all the facts *right now.* The trouble with this approach is that self-knowledge is often bought at the price of anxiety, and anxiety is a drinking trigger. What to do? Provide lots of support to counteract the initial anxiety caused by the acceptance of the reality of the drinking itself. Then, gradually, keep supporting the small increments in awareness that occur in the sober experience. It is always the temptation of a counselor or family to take denial personally, to think the alcoholic is "lying" to them. Remind yourself that the alcoholic has adopted this defense as protection against the massive pain that would go with facing the "cold, hard facts." Its function is to fool the self, not the others. It is difficult but very necessary to remember that the denial of some particular issue is serving a useful purpose at the time, keeping overwhelming pain and anxiety at bay until more strength is available. The counselor must decide how much of either the client can tolerate. The question facing the counselor is whether the denial is still necessary or whether it has become counterproductive, blocking further progress.

Guilt. Other problems occur over the issues of guilt and its fraternal twin, self-blame. It is clearly desirable to mitigate the degree of both. It is also necessary to avoid the pitfalls of their opposites, rejection of social values and blaming others. Although excessive guilt leads to the guilt/drinking spiral, some degree of conscience and sense of responsibility is necessary to function in society. The helper needs to be clear on this issue. A counselor must be able to point out unnecessary burdensome guilt on the one hand, and yet allow honest guilt its expression. Dealing with both kinds appropriately is essential. On the blame issue, the alcoholic needs help in accepting personal responsibility where necessary. However, it can be helpful to point out that the disease itself, rather than self/others, may be the true cause of some of the difficulties.

Compliance/rebellion. Two other unhealthy extremes are often seen, particularly early in treatment: compliance or rebellion. In either case, strong confrontation is not a good strategy to choose. It seems simply to produce more of either behavior. The compliant client becomes a more "model" client; the rebellious one says: "Aha! I was right. You are all against me," and drinks. Moderation is again the key. The aim is to help clients to acknowledge the alcoholism and accept the facts of their situation.

Feelings. Feelings, and what to do with them, provide another dual obstacle to be faced. The dry alcoholic is likely to repress feelings entirely. He does this to counteract their all too uncontrolled expression during the drinking experiences. Respect for this need to repress the emotions should prevail in the initial stages of recovery. But the eventual goal of the helper is to teach the alcoholic to recognize emotions and to deal with them appropriately. Alcoholics need to learn, or relearn, that feelings need not be repressed altogether or, conversely, wildly acted out. Instead, a recognition and acceptance of them can lead to better solutions. These are by no means the only examples of extremes to which alcoholics fall victim. The therapist needs to be wary when dealing with any extreme behavior or reaction in order to avoid having the client plunge into the opposite danger. It should be noted that some of these problems are continuing ones and may require different tactics at different stages in the recovery process.

Dependency issues. One of the most provocative points Wallace makes concerns dependency issues. Many articles, and indeed whole books, have been written about dependency and alcoholism. Sometimes the alcoholic is depicted as a particularly dependent type who has resolved conflicts inappropriately by the use of alcohol. It is doubtful that this point of view should be taken as a theoretical framework for the development of alcohol treatment programs. However, it must be noted that many alcoholics do tend toward stubborn independence versus indiscriminate dependence in their relationships. They seem to have an evil genius for attracting the very people they don't need— ones who, in fact, are harmful to them. The need for loving relationships, the development of unsatisfactory ones, and the consequent pain and misery are responsible in an unusually large number of instances for relapses. The alcoholic needs, maybe more than most, to realize that people are all interdependent to some degree. The trick is to recognize the dependent need, and to ask, 1. Upon *whom* should I be dependent? 2. For *what*? 3. At what *cost* to me? These questions should be asked in regard to all the relationships, not simply the primary love one. It may well turn out that dependency is being channeled into one relationship instead of spread out more effectively. Once these questions are squarely faced, selectivity and judgment stand a better chance; the extremes, with their threat to sobriety, can be more successfully avoided.

Another issue may well be encountered by single alcoholics, or those caught in unhappy marriages. It is not uncommon for them to find themselves "suddenly" involved in an affair or an extramarital relationship. With a little bit of sobriety, they are very ripe to fall in love. This may have several roots. They may be questioning their sexuality, and the attentions of another may well provide some affirmation of attractiveness. Also possible is that with sobriety comes a sense of being alive again. There is the reawakening of a host of feelings that have long been dormant, including sexual feelings. In this sense, it may be like the bloom and intensity of adolescence. A romantic involvement may follow very naturally. Unfortunately, it can lead to disaster if followed with abandon. The counselor needs to be alert to this general possibility, as well as the possibility of being the object of the crush.

Getting stuck. Speaking of dependency, anyone working with alcohol-troubled people is bound to hear this one some time: "Sending someone to AA just creates another dependency." The implication of this is that you are simply moving the dependency from the bottle to AA, and ducking the real issue. That the dependency shifts from alcohol to AA or a counselor for the newcomer is probably true. We think that is a plus. We also think no one should get stuck there. By "there," we mean in a life-style just as alcohol-centered as before. The only difference is that the center is "not drinking" instead of "how to keep drinking." Granted, physical health is less threatened, traumatic events are less frequent, and maybe even job and family stability have been established. Nonetheless, it is a recovery rut (maybe even a trench!). That some do get stuck is unfortunately true, but that is no reason to condemn the whole process. After all, weaning takes time, and no one implies it is easy or without the possibility of some setbacks. The infant doesn't usually go from the breast to the coffee mug in one easy jump.

Many factors probably account for the "stuckness." One might be an "I never had it so good, so I won't rock the boat" feeling, a real fear of letting go of the life preserver even when safely ashore. Another factor is that some recovering alcoholics, particularly those who began drinking as teenagers, have spent the bulk of their adult lives as active alcoholics. Therefore, they have no baseline of adult healthy behaviors to return to. They are confronted with gaining sobriety, growing up, and functioning as adults simultaneously. This is a tall order that can be an overwhelming prospect. To make it more manageable, it may well be tempting for these recovering alcoholics to keep their world narrowed down to alcoholism recovery. The only thing they now feel really competent to do, the only area where they have had support and a positive sense of self, is in getting sober. Giving up the status of "newcomer" to be replaced by that of "sober responsible adult" may be scary, so a relapse or drinking episode may ensue. They then can justify and ensure that they can keep doing the only thing they feel they do well—being a client, an AA newcomer, a recovering alcoholic.

Another factor could be that some counselors (and some AA members) are better equipped to deal with the crisis period of getting sober than with the later issues of growth and true freedom. Time constraints are too often the cause of the counselor's inability to encourage the letting go–stretching phase. They are quite often overwhelmed with numbers of clients truly in crisis. They simply have no time or energy to put out for the clients who are "getting along okay." Counselors who are not content with their clients' just getting by could aid the process by referring them to extra types of therapy and groups that promote personal exploration and growth. This is a delicate situation; the adjunctive treatments are not to be seen as substituting for whatever has worked so far. Rather, they are an addition to it, whether it is AA, individual counseling, or some other regimen.

The counselor who does have time and does work with clients on a long-term basis should beware of getting stuck in back-patting behavior. The phrase, "Well, I didn't do much today, but at least I stayed sober," is okay once in awhile. When it becomes a client's standard refrain, over a long period of time, it should be questioned as a satisfactory life-style. Those who work around treatment facilities are all too aware of groups of alcoholics who hang around endlessly, drinking coffee, talking to other alcoholics exclusively, and clearly going nowhere. For some who, for instance, may have suffered brain damage or some other disability, this may be the best that can be hoped for. However, we suspect that many are there simply because they are not being helped and encouraged to proceed any further. These are the alcoholics most clearly visible to the health care professionals; thus, they may be one reason for the low expectations professionals have for recovering alcoholics. They don't see the ones who are busy, involved, highly functioning individuals. Our contention is that counselors and caregivers can increase the number of the latter and unstick more and more, if they are sensitive to this issue.

Relapse. Any individual with a chronic disease is subject to relapses. For the alcoholic, relapse means the resumption of drinking. Why? The reasons are numerous. For the relatively newly sober person it probably boils down to a gross underestimation of the seriousness and severity of the disease. Thus, the alcoholic fails to really come to grips with his own impotence to deal with it single-handedly. Hence, while perhaps going through the motions of treatment, there may be a lingering notion that although other alcoholics may need to do this or that, somehow it is not applicable to them. This may show up in very simple ways, such as the failure to change the little things that are likely to make drinking easier than not drinking. "Hell, I've always ridden home in the bar car; after 20 years that's where my friends are"; "What would people say if ————"; "There's a lot going on in my life; getting to the couples group simply isn't possible on a regular basis." If families and close friends are not well informed about alcoholism treatment and are not willing to make adjustments, too, they can unwittingly support and even invite this dangerous behavior.

For the recovering alcoholic with more substantial sobriety, relapse is commonly tied to two things. Relapse may be triggered by the recovery rut already described. On the other hand, if things have been going really well with the recovering alcoholic's life proceeding quite swimmingly, there is the trap of thinking the alcoholism is a closed chapter.

As an aside, probably as a response to this danger, one sometimes hears alcohol counselors, AA members, or those well acquainted with alcoholism stating a preference for the phrase recovering alcoholic, rather than recovered. It serves as a reminder that one is not cured of alcoholism. From a medical standpoint, this is quite accurate. The evidence points strongly to biological–biochemical changes that occur during the course of heavy drinking. Even with long-term abstinence, in this respect there is no return to the "normal" or prealcoholic state. The body's biological memory of alcoholism remains intact, even if the recovered alcoholic has "forgotten." The addiction can be rapidly reinstated. The alcoholic who resumes drinking may very quickly, in days or a week, be drinking quantities equal to amounts prior to abstinence.

It is recommended that management of a relapse, should one occur, be discussed and incorporated into the continuing treatment plan. After all, relapse is not an unheard of occurrence. It is far better to discuss ahead of time how it shall be handled in an open discussion between client, family, and counselor. In the midst of the crisis of relapse neither the family nor client can do their most creative and clear-headed problem solving. Also, having gotten this taboo subject out in the open, it may be easier for all to attend to the work at hand, rather than worry about "what if." Any plan for responding to a relapse should be very concrete; for example, the family will contact the counselor, the client will agree to A, B, C.

Although one can look ahead in the abstract, it is during ongoing counseling that the counselor needs to be alert to possible signals of impending relapse. This can then be dealt with in individual sessions. Of course, part of the real meat of educational efforts is teaching the recovering alcoholic to become aware of danger signals. If a drinking episode occurs it does not have to be the end of the world; but neither should it be taken lightly. Whether it is one drink, or an evening of drinking, or a weekend, or a month, the alcoholic needs to be immediately reinvolved with a treatment center, a counselor, or— if active or previously active in AA—an AA member, or do several of these things. The important thing is not to sit back and do nothing. It is critical that a drinking cycle not be allowed to develop. Active intervention is needed to prevent this. If the alcoholic is still involved with you in treatment at the time of relapse, it is a clear sign that more help is needed. If the alcoholic is currently trying to become sober on an outpatient basis, while continuing to hold down a job and handle all the usual obligations, the drinking episode clearly shows that the approach is not working. A residential inpatient experience that allows and indeed forces the alcoholic to put full attention to alcoholism treatment may well be what is needed.

The alcoholic may instead have "played" at treatment, seen a therapist a few times, and decided things were under control. Fully resolved not to drink again, he then terminated counseling. However, willpower and determination, even with a dash of counseling, did not accomplish what the alcoholic had intended; so the answer is a commitment by the alcoholic to engage in more substantive treatment.

Seasoned alcohol counselors often say that the most dangerous thing for a recovering alcoholic is a "successful drunk." By this they refer to the recovering alcoholic who has a drink, does not mention it to anyone, and suffers no apparent ill effects. It wasn't such a big deal. A couple of evenings later it isn't a big deal either—and so forth. Almost inevitably, if this continues the alcoholic is drinking regularly, drinking more, and on the threshold of being reunited with all the problems and consequences of active alcoholism. The danger, of course, is that the longer the drinking continues, the less able the alcoholic is either to recognize the need for help or to reach out for it. The alcoholic who has had a difficult withdrawal in the past may also be terrified of the prospect of stopping again. It may be wise for you to make it clear that if the client has a drink—or a near encounter—that you both agree it will be discussed.

For the recovering alcoholic who has possibly attained substantial sobriety, reentry into treatment after relapse may be especially difficult. Among a host of other feelings there are embarrassment, remorse, guilt, a sense of letting others down. Recognition that alcoholism is a chronic disease, that it can involve relapses, may ease this. However, refrain from giving the impression that relapses are inevitable. Following a relapse, it is necessary to look closely at what led up to it, what facilitated its occurrence. The alcoholic can gain some valuable information about what is critical to maintaining his or her own sobriety. That is another reason it is so important to deal with a relapse openly. The counselor must also be sensitive to the issues that a relapse may evoke in the family.

For the moment—and we emphasize *the moment*—the family also may be thrown back into functioning just as it did during the old days of active drinking. The old emotions of hurt, anger, self-righteous indignation, to hell with it all, may spring up as strongly as before. This is true even if— especially if—the family scene has vastly changed and improved. All of that progress suddenly evaporates. There also may be the old embarrassment, guilt, and wish to pretend it isn't so.

It is important that you as a counselor maintain contact with your clients for an extended period of time to help reduce the likelihood of relapse. Though your contact may be less frequent, and possibly appointment times less than a full hour, don't allow the follow-up visits to become an empty ritual. Greeting clients with a "Hi, how are you?" and "You're looking great," and then escorting them to the door is not a very therapeutic style. If things are not going well, the client hasn't been given much opportunity to tell you! Be alert to the fact that clients may be reluctant to talk about difficult times. They may feel they should be able to handle it alone, or they may feel they are letting you down. So, in conclusion, don't be casual with follow-up care. It is as important as all the earlier sessions. By taking it seriously, you communicate this to your clients as well.

The reason for the emphasis on considerable treatment over a fairly long period of time throughout this treatment section is simple. The people most successful in treating alcoholism are those who recognize that anywhere from 18 to 36 months are necessary for the alcoholic to be well launched in a healthy lifestyle. It might be said that recovery requires an alcoholic to become "weller than well." To maintain sobriety and avoid developing alternate harmful dependencies, the alcoholic must learn a range of healthy alternative behaviors to deal with tensions arising from living problems. Nonaddicted members of society may quite safely alleviate such tensions with a drink or two. Because living, problems, and tensions go hand in hand, being truly helpful implies helping the alcoholic grow to a higher level of health than might be necessary for the general population.

WOMEN

The alcohol problems of women was a topic not much discussed until very recently. Alcoholism, heavy drinking, and problem drinking were long thought to be the province principally of men. Accordingly, a review of the scientific literature found that between 1928 and 1970 only 28 studies of women alcoholics had been published in the English language! For many years the estimates were that only 1 in every 7 alcoholics was a female; then the ratio cited became 1 in 4. More recently some authorities have claimed almost as many female alcoholics as males. Alcoholism and alcohol problems among women have been areas of fast-growing inquiry. Much has and is being written both in the scientific and popular literature about women and alcohol. Thus, here we wish to touch in very brief and admittedly cursory fashion on only some of the highpoints.

- Apparently more women then men can point to a specific trigger for the onset of heavy drinking. This might be a divorce, an illness, death of a spouse, children leaving home, or some other stressful event. If a woman seeks help at such a point, both a careful alcohol use history and education about the potential risks of alcohol use are warranted. The danger of relying upon alcohol or other drugs is that the crisis can take on a long-term life of its own. The challenge to those dealing with a woman in the face of any of the above difficulties is in providing empathy rather than sympathy. Either overtly or covertly, the danger is often to imply that if that had happened to us, we would probably have responded in the same fashion. The current dangerous misuse of alcohol and drugs can become lost in the forest of other problems.
- It has been suggested that women's alcoholism is often "telescoped"; the disease appears later and progresses more rapidly.

There is also evidence suggesting that women may be more susceptible to liver disease than men.

- Women are prescribed mood-altering drugs much more frequently then men. This suggests the need for a very careful drug use history, with a wary eye for multiple drug use patterns and possible cross-addiction.
- In a marriage in which one spouse is alcoholic, if the alcoholic is the woman there is a significantly greater likelihood of divorce. (A ninefold increase in divorce has been reported if the female is alcoholic as opposed to the male being alcoholic.) Therefore, the family and emotional support systems that are an asset in recovery are less likely to be present.
- Nonetheless, whatever the woman's marital situation, it has been found that women entering treatment do not receive the solid support for that decision that men generally receive from family and friends.
- If the woman alcoholic is unmarried or a divorced single parent, there are not only additional emotional demands but also economic burdens. Remember that in the aftermath of divorce, almost three quarters of women and their children are economically less well off, if not downright poverty stricken. Entry into treatment may stretch an already difficult financial situation.

Treatment issues

Beyond the items touched upon above which can influence the course of the disease process and when and how women are identified and diagnosed as alcoholic and involved in treatment, there are also issues relevant to the treatment process itself.

Mothering and sexuality. Mothering and female sexuality are two aspects of self-esteem unique to women. If the woman alcoholic has children, some of the questions she may well be asking herself are the following: "Am I a good mother?" "Can I be a good mother?" "Have I hurt my children?" "Can I ever cope with my children if I don't drink?" These may not be explicit in the alcohol counseling, but they do cross her mind. They begin to be answered, hopefully positively, as she gains sober time. Family meetings may also be one way she gains answers to these questions. However, in some cases where there has been child abuse or a child is having special difficulties, a referral to a children's agency, a family-service agency, or a mental health clinic may be important in dealing with these situations. One of the things any alcoholic mother will need to learn to regain her self-esteem as a mother is a sense of what the "normal" difficulties are in raising children.

In terms of her sexuality, there may be a number of potential questions. If there has been a divorce or an affair, she may well be wondering about her worth and attractiveness as a woman. Even if the marriage is intact, there may be sexual problems. On one hand, the sexual relationship may have almost disappeared as the drinking progressed. On the other, it may have been years since she has had sexual intercourse without benefit of a glass of wine or a couple of beers to put her "in the mood." Again, sober time may well be the major therapeutic element. But couples' therapy and/or sexual counseling may be needed if marital problems are not resolved. In cases where the sexual problems preceded the active drinking, professional help is certainly recommended. Sobering up is not likely to take away the existing problem in some miraculous fashion. To let it fester is to invite even more problems.

What about single women, or women caught in an unsatisfactory marriage? It is not uncommon for them to find themselves "suddenly" involved in an affair or an extramarital relationship. With a little bit of sobriety, they are very ripe to fall in love. This may have several roots. The woman may be questioning her femininity, and the attentions of a man may well provide some affirmation of her status as a woman. Also possible is that with sobriety comes a sense of being alive again. There is the reawakening of a host of feelings that have long been dormant, including sexual feelings. In this sense, it may be like the bloom and intensity of adolescence. A romantic involvement may follow very naturally. Unfortunately, it can lead to disaster, if followed with abandon. It should be noted that this can be equally true for men!

We would caution male counselors working with women that if you are the first person in many years to accept her, and if you have been making attempts to raise her self-esteem, she may mistake her gratitude for a personal emotional involvement with you. Your recognition of this "error" is imperative. If you provide contacts for her with other recovering women alcoholics, she may be better able to recognize this pitfall as well.

Another area of great concern when treating women is children. If an alcoholic woman has young children, long-term residential treatment may be very difficult to arrange. Many have no husbands in the home, and extended family members do not live down the street as was once the case. However, for that very reason, it may be all the more important. Models of treatment to overcome this problem are being tried in many areas throughout the country. But in most places the usual facilities are still the only ones available. You will need to stretch your creativity to the limit to deal with this problem. Potentially, friends, extended family—even if they are called in from a distance—or a live-in sitter can be used. There may be no way to allow her the optimum advantage of a 2- to 3-week stay in residential treatment. If this is the case, daily outpatient visits, intensive AA contact, or day treatment are possible options. Even if inpatient care can be arranged, you will be faced with her intense guilt over her children and her resistance to leaving them. There are no easy formulas, and the counselor is left to work out the best solution possible in each individual case.

Women and AA. The latest figures from the General Services Board of AA indicate that over one third of the new members coming into AA are women. It appears that whatever the differences between male and female alcoholics, AA manages to achieve the same rate of success with both. It is just as important to make a referral to AA for your female clients as for male clients. A few trips to local meetings should assure her that it is no longer the male stronghold it once was. In many communities one will also find AA groups that are predominantly women.

Being aware that alcoholism, alcohol problems, and treatment issues are not identical for men and women is important. An increasing body of literature on women alcoholics warrants your attention.

THE EMPLOYED

The majority of alcoholics are members of the work force. Probably a conservative estimate is that 8% of the nation's work force is adversely affected by the use of alcohol. Business and industry have begun to recognize the costs to them of employees with alcohol problems. As a result, there has been a rapid development of special programs by employers to identify problems and initiate alcohol treatment. These programs are generally termed either *employee assistance programs* or *occupational alcohol programs.*

Portrait of a man who stops in a bar for 3 drinks on his way home from work every night.

Drinking has long been interwoven into work. To offer just a few examples of its intrusion, consider the office party, the company picnic, and the wine and cheese reception....The martini lunches, the "drink date" to "review business," and the bar car on the commuter train....The old standby gift for a business associate? A fifth of good liquor. . . A round of drinks to celebrate the closing of a business deal.. . The construction crew stopping off for beers after work. But the meshing of drinking and business has come under fire. First, the IRS decreed the martini lunch was not a legitimate business expense. Then the growing interest in physical fitness took its toll. Concern about liability when alcohol is a part of company-sponsored parties has come into play. While receiving more attention recently, court cases addressing this go back to the mid-'70s.

Possibly most telling about the new attitudes is the very recent and growing discussion about the use of mandatory drug testing as a condition for initial hiring and continuing employment. This discussion has centered less on alcohol than other drugs; however, alcohol no longer enjoys a status of being "okay," whereas all other drugs are seen as "bad." To our minds this is evidence of the growing recognition by businesses that substance use can and does interfere with performance and productivity, and is therefore a legitimate concern.

Nonetheless for too long, drinking in many work situations was not only accepted but expected. Whenever the use of alcohol is tolerated, the potential for alcohol problems among susceptible individuals rises, and more so if drinking is subtly encouraged.

Occupational high-risk factors

The printout said if we couldn't bring it to the office party we should pour a fifth of vodka in its ink supply.

Although a job cannot be said to cause alcoholism, it can contribute to its development. Some of the factors that Trice and Roman, authorities in the area of occupational alcohol issues, have identified as job-based risk factors include:

- Absence of clear goals (and absence of supervision)
- Freedom to set work hours (isolation and low visibility)
- Low structural visibility (e.g., salespeople away from the businessplace)
- Work addiction
- Occupational obsolescence (especially common in scientific and technical fields)
- New work status
- Required on-the-job drinking (e.g., salespeople drinking with clients)
- Reduction of social controls (occurs on college campuses and other less structured settings)
- Severe role stress
- Competitive pressure
- Presence of illegal drug users (less an issue for alcohol abusers)

The workplace cover-up

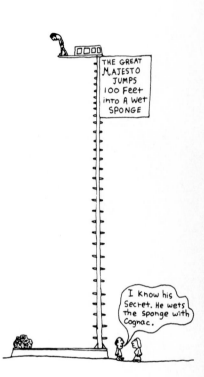

THE GREAT MAJESTO JUMPS 100 Feet into A Wet SPONGE

I know his Secret. He wets the sponge with Cognac.

If bringing up the drinking practices and potential problems of a family member or close friend makes someone squirm with discomfort, the idea of saying something to a coworker is virtually unthinkable. Almost everyone accepts a separation between work and home or professional and private life. So until the alcohol problem flows into the work world, the worker's use of alcohol is considered no one else's business. That does not mean that no one sees a problem developing. Our suspicion is that someone with even a little savvy can often spot potentially dangerous drinking practices. The office scuttlebutt or work crew's bull sessions plus simple observation make it common knowledge who "really put it away this weekend," or the "poor devil who just got picked up DWI," or "you can always count on Sue to join in whenever anyone wants to stop for a drink after work."

Even if an employee does show some problems on the job, whether directly or indirectly related to alcohol use, coworkers may try to "help out"—by doing extra work, or not blowing the whistle. Because employee assistance programs, if they are present, are based on identifying work deterioration, any attempt by coworkers to help cover up job problems makes spotting the alcohol problem all the more difficult. If a company does not have a program to help alcoholics, odds for a cover-up by coworkers are even greater. Another important party in this concealment strategy is predictably the spouse, who usually doesn't want to do anything to threaten the paycheck.

There are two things that will be believed of any man whosoever, and one of them is that he has taken to drink.

BOOTH TARKINGTON

In the past when the cover-ups no longer could hide a problem, the alcoholic usually got fired; this may still happen in many companies. In such instances, the company loses a formerly valuable and well-trained worker, statistically a costly "solution." The current thinking is that it is cheaper for a company to identify problems earlier and to use the job as leverage to get the employee into treatment and back to work.

Employee assistance programs

Facts and experience suggest that the occupational environment may be one of the most efficient and economical means of providing an opportunity for early identification and treatment of alcoholism and alcohol-related problems.

Chances for recovery are increased by reaching the alcoholic at an earlier stage for the following reasons:
- Physical health has not deteriorated significantly
- Financial resources are not as depleted
- Emotional supports still exist in the family and community
- Threat of job loss is present as a motivator

Employee assistance programs are organized in a variety of ways, from an in-house counselor to contracts with outside groups for these services. Programs may also be structured as "broad brush," that is, dealing with any of the many problems that may affect employee's performance, or be more narrowly restricted to alcohol and drugs only.

Whatever the program structure, the following are among the common signs and symptoms used to identify the problem drinker or substance abuser:
- Chronic absenteeism
- Change in behavior
- Physical signs
- Spasmodic work pace
- Lower quantity and quality of work
- Partial absences
- Lying
- Avoiding supervisors and coworkers
- On-the-job drinking
- On-the-job accidents and lost time from off-the-job accidents

Training supervisors and others to recognize these signs is important so that early detection can occur. Training is also critical to helping employers to document and not diagnose. Where there have been broad educational efforts through information sessions, posters, pamphlets, and so forth, there has been an increase in peer or self-referrals. Such referrals may often comprise the bulk of referrals to a program. For whatever reasons, supervisor referrals are still rare.

An important technique in dealing with the alcoholic employee is called either *intervention, constructive coercion, or confrontation.* The technique, based on the Johnson intervention model, is used in the work setting to motivate the individual to seek help to improve job performance and retain the job. In the context of a formal program, the procedure is to identify, document, and then confront the employee with the facts and an informal offer of referral for help. Confrontation occurs within the company's normal evaluation and disciplinary procedures. A supervisor, manager, or union steward who notes certain behaviors and signs of deteriorating job performance documents them. If the "confrontation" is unsuccessful, the next phase would be a stepped-up disciplinary procedure, including a time limit and a formal referral with the "threat" of job loss if performance is not improved.

Implications for alcohol treatment

It is important for alcohol counselors to be knowledgeable about occupational programs. Counselors can thereby better coordinate treatment efforts for the employed alcoholic or problem drinker. Does the client's employer have a program? If so, who is the counselor, what services are offered? For any client it is important to know if there have been any work-related problems. If so, what is the current job status? Has a disciplinary procedure been instituted, or has the employee been informally warned and referred for treatment? In addition, to avoid future conflict, learn about any union involvement. Such information can help in formulating realistic treatment plans.

It is important for the counselor to be sensitive to the policies and politics of the employed alcoholic's work setting. Without this knowledge and awareness, there is the danger of violating the client's confidentiality or, conversely, of not taking full advantage of the opportunity to cooperate with the employer on the client's behalf. If there is a company policy, learn about it in order to plan realistically and avoid treatment/work conflicts. The type of medication, if any, will also be affected by the nature of the client's work. A follow-up plan must consider the working person's hours and geographical location. The flexibility and accessibility of the treatment facility can be a key factor in the successful rehabilitation of the employed alcoholic. Evening office hours

Portrait of a man who thinks he's clever when he's drunk

It would take 14,931,430 six-packs of 12 oz. cans to float a battleship.

NATHAN COBB
Boston Globe

and early-morning and weekend appointments may have to be arranged by the counselor, so that treatment will not interfere with the individual's job.

You may also find that some clients will have to receive outpatient care even when inpatient services are more appropriate. The employee may not be able to take the time off or may not have adequate insurance coverage. In fact, insurance companies who have been covering inpatient alcholism treatment are now attempting to change their policies to cover outpatient care exclusively, or at least preferentially. They cite the fact that it is less expensive and that little or no evidence indicates that inpatient care provides better treatment outcomes. As we hope this text has made clear, all alcoholics are not alike, and blanket assumptions regarding their treatment should not be made.

Occupational programs have made significant progress in demonstrating that the "human approach" is good business. Yet there is still a great deal to be done, and it can be better accomplished with cooperation among those involved in the occupational program field and alcohol clinicians.

RESOURCES AND FURTHER READING

Blume, S.: Women and Alcohol: A Review. *JAMA*, Sept. 19, 1986. Vol. 256, No. 11.

Brown, S.: *Treating the Alcoholic: A developmental model of recovery.* New York: Wiley Interscience Publication, 1985.

Clark, W.D.: Alcoholism: Blocks to diagnosis and treatment. *Am J Med* (71):275, 1981.

Clark, W.D.: The medical interview: Focus on alcohol problems. *Hosp Pract* 20(11):59–68, 1985.

Corrigan, E.M.: Alcoholic women in treatment. New York: Oxford Press, 1980.

Ewing, J.A.: Detecting alcoholism, the CAGE questionnaire. *JAMA* 252(14):1905–1907, 1984.

Gitlow, S., and Peyser, H. (Eds.): *Alcoholism: A Practical Treatment Guide.* New York: Grune & Stratton, 1980.

Kinney, J., and Peltier, D.: A model alcohol program for the college health service. *J Am Coll Health*, Vol. 34. April, 1986.

Selzer, M.L.: The Michigan Alcoholism Screening Test: the quest for a new diagnostic instrument. *Am J Psychiatry* 127(12):1653–1658, 1971.

Skinner, H.A., et al.: Identification of alcohol abuse using laboratory tests and a history of trauma. *Annals Intern Med* 101(6):847–851, 1984.

Wallace, J.: Between Scylla and Charybdis: issues in alcoholism therapy. *Alcohol Health and Res. World.* 4(1):15–22, 1977.

Wilsnack, S., and Beckman, L.J.: Alcohol problems in women: antecedents, consequences, and intervention. New York: Guilford Press, 1984.

Treatment techniques and approaches

9

INDIVIDUAL COUNSELING

Earlier we defined treatment as all the interventions intended to short-circuit the alcoholism process and to introduce the alcoholic to effective sobriety. This could be put in equation form as follows: Treatment = individual counseling +family therapy +family education +client education +group therapy +medical care +AA +Al-Anon +Antabuse +vocational counseling +activities therapy +spiritual counseling +....As you can see, individual counseling is only a small part of the many things that comprise treatment. So what is it? A very simple way to think of individual counseling is simply the time and place and space in which the rest of the treatment is organized and planned. One-to-one counseling is a series of interviews. During the interviews the counselor and client work together to define problems, explore possible solutions, and identify resources, with the counselor providing support, encouragement, and feedback to the client as he takes action. Before proceeding to a discussion of how the counselor does this, we would like to digress for a moment.

One of the difficulties in thinking about, discussing, or writing about counseling is knowing where to begin. It all seems more than a little overwhelming. One of the problems is that most of us have never seen a real counselor at work. We have all seen police officers, telephone lineworkers, carpenters, or teachers busily at work. So we have some sense of what is involved and can imagine what it would be like. The counselor's job is different. It is private and not readily observable. Unfortunately, most of our ideas about counselors come from books or television. Now it doesn't take too much television viewing to get some notion that a good counselor is almost a magician, relying on uncanny instincts to divine the darkest, deepest recesses of the client's mind. You can't help thinking the counselor must have a T-shirt with a big letter **S** underneath the button-down collar. Television does an excellent job of teaching us that things are not always as they seem. Yet, remember, in real life they often—indeed usually—are. Everyone is quite adept at figuring out what is going on.

"It's SUPERCOUNSELOR! He's STRONGER THAN A DOUBLE MARTINI."

Observation

Each day we process vast amounts of information without much thought. Our behavior is almost automatic. Without benefit of a clock, we can make a reasonable estimate of the time. When shopping, we can without too much trouble distinguish the clerk from fellow customers. Sometimes, though, we cannot find a person who seems to be a clerk. Take a couple of minutes to think about the clues you do use in separating the clerk from the customers. One of the clues might be dress. Clerks may wear a special outfit, such as smock, apron, or shirt with the store's logo. In colder weather, customers off the street will be wearing or carrying their coats. Another clue is behavior. The clerks stand behind counters and cash registers, the customers in front. Customers stroll about casually looking at merchandise, whereas clerks systematically arrange displays. Another clue might be the person's companions. Clerks are usually alone, not hauling children or browsing with a friend. Although we have all had some experience of guessing incorrectly, it happens rarely. In essence, this is *the good guys wear white hats* principle. A person's appearance provides us with useful, reliable information about that person. Before a word of conversation is spoken, our observations provide us with some basic data to guide our interactions.

We hope that you are convinced everyone indeed has keen observational powers. Usually people simply do not reflect on these skills. The only difference between a counselor and others is that a counselor will cultivate these observational capacities, will listen carefully, and will attend to *how* something is said and not merely the content. The counselor will ask: "What is the client's mood?" "Is the mood appropriate to what is being said?" "What kinds of shifts take place during the interview?" "What nonverbal clues, or signs, does the client give to portray how she feels?"

So, in a counseling session, from time to time, momentarily tune out the words and take a good look. What do you *see*? Reverse that. Turn off the picture and focus on the sound. One important thing : the questions you ask yourself (or the client) are not *why* questions. They are *what* and *how* questions that attempt to determine what is going on. Strangely enough, in alcohol counseling, successful treatment can occur without *ever* tackling a why question. Ignoring what or how issues, however, may mean you'll never even get into the right ball park.

So what is the importance of observation? It provides data for making hypotheses. A question continually before the counselor is: "What's going on with this person?" What you see provides clues. You do not pretend to be a mind reader. Despite occasional

An alcohol counselor's first task is to observe the client.

lapses, you do not equate observations, or hunches, with ultimate truth. Your observations, coupled with your knowledge of alcohol, suggest where you might focus attention. An example: a client whose coloring is awful, who has a distended abdomen and a number of bruises, will alert the counselor to the strong possibility of serious medical problems. The client may try to explain this all away by "just having tripped over the phone cord," but the counselor will urge the client to see a physician.

You do your work by observing, by listening, and by asking the client (and yourself) questions to gain a picture of the client's situation. The image of a picture being sketched and painted is quite apt to capture the counseling process. The space below is the canvas. The total area includes everything that is going on in the client's life.

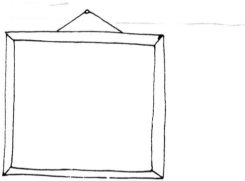

As the client speaks with the counselor, this space is filled in. Now the counselor is getting a picture of the client's situation. Not only do you have the "facts" as the client sees them; you can also see the client, his mood and feelings, and get a sense of what the world and picture *feel* like as well. As this happens, the space gets filled in and begins to look like this:

You have a notion of the various areas that make up the person's life: family, physical health, work, economic situation, community life, how the person feels about himself, and so on.

You are also aware of how alcohol may affect these areas. As you find it necessary, you will guide the conversation to insure that you have a total picture of the client's life. You are also aware that if the client is experiencing difficulty, having a problem, it means that the pieces are not fitting together in a way that feels comfortable. Maybe some parts have very rough edges. Maybe one part is exerting undue influence on the others. So you also attempt to see the relationship and interaction between the parts.

Confrontation

Confrontation is a technique used by the counselor to help the client make the essential connections. Confrontation does *not* equal attack. According to *Webster's*, to confront means "to cause to meet: bring face to face." Several examples of what the counselor may do to bring the client face to face with the consequences of his behavior are having a family meeting, so that the family's concerns can be presented; making a referral to a physician for treatment and consultation on the "stomach problems"; or referring the client to an alcohol discussion group. The counselor endeavors to structure situations in which the client is brought face to face with facts.

Feedback

In assisting the alcoholic to "see" what is going on, the counselor's observation skills pay off. The alcoholic has a notoriously warped perception of reality. The ability of the counselor to "merely" provide accurate feedback to the client, giving specific descriptions of behavior, of what the client is doing, is very valuable. The alcoholic has lost the ability for self-assessment. It is quite likely that any feedback from family members has also been warped and laced with threats, so that it is useless to the alcoholic. In the counseling situation, it may go like this: "Well, you say things are going fine. Yet, as I look at you, I see you fidgeting in your chair, your voice is quivering, and your eyes are cast down toward the floor. For me, that doesn't go along with someone who's feeling fine." *Period.* The counselor simply reports the observations. There is no deep interpretation. There is no attempt to ferret out hidden unconscious dynamics. The client is not labeled a liar. Your willingness and ability to simply describe what you see is a potent therapeutic weapon. The alcoholic can begin to learn how he does come across, how others see him. Thus, your use of observation serves to educate the client about himself.

Education

In addition to self-awareness, the client also needs education about alcohol, the drug, and the disease of alcoholism. Provide facts and data. A host of pamphlets are available from state alcohol agencies, insurance companies, and AA. Everyone likes to understand what is going on with them. This is becoming increasingly apparent in all areas of medicine. Some institutions have hired client educators. Client education sessions on diabetes, heart disease, cancer, and care of newborns are becoming commonplace. The importance of education has two thrusts in alcoholism. The first is to help instill new attitudes toward alcoholism: that it is a disease, has recognizable signs, and is treatable. The hope is to elicit the alcoholic's support in helping to manage and treat his problem. The other reason for educating alcoholics is to handle feelings of guilt and low self-esteem. The chances are pretty good that the alcoholic's behavior has been downright crazy, and not just to others. It has also been inexplicable to the alcoholic. The fact that he has been denying a problem confirms this. There is no need to deny something unless it is so painful, so out of step with values, that it cannot be tolerated. Learning facts about alcohol and alcoholism can be a big relief to the alcoholic. Suddenly, things make sense. All the crazy behavior becomes normal, at least for an active alcoholic. That makes a significant difference. Successful recovery appears to be related to a client's acceptance of the disease concept. Energy can be applied to figuring out how one can live around the disease, live successfully, now. The client is relieved of the need to hash around back there, in the past, to uncover causes, to figure out what went wrong. He need not dwell on his craziness; it becomes merely a symptom, one that he isn't doomed to reexperience if he works on maintaining sobriety.

Self-disclosure

At this juncture it seems appropriate to add some cautionary word about the technique of self-disclosure. And make no mistake about it, we consider this to be a *counseling technique*. As such, it requires the same thoughtful evaluation of its usefulness as any other counseling tool. It is important to recognize that "self-disclosure" is not limited to sharing information of one's own alcoholism. Self-disclosure in counseling or therapy refers to sharing not only the facts of one's life, but one's feelings and values as well. The point of contrast would be the style of the early psychoanalyst who never revealed information about himself, nor in any way presented himself as an individual to his clients. Counselors are self-disclosing when they express empathy, or when they note that the client's concerns are those with which other clients of the counselor have also struggled. But the phrase does have special meaning in alcohol counseling. The counselor may also be a recovering alcoholic in private life. As one, he or she may have participated nonprofessionally in interventions or AA Twelfth Step calls when self-disclosure was called for and effective and also clear cut. In a professional individual counseling or group therapy session when, or indeed, *if*, to use self-disclosure may not be so clear-cut.

Particularly at the early stages of the client's treatment, or in the assessment process, it may seem only natural to allay some of the client's nervousness or resistance with the news that you, as a counselor, have been there and know just how they feel and furthermore can testify to the possibility of a happy recovery. What seems natural may, however, be totally inappropriate or even countertherapeutic. Counselors need to remember that their professionalism is important to the client, particularly in the early days of treatment. That professionalism is comforting! The patient in an intensive cardiac care unit is interested in his physician's medical assessment of his condition, the physician's treatment recommendations, and the probable outcome. He is in no condition to appreciate the physician's personal story of his own heart attack.

This is not to imply that self-disclosure shouldn't ever be used, or that it is ineffective. In the example of the physician above, if the patient were so frightened he couldn't hear the physician's medical assessment or, at some point, in despair and seemingly abandoning hope, the physician *might* decide to reassure the patient by the example of his own recovery and obvious present robust good health. But we see the technique too often used as a matter of course without proper thought given to the possible ramifications of it in a particular instance. Because we do, indeed, see it as a sometimes very powerful aid in certain cases, we recommend that great care be taken to see that it is used at the best possible time for the best possible reason—the benefit of the client. It should never be used to make the counselor feel more comfortable by getting "everything out in the open."

Client responsibility

The counselor expects the client to assume responsibility for his actions. You do not buy into the client's view of himself as either a pawn of fate or a helpless victim. An ironic twist is present. You make it clear that you see the client as an adult who is accountable for his choices. Simultaneously, you are aware that an alcoholic, when consuming alcohol, is abdicating control of his life to a drug. By definition, an alcoholic cannot be responsible for what transpires after even one or two drinks. Therefore, being responsible ultimately means that the attempt to manage alcohol must be abandoned. Here again, facts about the drug, alcohol, and the disease, alcoholism, are important. A large chunk of the client's work will be to examine the facts of his own life in light of this information. People's ability to alibi, to rationalize, and to otherwise explain away the obvious varies. But the counselor consistently holds up the mirror of reality. You play back to the client the client's story. You share your observations. In this way the client is enabled to move toward the first step of recovery: admitting the inability to control alcohol.

A word of caution

One word of caution to the newcomers to the field: alcoholics are sometimes described as notorious "con artists." They've had to be. Anyone who has managed to continue drinking alcoholically in spite of the consequences has learned many sneaky little tricks. These do not disappear with the first prod, push, or pull toward treatment. Habits die hard. The habit of protecting the right to drink (even to death) is a longstanding one for most alcoholics. When he finds that you are probably not going to hand out a simple "three-step way to drink socially," all the considerable cunning at his command will rise up in defense.

"Gee, you've really helped me to see exactly what I have to do. I'll ————, ————, and ————, and everything will be just fine. Thanks so much. You've made my life for me.

"Well, you know, both my parents were alcoholics. I even had a grandfather who was. But you know, I really don't drink like that at all! It really only started when Johnny had that awful operation, and I spent hours at the hospital, and then my husband was called away to South America, and I needed *something* to just boost me over those awful times. But my husband's due home next week, and I'm just sure now that I know all the facts you've given me, that I'll just stop by myself, and everything will be just fine! Thank you so much. You've changed my life.

"I can't imagine why my wife says what she does about my drinking. She must really be down on me, or jealous, or something....After all, I only have a couple of beers with the guys after work....

"Speaking of ————, did you hear about that new research they've been doing? You know, the stuff that talks about having a

I've heard him renounce wine a hundred times a day, but then it has been between as many glasses.

DOUGLAS JERROLD

dog helps. I bet if I just get a dog and take something for my nerves (after all, my nerves are the *real* problem), I'll be just fine! Etc., etc., etc.

Most alcoholics are far more inventive than these examples show. Add tears, or a charming smile, or bruises from a beating, and you've been exposed to quite a smoke screen. If they're not at the moment falling down, slobbering, throwing up, or slurring their words, it is hard not to believe them. There they sit—full of confidence, hopeful, and very friendly. Experience has shown that at some point, you will either see, hear from, or hear about these people, and their situations will have gone downhill. They don't know how familiar their stories are—to them, they are unique. They are not lying. They are simply trying to hang on to the only help they feel they have— the bottle. Also, always keep in mind that the purpose of the "con" is not to deceive you. The alcoholic is trying above all to maintain his or her own self-deception. You may be able to help them loosen their grip by not allowing these pat replies to go unchallenged, by giving them something else to grasp.

Problem identification and problem solving

In counseling, problem identification and problem solving constitute a recurring process. No matter what the problem, two kinds of forces are always in action: some factors help maintain the problem; other factors are pushing toward change. These can be sketched out in a diagram, as shown below. Suppose the problem being presented is: "I don't like my job." The line going across represents the current situation. The arrows pointing upward stand for the factors that ease or lighten the problem. The arrows pointing downward represent the factors aggravating the problem.

If the goal of the client is to be more content at work, this might happen in several ways. The positive forces can be strengthened or others added; or attempts can be made to diminish the negative ones. A similar sketch might be made for alcoholic drinking. This kind of chart can help the counselor decide what factors might be tackled to disturb the present equilibrium.

Left to his own devices, the alcoholic would piddle along for years. The fact that he is sitting in front of you indicates that something has happened to jiggle the equilibrium. This can be a force for change. Take advantage of it. Jiggle the equilibrium further. In the example just given, to take away the family denial or coworker cover-up would blow his whole act. It is becoming widely acknowledged that for the counselor to precipitate such a crisis is the most helpful thing to do.

The counselor–client relationship

Whole volumes have been written on the nature and components of the therapeutic relationship. This book cannot even begin to summarize what has been set forth. Some of the attributes of the helping relationship were alluded to at the begin-

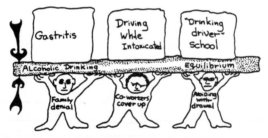

ning of the previous chapter on treatment. The counselor is a guide. The counselor cannot do the work, but only attempt to bring the client's attention to the work that needs to be done. The counselor may provide some "how to" suggestions but will proportionally provide more support as the client goes to it.

Although an exposition of the therapeutic relationship is beyond this book, several items are common points of confusion for newcomers. First, whatever the peculiar thing is that is the client–counselor relationship, it is not a friendship. It is not based on liking one another. The value of the counselor to the client is paradoxically that he is not a friend, the counselor is not exacting or needing anything from the client. Indeed, if that sneaks into the equation, then the potential value of the counselor has accordingly been diminished. Beyond a knowledge of alcohol and its effects, what the counselor offers the client is someone who can be trusted to be candid, open, and who strives for objectivity. She or he is one who can be counted upon to say what needs to be said and trusted to hear the difficult things a client must say without scolding or thinking any the less of the person. Although it may initially sound demeaning, in point of fact the counselor is most effective with clients when the relationship is "just part of the job."

With the client–counselor relationship outside the realm of friendship, several potentially difficult situations for the counselor are more easily avoided. A predictable difficult situation is what to do when the client becomes angry, or threatens to drop out of counseling, or claims you are taking someone else's side, or that you don't care or understand. It's very tempting and ever so easy to experience such situations as personally (and undeservedly) directed toward you. So first, take a deep breath. Secondly, remind yourself it isn't you who's being attacked. This is not an occasion for either reminding the client of "everything you've done for him," or just how experienced you are, even if he doesn't appreciate it. As quietly and calmly as possible, discuss what's going on, which includes acknowledging the feelings the client is experiencing. Resist trying to make him feel "better" or talk him out of those feelings. Expression of negative emotion is something to be anticipated. Indeed, if it never occurs, it may mean that the counselor is sending signals that it is not permitted. Allowing negative feelings to be expressed doesn't mean being a sponge for everything, or not setting limits, or not stating a different perspective if you have one. One of the most important lessons the client may need to learn during treatment is that negative emotions can be expressed and the world doesn't fall apart. Nor will others immediately try to placate or run away.

The other side of the "emotions coin" can present a different trap. It is difficult not to respond to: "You are so wonderful," "You are the only person who really understands," or that "you are the only person I can say this to." Beyond the danger of inflating the counselor's ego, there is the danger for the client that all the power is invested in the counselor. In the process of treatment, it is important that the client experience, and take credit for, the work that he has done. So, for example, in responding to "You are the only person who really understands," a gentle reminder of his share of the work is appropriate. You might ask if there are others he'd like to share with and help him decide how best to do that.

Administrative tasks

Now to sound a very different note. An inevitable and necessary part of a counselor's work is adminstrative. Writing notes in the chart....Contacting agencies or counselors for previous re-

cords....Dictating discharge summaries....Contacting the referring party or others to whom a client will be referred....This is often perceived as a pain in the neck and the portion of one's job most likely to get short shrift. However, attending to these details is an important part of good clinical care. Alcohol treatment is almost never a solo act, but instead involves the efforts of a team. How effectively the team functions often depends on the counselor who orchestrates and coordinates the various efforts.

The client's chart or medical record is one very important vehicle for communicating information. This is especially true in a residential facility, with multiple staff working different shifts. There are often questions as to what should and shouldn't go in a chart. To handle things that should be noted but are particularly sensitive, some agencies have adopted a set of confidential files, separate from the main record. Although not wishing to dismiss lightly the concern for confidentiality, nevertheless, it can be a red herring. In thinking about what to include in the chart, ask yourself "What do others need to know to respond therapeutically?" Rarely does this have anything to do with "deep dark secrets." More often it has to do with the everyday nuts and bolts—worrying over a date for discharge, preoccupation with an upcoming court appearance, a strained family meeting. The chart is not the place for putting forth verbatim accounts of individual sessions. But notation of any general themes, plus any modification of treatment plans is needed.

In addition to charting, it will also fall to the counselor to present cases at team planning meetings. On such occasions, a little preliminary thought helps: Are there special questions you have that you'd like to discuss with others? Along with these formal routes of communication, there are also informal channels. Take the opportunity to brief others.

Beyond orchestrating the activities of the treatment team, it falls to the counselor to be a liaison, and sometimes an advocate, with external groups such as employers, welfare workers, the courts. In these situations you must have the client's permission before acting. Also, it is important not to do for the client what he can do for himself. Generally, it is more therapeutic to do a lot of handholding as the client takes care of business, rather than, in the interest of efficiency, doing it yourself.

GROUP WORK

Group therapy has become an increasingly popular form of treatment for a range of problems, including alcohol abuse. (Of course, with AA dating back to 1935, alcoholics have been recovering in groups, long before group therapy became popular or alcohol treatment was even known.) Why the popularity of group treatment methods? The first response often is: "It's cheaper," or "It's more efficient; more people can be seen." These statements may be true, but a more fundamental reason exists. Group therapy works. It works very well with alcoholics. Some of the reasons for this can be found in the characteristics of alcoholism, plus normal human nature.

For better or worse, people find themselves part of a group. And whatever being a human being means, it does involve other people. We think in terms of our family, our neighborhood, our school, our club, our town, our church. On the job, at home, on the playground, wherever, it is in group experiences where we feel left out or, conversely, find a sense of belonging. Through our contacts with others, we feel okay or not okay. As we interact, we find ourselves sharing our successes or hiding our supposed failures. Through groups we get strokes on the head or a kick in the pants. There is no avoiding the reality that other people play a big part in our lives. Just as politicians take opinion polls to see how they're doing with the populace, so do each of us run our surveys. The kinds of questions we ask ourselves about our relationships are: "Do I belong?," "Do I matter to others?," "Can I trust them?," "Am I liked?," "Do I like them?" To be at ease and comfortable in the world, the answers have to come up more ayes than nays. The practicing alcoholic doesn't fare so well when taking this poll. For the myriad reasons discussed before, relationships with other people are poor. Isolated and isolating, rejecting and rejected, helpless and refusing aid—with such a warped view of the world, alcoholics are oblivious to the fact that the drinking has been causing the trouble. When one is wed to the bottle, other bonds cannot be formed. Attempts to make it in the world sober will require reestablishing real human contacts. Thus groups, the setting in which life must be lived, become an ideal setting for treatment.

Of course I have friends — Jack Daniels, Chivas Regal, Kahlua

Group as therapy

Being a part of a group can do some powerful therapeutic things. The active alcoholic is afraid of people "out there." The phrase "tiger land" has been used by alcoholics to describe the world. That's a fairly telling phrase! Through group treatment, the alcoholic will ideally *reexperience* the world differently. The whole thing need not be a jungle—other people can be a source of safety and strength. Another big bonus from a group experience is derived from the alcoholics' opportunities to become *reac-*

quainted with themselves. A group provides a chance to learn who they are, their capabilities, their impact on and importance to others. Interacting honestly and openly provides opportunity to adjust and correct their mental pictures of themselves. They get feedback. Group treatment of those in a similar situation reduces the sense of isolation. Acoholics tend to view themselves very negatively and have an overwhelming sense of shame for their behavior. Coming together with others proves that one is not uniquely awful. Yet, mere confession is not therapeutic. Something else must happen for healing to occur. Just as absolution occurs in the context of a church, in a group that functions therapeutically, the members act as priests to one another. Members hear one another's confession and say, in essence: "You are forgiven, go and sin no more." (A short lesson in linguistics: the word *sin* is derived from the Greek word meaning "to miss the target." It is what the person standing by the target called back to the archer, so that the archer could readjust his aim. It does not imply evil, or bad, as is so often assumed.) That is to say, group members can see one another apart from the alcoholic behavior. They can also often see a potential that is unknown to the individual. This is readily verified in our own lives. Solutions to other people's problems are so obvious, but not so solutions to our own. Members of the group can see that people need not be destined to continue their old behaviors. Old "sins" need not be repeated. Thus, they instill hope in one another. Interestingly enough, one often finds that people are more gentle with others than with themselves. In this regard, the group experience has a beneficial boomerang effect. In the process of being kind and understanding of others, the members are in turn forced to accord themselves similar treatment.

What has been discussed is the potential benefit that can be gleaned from a group exposure. How this group experience takes place can vary widely. Group therapy comes in many styles and can occur in many contexts. Being a resident in a halfway house puts the alcoholic in a group, just like the person who participates in outpatient group therapy. Group therapy means the use of any group experience to promote change in the members. Under the direction of a skilled leader, the power of the group processes is harnessed for therapeutic purposes.

Group work with alcoholics

In contemplating group work with alcoholics, the leader will need to consider several basic issues. What is the purpose of the group? What are the goals for the individual members? Where

will the group meet? How often? What will the rules be? The
first question is the key. The purpose of the group should be clear
in the leader's mind. There are many possible legitimate purposes. Experience shows that not all can be met simultaneously.
It is far better to have different types of groups available, with
members participating in several, than to lump everything into
one group and accomplish nothing.

Some of the major group focuses include education, self-
awareness of alcohol use, support for treatment, problem solving, and activity/resocialization.

Educational groups attempt to impart factual information
about alcohol, its effects, and alcoholism. There is a complex relationship between knowledge, feelings, and behavior. Correct
facts and information do not stop alcoholic drinking, but they
can be important in breaking down denial, which protects the alcoholic drinking. Besides battering denial, educational efforts assist the already motivated person. Information provides an invaluable framework for understanding what has happened and
what treatment is about. Alcoholics acquire some cognitive tools
to better participate in their own treatment. Educational groups
generally include a lecture, film, or presentation by a specialist
in the alcohol field, followed by a group discussion.

Another kind of educational activity developed by Leona M.
Kent in California, is the AA Training Group. In a series of ten sessions, the clients are introduced to the structure, philosophy, and
jargon of AA. The intent is to help the referral process to AA of persons in treatment programs. Many of these clients are resistive, or
confused, and apprehensive about AA. Normally, in AA this kind
of information is shared informally between a sponsor and a newcomer. Without an introduction, some clients would never get
close enough to understand how the AA program works.

Self-awareness and support groups are intended to assist the
members to grapple honestly with the role of alcohol in their
lives. The group function is to support sobriety, to identify the
characteristic ways in which people sabotage themselves. In
these groups, the emphasis is on the here and now. The participants are expected to deal with feelings as well as facts. The goal
is not intellectual understanding of why things have, or are, occurring. Rather, the hope is to have members discover how they
feel and learn how feelings are translated into behavior. They
then choose how they would prefer to behave, and try it on for
size.

A *problem-solving* group is directed at tackling specific problem or stress areas in the group members' lives. Either discus-

sion, role play, or a combination may be used. For example, how to say no to an offer to have a beer or how to handle an upcoming job interview could be appropriate topics. The goal is to develop an awareness of potential stress situations, to identify the old response pattern and how it created problems, and then to try new behaviors. These sessions thus provide practice for more effective coping behaviors.

Activity groups are least likely to resemble the stereotype of group therapy. In these groups an activity or project is undertaken, such as a ward or client government meeting or a planning session for a picnic. The emphasis is on more than the apparent task. The task is also a sample of real life; thus it provides a practice arena for the clients to identify areas of strength and weakness in interpersonal relationships. Here, too, the people have a safe place to practice new behaviors (see Activities Therapy, p. 269).

Group functions

Wine is a mocker, strong drink is raging.
PROVERBS 28:29–30

No matter what the kind of group, a number of functions will have to be performed. For any group to work effectively, there are some essential tasks, regardless of the goal. Initially the leader may have to be primarily responsible for filling these roles:

- Initiating—suggesting ideas for the group to consider, getting the ball rolling
- Elaborating or clarifying—clearing up confusions, giving examples, expanding on contributions of group members
- Summarizing—pulling together loose ends, restating ideas
- Facilitating—encouraging others' participation by asking questions, showing interest
- Expressing group feelings—recognizing moods and relationships within the group
- Giving feedback—sharing your response to what is happening in the group
- Seeking feedback—asking for others' responses to what you are doing

As time goes on, the leader does need to teach the group members to share the responsibility for these functions. Giving a lecture or showing a film on how to be a group member won't do it. Instead, through your own behavior, you serve as a model. You not only set the example of how to act in a group, but you also demonstrate more generally what healthy behavior looks like.

Different types of group therapy can be useful at different times during recovery. During the course of an inpatient stay, a client might well attend an educational group, an AA Training

Group, a problem-solving group, and a self-awareness group. In addition, the person could attend outside AA meetings. In this example, the client would be participating in five different types of groups. On discharge from the residence, the person would return for weekly group sessions as part of follow-up, and with his spouse might join a couples group. None of these group experiences would be intended to substitute for AA. The most effective treatment plans will prescribe AA plus alcohol-related group therapy. They are no more mutually exclusive than is AA or group therapy, along with medical treatment of cirrhosis.

Groups as a fad

A word of caution is in order. Group experiences have become something of a fad. Marathon, encounter, TA, gestalt, sensitivity, EST, and many other forms are seemingly offered everywhere: school, church, job, women's clubs. The emphasis placed on groups here does not imply that the alcoholic should ride the group therapy circuit! On the contrary, alcoholics seeking alcohol treatment in a group not restricted to alcoholics are likely to waste their own and other people's time. As was stated earlier, until one has taken some step to combat the alcohol problem, there is little likelihood of working on other problems successfully. Inevitably, the still drinking alcoholic will raise havoc in a mixed group. Our prediction is that the alcoholic will have others running in circles figuring out the whys, get gobs of sympathy, and remain unchanged. Eventually the other group members will wear out, end up treating the alcoholic just as the family does, and experience all the same frustrations as the family. In a group with other alcoholics and a leader used to the dynamics of alcoholism, however, it's a different story. The opportunity to maintain the charade is diminished to virtually zero because everyone knows the game thoroughly. The agenda, in this latter instance, is clearly how to break out of the game.

When you ask one friend to dine,
Give him your best wine!
When you ask two,
The second best will do!

LONGFELLOW

FAMILY TREATMENT

Historically, all too often the family of the alcoholic has been shortchanged. If a family member contacted an alcohol agency about an alcohol problem, what was likely to happen? They may have been told to have the alcoholic call on his or her own behalf, or have heard a sympathetic "Yes, it's awful," or have been told to call Al-Anon. It was unusual that families or family members were invited to come in as clients in their own right. In instances in which the alcoholic was seeking help, the family may have been called in to provide some background information, and then subsequently ignored. The only further attention they got was if a problem arose, or if the counselor believed that the spouse or family wasn't being supportive. Treatment efforts did not routinely take into account the problems the spouses faced and their need for treatment.

Although the aforementioned events may still take place, nonetheless very few in the alcohol field would claim that this approach is adequate. By definition, alcohol treatment that ignores the family has come to be seen as second-rate care! Although larger treatment programs may have staff whose speciality is family work, every alcohol counselor needs to have some basic understanding of the issues that confront families and develop some basic skills for working with family members. Members of an alcoholic's family do need treatment as much as the alcoholic. More and more often they are coming to this conclusion themselves and seeking help. Alcohol counselors are likely to find that more and more of their clients are in fact family members.

Working with families of active alcoholics

The most important thing the counselor needs to keep in mind is that the client being treated is the person in the office. In this case it is the family. The big temptation for the counselor may be to try treating the alcoholic in absentia, through the family member. This may be the family member's wish, too, but it would be futile to attempt it.

What does the family need? One important need is for education about alcoholism, the disease, including its impact on the family. Another is aid in sorting out their own behavior to see how it fits into, or even perpetuates the drinking. Also, they need to sort out their feelings, and realistically come to grips with the true dimensions of the problem and the toll being exacted from them. As well, there is the need to examine what their options are for dealing with the problem. Most importantly family members require support to live their own lives *despite the alcoholic*. Paradoxically, by doing this, the actual chances of short-circuiting the alcoholism are enhanced.

Family assessment. Just as all alcoholics do not display the identical symptoms or have the same degree of chronicity and extent of impairment, the same is true of family members. In the assessment process many of the same questions the counselor asks in dealing with the alcoholic should be considered. What has caused the family member to seek help now? What is the family's understanding of the problem? What supports do they have?

What is the economic, social, and family situation like? What coping devices do they use? What are their fears? What do they want from you? Where the counselor goes in working with the family will depend on the answers to these questions. Treatment plans for family members might include individual counseling, support groups, Al-Anon, or other agencies.

You will notice that we have been speaking interchangeably about families and family members. Contact with a counselor is typically made by a single individual. Efforts to include other nonalcoholic members of the family (or the alcoholic) usually fall to the counselor. In some cases all it takes is the suggestion. In other cases, the family member may resist. This resistance may be due to a sense of isolation, that no one else in the family cares. It may instead be fear of the other family members' disapproval for having "spilled the beans" about the family's secret. Although the ideal might be having the family member approach the others, as the counselor, you (with the client's permission) can contact other family members to ask them to come in for at least one session. Almost universally others will come in at least once (and this includes the alcoholic), if you tell them you are interested in their views of what is happening.

Family intervention. The initial focus has to be working with the family or family members on their own problems. Nonetheless, the indisputable fact is that the alcoholism is a central problem and that the family would like to see the alcoholic receive help. It is important to recognize that, ineffective as their efforts may have been, still much of a family's energy has gone into "helping." Now, as a result of education about the disease, plus assistance in sorting out their own situation, they in essence have become equipped to act more effectively in relation to the alcoholic. At the very least the family has been helped to abandon its protective, manipulative, enabling behavior. However, more is possible. A very successful technique, developed by the Johnson Institute in Minneapolis, consists of an intervention that involves the family and can be used to help move the alcoholic into treatment. This intervention technique and the rationale underpinning it was first described in *I'll Quit Tomorrow*.

The intervention process involves a meeting of family, other concerned persons, and the alcoholic, conducted under the direction of a counselor. Each individual, in turn, provides the alcoholic with a list of specific incidents related to drinking that have caused concern. These facts must be conveyed in an atmosphere of genuine concern for the alcoholic. In so doing, the alcoholic is helped to see both the true nature of the problem and

the need to seek assistance. Each person also expresses the hope that the alcoholic will seek treatment. By cutting through the denial, by providing the painful details, the intervention process can be thought of as precipitating a crisis for the alcoholic.

The counselor who is involved in family work is well advised to become skilled in conducting interventions, either by attending workshops or by "apprenticing" to someone trained in this technique. We should be clear that conducting an intervention is not something you do on the spur of the moment. It is not something to be done impromptu, just because you happen to have the family together. Nor is it something you describe to the family and suggest they do on their own after supper some evening!

The effectiveness of intervention depends on the participants' ability to voice a genuine concern and describe incidents that have caused concern in an objective, straightforward manner. This takes briefing and preparatory work. Typically, this will entail several meetings with the family. The family members must become knowledgeable about the disease of alcoholism, so that the behaviors that previously were seen as designed to "get them" can be seen for what they are, symptoms. The preparation will usually involve a rehearsal during which each of the participants goes through the things that they would like to convey to the alcoholic. The participants also need to discuss what treatment options are to be presented, and the actions they will take if the alcoholic does not seek help. Is the spouse ready to ask for a separation? Is the grown daughter ready to say she will not be comfortable allowing Mom to babysit for the grandchildren anymore. Beyond preparing the participants, a successful intervention also requires that the counselor be supportive to *all* present, equally, and deflect the alcoholic's anxiety and fears, which may surface as anger.

Family treatment in conjunction with the alcoholic's treatment

Work with the family is equally important for the alcoholic who enters treatment. The family should be included as early as possible. The family members' views of what the problem is, their understanding of alcoholism as a disease, their ability to provide support, and their willingness to engage in the treatment as well will have a bearing on the treatment plans for the alcoholic. If the family is in pure chaos, at a point at which concern for the alcoholic is lost under feelings of anger and frustration, inpatient care may be far preferable to outpatient treatment. On the other hand, if the family is very supportive and is able to marshal its collective resources on the alcoholic's behalf, outpatient treatment may be the treatment of choice.

For these reasons a family meeting is becoming a routine part of any assessment process. At this time, the counselor will be seeking their view of what is happening. When this meeting is held will be determined by the alcoholic's status, the severity of the alcohol problem, what is going on with the family, the receptivity and/or resistance to treatment. Say alcoholism is clearly evident—at such a stage it is diagnosable even by the parking lot attendant. In this situation, the family may be the only reliable source of even the most basic information, such as how much alcohol is being consumed, past medical history, prior alcohol treatment. The alcoholic's judgment may be so severely impaired that realistically others will need to make the decision about admission for treatment. The postponement of formal family involvement may be indicated when the alcoholism is in the early stages, and the alcoholic's life still has some semblance of order. In such circumstances the counselor may want to explore with the alcoholic his view of the world and develop a working relationship, before introducing possibly opposing views.

It is important to keep in mind that in initial contact with the family you don't go into a family therapy routine. It is data-collecting time. The task is to understand how the alcoholic family sees and deals with the alcoholism in its midst. In joint meetings, be prepared to provide the structure and lay the ground rules. For example, explain that people often see things differently, and that you want to know from each of those present what has been going on. If need be, reassure them that everyone gets equal time, but no interruptions, please.

During the alcoholic's treatment the family may become involved in regularly scheduled family counseling sessions, or participate in a special group for family members, or a couples' group, in addition to attending Al-Anon. Some residential treatment programs are beginning to hold "family weekends." The family joins the alcoholic in residence and participates in a specially structured family program of education, group discussion, and family counseling.

Issues of the family

The alcoholic's entering treatment, especially residential treatment, may impose very real immediate problems for the family. The spouse may be concerned about even more unpaid bills, problems of child care, fears of yet more broken promises,

That is a treacherous friend against whom you must always be on your guard. Such a friend is wine.

C.N. BOVEE

> I'll be glad if Hubert is better in 30 days, but they are going to turn off our electricity in 7 days and our water in 14. Hubert will be in here with all the comforts and we'll be out on the street freezing.

and so on. In the face of these immediate concerns, long-range benefits may offer little consolation. Attention must be paid to helping the family deal with the nitty-gritty details of everyday living. Just as the alcoholic is requiring a lot of structure and guidance, so is the family.

Another issue for the family will be to develop realistic expectations for treatment. On one hand, they may think everything will be rosy, that their troubles are over. On the other, they may be exceedingly pessimistic. Probably they will initially bounce back and forth between these two extremes.

The family at some point will also have a need to have the alcoholic "really hear" what it has been like for them at the emotional level. If there has been an intervention, it stressed objective factual recounting of events and being sympathetic to the alcoholic. Although a presentation to the alcoholic of the family's emotional reality may not be apropos at the time of the intervention, it must take place at some point. If the alcoholic and family are to be reintegrated into a functioning unit, it is going to require that both "sides" gain some appreciation of what the alcoholism felt like for the other. How this occurs will vary. Within some family weekend programs there may be a session specifically devoted to "feelings," led by skilled family therapists. These sessions can be very highly charged, "tell-it-like-it-is" cathartic sessions. To do this successfully requires a lot of skill on the therapist's/counselor's part, as well as a structure that provides a lot of support for the family members. For the alcoholic, the pain and remorse and shame can be devastating. For the family this, in turn, can invoke guilt and remorse, as well. These responses must be dealt with; a session cannot be stopped with the participants left in those emotional states. More commonly this material will be dealt with over time, in "smaller doses." It may occur within family sessions and frequently also within the context of working in the AA program.* Again, the important issue is that you recognize this as a family task that must be dealt with in some way at some time. Otherwise, the family has a closet full of "secrets" or "skeletons" that will haunt them, come between them, and interfere with their regaining a healthy new balance.

Suggestions for working with families during treatment

The data gathering completed, the task turns to helping the family make the readjustments necessary to reestablish a new

---

*Dealing with the effects of the alcoholic's drinking on the family may be part of taking an inventory (Step 4) and part of making amends (Step 8). See the Twelve Steps of AA later on in this chapter (pp. 255-257).

balance. Here are some concrete suggestions for dealing with alcoholic families at this treatment stage. You are the most objective person present; therefore, it is up to you to evaluate and guide the process.

Concentrate on the interaction, not on the content. Don't become the referee in a family digression.

Teach them how to check things out. People tend to guess at other peoples' meanings and motivations. They then respond as though the guesses were accurate. This causes all kinds of confusion and misunderstandings and can lead to mutual recriminations. The counselor needs to put a stop to these mind-reading games, and point out what is going on.

The counselor must *be alert to "scapegoating."* A common human tendency is to lay it all on George. This is true whatever the problem. The alcoholic family tends to blame the drinker for all the family's troubles, thereby neatly avoiding any responsibility for their own actions. Help them see this as a no-no.

Any good therapy stresses *acceptance of each person's right to his own feelings.* One reason for this is that good feelings get blocked by unexpressed bad feelings. One of the tasks of a therapist is to bring out the family's strengths. The focus has been on the problems for so long that they have lost sight of the good points.

Be alert to avoidance transactions. This includes such things as digressing to Christmas 3 years ago in the midst of a heated discussion of Daddy's drinking. It is up to you to point this out to them and get them back on the track. In a similar vein, it may fall to you to "speak the unspeakable," to bring out in the open the obvious, but unmentioned, facts.

In making these patterns clear to the family, you can *guide them into problem-solving techniques as options.* You can help them begin to use these in therapy, with an eye to teaching them to use them on their own.

After a time of success, when things seem to be going better, there may be some resistance to continuing therapy. The family fears a setback and wants to stop while they're ahead. Simply point this out to them. They can try for something better or terminate. If they terminate, leave the door open for a return later.

Pregnancy in the alcoholic family

You may recall some of the particular family problems that relate to pregnancy and the presence of young children in the family. A few specific words should be said about these potential problematic areas. The first is contraceptive counseling. Pregnancy is not a cure for alcoholism in either partner. In a couple in which one or both partners are actively drinking, they would be advised to make provision for the prevention of pregnancy until the drinking is well controlled. It is important to remember that adequate birth control methods for an ordinary couple may be inadequate when alcoholism is present. Methods that require planning or delay of gratification are likely to fail. Rhythm, foam, diaphragms, or prophylactics are not wise choices if one partner is actively drinking. A woman who is actively drinking is not advised to use the pill. So the alternatives are few: the pill for the partner of an active male alcoholic, a condom for the partner of a sexually active female alcoholic. In the event of an unwanted pregnancy, the possibilities of placement or therapeutic abortion should be considered. If the woman is alcoholic, a therapeutic abortion certainly should be considered. At the moment, no amniotic fluid assay test exists that can establish the presence of fetal alcohol syndrome, but the possibility is there when the mother is actively drinking.

Should pregnancy occur and a decision be made to have the baby, intensive intervention is required. If the expectant mother is the alcoholic, every effort should be made to get her to stop drinking. Regular prenatal care is also important. Counseling and support of both parents if alcohol is present is essential to handle the stresses that accompany any pregnancy. If the prospective father is the alcoholic, it is important to provide additional supports for the mother.

The above touches on the problems of pregnancy with active alcoholism. Contraceptive counseling should also be considered for alcoholics in early recovery. At that point the family unit is busy coping with sobriety, and the alcoholic is engaged in establishing a solid recovery. Pregnancy is always a stress for any couple or family system.

Children in the alcoholic family

A few words are in order on behalf of older children in an alcoholic family. In many cases, children's problems are related to stress in the parents. Children may easily become weapons in parental battles. With alcoholism, children may think their behavior is the cause of the drinking. A child needs to be told that this is not the case. In instances where the counselor knows that physical or severe emotional abuse has occurred, child welfare authorities must be notified. In working with the family, additional parenting persons may be brought into the picture. Going to a nursery school or day-care center may help the child from a chaotic home.

What cannot be emphasized too strongly is that children not be "forgotten" or left out of treatment. Sometimes parents consider a child too young to understand, or feel the children need to be "protected." What this can easily lead to is the child's feeling even more isolated, vulnerable, and frightened. Children in family sessions tend to define an appropriate level of participation for themselves. Sometimes the presence of children is problematic for adults not because they won't understand, but because of their uncanny ability to see things exactly as they are: for example, without self-consciousness the child may say what the rest are only hinting at, or may ask the most provocative questions. Along the same line, while a parent is actively drinking, the inevitable concerns and questions of the child must be addressed. Children may not need all the details, but pretense by adults that everything is okay is destructive. When initially involving the family, consider the children's needs in building a treatment plan. Many child welfare agencies or mental health centers conduct group sessions for children around issues of concern to children, such as a death in the family, divorce, or alcoholism. Usually these groups are set up for children of roughly the same age, and run for a set period, such as 6 weeks. The goal is to provide basic information, support, and the chance to express feelings the child is uncomfortable with or cannot bring up at home. The subliminal message of such groups is that the parents' problems are not the child's fault, and talking about it is okay. In family sessions you can make that message clear, too. You can provide time for the child to ask questions and also provide children with pamphlets that may be helpful for them.

Occasionally a child may seem to be "doing well." In fact, the child may reject efforts by others to be involved in alcohol discussions or treatment efforts. If the alcoholic parent is actively drinking, the resistance on the child's part may be part of the child's way of coping. Seeing you may be perceived by the child as taking sides; it may force the child to look at things he is trying to pretend are not there. (Resistance also may surface to joining the family treatment when the alcoholic has become sober, for many of the same reasons.) Listen to the child's objections for clues to the child's concerns. Feel free to seek advice from a child therapist if you feel you are in danger of getting in over your head. What is important here is not to let a child's assertion that "everything is fine" pass without some question.

Portrait of a young child whose father is nice to him when sober, but beats him when drunk.

I know I promised we would play Cowboys and Indians today, but I have to go to my AA meeting.

Recovery and the family

A common mistake when working with an alcoholic family is to assume that once the drinking stops things will get better. Yet when the alcoholic stops drinking the family again faces a crisis and time of transition. Such crises can lead to growth and positive changes, but not automatically or inevitably. In the alcoholic family there has been a long period of storing up anger, of mistrust and miscommunication. This may have been the children's only experience of family life. At times children who previously were well behaved may begin acting out when a parent becomes sober. Children may feel that earlier their father loved alcohol more than them, and that now he loves AA more. He may have stopped drinking, but in the children's eyes they're still in second place.

Recovering families have a number of tasks to accomplish before they return to healthy functioning. They must strengthen generational boundaries. They must reassume age- and sex-appropriate roles in the family. They must learn to communicate in direct and honest ways with one another. They must learn to trust one another. And finally they must learn to express both anger and love appropriately.

It might be expected, if one considers the family as a unit, that there are stages or patterns of a family's recovery from alcoholism. This has not yet been adequately studied. No one has developed a "valley chart" that plots family disintegration and recovery. Counselors who have had considerable involvement with families of recovering alcoholics have noticed and are now beginning to discuss some common themes of the family's recovery.

One observation suggests that the family unit may experience growth pains that parallel those facing the alcoholic. It has long been a part of the folk wisdom that the alcoholic's psychological and emotional growth ceases when the heavy drinking begins. So when sobriety comes, the alcoholic is going to have to face some growing-up issues that the drinking prevented him from attending to. In the family system, what may be the equivalent of this Rip Van Winkle experience? Consider an example of a family in which the father is an alcoholic, whose heavy drinking occurred during his children's adolescence, and who begins recovery just as the children are entering adulthood. If he was basically "out of it" during their teenage years, they grew up as best they could, without very much fathering from him. When he "comes to," they are no longer children but adults. In effect, he was deprived of an important chunk of family life. There may be regrets. There may be unrealistic expectations on the father's part about his present relationship with his children. There may be inappropriate attempts by him to "make it up," regain the missing part. Depending on the situation, the counselor may need to help him grieve. There may be the need to help him recognize that his expectations are not in keeping with his children's adult status. He may be able to find other outlets to experience a parenting role or reestablish and enjoy appropriate contacts with his children.

Divorced or separated alcoholics

Vaillant, in examining the course of recovery from alcoholism, found that quite commonly those who recovered "acquired a new love object." Basically, those who recovered found someone to love and be loved by, someone who had not been part of the active alcoholism. This cannot be used as evidence that family treatment is not warranted because there has been too much water over the dam, too much pain, and too much guilt. The sample he studied were those who were treated prior to the time in which family involvement in treatment was commonplace. So who knows what the outcome would have been had attention been directed to family members as well. Early intervention was not the rule then either. His sample consisted of long-established cases of alcoholism. However, it does serve to remind us of an important fact. Not all families will come through alcoholism treatment intact. Divorce is not uncommon in our society. Even if alcoholics had a divorce rate similar to that for nonalcoholics, it would still mean a substantial number of divorces. Therefore, for some families, the work of family counseling will be to achieve a separation, with the least pain possible and in the least destructive manner for both partners and their children.

Issues of family relationships are not important just for the alcoholic whose family is intact. For the alcoholic who enters treatment divorced and/or estranged from the family, the task during the early treatment phase will be to help him make it without family supports. Other family members may well have come to the conclusion long ago that cutting off contacts with the alcoholic was necessary for their welfare. Even if contacted when the alcoholic enters treatment, they may refuse to have anything to do with him or his treatment. However, with many months or years of sobriety, the issue of broken family ties may emerge. The recovering alcoholic may desire a restoration of family contacts and have the emotional and personal stability to attempt it, be it with parents, siblings, or the alcoholic's own children.

If the alcoholic remains in follow-up treatment with a counselor, the counselor ought to be alert to this. If the alcoholic is successful, it will still involve stress; very likely many old wounds will be opened. If the attempt is unsuccessful, the counselor will be able to provide support and help the person find a new adjustment in the face of those unfulfilled hopes. As family treatment becomes an integral part of treatment for alcoholism, the hope is that fewer families will experience a total disruption of communications in the face of alcoholism. It is hoped that a more widespread knowledge of the symptoms of alcoholism may facilitate reconciliation of previously estranged families.

Al-Anon

Long before alcoholism was widely accepted as a disease, much less one that also affected family members, wives of the early members of AA recognized disturbances in their own behavior. They also encountered problems living with their alcoholics whether sober or still drinking. They saw that a structured program based on self-knowledge, reparation of wrongs, and growth in a supportive group helped alcoholics to recover from their disorder; so why not a similar program for spouses and other family members?

Al-Anon was formed and soon became a thriving program in its own right. The founders were quick to recognize that patterns of scapegoating the alcoholic and trying to manipulate the drinking were nonproductive. Instead, they based their program on the premise that the only person you can change or control is yourself. Family members in Al-Anon are encouraged to find an acceptable life-style for themselves regardless of the actions of the alcoholic.

Using the Twelve Steps of AA (described in detail on pp. 255–257) as a starting point, the program also incorporated the AA slogans and meeting formats. The major difference is in Al-Anon members' powerlessness over others' alcohol use rather than being powerless over their own personal alcohol use. Effort is directed at gaining an understanding of their own inappropriate responses and substituting behavior that will lead them to health. They are not encouraged to dodge responsibility for themselves by continuing to focus on the alcoholic as "the problem." Instead, they can see by shared example the effectiveness of changing themselves, of "detaching with love" from the drinker. Although no promises are made that this will have an impact on a still-drinking alcoholic, there are many examples of just such

an outcome. At the very least, when family members stop behaviors that tend to perpetuate the alcoholic drinking, not only
will their lives be better, the odds are increased for a break-
through in the alcoholic's denial system.

Many people have found support and hope in the Al-Anon
program for personal change and growth, through education
about the disease and its impact on families, coupled with the
sharing of experiences with others who have lived with the
shame and grief caused by alcoholism and the attached stigma.

Al-Ateen

Al-Ateen is an outgrowth of Al-Anon set up for teenagers with
an alcoholic parent. Their problems are different from those of
the spouse of the alcoholic, and they need a group specifically to
deal with these. Under the sponsorship of an adult Al-Anon or
AA member, they are taught to deal with their problems in much
the same manner as the other programs.

Even with the currently more widespread information about
alcoholism, alcoholics and their families still feel a sense of
stigma. Most of them feel completely alone. It is such a hush-
hush issue that anyone experiencing it thinks they are unique in
their suffering. The statistics mean little if your friends and
neighbors never mention it and seem "normal" to you. It is very
painful to have a problem about which you are afraid to talk because of the shame of being "different." One of the greatest benefits of both Al-Anon and Al-Ateen is the lessening of this shame
and isolation. Hard as it may be to attend the first meeting, once
there, people find many others who share their problems and
pain. This alone can begin a healing process.

Although Al-Anon or Al-Ateen can be a tremendous assistance to the family, you may need to point out what they are *not*
designed to do. Frequently confusion is introduced because all
family treatment efforts may be erroneously referred to as "Al-
Anon." Al-Anon is a self-help group. It is not a professional program whose members are trained family therapists, any more
than AA members are professional counselors. However, Al-Anon
participation can nicely complement other family treatment efforts. Referral to Al-Anon or Al-Ateen is recommended as part of
the treatment regimen for families.

ALCOHOLICS ANONYMOUS

Volumes have been written about the phenomenon of AA. It
has been investigated, explained, challenged, and defended by

laypeople, newspapers, writers, magazines, psychologists, psychiatrists, physicians, sociologists, anthropologists, and clergy. Each has brought a set of underlying assumptions and a particular vocabulary and professional or lay framework to the task. The variety of material on the subject reminds one of trying to force mercury into a certain-sized, perfectly round ball.

In this brief discussion, we certainly have a few underlying assumptions. One is that "experience is the best teacher." This text will be relatively unhelpful compared to attending AA meetings over a period of time, watching and talking with people in the process of recovery actively using the program of AA. Another assumption is that AA works for a wide variety of people caught up in the disease and for this reason deserves a counselor's attention. Alcoholics Anonymous has been described as "the single most effective treatment for alcoholism." The exact whys and hows of its workings are not of paramount importance, but some understanding of it is necessary to genuinely recommend it. Presenting AA with such statements as "AA worked for me; it's the only way," or, conversely, "I've done all I can for you, you might as well try AA," might not be the most helpful approach.

History

Alcoholics Anonymous had its beginnings in 1935 in Akron, Ohio, with the meeting of two alcoholics. One, Bill W., had had a spiritual experience that had been the major precipitating event in beginning his abstinence. On a trip to Akron after about a year of sobriety, he was overtaken by a strong desire to drink. He hit upon the idea of seeking out another suffering alcoholic as an alternative. He made contact with some people who led him to Dr. Bob, and the whole thing began with their first meeting. The fascinating story of this history is told in *AA Comes of Age*. The idea of alcoholics helping each other spread slowly in geometric fashion until 1939. At that point, a group of about a hundred sober members realized they had something to offer the thus far "hopeless alcoholics." They wrote and published the book *Alcoholics Anonymous*, generally known as the Big Book. It was based on a retrospective view of what they had done that had kept them sober. The past tense is used almost entirely in the Big Book. It was compiled by a group of people who over time, working together, had found something that worked. Their task was to present this in a useful framework to others who might try it for themselves. This story is also covered in *AA Comes of Age*. In

1941, AA became widely known after publication of an article in a national magazine. The geometric growth rapidly advanced, and in 1983 there were an estimated 1 million active members world wide.

Goals

Alcoholics Anonymous stresses abstinence and contends that nothing can really happen for a drinker until "the cork is in the bottle." Many other helping professionals tend to agree. A drugged person—and an alcoholic is drugged—simply cannot comprehend, or use successfully, many other forms of treatment. First, the drug has to go.

The goals of each individual within AA vary widely; simple abstinence to a whole new way of life are the ends of the continuum. Individuals' personal goals may also change over time. That any one organization can accommodate such diversity is in itself something of a miracle.

In AA, the words *sober* and *dry* denote quite different states. A dry person is simply not drinking at the moment. Sobriety means a more basic, all-pervasive change in the person. Sobriety does not come as quickly as dryness and requires a desire for, and work toward, a contented, productive life without reliance on mood-altering drugs. The Twelve Steps provide a framework for achieving this latter state.

The Twelve Steps

The Twelve Steps function as the therapeutic framework of AA. They were not devised by a group of social scientists; nor are they derived from a theoretical view of alcoholism. The Twelve Steps of AA grew out of the practical experience of the earliest members, based on what they had *done* to gain sobriety. They do, indeed, represent a doing: AA is not a passive process.

The initial undrugged view of the devastation can, and often does, drive the dry alcoholic back to the bottle. However, the Twelve Steps of AA, as experienced by the sober members, offer the possibility of another solution: hope for another road out of the maze.

Step 1, "We admitted we were powerless over alcohol—that our lives had become unmanageable," acknowledges the true culprit, alcohol, and the scope of the problem, the whole life. Step 2, "Came to believe that a Power greater than ourselves could restore us to sanity," recognizes the craziness of the drinking behavior, and allows for the gradual reliance on some agent

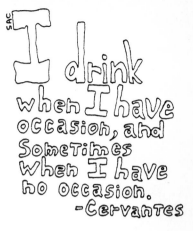

I drink when I have occasion, and sometimes when I have no occasion.
—Cervantes

Green Mountain Chablis

60 proof
bottled in island pond
vermont

outside (God, the AA group, the therapist, or a combination) to aid an about-face. Step 3, "Made a decision to turn our will and our lives over to the care of God as we understood Him," enables the alcoholic to let go of the previous life preserver, the bottle, and accept an outside influence to provide direction. It has now become clear that as a life preserver, the bottle was a dud, but free floating cannot go on forever either. The search outside the self for direction has now begun.

Step 4, "Made a searching and fearless moral inventory of ourselves," allows a close look at the basic errors of thinking and acting that were part of the drinking debacle. It also gives space for the positive attributes that can be enhanced in the sober state. An inventory is, after all, a balance sheet. Step 5, "Admitted to God, to ourselves, and to another human being the exact nature of our wrongs," provides a method of cleaning the slate, admitting just how awful it all was, and getting the guilt-provoking behavior out in the open instead of destructively "bottled up."

Steps 6 and 7, "Were entirely ready to have God remove all these defects of character," and "Humbly asked Him to remove our shortcomings," continue the mopping-up process. Step 6 makes the alcoholic aware of the tendency to cling to old behaviors, even unhealthy ones. Step 7 takes care of the fear of repeated errors, again instilling hope that personality change is possible. (Remember, at this stage in the process, the alcoholic is likely to be very short on self-esteem.)

Steps 8 and 9 are a clear guide to sorting out actual injury done to others and deciding how best to deal with such situations. Step 8 is "Made a list of all persons we had harmed and became willing to make amends to them all." Step 9 is "Made direct amends to such people wherever possible, except when to do so would injure them or others." They serve other purposes, too. First, they get the alcoholic out of the "bag" of blaming others for life's difficulties. They also provide a mechanism for dealing with presently strained relationships and for alleviating some of the overwhelming guilt the now-sober alcoholic feels.

Steps 10 to 12 are considered the continuing-maintenance steps. Step 10, "Continued to take personal inventory and when we were wrong promptly admitted it," ensures that the alcoholic need not slip back from the hard-won gains. Diligence in focusing on one's own behavior and not excusing it keeps the record straight. Step 11, "Sought through prayer and meditation to improve our conscious contact with God as we understood Him, praying only for knowledge of His will for us and the power to carry that out," fosters continued spiritual development. Finally,

Step 12, "Having had a spiritual awakening as a result of these steps, we tried to carry this message to alcoholics and to practice these principles in all our affairs," points the way to sharing the process with others. This is one of the vital keys Bill W. discovered to maintain sobriety. It also implies that a continued practice of the new principles is vital to the sober life.

A word can be said here about "Two Steppers." This phrase is used to describe a few individuals in AA who come in, admit they are alcoholics, dry out, and set out to rescue other alcoholics. However, it is often said in AA that "you can't give what you don't have." This refers to a quality of sobriety that comes after some long and serious effort applying the entire Twelve Steps. It is interesting to note that "carrying the message" is not mentioned until Step 12.

No AA member serious about the program and sober for some time would ever imply that the steps are a one-shot deal. They are an ongoing process that evolves over time (a great deal of it) into ever-widening applications. When approached with serious intent, the steps enable a great change in the individual. That they are effective is testified to not only by great numbers of recovering alcoholics, but also by their adoption as a basis for such organizations as Overeaters Anonymous, Gamblers Anonymous, and Emotions Anonymous. These other organizations simply substitute their own addiction for the word alcohol in Step 1.

A therapist/counselor/friend should be alert to the balance required in this process. The newly dry alcoholic who wants to tackle all Twelve Steps the first week should be counseled "Easy does it." The longer dry member hopelessly anguished by Step 4, for instance, could be advised that perfection is not the goal and a stab at it the first time through is quite sufficient. The agnostic having difficulty with "the God bit" can be told about using the group or anything else suitable for the time being. After all, the spiritual awakening doesn't turn up until Step 12 either.

Organization

AA has very little structure as an organization. It describes itself as a fellowship and functions around the Twelve Steps and Twelve Traditions. The traditions cover the organization as a whole, setting forth the purpose of the fellowship, to carry its message to the still-suffering alcoholic, and defining principles of conduct; for example, AA does not affiliate with other groups, nor lend its name; it should not be organized and should remain forever nonprofessional. Individual groups are autonomous and decline outside contributions. Thus, all care has been taken not to obscure or lose sight of the organization's purpose. The individual groups function in accord with these principles; their focus is on sobriety, anonymity, and individual application of "the program," which includes meetings, attempting to work the Twelve Steps, and service to other alcoholics.

Anonymity

Before discussing the meetings, a special word about anonymity. Alcoholics Anonymous' Tradition 12 reads as follows: "Anonymity is the spiritual foundation of all our traditions ever reminding us to place principles above personalities." This concept evolved out of the growth pains of the organization. Early members admit candidly that fear of exposure of their problem was their *original* motivation for remaining anonymous: the need "to hide from public distrust and contempt." The practice of anonymity that was introduced out of that fear began to provide evidence of its value on a totally different level.

This evolutionary process tends to occur for most individual members of AA. At first, the promise of anonymity is viewed as a safeguard against exposure. The stigma attached to alcoholism has not yet disappeared. Added to this are the alcoholic's own guilt, sense of failure, and low self-esteem. It is vital to maintain this concept to encourage fearful newcomers to try out the program while assuring them of complete confidentiality. As they progress in sobriety, fear gives way to the deeper understanding revealed in the practice. To be simply Joe or Mary, one alcoholic among many, has therapeutic value.

In practice, anonymity takes the form of first names only during the meetings, not identifying oneself through the media as a member of AA, and being careful not to reveal anyone else's attendance at meetings. Some meetings end with the reminder that "Who you see here and what is said here, stays here." It is important to the ability of AA to continue its healing mission to suffering alcoholics that this principle of anonymity be respected.

Meetings plus...

There are open meetings (open to any spouses, interested parties, etc.) and closed meetings (only professed alcoholics attend the latter). Both types divide into speaker or discussion meetings. The former format has one to three speakers who tell what it was like drinking (for the purpose of allowing newcomers to identify), what happened to change this, and what the sober life is now like. A discussion meeting is usually smaller. The leader may or may not tell his story briefly as just described, or "qualify" in AA jargon. The focus of the meeting is a discussion of a particular step, topic, or problem with alcohol, with the leader taking the role of facilitator.

Attendance at meetings is not all there is to AA. An analogy to medical care may help. The AA meeting might be like a patient's visit to a doctor's office. The office visit doesn't constitute the whole of therapy. It is a good start; but how closely the patient follows the advice and recommendations and acts on what is prescribed makes the difference. Sitting in the doctor's office doesn't do it. So too with AA. The person who is seriously trying to use AA as a means of achieving sobriety will be doing a lot more than attending meetings. Those successful in AA will spend time talking to and being with other more experienced members. Part of this time will be spent getting practical tips on how to maintain sobriety. Time and effort go into learning and substituting other behaviors for the all-pervasive drinking behavior. Alcoholics Anonymous contacts will also be a valuable resource for relaxation. It is a place a newly recovering alcoholic will feel accepted. It is also a space in which the drinking possibilities are greatly minimized. A new member of AA may spend a couple of hours a day phoning, having coffee with, or in the company of, other AA members. Although it is strongly recommended that new members seek sponsors, they will be in touch with a larger circle of people. Frequent contact with AA members is encouraged, not only to pass on useful information. Another key reason is to make it easier for the new members to reach out at times of stress, when picking up a drink would be so easy and instinctively natural. The new member's contacting a fellow AA member when a crunch time comes makes the difference in many cases between recovery and relapse.

Slogans

Slowly the new member's life is being restructured around not drinking, and usually the slogans are the basis for this: "One day at a time," "easy does it," "keep it simple," "live and let live," "let go and let God," and more. Although they sound trite and somewhat corny, remember the description of the confused, guilt-ridden, anxious product of alcoholism. Anyone in such a condition can greatly benefit from a simple, organized, easily understood schedule of priorities. A kind of behavior modification is taking place in order that a growth process may begin. Some new members feel so overwhelmed by the idea of a day without a drink that their sponsor and/or others will help them literally plan every step of the first few weeks. They keep in almost hourly touch with older members. Phone calls at any hour of the day or night are encouraged as a way to relieve anxiety.

Resistances

Some alcoholics and their families may be quite resistant to AA. A counselor often finds they may agree to anything, as long as it isn't AA. This resistance probably has a number of sources. It may be based on very erroneous information and myths about AA. Quite likely it is embarrassment, plain and simple. The alcoholic may have been notorious at office parties, or been a regular in the newspaper column for drinking and driving offenses, or almost single-handedly been keeping the neighborhood general store solvent with beer purchases; but heaven forbid being seen entering a building where an AA meeting is held! Also, going to an AA meeting represents, if not a public admission, at least a private one that alcohol is a problem. Seeing a counselor, even an alcohol counselor, may allow the alcoholic multiple interpretations, at least for a while. Going to AA is clear-cut and in that respect a big step.

In dealing with this resistance education is useful, but also required is a certain insistence that going at least for a reasonable "experimental" period is expected to get firsthand knowledge.

Sometimes alcoholics will have had some limited prior exposure to AA, which they use for the basis of their objections. Commonly this is coupled with the similarly "negative" experiences of their best drinking buddies, who also agree AA doesn't work. Usually these alcoholics say they tried it once, but it wasn't for them, and they didn't like it. Any examination of what was going on in their lives generally reveals at best a very halfhearted "try." The liking or not liking is not an issue. Usually we care little if people like any other prescribed treatments as long as the treatment produces positive results. No one *likes* braces or casts on broken limbs or hospital stays for any reason, but they are accepted as necessary to produce a desired result. Feel free to point this out, that the ultimate criteria are the results.

The alcoholic may have found some professionals who will support the resistances. If the alcoholic remains in treatment with such a person, you had better get in touch with another professional. Possibly the alcoholic is misinterpreting what has been

"What I said was "Join AA." not "Join AAA." No wonder you couldn't find the meeting.

I didn't mind that, Doc. It was getting hauled out of a bar by a tow truck that embarassed me.

said. If not, you need to do a bit of informal education, explaining why you think AA is indicated, and dispelling misconceptions.

An objective opinion of AA is hard to find. Quite honestly, some workers do show resistances to AA. At times one gets the sense that AA is not considered to be "real" treatment. Why these feelings? Often, we don't have the foggiest notion. Nonetheless, our suspicion is that a number of factors may feed into this attitude. One reason is that any worker in the field of alcoholism will periodically lose touch with what the disease of alcoholism is really like. The literal hell that is the life of the active alcoholic is forgotten. That is who AA is for. Yet at times, we forget that the primary purpose of AA is to help people to escape their hell. Then we begin to act as if AA were supposed to do other things, for example, be a growth group or handle marital problems. Another point of possible professional resistance is that we sometimes take our resistive clients' objections too seriously. We buy their criticisms of AA. We accept their not "liking" AA as a valid reason for their not going. But we do not expect them to "like" to see their physicians, or "like" to use other forms of treatment! Similarly, treatment people do not usually see the people who try AA and succeed the first time around, who don't need other kinds of help. There is a natural human tendency, when we see someone operating differently, to think one of us must be wrong. If I don't want it to be me, that means it must be you—or AA. Another point of friction seems to be connected to the fact that AA does not build termination into the program. More will be said about this later. Professional workers forget that any chronic disease is only terminated by death. Even when the disease is under control, regular checkups are routine practice. Finally, professionals sometimes have mistakenly gotten the impression that AA, as an organization, holds AA and other therapies to be incompatible. This is not true. Nothing in the AA program would support this. Certainly, an occasional client member will give this impression in which case as a counselor, you can help clear up this misconception. So much for the friction points; let us return to AA.

View of recovery

One thing assumed in AA is that recovery is a serious, lifelong venture. Safety does not exist, and some kind of long-term support is necessary. This seems to be the case, and a lot of experience supports the assumption. Alcoholics, like all of us, have selective memories and are inclined, after varying periods of dryness, to remember only the relief of drinking and not the

Against diseases the strongest fence is the defensive virtue, abstinence.

ROBERT HERRICK

consequent problems. Some kind of reminder of reality seems to be necessary. Any alcoholic of long-term sobriety will be able to tell about the sudden desire to drink popping up out of nowhere. Those who do not succumb are grateful, for the most part, to some aspect of their AA life as the key to their returning stability. No one knows exactly why these moments occur, but one thing is certain: they are personally frightening and upsetting. They can reduce the reasonably well-adjusted recovering alcoholic to a state very like that first panic-ridden dryness. The feelings could be compared to the feelings after a particularly vivid nightmare. Whatever the reason for the phenomenon, these unexpected urges to drink do spring up. This is one reason continued participation in AA is suggested. Another is the emphasis (somewhat underplayed from time to time) on a continued growth in sobriety. Certainly, groups will rally around newcomers with a beginner's focus and help them learn the basics. In discussion meetings with a group of veterans, however, the focus will be on personal growth within the context of the Twelve Steps. Alcoholics Anonymous may advertise itself as a "simple program for complicated people," but an understanding of it is far from a simple matter. It involves people, and people are multifaceted. Its simplicity is deceptive and on the order of "Love thy neighbor as thyself." Simple, and yet the working out of it could easily take a lifetime.

In closing, we again strongly urge you to attend a variety of AA meetings and speak at some length with veteran members. So much has been written about AA—and besides, in some respects it is so understandable an approach—that people assume they know what it's about without firsthand knowledge. Just as you would visit treatment programs or community agencies to see personally what they are about, so, too, go to AA.

Referral

A few words are in order about making an effective referral to AA. Simply telling someone to go probably won't work in most cases. The worker needs to play a more active role in the referral. Alcoholics Anonymous is a self-help group. What AA can do and offer is by far best explained *and* demonstrated by its members. The counselor can assist by making arrangements for the client to speak to a member of AA or can arrange for a client to be taken to a meeting. Helping professionals, whether concentrating on alcoholics or not, often have a list of AA members who have agreed to do this. Even if the counselor is an AA member, a separate AA contact is advisable. It is less confusing to the client if AA is seen as distinct from, although compatible with, other therapy. The counselor need not defend, proselytize for, or try to sell AA. Alcoholics Anonymous speaks for itself eloquently. You do your part well when you persuade clients to attend, to listen with an open mind, and to stay long enough to make their own assessments.

A standard part of many treatment programs is an introduction and orientation to AA. This would seem to be very important, as is shown below, because treatment programs are an ever-growing source of referrals to AA. Many treatment programs include AA meetings on the grounds or transport clients to outside meetings. It is not unusual for AA to be presented in educational sessions or AA referred to in counseling or group therapy. One of the challenges for treatment programs is to help clients distinguish between formal treatment and AA. Nowhere may this be more important than in terms of aftercare. It needs to be pointed out that attending a treatment program's alumni group is not the same as going to AA. Nor for that matter is a chat with a sponsor necessarily a substitute for an appointment with a counselor. Although wishing to be supportive of AA, treatment programs also need to respect the boundaries between AA and treatment, which AA has long acknowledged.

AA membership

The General Service Office of AA, going back to 1968, has conducted a triennial survey of its members. The most recent survey conducted in 1983, provides some interesting information. Men in AA continue to outnumber women by 2 to 1. Younger members, under age 30, are continuing to grow in numbers. They now represent 20% of all AA members. Among this younger group, there are more women, 42%; there is more addiction to other drugs, 40% (and 79% of those under age 21); and half credit a rehab facility or counselor for their affiliation with AA. Of all those coming into AA, almost a third acknowledge a treatment program for the referral. That represents an increase of almost 63% since 1977. Thus, it appears that AA members represent an increasingly diverse group.

SPIRITUAL COUNSELING

There is increasing effort to educate and inform clergy members about alcohol abuse and alcoholism. The focus of the effort is to equip pastors, priests, rabbis, ministers, and chaplains who come into contact with alcoholics or their families to assist in early identification and help get the alcoholic into treatment. Presumably the merits of this effort are self-evident. There is plenty of room in the alcohol field for many different kinds of care providers. This section on spiritual counseling is not about this educational outreach to clergy members. Instead, we wish to discuss the contribution that clergy members, priests, or rabbis may make to the recovery process in their pastoral roles.

Alcoholics may have a need for pastoring, "shepherding," or spiritual counseling, as do other members of the population. In fact, their needs in this area may be especially acute. Attention to these needs may play a critical part in the recovery process.

It is not easy to discuss spiritual matters. Medical, social work, psychology, or rehabilitation textbooks do not include chapters on spiritual issues as they affect prospective clients and patients. The split between spirituality and the "rest of life" has been total. In our society, that means for many it has become an either/or choice. Because defining crisply what we mean by spiritual issues is not easy, let us begin by stating what it is not. By spiritual we do not mean the organized religions and churches. Religions can be thought of as organized groups and institutions that have arisen to meet spiritual needs. The spiritual concern is more basic than religion, however. In our view, the fact that civilizations have developed religions throughout history is evidence of a spiritual side to human beings.

There are also experiences, difficult to describe, that hint at another dimension different from but as real as our physical nature. They might be called "intimations of immortality," and they occur among sufficient numbers of people to give more evidence for the spiritual nature of humankind.

It is hard to believe in God, but it is far harder to disbelieve in Him.
EMERSON

In a variety of ways we can see an awakened interest in spiritual concerns in contemporary America. Whether it is transcendental meditation, Zen Buddhism, Indian gurus, Jesus "freaks," the "Moonies," mysticism, the Moral Majority, or the more traditional Judeo–Christian Western religions, people are flocking in. They are attempting to follow these teachings and precepts, with the hope that they will fill a void in their lives. It is being recognized that "making it," in terms of status, education, career, or material wealth, can still leave someone feeling there is something missing. This "something" is thought by many to be of a spiritual nature. This missing piece has even been described as a "God-shaped hole."

Alcoholism as spiritual search

How does this fit in with alcohol and alcoholism? First, it is worth reflecting on the fact that the very word most commonly used for alcohol is "spirits." This is surely no accident. Indeed, consider how alcohol is used. It is often used in the hope it will provide that missing something or at least turn off the gnawing ache. From bottled spirits, a drinker may seek a solution to life's problems, a release from pain, an escape from circumstances. For awhile it may do the job; but eventually it fails. To use spiritual language, you can even think of alcoholism as a pilgrimage that dead-ends. Alcohol is a false god. To use the words of the New Testament, it is not "living water."

If this is the case, and alcohol use has been in part prompted by spiritual thirst, the thirst remains when the alcoholic sobers up. Part of the recovery process must be aimed at quenching the thirst. Alcoholics Anonymous has recognized this fact. It speaks of alcoholism as a threefold disease, with physical, mental, and spiritual components. Part of the AA program is intended to help members by focusing on their spiritual needs. It is also worth noting that AA makes a clear distinction between spiritual growth and religion.

Clergy assistance

How can the clergy be of assistance? Ideally, the clergy are people within society who are the "experts" on spiritual matters. (Notice we say ideally.) In real life, clergy are human beings, too. The realities of religious institutions may have forced some to be fund raisers, social directors, community consciences, almost everything but spiritual mentors. Yet there are those out there who do, and maybe many more who long to, act as spiritual counselors and advisors. One way the clergy may be of potential assistance is to help the alcoholic deal with "sin" and feelings of guilt, worthlessness, and hopelessness. Many alcoholics, along with the public at large, are walking around as adults with virtually the same notions of God they had as 5-year-olds. He has a white beard, sits on a throne on a cloud, checks up on everything you do, and is out to get you if you aren't "good." This is certainly a caricature but also probably very close to the way most people really feel if they think about it. The alcoholic getting sober feels remorseful, guilt-ridden, worthless, endowed with a host of negative qualities, and devoid of good. In his mind, he certainly does not fit the picture of someone God would like to befriend or

hang around with. On the contrary, he probably feels that if God isn't punishing him, He ought to be! So the alcoholic may need some real assistance in updating his concept of God. There's a good chance some of his ideas will have to be revised. There's the idea that the church, and therefore (to him) God, is only for the "good" people. A glance at the New Testament and Christian traditions doesn't support this view, even if some parishes or congregations act that way. Jesus of Nazareth didn't exactly travel with the smart social set. He was found in the company of fishermen, prostitutes, lepers, and tax collectors! Whether a new perspective on God or a Higher Power leads to reinvolvement with a church, assists in affiliation with AA, or helps lessen the burden of guilt doesn't matter. Whichever it does, it is potentially a key factor in recovery.

Again, to use spiritual language, recovery from alcoholism involves a "conversion experience." The meaning of conversion is very simple: "to turn around" or "to transform." Contrasting the sober life to the alcoholic's drinking days certainly testifies to such a transformation. A conversion experience doesn't necessarily imply blinding lights, visions, or a dramatic turning point, although it might. Indeed, if it does involve a startling experience of some nature, the sober alcoholic will need some substantial aid in dealing with and understanding this experience.

Carl Jung

It is interesting to note that an eminent psychiatrist recognized this spiritual dimension of alcoholism and recovery over 40 years ago, in the days when alcoholism was considered hopeless by the medical profession. The physician was Carl Jung. Roland H., who had been through the treatment route for alcoholism prior to this, sought out Jung in 1931. He saw Jung as the court of last resort, admired him greatly, and remained in therapy with him for about a year. Shortly after terminating therapy, Roland lapsed back into drinking. Because of this unfortunate development, he returned to Jung. On his return, Jung told Roland his condition was hopeless as far as psychiatry and medicine of that day were concerned. Very desperate and grabbing at straws, Roland asked if there was any hope at all. Jung replied that there might be, provided Roland could have a spiritual or religious experience—a genuine conversion experience. Although comparatively rare, this had been known to lead to recovery for alcoholics. So Jung advised Roland to place himself in a religious atmosphere and hope (pray) for the best. The "best" in fact occurred.

The details of the story can be found in an exchange of letters between Bill W. and Jung, published in the AA magazine, *The Grapevine*.

In recounting this story many years later, Jung observed that unrecognized spiritual needs can lead people into great difficulty and distress. Either "real religious insight or the protective wall of human community is essential to protect man from this." In talking specifically of Roland H., Jung wrote: "His craving for alcohol was the equivalent, on a low level, of the spiritual thirst of our being for wholeness, expressed in medieval language; the union with God."

You would be hard pressed to find a drinker who would equate the use of alcohol with a search for God! Heaven only knows they are too sophisticated, too contemporary, too scientific for that. Yet an objective examination of their use of alcohol may reveal otherwise. Alcohol is viewed as a magical potion, with the drinker expecting it to do the miraculous.

Counselor's role

If convinced that a spiritual dimension may be touched by both alcoholism and recovery, what do you as a counselor do? First, we recommend cultivating some members of the clergy in your area. It seems that many communities have at least one member of the clergy who has stumbled into the alcohol field—and we do mean stumbled. It was not a deliberate, intellectual decision. It may have occurred through a troubled parishioner who has gotten well, or one whom the clergy member couldn't tolerate watching drink himself to death any longer and so blundered through an intervention. The pastor may have aided some alcoholics and finds more and more showing up on his doorstep for help. This is the one you want. If you cannot find him, find one with whom you are comfortable talking about spiritual or religious issues. That means one with whom you don't feel silly or awkward and, equally important, who doesn't squirm in his seat either at talk of spiritual issues. (Mention of God and religion can make people, including some clergy, as uncomfortable as talk of drinking can!)

Once you find a resource person, it is an easy matter to provide your client with an opportunity to talk with that person. One way to make the contact is simply to suggest that the client sit down and talk with Joe Smith, who happens to be a Catholic priest, or a Jewish rabbi, or something else. It may also be worth pointing out to the client that the topic of concern is important and that the individual mentioned may be helpful in sorting it out. Set up the appointment and let the clergy member take it from there. Some residential programs include a clergy member as a resource person. This person may simply be available to counsel with clients or may take part in the formal program, for example, by providing a lecture in the educational series. What is important is that the presence and availability of this person gives the message to clients that matters of the spirit are indeed important and not silly.

How do you recognize the person for whom spiritual counseling may be useful? First, let us assume you have found a clergy member who doesn't wag a finger, deliver hellfire and brimstone lectures, or pass out religious tracts at the drop of a hat. Rather, you have found a warm, caring, accepting, and supportive individual. A chat with someone like that isn't going to hurt anyone. So don't worry about inappropriate referrals. Nonetheless, for some clients the contact may be particularly meaningful. Among these are individuals who have a spiritual or religious background and are not experiencing it as a source of support, but rather as a condemnation. Others may, in their course of sobriety, be conscientiously attempting to work the AA program, but have some problem that is hanging them up. Another group who may experience difficulty are Jewish alcoholics. "Everyone knows Jews don't become alcoholics." This presents a problem for those who do. It has been said that there is double the amount of denial and consequent guilt for them. Because the Jewish religion is practiced within the context of a community, there may also be a doubled sense of estrangement. A contact with a rabbi may be very important. It is worth pointing out that someone can be culturally or ethnically Jewish, but not have been religiously Jewish. The intrusion of an alcohol problem may well provide the push to the Jewish alcoholic to explore his spiritual heritage. The alcohol counselor is advised to be sensitive to this as well as supportive.

The counselor, as an individual, may or may not consider spiritual issues personally important. What the caregiver needs is an awareness of the possibility (even probability) of this dimension's importance to a client, as well as a willingness to provide the client with a referral to an appropriate individual.

ACTIVITIES THERAPY

Activities therapy has been a mainstay of inpatient psychiatric treatment for a long time. It includes recreational therapy and occupational therapy. To those unfamiliar with this field, the activities that are encompassed may look like "recreation" or "free time" or diversionary activities, not *real* treatment. For the activities therapist, the event, such as a picnic—with the associated menu planning, the food preparation, the set up and clean up afterwards—is of far less importance than the process.

Recall that the alcoholic's repertoire of social skills has been depleted. Plus, it may have been a long time since there have been social interactions without alcohol, or tasks completed, and responsibilities assumed and fulfilled. Then too, during treatment, the alcoholic can only spend so many hours a day in individual counseling, or group therapy sessions, or listening to lectures and films. Activities therapy programs can be the forum in which the alcoholic has the opportunity, with support and guidance, to try on some of the new behaviors that may have been discussed elsewhere and will be necessary in sobriety. It's the portion of the therapeutic program that will most closely approximate real life.

A common dilemma for recovering alcoholics is how to fill the time that they used to spend drinking. A part of the activity therapist's task will be in identifying past interests or activities, which can be reawakened, resumed, not only to fill time, but to provide a sense of accomplishment and belonging. The activities therapist will be sensitive to the client's limitations. The person who used to have a half-acre garden and is now going to make up for lost time by plowing up another half acre can be cautioned to take it easy. One or two tomato plants, plus a few lettuce and radish plants may be the place to start.

One of the more imaginative adaptations of activities therapy in alcohol treatment has been the use of Outward Bound programs. Outward Bound grew out of the experience of the British Merchant Navy in the Second World War. It was discovered that among the merchant marines who were stranded at sea, those who survived were not the youngest and most physically fit, but their older "life-seasoned" comrades. From that observation, an attempt was made to provide a training experience, which incorporated physically challenging and psychologically demanding tasks to demonstrate to people their capacities.

Outward Bound was introduced in this country in 1961. Since that time, its programs have been conducted in a range of settings from rehabilitation programs for the physically handicapped to training for corporation executives. The programs can be a day or several days or a week in length. Typically, an Outward

Bound experience combines both group exercises, such as a group being confronted with the task of getting all of its members over a 10-foot wall, with individual activities, such as rock climbing. Within alcohol treatment programs, Outward Bound has been made available to individual clients, and clients with their families, and has been used particularly with adolescents. The staff often includes an alcohol counselor as well as the Outward Bound instructors. Integral to Outward Bound is discussing and processing what transpires. Alcoholics Anonymous adages such as "one step (day) at a time," or "easy does it," might be the topic of a group meeting. These take on new meaning to someone who has been involved in scaling a cliff or negotiating a ropes course 20 feet off the ground.

BEHAVIORAL THERAPY

The terms *behavioral therapy* and *behavior modification* have been bandied about by many folks, some of whom are poorly informed about them. Unfortunately, in too many facilities the terms have been used so casually and imprecisely that what is being discussed is not correctly termed behavior modification at all. Here we would like to give you a brief rundown of the pertinent factors, as well as point out some of the things that have muddied the waters.

Obviously, any therapy has as its goal the modification of behavior. However, behavioral therapy is the clinical application of the principles psychologists have discovered about how people learn. The basic idea is that if a behavior can be learned, it can also be changed. This can be done in several ways. To put it very simply, one way is to introduce new and competing behavior in place of the old or unwanted behavior. By using the principles by which people learn, the new behavior is reinforced (the person experiences positive results), and the old behavior is in effect "squeezed out." Another technique is to negatively reinforce (punish) the unwanted behavior; therefore, it becomes less frequent. Recall the discussion of Johnson's model for the development of drinking behavior in Chapter 6. That explanation was based on learning principles. People *learn* what alcohol can do; alcohol can be counted on in anyone's early drinking career to have dependable consequences. Therefore, drinking is reinforced and the behavior continues.

Behavioral therapy is a field of psychology that developed rapidly over the past 20 years. In the course of this development, its techniques have been applied to the treatment of alcoholism.

However, the early behavioral approaches fared no better than did other psychological approaches, which were unable to offer by themselves a full explanation of alcoholism, nor alone were sufficient to guide treatment.

Historically, one of the first behavioral methods to be used in alcohol treatment was *aversion therapy*. In this case, a form of punishment was used to modify behavior. The behavior was drinking and the goal was abstinence. Electric shock and chemicals were the things primarily used. The alcoholic would be given something to drink and as he swallowed the alcohol, the shock would be applied. Alternatively, a drug similar to disulfiram would induce sickness. The procedure was repeated periodically until it was felt that the drinking was so thoroughly associated with unpleasantness in the subject's mind that the person would be unlikely to continue drinking alcohol. Although short-term success was assured, those results were not maintained over the long haul. Aversion therapy of this form is now used very rarely.

As one author noted in reviewing behavioral approaches toward alcoholism,

> Historically there have been many fads in the treatment of alcoholism....Behavioral therapists have also been guilty of this faddism in the form of aversion therapy. There is a recent awareness on the part of behavior therapists that this rather naive approach to a complex clinical problem such as alcoholism is unwarranted.

As the field became more sophisticated, it became clear that an effective behavioral treatment program could not be based on a single behavioral technique. One cannot expect all clients to be successfully treated by the routine application of the same procedure. Just as not all clients are given the same kind and dose of a medication, neither can they be given the same behavioral treatment. Thus, efforts were then made to devise total alcohol treatment programs based on a variety of behavioral techniques.

One such approach received considerable attention and generated much controversy. It centered on efforts by behavioral psychologists in the early 1970s to teach controlled drinking to alcoholics. The Sobells (Linda and Mark) are the researchers most closely identified with this. The initial reports were quite positive. Controlled drinking as an alternative to abstinence seemed to be further supported by several studies that followed up on individuals who had been treated for alcoholism. Though the programs the clients had been involved in were generally abstinence oriented, a portion of these clients (although nowhere near a majority) were found to have returned to moderate drinking without problems. The report that generated the most attention (in part because its findings were released at a news conference rather than being reported in a scientific journal) was the Rand study, funded by the federal government to explore the outcomes of clients in NIAAA-funded treatment programs.

The optimism about controlled drinking as an alternative to abstinence could not be sustained. Several researchers very painstakingly tracked down the subjects of the Sobells' study to see how they had fared over the long haul. Of the original group, only one was described as continuing as a moderate drinker. All of the others had serious problems and relapses, and four had died of alcohol-related problems. Similarly, Vaillant's work suggested that once an addictive state has been established, a return to moderate, controlled drinking is very rare. If one follows people over time as he did, the proportion who can maintain a controlled drinking pattern declines. It must also be noted that "controlled" drinking is not to be confused with "social" drinking. Most social drinkers do not need to invest considerable attention and energy to maintain a moderate level of alcohol use.

At this point, designing treatment programs exclusively on behavioral methods has largely been abandoned. What has now become far more commonplace is the use of behavioral methods to treat particular aspects of an alcohol problem. These will be described next.

Behavioral techniques

A recovering alcoholic is likely to face a multitude of problems. One of these is a high level of anxiety. It can be of a temporary nature, the initial discomfort with the nondrinking life, or more chronic if one is the "nervous" type. Whether temporary or chronic, it is a darned uncomfortable state, and the alcoholic has a *very* low tolerance for it. Many alcoholics have used alcohol for the temporary and quick relief of anxiety. What is now remembered (and longed for!) is the almost instant relief of a large swig of booze. When alcohol or drugs are no longer an option, the alcoholic has quite a problem: how to deal with anxiety. Many simply "sweat it out"; some relapse over it.

Some positive things can be done to alleviate their anxiety, or anyone's, for that matter. One is *relaxation therapy*. It is based on the fact that if the body and breathing are relaxed, it is impossible to *feel* anxious. The mind rejects the paradox of a relaxed body and a "tense" mind. Working with this fact, some techniques have evolved to counter anxiety with relaxation. Generally, the therapist vocally guides a person through a progressive tensing and relaxing of the various body parts. The relaxing can start with the toes and work up, or with the scalp and work down. The process involves first tensing the muscles, then relaxing them at the direction of the therapist. These directions are generally given in a modulated, soft voice. When the client is quite relaxed, it is suggested a soothing picture be held in her mind. The client is then given a tape of the process to take home, with instructions on its use, as an aid in learning the relaxation. With practice, the relaxed state is achieved more easily and quickly. In some cases, the client may finally learn to totally relax with just the thought of the "picture." Once thoroughly learned, the relaxation response can be substituted for anxiety at will. The response once learned can be used by the recovering alcoholic to deal with those situations in which taking a drink might be almost second nature.

Another behavioral approach to deal with anxiety, *systematic desensitization*, builds upon the relaxation response. This technique has been found quite useful in treating people with phobias. This is an appropriate approach for recovering alcoholics who may feel panic at the mere thought of a particular situation. We mean real panic, so that even the idea gets them so uptight that the temptation to drink may be overwhelming.

In this process, with the aid of a therapist the recovering alcoholic approaches the situation that leads to anxiety in his imagination. As the anxiety builds up, he is directed to use relaxation techniques he has been taught. Gradually, going step by step, he uses the relaxation to turn off the anxiety, and eventually the situation itself becomes much less anxiety provoking. In alcohol treatment, this approach has been used for persons whose drinking has been partially prompted by stressful, anxiety-producing situations. Given another option, they are better equipped to avoid drinking when such situations arise.

Assertiveness training, another technique that has evolved from behavioral methods, is also sometimes used in alcoholism treatment. One of the more common applications is to help recovering alcoholics learn how to say no comfortably to a drink in social situations, or say no to other things that might threaten sobriety.

Record keeping is another tool borrowed from behavioral psychology. Not uncommonly, recovering alcoholics may report finding themselves with some regularity "suddenly" in the midst of some kind of troubling situation (e.g., an argument with a spouse), with no idea as to what led up to it. There may instead be periods of inexplicable despondency. Often there is a pattern, but the key elements may not be apparent. Record keeping, a personal log or diary, of one's daily routine sometimes is used to help identify the precursors that lead up to difficult moments. Recovery requires all kinds of readjustments to routines. By keeping a daily log, over time, one may have a far better sense of what areas need attention.

MEDITATION

Meditation is frequently suggested as an aid in achieving and maintaining sobriety. Any number of approaches are available to those wishing to try it, and many treatment centers include an introduction to one or more. Although meditation has different goals depending on the type practiced, the process of reaching a meditative state is somewhat similar to relaxation. A fairly relaxed state is necessary before meditation can begin. Some schools of meditation use techniques quite similar to relaxation methods as a lead-in to the meditation period. In yoga, physical exercises are coupled with mental suggestions as a precursor. Studies have shown that altered physiological states accompany meditation or deep relaxation. Altered breathing patterns and different brain-wave patterns are examples. These changes are independent of the type of meditation practiced. The real physical response in part accounts for the feelings of well-being after meditation periods. Those who practice meditation find it, on the whole, a rewarding experience. Many also find in the experience some form of inspiration or spiritual help. Several highly advertised schools of meditation are receiving attention these days. You might investigate those that are available for clients who express an interest in meditation.

A word of caution is needed here. Alcoholics tend to go overboard. Meditation should never be a substitute for their other prescribed treatment. Also, there are extremists in every area of life, and meditation is no exception to exploitation. That is why some personal knowledge of what is available, who is using it, and how it affects those who do use it is necessary before advising your alcoholic client to try it. Meditation is only helpful if it alleviates the alcoholic's anxiety and allows him to continue learning how to function better in the world, not out of it.

What is a meditation?
Perhaps a meditation is a daydream, a daydream of the soul as the beloved and God, the lover, their meeting in the tryst of prayer, their yearning for one another after parting; a daydream of their being united again.

Or perhaps a meditation is the becoming aware of the human soul of its loneliness and the anticipation of its being united with the One who transcends the All and is able to come past one's own defenses.

Or perhaps, again, it is a standing back with the whole of the cosmos before one's mind's eye as one's heart is being filled with the sheer joy of seeing the balances of the All and one's own self as part of it.

Or perhaps a searching into one's own motives, values, and wishes, with the light of the Torah against the background of the past.

Or perhaps...[2]

DISULFIRAM (ANTABUSE)

In the late 1940s, by a series of accidents, a group of Danish scientists discovered that a drug they were testing for other purposes, disulfiram, led to a marked reaction when alcohol was ingested by a person exposed to it. Disulfiram alters the metabolism of alcohol by blocking out an enzyme necessary for the breakdown of acetaldehyde, an intermediate product of alcohol metabolism. Acetaldehyde is normally present in the body in small amounts, in somewhat larger ones when alcohol is ingested, and in toxic amounts when alcohol is taken into the body after disulfiram medication.

This adverse physical reaction is characterized by throbbing in the head and neck, flushing, breathing difficulty, nausea, vomiting, sweating, tachycardia (rapid heartbeat), weakness, and vertigo. The intensity of the reaction can vary from person to person and varies also with the amount of disulfiram present and the amount of alcohol taken in. Disulfiram is excreted slowly from the body, so the possibility of a reaction is present for 4 to 5 days after the last dose and in some cases longer. Because of this reaction, Antabuse, the trade name for disulfiram, has been widely used in the treatment of alcoholism.

Prescription, administration, and use

Over the years since disulfiram's discovery, trial and error and research have led to some suggestions for its prescription, administration, and use in alcohol treatment. Disulfiram is not a cure for alcoholism. At best, it can only postpone the drink for the alcoholic. If the recovering alcoholic chooses to use disulfiram as an adjunct to AA, psychotherapy, group therapy, and so forth, it can be most useful in helping him not take an impulsive drink. Because it stays in the system for such a long time, whatever caused the impulsive desire for a drink can be examined. It possibly could be worked through during the 5-day grace period to forestall the need for the drink entirely.

Anyone who wishes to use it should be allowed to do so, provided they are physically and mentally able. The client should first be thoroughly examined by a physician to determine physical status. Some conditions contraindicate disulfiram usage. There is still some debate as to the need for such caution with lower doses, but only the client's physician can decide this point. In some cases physicians consider the risks of a disulfiram reaction not as dire as continued drinking certainly would be. Its administration should usually be supervised for at least a short time. Preferably the spouse should *not* be the one expected to do this. Ideally, a visit to an outpatient clinic for the doses is desirable. Also ideally, it should be used in combination with other support therapies.

The client taking disulfiram should be thoroughly informed of the dangers of a possible reaction. A variety of substances (such as cough syrup, wine sauces, paint fumes) that contain some alcohol can cause a reaction. Clients taking disulfiram should be provided a list of such substances. They should carry a card or wear a "Med-Alert disk" stating they are taking disulfiram. Some medications given to accident victims or in emergency situations could cause a disulfiram reaction compounding whatever else is wrong. There is no way to be able to tell if an unconscious person has been taking disulfiram without such a warning.

A client who wishes to use disulfiram often begins taking the drug in a hospital setting after primary detoxification. Generally, one tablet (0.5 gm) daily for 5 days is given, then half a tablet daily thereafter. During the initial 5 days the client is carefully monitored for side effects. Once the client is receiving the maintenance dosage, he can continue for as long as he and his therapist feel it to be beneficial.

Disulfiram seems also to free the alcoholic's mind from the constant battle against the bottle. When someone decides to take the pill on a given day, that person has made one choice that will postpone that drink for at least 4 or 5 days. If he continues to take it daily, that fourth or fifth day is always well out ahead. He can then begin to acquire or relearn behaviors other than drinking behaviors, and the habits of sobriety can take hold.

Disulfiram has been described as a crutch (which is not really out of place when one's legs are impaired!). Instead, one might think of it as buying sober time until the alcoholic's "legs"

TABLE 3

Some alcohol-containing preparations for coughs, colds, and congestion

Drug	Manufacturer	Percentage of Alcohol
Actol Expectorant	Beecham Labs	12.5
Ambenyl Expectorant	Parke-Davis	5.0
Calcidrine Syrup	Abbott	6.0
Chlor-Trimeton Syrup	Schering	7.0
Citra Forte Syrup	Boyle	2.0
Coryban-D Syrup	Pfipharmecs	7.5
Demazin Syrup	Schering	7.5
Dilaudid Cough Syrup	Knoll	5.0
Dimetane Elixir	Robins	3.0
Dimetane Expectorant	Robins	3.5
Dimetane Expectorant-DC	Robins	3.5
Dimetapp Elixir	Robins	2.3
Hycotuss Expectorant and Syrup	Endo	10.0
Lufyllin-GG	Mallinckrodt	17.0
Novahistine DH	Dow Pharmaceuticals	5.0
Novahistine DMX	Dow Pharmaceuticals	10.0
Novahistine Elixir	Dow Pharmaceuticals	5.0
Novahistine Expectorant	Dow Pharmaceticals	7.5
Nyquil Cough Syrup	Vicks	25.0
Ornacol Liquid	Smith Kline & French	8.0
Periactin Syrup	Merck Sharp & Dohme	5.0
Pertussin 8-Hour Syrup	Cheeseborough-Ponds	9.5
Phenergan Expectorant, Plain	Wyeth	7.0
Phenergan Expectorant, Codeine	Wyeth	7.0
Phenergan Expectorant VC, Plain	Wyeth	7.0
Phenergan Expectorant VC, Codeine	Wyeth	7.0
Phenergan Expectorant, Pediatric	Wyeth	7.0
Phenergan Syrup Fortis (25 mg)	Wyeth	1.5
Polaramine Expectorant	Schering	7.2
Quibron Elixir	Mead Johnson	15.0
Robitussin	Robins	3.5
Robitussin A-C	Robins	3.5
Robitussin-PE and DM	Robins	1.4
Robitussin-CF	Robins	4.75
Rondec-DM	Ross	0.6
Theo-Organidin Elixir	Wampole	15.0
Triaminic Expectorant	Dorsey	5.0
Triaminic Expectorant DH	Dorsey	5.0
Tussar-2 Syrup	Armour	5.0
Tussar SF Syrup	Armour	12.0
Tussi-Organidin	Wampole	15.0
Tuss-Orande	Smith Kline & French	7.5
Tylenol Elixir	McNeil	7.0
Tylenol Elixir with Codeine	McNeil	7.0
Tylenol Drops	McNeil	7.0
Vicks Formula 44	Vicks	10.0

TABLE 4

Other commonly used drugs containing alcohol

Drug	Manufacturer	Percentage of Alcohol
Alurate Elixir	Roche	20.0
Anaspaz-PB Liquid	Ascher	15.0
Aromatic Elixir	Circle	22.0
Asbron Elixir	Dorsey	15.0
Atarax Syrup	Roerig	0.5
Belladonna, Tincture of	Purepac	67.0
Benadryl Elixir	Parke-Davis	14.0
Bentyl-Phenobarbital Syrup	Merrell-National	19.0
Carbrital Elixir	Parke-Davis	18.0
Cas-Evac	Parke-Davis	18.0
Choledyl Elixir	Warner/Chilcott	20.0
Decadron Elixir	Merck Sharp & Dohme	5.0
Dexedrine Elixir	Smith Kline & French	10.0
Donnagel	Robins	3.8
Donnagel-PG	Robins	5.0
Donnatal Elixir	Robins	23.0
Dramamine Liquid	Searle Labs	5.0
Elixophyllin	Cooper	20.0
Elixophyllin-KI	Cooper	10.0
Feosol Elixir	Smith Kline & French	5.0
Gevrabon	Lederle	18.0
Ipecac Syrup	Lilly	2.0
Isuprel Comp. Elixir	Winthrop	19.0
Kaochlor S-F	Warren-Teed	5.0
Kaon Elixir	Warren-Teed	5.0
Kay Ciel	Cooper	4.0
Kay Ciel Elixir	Cooper	4.0
Marax Syrup	Roerig	5.0
Mellaril Concentrate	Sandoz	3.0
Minocin Syrup	Lederle	5.0
Modane Liquid	Warren-Teed	5.0
Nembutal Elixir	Abbott	18.0
Paregoric Tincture		45.0
Parelixir	Purdue Frederick	18.0
Parepectolin	Rorer	0.69
Propadrine Elixir	Merck Sharp & Dohme	16.0
Serpasil Elixir	CIBA	12.0
Tedral Elixir	Warner/Chilcott	15.0
Temaril Syrup	Smith Kline & French	5.7
Theolixir (Elixir Theophylline)	Ulmer	20.0
Valadol	Squibb	9.0
Vita-Metrazol Elixir	Knoll	15.0

TABLE 5

Some nonalcoholic preparations for coughs, colds, congestion

Drug	Manufacturer
Actifed-C Expectorant	Burroughs Wellcome
Actifed Syrup	Burroughs Wellcome
Hycodan Syrup	Eaton Labs.
Ipsatol Syrup	Key
Omni-Tuss	Pennwalt
Orthoxicol Syrup	Upjohn
Sudafed Syrup	Burroughs Wellcome
Triaminic Syrup	Dorsey
Triaminicol Syrup	Dorsey
Tussionex Suspension	Pennwalt

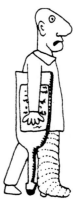

are steadier and other healthy supports are found. The supports may be available already, but the alcoholic has to be able to use them successfully. Until then, these supports would fit him no better than a basketball player's crutch would fit a 10-year-old boy!

Medications containing alcohol

Alcohol, in one or another of its many forms, was for centuries virtually *the* pharmacological agent available to physicians. In the twentieth century, alcohol has had rather limited uses. Now, in addition to being used externally as an antiseptic (e.g., to wash the skin before giving an injection or taking a blood sample—*except* when this sample is being obtained to measure blood alcohol levels), its only other major use is as an "inert" medium or carrier for liquid medications. Alcohol is an almost universal ingredient of cough medicines and liquid cold preparations sold over the counter or by prescription (see Table 3). Moreover, the percentage of alcohol is often not insignificant. Nyquil, for example, contains 25% alcohol. That's 50 proof! Alcohol is also an ingredient in a variety of other kinds of commonly used liquid medication (see Table 4).

Recovering alcoholics in general are well advised to avoid alcohol-containing preparations. For those taking disulfiram (Antabuse), it is imperative.

Some preparations available for coughs and colds do not contain alcohol. These are listed in Table 5. However, some of these contain substances also having psychoactive properties. Although using such agents will avoid the danger of Antabuse reactions, the recovering alcoholics may wish to carefully monitor their exposure to the effects of any such drugs—by carefully measuring the medication, taking it only at specified intervals, or settling for hot lemonade with honey and consoling themselves that this cold too shall pass.

RESOURCES AND FURTHER READING

Alcoholics Anonymous. New York: Alcoholics Anonymous Publishing, 1955.

Gitlow, S., Peyser, H.S.: Alcoholism: A Practical Treatment Guide. New York: Grune & Stratton, 1980.

Kaufman, E., and Pattison, E.M.: Differential Methods of Family Therapy in the Treatment of Alcoholism. *J Stud Alcoh* 42(11):951–971, 1981.

Keiter, R.H.: Principles of disulfiram use. *Psychosomatics* 24(5):483–487,1983.

Lawson, G., Peterson, J.S., Lawson, A.: Alcoholism and the Family. Rockville, MD: Aspen Publication, 1983.

Pattison, E.M., Kaufman, E. (Eds.): Encyclopedic Handbook of Alcoholism. New York: Gardner Press, 1982.

Pendry, M.L., Maltzman, I.M., West, L.J.: Controlled drinking by alcoholics? New findings and a reevaluation of a major affirmative study. *Science* 217:169-175, 1982.

Sobell, M.L., Sobell, L.C.: Second-year treatment outcome of alcoholics treated by individualized behavior therapy: Results. *Behavioral Research Therapy* 14:195–215, 1976.

Thiebout, H.: Surrender vs. compliance in therapy. *J Stud Alcoh* 14:58–68, 1953.

Zimberg, S., Wallace, J., Blume, S.B: Practical Approaches to Alcoholism Psychotherapy. New York: Plenum Press, 1978.

Special considerations

10

In this chapter we wish to focus upon other issues warranting a counselor's attention: the special characteristics of special populations, particularly adolescents and the elderly; the interface of alcohol problems and psychiatric concerns; and the issues of multiple drug use.

SPECIAL POPULATIONS

Although not quite the "hot topic" it was several years ago, the unique characteristics of client subgroups need to be appreciated and acknowledged. There may be remarkable similarities between the 15-year-old alcohol abuser, who also dabbles with cocaine, and the 72-year-old retired schoolteacher, who never drank anything stronger than sherry. But that should not blind us to the equally significant differences! We cannot begin to touch upon the central points to bear in mind if one is involved with clients from particular ethnic or racial or religious groups. We must be content to urge you to speak with more experienced colleagues as well as to seek out articles and books, which are becoming available in ever greater numbers. However, two groups warrant special mention—due to their numbers in the population and because they crosscut any ethnic, racial, or religious groupings—adolescents and the elderly.

Adolescents

Adolescence is indeed a special period of life. It lies at the back door of childhood yet at the very doorstep of adulthood. At no comparable time in life do more physical and emotional changes take place in such a narrow span of time.

Adolescence as a term is less than 150 years old. Prior to that time, one grew straight from childhood into adulthood. The needs of family and culture demanded earlier work and community responsibilities. Survival depended on it. With increasing industrialization, children left the factories and fields to spend more time in school, play, and idle time. Society became increasingly aware of the presence of teenagers as a group who had and still have as yet fairly undefinable roles and rights. Most texts define adolescence as the period from 12 to 21. Physical and legal determinants would suggest otherwise. Physical changes indicative of the beginning of adolescence may begin as early as age 7 and not end until the mid-20s.. Legal age differs between state and federal jurisdictions. Varied drinking ages, youthful draft requirements, and the 18-year-old voting age have clouded the definition.

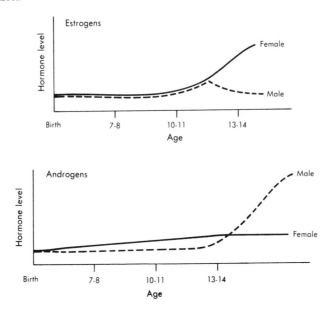

Physical changes. The most striking aspect of adolescence is the rapid physical growth. These changes are mediated by the sex hormones. The rough charts above indicate that the first recognizable change in the male is due to fat increase dictated by a small but gradual increase in estrogen. Every boy gains weight at the expense of height during these years. Some boys due to become tall and muscular men are actually chubby and effeminate-looking during these early adolescent years. To add insult to injury, the next body part to grow is the feet, then thighs, which

make him appear short waisted and gawky. This slows, allowing the rest of the body to catch up. Androgen influence may not come for a few years, with often unrecognizable pigment changes in the scrotal sac, then enlargement of the penis, testes, the beginning of pubic hair, and early voice changes. The first nocturnal emission or "wet dream" may occur as early as age 10 or as late as age 15. Even so, the majority of boys remain "relatively sterile" till age 15. The major male growth spurt appears at age 14 1/2 and is due to growth in the backbone. This averages 4 to 4 1/2 inches over an 18-month period. Some boys will shoot up 8 to 10 more inches during this time. Axillary and facial hair soon follow. Facial hair may develop entirely in 1 year. Other boys, equally normal but with different genes, may not complete the facial and body-hair growth till the mid to late 20s.

We are indeed taller than our ancestors, which can be shown from historical evidence. Clothing, doorways, and furniture were made for shorter men and women. Better nutrition is mainly responsible for the changes seen.

A girl's first hormonal response is around age 7 or 8 with a normal vaginal discharge called *leukorrhea*. The feet then grow, but this is rarely as noticeable a change as in the male. A breast "button" begins about age 11 under the skin of one breast first, to be followed in weeks or months under the remaining breast. The breasts develop into adult breasts over a span of 4 to 5 years. Pubic hair begins approximately 6 months after the breast button stage. The hips widen, and the backbone gains 3 to 4 inches before she is ready for her menses. Although a critical body weight is not the only initiator, the body is influenced by this. If other criteria are met, such as developing breasts, pubic hair, widened hips, and growth spurt, a sample of American girls will begin their menses weighing from 100 to 105 pounds. Nutrition has a great deal to do with the menarche (first menses); girls in countries with poor nutritional standards begin their menses 2 to 3 years later. The mean age for menarche in America is 12. (Pilgrim girls, who suffered from many nutritional deprivations, often had menarche delayed until age 17.) A regular menstrual cycle is not established immediately. Quite commonly a girl will have anovulatory (no egg) periods for 6 to 18 months before having ovulatory periods. This change may bring an increased weight gain, breast tenderness, occasional emotional lability, and cramps at the midcycle. These are consequences of progesterone, a hormone now secreted by the ovary at the time of ovulation. An adult pattern in ovulation will not be completed till the early 20s.

Until puberty, boys and girls are equally strong in muscle strength (if corrected for height and weight). Total body fat increases in girls by 50% from ages 12 to 18, whereas a similar decrease of 50% occurs in boys. Muscle cell size and number increase in boys; muscle cell size alone increases in girls. Internal organs, such as the heart, double in size. Blood pressure increases with demands of growth. Pulse rate decreases, and the ability to break down fatigue metabolites in muscle prepares the male, especially, for the role of hunter and runner that was so important for survival centuries ago.

Marked fatigue coupled with overwhelming strength is often difficult to fully appreciate. An adolescent may wolf down several quarts of milk, a full meal or two, play many hours of active sports, and yet complain bitterly of severe fatigue at all times! This human metabolic furnace needs the food and rest as well as the drive to have the machine function and test itself out. These bodily inconsistencies often show in mood swings and unpredictable demands for self-satisfaction and physical expression.

The rapidity of these changes tends to produce almost a physiological confusion in many adolescents. Quite commonly, they become preoccupied with themselves. This can lead to an overconcern with their health. In some instances it is almost hypochondriacal. Adolescents may complain of things that to an adult appear very minor. The thing to remember is that their concern is very real and deep. Attention should be paid to their concerns. Remembering the rapid rate of physical changes that confront adolescents makes their preoccupation with their bodies understandable.

Characteristics. Adolescence characteristically is an extremely healthy time of life. In general, adolescents do not die off from the kinds of things that strike the rest of us, such as heart disease. The major causes of adolescent deaths are accidents and suicide. The result of this healthiness is that adults tend to assume that adolescents with problems are not really sick, and thus do not give their complaints the hearing they deserve. Another characteristic of adolescence is a truly tremendous need to conform to their peers. There is the need to dress alike, wear the same hairstyle, listen to the same music, and even think alike. A perpetual concern of the adolescent is that he or she is different. Although the sequence of physical development is the same, there is still variation in the age of onset and the rate of development. This can be a big concern for adolescents, whether the teenager is ahead, behind, or just on the norm. Worry about being different is a particular concern for the adolescent who

Let us eat and drink for tomorrow we shall die.

ISAIAH 22:13

may want or need professional help. The adolescent will not go unless it is "peer acceptable." Kids often stay away from caregivers out of fear. A big fear is that if they go, sure enough something really wrong will be found. This, to their minds, would officially certify them as different. They cannot tolerate that.

Also characteristic of adolescence is wildly fluctuating behavior. It frequently alternates between wild, agitated periods and times of quiescence. A flurry of even psychotic-type thinking is not uncommon. This does not mean that adolescents are psychotic for a time and then get over it. There are just some periods when their thinking really only makes sense to themselves and possibly to their friends. For example, if not selected for the play cast, he may be sure that "proves" he will be a failure his entire life. If she is denied the use of the family car on Friday, she may overreact. With a perfectly straight face, she may accuse her parents of *never* letting her have the car, even as she stands there with the car keys ready to drive off.

Adolescence is very much a time of two steps forward and one back, with an occasional jog to one side or the other. Despite the ups and downs, it is usually a continuing, if uneven, upward trip to maturity.

Another point of importance: in early adolescence, girls are developmentally ahead of boys. At the onset of puberty, girls are physically about 2 years ahead. This makes a difference in social functioning because social development takes place in tandem with physical development. This can cause problems in social interactions for boys and girls of the same age. Their ideas of what makes a good party or what is appropriate behavior may differ considerably. The girls may consider their male peers dumbos. The boys, aware of the girls' assessments, may be shaken up, while the girls feel dislocated, too. With the uneven development of boys and girls during early adolescence, girls have an edge in school. In reading skills, for example, girls may be a year ahead of boys. There is a catching-up period later, but in dealing with younger adolescents, keep this disparity in mind.

Four tasks. When does adolescence end? There are fairly clear-cut signs that mark the beginnings of the process. There is more to adolescence than just physical maturation. Defining the end can lead to philosophical discussions of "maturity." Doesn't everyone know a 45- or 65-year-old "adolescent?" There is more to assigning an end point than just considering a numerical age.

One way of thinking about the adolescent period is to assign to it four tasks. From this point of view, once the tasks have been reasonably accomplished, the person is launched into adulthood. These tasks are not tackled in any neat order or sequence. It is not like the consistent pattern of physical development. They are more like four interwoven themes, the dominant issues of adolescence.

One task of adolescence is *acceptance of the biological role.* This means acquiring some degree of comfort with your identity as either male or female. It is an intellectual effort that has nothing to do with sexuality or experimentation with sexuality.

A second task is the *struggle to become comfortable with heterosexuality.* This does not mean struggling with the question of "how to make out at the drive-in!" It is the much more important question: "How do you get along with the opposite sex at all, ever?" Prior to adolescence, boys and girls are far more casual with one another. With adolescence, those days are over. Simply to walk by a member of the opposite sex and say "Hi" without blushing, giggling, or throwing up can be a problem. To become a heterosexual person—able to carry on all manner of social and eventually sexual activities with a member of the opposite sex—does not come easily. It is fraught with insecurity and considerable self-consciousness. If you force yourself to remember your own adolescence, some memories of awkwardness and uncertainty come to the fore. Thus, there is the adolescent who does not ask for a date because of the anticipated no. Being dateless is much more tolerable than hearing a no.

Another task is the *choice of an occupational identity.* It becomes important to find an answer to "What am I going to do (be)?" There are usually several false starts to this one. Think of the 5-year-old who wants to be a fireman. He probably never will be, but he gets a lot of mileage for awhile just thinking he is. It is not so different for adolescents. It is not helpful to pooh-pooh the first ideas they come up with. Nor is handing over an inheritance and saying "Go ahead" recommended. They need some time to work it out in their heads. A fair amount of indecision, plus some real lulu ideas are to be expected.

The fourth task is the *struggle toward independence.* This is a real conflict. There is the internal push to break away from home and parents, and, at the same time, the desire to remain comfortably cared for. The conflict shows up in rebellion, because there are not many ways to feel independent when living at home, being fed, checked on, prodded, and examined by parents. Rebellion of some type is so common to this period of life that an adolescent who does not rebel in some fashion should be suspect.

Rebellion. Rebellion can be seen in such things as manner of dress and appearance. It is usually the opposite of what the parents' generation accepts. Little ways of testing out crop up in being late from a date, buying something without permission, arguing with the parents over just anything. The kids are aware of their dependency, and they don't like it. There is even some shame over being in such a position. It is important that the parents recognize the rebellion and respond to it. In this era of "Be friends with your kids," some well-meaning parents have accepted *any* behavior from their kids. For example, if the kids, for the sake of rebellion, brought home some grass to smoke, their parents might light up, too. Often the kids will do whatever they can, just to get their parents angry. They are so often reminded by others of how much they look or act like their father or mother. They don't want that. *Adolescents want to be themselves.* They do not want to be carbon copies of their parents, whom they probably don't much like at the moment. Going out and doing some drinking with the gang, doing something weird to their hair that Mom and Dad will hate, not cleaning their rooms, helping the neighbors but not their parents, are all fairly common ways of testing out and attempting to assert independence.

Destructive rebellion can occur when the parents either do not recognize the rebellion or do not respond to it. It can take many forms, such as running out of the house after an argument and driving off at 80 or 90 miles per hour, getting really drunk, running away, or, for girls, getting pregnant despite frequent warnings from their overrestrictive parents to avoid all sexual activities.

There are many roadblocks to completion of these four basic tasks. One results from a social paradox. Adolescents are physically ready for adult roles long before our society allows it. Studies of other societies and cultures point this out. In some societies adolescence doesn't cover a decade or more. It is about a 1-hour trip! Light a fire, beat a gong, send the boy into the woods to pray to the moon; when he returns, hand him a spear and a wife, and he's in business. Our society dictates instead that people stay in an adolescent position for a frightfully long time: junior high school, senior high school, college, graduate school. Another social paradox comes from the mixed messages. On the one hand, it's "Be heterosexual, get a date," "Get a job," "Be grown up." On the other, it's "Be back by 1 AM," "Save the money for college," "Don't argue with me." The confusion of "Grow up, but stay under my control" can introduce tensions.

Another roadblock can be posed by alcohol and drug use. It should be pointed out that of all groups, adolescents are those most likely to be involved with drugs other than alcohol. In considering adolescents it is imperative to think broadly, in terms of substance use and abuse, or chemical dependency, not just in terms of alcohol and alcoholism.

This has been a very brief overview of adolescence. There are many excellent books on the subject should you want a more in-depth study. For our purposes here, it will suffice as a context in which to consider alcohol use.

Alcohol use. Alcohol use is common in adolescence. By age 13, 30% of boys and 22% of girls drink alcohol. By age 18, the number has jumped dramatically: 92% of boys and 73% of girls are drinkers.

Despite widespread alcohol use, adolescents tend to be uninformed about the effects of alcohol as a drug. Short on facts, adolescents tend more than adults to rely on myths. For example, beer, the overwhelming favorite beverage, is thought to be less intoxicating than distilled spirits. One study showed that 42% thought five to seven cans of beer could be drunk in 2 hours without risk of intoxication. Seventy percent believed cold showers could sober someone up, and 62% thought coffee would do it. Also, adolescents minimize the consequences of drinking. Only 8% thought their driving ability would be "much worse" under the influence. They also do not consider their being in an accident a real possibility, much less one that might result in serious injury or death.

Adolescents use alcohol in many different ways. Some of these ways are a normal part of the whole process. The "try it on" thread runs throughout adolescence. Alcohol is just one of the things to be tried. With drinking being a massive part of adult society, it is natural that the adolescent struggling toward adulthood will try it. Drinking is also attractive for either rebellious or risk-taking behavior.

Adolescent alcohol problems. Not unexpectedly accompanying adolescent drinking there are also alcohol problems. To cite just a few of the statistics from the ever-growing pile:

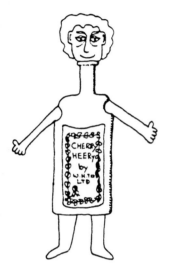

- In the 13 to 17 year age group, it is estimated there are three million problem drinkers, and over three hundred thousand teenage alcoholics
- Drinking is a significant problem for between 10% and 20% of adolescents.
- 11% of adolescents and 28% of high school seniors drink 5 or more drinks at least once a week.
- 97% of drug-abusing adolescents also use alcohol.
- Over the last 20 years, life expectancy has increased for all age groups *except* ages 15 to 24. The three leading causes of death in this age group are accidents, suicide, and homicide, all closely linked to alcohol and drug use.
- The *leading cause of death* between ages 16 and 24 is driving while impaired.
- Drivers age 16 to 24 years constitute 17% of the population; they are involved in 48% of fatal accidents.
- Daily, 14 adolescents, age 15 to 19 years, die and 360 are injured in alcohol-related traffic accidents.

One way to understand the high incidence of problems with substance abuse in adolescence is in terms of the adolescent developmental tasks cited earlier. The first task mentioned was the acceptance of one's biological role. For women the onset of their menstrual cycle provides clear biological evidence of their transition to adult functioning. For males the transition may be more difficult. But for both in contemporary America the question of how to know you are an adult is often difficult. For many adolescents drinking serves as a rite of passage. Not only is it an adult activity, it is also one way to be "one of the crowd." Drinking can provide entry to a group of peers. Even as an adult one is often encouraged to drink and given messages that not to drink is to be antisocial. For adolescents with their intolerance of differences and their increased vulnerability to following along with peers' behavior, not drinking at a party where others are drinking may be even harder for teenagers than for adults.

Also, an important part of accepting one's biological role is learning to be intimate with those of the opposite sex. This can be threatening to many adolescents. Alcohol can be used to avoid intimacy, or to seek intimacy without responsibility. "I wasn't myself last night, I was really plastered" can be said by either boys or girls to disavow what happened the night before. The same is true in the sexual realm, as a means of experimenting without taking responsibility. In our society being drunk has long provided a "way out." Often people are not held accountable for actions that occur when they are drunk. Thus, getting drunk can often help adolescents express these increasingly powerful impulses, without really taking direct responsibility for their behavior.

Part of the task of attaining independence is learning to set limits for themselves, to develop self-control. For some adolescents this is more difficult than for others. It is particularly difficult about issues like drinking where societal messages and alcohol advertising suggest that "having more than one" is appropriate adult behavior. In the process of learning self-control, adolescents react negatively to adults setting limits. If parents are too aggressive in forbidding alcohol use, it may backfire. Further confusing matters is that adolescent development is characterized as well by changes in patterns of thinking. Prior to age 12 to 13, adolescents generally adhere to concrete rules for behavior. From ages 13 to 15 years, adolescents are likely to question the justification of set rules. They feel that conventions are arbitrary, hence rules supporting them are invalid. By the age of 16 most of them begin to realize that some rules are necessary.

Another important task mentioned earlier is the development of a sense of identity. Part of the task of gaining an independent identity involves experimentation in all realms. Adolescents may use alcohol for help in experimenting with different roles and identities. Closely connected to this experimentation is risk taking. Some of this risk taking involves physical danger. Adolescents are said to have a "sense of invulnerability." Unfortunately, alcohol can further increase this sense of invulnerability and lead to risk taking with dangerous consequences. It is not surprising, as mentioned earlier, that accidents are the leading cause of death in adolescents, and that alcohol use and abuse is heavily implicated in fatal accidents from all causes.

As these adolescent developmental tasks are accomplished, the number of problem drinkers decreases. But for a significant proportion of problem drinkers, these problems will persist and grow worse. For far too many, the problem drinking may end in death or disability, long before either outcome.

Diagnosing alcohol/substance abuse. Often the temptation is to disregard adolescent alcohol or drug problems as "just a stage," or a normal feature of adolescence. The criteria for a diagnosis of alcohol abuse in adolescents are the same as those for adults. It involves a pattern of pathological use and impairment in social or occupational functioning due to use. Common signs of adolescent alcohol/substance abuse include the following:

- unexplained drop in grades
- irregular school attendance
- unaccounted for personal time
- wearing "druggie" clothing or jewelery
- increased money or poor justification of how money was spent
- change in personal priorities
- new group of friends
- change in health or grooming
- failure to provide specific answers to questions about activities
- possession of "drug" materials
- desire to be secretive or isolated
- unexplained disappearance of possessions in the home

Other symptoms one may see in adolescents are:

- decreased interest in school or family social activities, sports and hobbies
- attending parties where parents are not home to monitor behavior
- frequent "flu" episodes, chronic cough, chest pains, "allergy symptoms"
- impaired ability to fight off common infections, fatigue, and loss of vitality
- strange phone calls
- not returning home after school
- not bringing friends home
- collecting beer cans, pot paraphernalia, etc.
- drop in school performance
- inexplicable mood changes—irritability, hostility
- verbal (or physical) mistreatment of younger siblings
- impaired short term memory,
- frequent accidents
- feelings of loneliness, paranoia, and depression

Indicators of a significant problem would include any "covering up" or lying about drug and alcohol use or about activities, losing time from school because of alcohol or drug use, being hospitalized or arrested because of drinking/drug-related behavior, or truancy plus alcohol or drug use. Alcohol or drug use at school generally indicates heavy use. One should be particularly alert to the above signs and symptoms in children of alcoholics, who may have a genetic predisposition and the added pressures such a parent brings to the already laden tasks of this period.

Treatment

General considerations in working with adolescents. In working with an adolescent, it is wise to avoid obvious authority symbols, such as white coats, framed diplomas dripping off the walls, and a remote clinical attitude. Adolescents are probably already having some degree of difficulty with authority figures anyway, and they don't need you added to that list. Being somewhat informal in dress and setting can remove one barrier. On the other hand, spiked hair, playing tapes, sitting on a floor cushion, and sucking on a "roach" when they arrive won't go down very well either. They want you to know about those things, but not be into them; unless, of course, you really are (even then, leave the roach at home). An attempt to fake out the adolescent will fail. They are a hard group to fool, and they place a high premium on honesty. Respect this and honestly be yourself. This means asking for a translation of their vocabulary if you are not familiar with the lingo.

Empathy rather than sympathy is the goal. This is true of all therapeutic relationships. Sympathy is feeling like the other person. Empathy is knowing how the person feels, understanding it, but not feeling like he does at the moment. For instance, it is simply not helpful to be depressed along with the person.

In general, three types of therapy are done with adolescents. One involves *manipulation of the environment*. This can include arranging for the father to spend more time with his child, getting the kid who hates Shakespeare into a different school program, or organizing a temporary placement for the child whose parents are nonsupportive at the time. These can be very valuable interventions.

Standard insight therapy—psychological, psychiatrically oriented traditional therapy—is not often used. Not many adolescents are ready for, or even could benefit from, this kind of therapy. The ones who can benefit from it tend to be "bright," advantaged young people, who seem more capable and older than their peers or their chronological age would suggest.

The most commonly productive therapy is what could be termed a *relational approach*. This requires time for you to become well acquainted and for the adolescent to feel comfortable with you. The counselor is supportive of the person without doing it for him. The counselor is a neutral person, available to the adolescent in a very different way than are parents or peers.

The issue of confidentiality always comes up. It can be a mistake to guarantee that "nothing you say will ever leave this room." The counselor does have the responsibility for others as well as the adolescent client. Given blanket protection, what happens when the kid announces he plans to rob the local deli, or another says she plans to drive the family car off the road at the first opportunity? A different approach was suggested by Dr. Hugh MacNamee. His practice was to tell whomever he saw that though most of what they said would be held in confidence, if they told him anything that scared him about what they might do, that would be harmful to themselves or others, he was going to blow the whistle. He made it clear he would not do so without telling them; nonetheless, he would do it. In his experience, adolescents accept this, maybe even with relief. It may help to know that someone else is going to exert some control, especially if they are none too sure about their own inner controls at the moment.

In a similar vein, Dr. MacNamee would suggest keeping the adolescent posted on any contacts you have with others about him. If a parent calls, start off the next session by informing the adolescent, "Hey, your Dad called me, and he wanted...." If a letter needs to be written to a school, probation officer, or someone else, share what you are writing with the adolescent. The chances are fairly good his fantasy about what you might say is worse than anything you would actually say, no matter what the problem. Because trust is such an issue with adolescents, it is important that you be willing to say *to* them what you would say *about* them behind their backs.

Although the aforementioned is a good general approach to the issue of confidentiality, you may need to be aware of other complicating factors. In particular, we refer to the legal issues of a child's right to care versus parental rights to be informed. There may be circumstances in which an adolescent has a legal right to be seen and treated without parental knowledge or consent. In any case, the ground rules you are following must be clear to the adolescent client.

Alcohol/drug assessment. Once the issue of confidentiality has been cleared up, it is important to take a family history. Ask about alcohol or drug problems, prescription or nonprescription. Include the grandparents, uncles, aunts, brothers and sisters, and cousins, as well as the parents. Other important parts of the history include asking the adolescent how he spends his time. Ask him to describe a typical day. Ask what he and his friends do Saturday night. Ask about his peer group, about their age, activities, drug and alcohol use. Ask how they are seen and described by other groups in the high school, and then ask about his own use of drugs and alcohol. Ask about parental relationships. Ask about sleep, appetite, depression.

The fact that adolescent alcohol abuse can go on for as long as 6 years without being diagnosed is a tribute to the ability of these adolescents to hide their problems, to the ability of parents to avoid recognizing problems in their children, and to the ability of school systems to ignore or expel problem children. It is not unusual for parents to be actively protecting, rescuing, and taking care of a substance-abusing adolescent without realizing that this supports and prolongs the abuse. They make good on forged checks. They hire lawyers or pay to have legal charges dropped. They go to bat for them at school or blame school authorities for the problems. In our experience, parents must stop protecting these children and seek help for them instead.

When asking about drug and alcohol use begin by asking about the first time he or she was drunk, how much they drink now, how often, if they have ever tried to stop or cut down. Ask about blackouts, legal problems, and school problems. Finally, don't assume that an adolescent is providing a wholly accurate history about drug and alcohol use. Denial is a central characteristic of adolescent alcohol or drug abuse. It is important to get information from parents and teachers whenever you are concerned about adolescent alcohol or drug problems.

Getting adolescents into treatment. Although occasionally adolescents will spontaneously request treatment, more often they come to treatment under some duress. In working with them it is important to make it clear that your task is to help them, and that you are not an agent of their parents, of the law, or of the school system. At the same time, part of helping them may involve an intervention, which entails confrontation, and, as was mentioned earlier, total confidentiality cannot be assured.

In dealing with adolescents, the importance of working with the family cannot be overemphasized. The parents need to deal with their child's alcohol/substance abuse. And they must consider their behaviors which may have protected, covered up, or excused the problem. When it is clear that there is a significant problem, and all efforts to involve the adolescent in treatment have failed, the parents may need to seek legal help. Most states allow for parents to request state assistance if they feel they cannot enforce safe limits for their child. Although this is a very drastic and difficult step to take, it can be important when alcohol-abusing adolescents are acting in ways that endanger their lives. Probation can also be a way of mandating treatment for adolescents, but again this only works if the parents can stop protecting the adolescent from the consequences of his behavior.

Adolescent alcohol/substance abuse treatment. Once it has been determined that an adolescent needs treatment and the adolescent has agreed to treatment, it is important to proceed in a careful way. Because medical and psychiatric complications frequently accompany adolescent substance abuse, a thorough medical and psychiatric evaluation should precede or be an early part of any treatment plan. Treatment options include outpatient, residential, or hospital-based care and can involve individual, group, and family counseling, plus self-help groups such as AA or NA (Narcotics Anonymous). Halfway houses may also be helpful for adolescents who are not ready to return home from a hospital-based program, but who no longer need the structure of a hospital.

There are very good alcohol/drug treatment programs for adolescents. There are those, on the other hand, which might most kindly be described as "nontraditional," or those less concerned with therapeutics than with turning a profit. Don't forget the standard questions before referring an adolescent to any program: "Does the program work?" "Is the program drug free?" "Is there a strong family component?" "Is there a strong therapeutic component?" "Is there a strong educational component?" "Is the adolescent involved in treatment planning?" "Is there a peer component?" "Are there provisions for aftercare?" "What are the costs and risks of treatment, including both financial cost and time cost?" "What beliefs are instilled?" "What are the staff credentials, including training, experience, licensure and certification?" "Is there a full range of services, including pediatric, psychiatric, educational, psychological, and alcohol counselors?" "Is there involvement with AA?" "How does the program feel when you visit it?" "Does the program evaluate itself?" "Is the program accredited?" "If so, by whom?"

When referring an adolescent for treatment, it is important to remember that alcoholism is a chronic disease. Treatment does not end with discharge. The conceptual model to use is not that of an acute illness like appendicitis, where the offending tissue can be surgically removed and the problem will never recur. It is rather a chronic illness like asthma, or arthritis, where ongoing monitoring is always essential, and whereas some cases are mild and require only outpatient treatment, others may require hospitalization.

Adolescents and AA. For the adolescent with an alcohol/substance problem, how might AA be of use? The first thought might be that the adolescent would never identify with a group of predominantly 35- to 55-year-olds. In many areas, that stereotype of the AA group does not necessarily hold true; there are now in some locales what are called "young people's groups." There the average age is the low to mid-20s. Even if there are no young people's groups in your vicinity, age need not be a barrier to an adolescent's affiliating with AA. On the contrary, several features of AA might attract and intrigue the adolescent. It is a group of adults who will definitely not preach at him. Furthermore, given the collective life experiences within AA, the members are not likely to be shocked, outraged, or, for that matter, impressed by any of the adolescent's behavior. The members will generally treat the adolescent as an adult, presumably capable of making responsible choices, although cognizant that to do so isn't easy for anyone. There is within AA a ready assortment of potential surrogate parents, aunts, uncles, and grandparents. The intergenerational contact, possibly not available elsewhere to the adolescent, can be a plus. Also, AA remains sufficiently "unacceptable" so as not to be automatically written off by the adolescent wary of traditional, staid, "establishment," and out-of-it adult groups. Because being alcoholic or a drug abuser is still a stigmatized condition, the parents may be more uncomfortable than their children about AA attendance for adolescents. The counselor may need to help parents with this. In making a referral, the same guidelines outlined in the section on AA would apply. The adolescent is full of surprises; his receptivity to AA may well be another.

Prevention. One important task for anyone working with adolescents is to be aware of the potential problems that virtually any adolescent may encounter with respect to alcohol and drugs. Even if adolescents are not currently into drugs or alcohol, anticipatory discussion with them as to how they might handle the situation when it inevitably arises can be very helpful. For the adolescent who is having a problem of some kind, an alcohol/drug history is imperative. In many communities there are efforts underway through parent groups and groups of adolescents to support the development of healthy peer values and norms about alcohol/drug use.

The elderly

Dishonor not the old: we shall all be numbered among them.

APOCRYPHA: BENSIRA 8:6

On his show many years ago, Art Linkletter was interviewing children, and they came up with the following answers to a question he posed: "You can't play with toys anymore…the government pays for everything…you don't go to work…you wrinkle and shrink." The question was "What does it mean to grow old?" The responses of the children contain many of the stereotypes our society attributes to the elderly. They also show that this negative picture develops from a very early age. There is a stigma to growing old. The notion is that for the elderly there is no play or fun, no money, no usefulness, and no attractiveness.

It is important to recognize that in considering the elderly, we all really are talking about ourselves. It is inevitable: we will all age; we will all become the elderly. A participant at a recent geriatric conference reported being asked by a friend, "Give me the inside scoop…what can I do to keep from getting older?" The response the person received was simple: "Die now!" There is no other way to avoid aging. So, for those not themselves among the elderly, in thinking about the older person, imagine yourself years in the future, because many of the circumstances will probably be the same.

You are as young as your faith, as old as your doubt; as young as your self-confidence, as old as your fear; as young as your hope, as old as your despair.

S. ULLMAS. *From the Summit of Four Score Years*

Of the approximately 240 million people in the United States, 29 million are over age 65. This is the group arbitrarily defined as the elderly, or aged. Each day, 3000 die and 4000 reach their 65th birthday, so there is a net gain of 1000. By the year 1990, it is estimated that over 35 million persons will be over age 65; this will represent a larger percentage of the population than ever before. Consequently, the problems of the elderly, including alcoholism, that will be discussed are going to become a growing concern for our society.

Coping styles. Despite the inevitability of aging and despite the inevitability of physical problems arising as the years pass, there is an important thing to keep in mind. It has been said many times and in many different ways that you are as young as you want to be. This is only possible, however, if the person has some strengths going for him. The best predictor of the future, specifically how someone will handle growing old, is how the individual has handled the previous years. Individuals who have demonstrated flexibility as they have gone through life will adapt best to the inevitable stresses that come with getting older. These are the people who will be able to feel young, regardless of the number of birthdays they have celebrated.

Interestingly, as people get older, they become less similar and more individual. The only thing that remains alike for this group is the problems they face. There is a reason for this. Everyone going through life relies most heavily on the coping styles that seem to have served them well previously. With years and years of living, gradually individuals narrow down their responses. What looks, at first glance, like an egocentricity or eccentricity of old age is more likely a life-long behavior that has become one of the person's exclusive methods for dealing with stress. An example illustrating this point arose in the case of an elderly surgical patient for whom psychiatric consultation was requested. This man had a constant smile. In response to any question or statement by the nurse or doctors, he smiled, which was often felt to be wholly inappropriate. The treatment staff requested help in comprehending the patient's behavior. In the process of the psychiatric consultation, it became quite understandable. Friends, neighbors, and family of the man consistently described him as "good ole Joe, who always had a friendly word and a smile for everyone, the nicest man you'd ever want to meet." Now under the most fearful of situations, with many cognitive processes depleted, he was instinctively using his faithful, basic coping style. Very similarly, the person who goes through life with a pessimistic streak may become angry and sad in old age. People who have been fearful under stress may be timid and withdrawn in old age. On the other hand, people who have been very organized and always reliant on a definite schedule may try to handle everything by making lists in old age. What is true in each case is that the person has settled into a style that was present and successful in earlier life.

Main stresses. In working with the elderly, in order to understand what is evolving in an individual case, it is imperative for helping professionals to consider every possible piece of information. Integration of data from the social, medical, and emotional realm is essential for understanding what makes the elderly person tick in order to make an intelligent treatment plan. Four areas of stress should be considered in dealing with the elderly: stresses that arise from social factors; psychological factors; biological or physical problems; and, unfortunately, iatrogenic stresses due to the helping professions as they serve (or inadequately serve) the elderly.

Social stresses. These can be summarized under the phenomenon of the national addiction to youth. Television commercials highlight all types of products that can be used to disguise the process of aging. There is everything from hair colorings to dish detergents, which if used will make a mother's hands indistinguishable from her daughter's. Look around you. Who is being hired and who is being retired? Aging is equated with obsolescence and worthlessness. People who have been vital, contributing members of an organization suddenly find themselves with the title "honorary." It is often not an honor at all! It means these people have become figureheads; they have been replaced. The real work has been taken over by someone else.

Next, let us consider social stresses due to the biases of the helping professions. The National Institute of Mental Health only a decade ago spent a mere 1.1% of its budget for research on problems of the elderly. Only 1% of its budget for services went to provide for care of the elderly. This is now changing, but it gives a graphic picture of the relative importance placed on this group of people in the recent past. The real issue is one of *attitude*. If one examines the dynamics behind this attitude, then one can see why there has been "disinterest" and "avoidance." Generally, the medical profession and other helping people, including family and friends, are overwhelmed by the multiplicity, chronicity, and confusing nature of the disorders of aging. Caregivers often feel helpless with the elderly and harbor self-doubts about whether they can contribute, both in a satisfactory manner and in a manner that is personally gratifying. To put it another way, most of us like to see results, to see things happen, to believe there is a "before" and "after" picture, in which the difference is clear. Also, it is important to feel that the part we have played, however big or small, has influenced this difference.

Helpers like it when someone puts out her hand and says "thank you," and the elderly often say, "Don't bug me....I don't want help." If you consider who it is that voluntarily comes into most clinical agencies, it is not the elderly. Those who do come are usually coerced into it. Helpers do not like complainers. What do the elderly say? "This hurts; that hurts...you're not nice enough...you don't come soon enough...my old doctor was much better...do this, do that." Helpers like patients who receive maximum cures in the minimum of time. This certainly is not the elderly. There are more visits, more problems, more time. Helpers like patients who get well. How many of the elderly are cured? How can you take away their diabetes, their arthritis, the pain from the memory of a lost spouse? Helpers like patients who take their advice. With the elderly, you suggest A, and they'll often do B.

These interactional dynamics are understandable but only aggravate the problem. They may rub the helpers' instincts the wrong way. The result is that many potential caregivers decide they do not like working with the elderly, and it shows. Very few clinicians volunteer to take on elderly clients. If an elderly client comes into a helping agency, the chances are good that the person who sees the client may soon decide to transfer the case to someone more "appropriate" or refer the client to another agency.

Another factor that gets in the way of their receiving adequate care from helping people is that they *may resent the helper's youth, just as the helper fears their elderliness*. Also, the elderly generally dislike the dependent status that goes along with being a client or patient. It is the opposite of what they want, which is to be independent and secure and feel a sense of worth. Being in treatment implies that something is wrong with them. It also means that someone else is partially in charge and telling them how to run their lives.

Psychological stresses. The common denominator is loss. No matter how you slice it, the elderly must constantly deal with loss. The elderly may try to handle loss in a number of ways. One is the widely used defense of *denial*. In response to an observation that a client's hand is more swollen, he may well say, "Oh no, it's no different than it's always been." If a close friend is in the hospital and very seriously ill, she may dismiss the seriousness and claim it is "just another of her spells, she'll be out, perky as ever in a day or two." Another common way of handling loss is by *somatization*. This means bringing the emotional content out in the open, but "saying" it in terms of the body hurts. This is why so many of the elderly are labeled hypochondriacal. When he says his knee hurts and he really cannot get up that day, what he also may be saying is that he hurts inside, emotionally. Because he may not get attention for emotional pains, having something wrong physically or "mechanically" is socially more acceptable. Another way of handling loss is *restricting affect*. Instead of saying it does not exist, as with denial, there is a withdrawing. They become less involved, so they do not hear about the bad things happening. By being less a part of the world, they are less vulnerable. Unfortunately, all these defenses boomerang and work against the elderly. How are love, affection,

and concern expressed? Through words, behavior, and many nonverbal cues—a smile, a nod, a touch. After so many years of living, the elderly certainly know the signs of affection and caring or of distancing and detachment. By withdrawing when they are fearful, they may well see others reciprocally withdrawing; the elderly may then be left without any source of affection, interest, and caring. This they, in turn, read as dislike, and they may feel their initial withdrawing was justified. Therefore, one of the prime treatment techniques with the elderly is to reach out to them, literally. Smile, touch them, sit close to them. Attempt to reach through the barrier they may have erected with the "protective" psychological defenses mentioned.

The elderly frequently overinterpret what helping people instinctively say when reaching out to the aged. There are often statements like "you're lucky to be alive…quit worrying about things…grow old gracefully." What the elderly hear is someone telling them to ignore their losses, or that the person making such statements does not want to get close to them. The elderly's response is that they do not want to grow old gracefully, they do not want to be "easy to manage," they want to go out with a bang, leave a mark—they want to be individuals to the last day.

Loss. In the geriatric population losses are steady, predictable, and often come in bunches. And even if they do not, they are still numerous. What are the specific losses?

There is the loss that comes from the *illnesses* and *deaths* of family and friends. The older you get, statistically the more likely that those about you will begin to falter. So there are the obvious losses of supports and companionship. Not necessarily as obvious is that the deaths of others also lead to questioning about loss of self, anticipation of one's own death. This may sometimes be the source of anxiety attacks among the elderly.

There is the loss that comes from the geographical *separations of family.* This begins earlier in life, as children go to school and later leave home for college, the service, and eventually to marry. For the elderly, this may be especially difficult, because 50% of all grandparents do not have their grandchildren living close by. As new generations are being born, they are not accessible to the older generation whose lives are coming to a close.

There is the loss of *money* through earned income. Whether income is supplemented through pensions, social security, or savings, the elderly usually do not have as much money as they did earlier in their lives. Dollars not only represent buying power; they also have symbolic values. Money represents power, stature, value, and independence. Lack of money has obvious implications in vital areas of self-esteem.

There are the losses that accompany *retirement*: loss of status, gratification, and often most important, identity. With retirement, you lose who you have been. This refers not only to retirement from a job; it includes retirement from anything, from being a mother, or a grandmother, or from being a person who walked around the block. Often accompanying retirement is a loss of privacy. For married couples, retirement may mean more togetherness than they have had for years. Both will have to change routines and habits and be forced to accommodate the presence of the other. The expectations may also be tremendous. Retirement, in most people's fantasies, is thought to usher in the "golden years," provide the opportunity to do the things that have been put off. There may well be a letdown.

There is also the loss of *body functions and skills*, which may include a loss of attractiveness. Older people may develop body odors. They lose their teeth. They are more prone to infection. For women, the skin may become dry, including the skin of the vagina, which can lead to vaginal discharges and dyspareunia (painful intercourse). For men, there is a general loss of muscle tone. Everything begins to stick out where it shouldn't. As physical problems arise, this may lead to loss of skills. The carpenter with arthritis or the tremors of Parkinson's disease will be unable to do the things that were formerly possible and rewarding.

How about sex and the elderly? The most prevalent lay myth is that the elderly have no interest in sex. Physiologically, aging of itself need not greatly affect sexual functioning. With advancing years, it takes a little longer to achieve an erection, a little more time to the point of ejaculation, orgasm is a little less intense, and a little more time is required before orgasms can be reexperienced. However, if the elderly are physically healthy, there is no reason why they should not be sexually active. The biggest factors influencing sexual activity in the elderly are the availability of a partner and social pressures. Among the elderly, when a partner dies, the survivor is often not encouraged to date or remarry. What is considered virility at age 25 is seen as lechery after age 65. Even when both partners are alive, if they are living in an institution or in the home of children, sexual activity may well be frowned on, or "not allowed."

Another loss is of *sensation*. With aging, the senses become less acute. What this means is that the elderly are then deprived of accurate cues from their environment. This may be a big factor in the development of suspiciousness in older persons. Any paranoid elderly person should have hearing and vision evaluated. The most powerful loss, the loss no elderly person is prepared to understand or accept, is the loss of thinking ability. This may happen imperceptibly over a period of time. It comes from the loss of cortical brain function. Suddenly a person who has been an accountant or a schoolteacher, for example, is adding $2 + 2$ and it doesn't equal 4 every time. This is embarrassing and scary and, though they may be able to stand losing other things, to "lose one's mind" is the ultimate indignity.

The result of all or any of these losses is that self-respect, integrity, dignity, and self-esteem are threatened. The implication can be that usefulness is questioned and life is ebbing away. The feeling may well be that "my work is over."

Biological stresses. Of the elderly, only 5% are institutionalized in nursing homes, convalescent centers, or similar facilities. However, 45% of the elderly have some serious physical disability, such as heart disease, diabetes, lung disease, or arthritis. About 25% also have a significant functional psychological problem, with depression the most prevalent. Understandably, as life expectancy increases and we live longer, there is more vulnerability to the natural course of disease. For this part of the population, receiving medical care and paying medical bills can mean additional big problems. The elderly have twice as many visits to a physician, their average hospital stay is three and one-half times longer than for person under age 65, and the hospital stay costs five times more than for the under-65 group. Ironically, for this medically fragile group, insurance coverage (including Medicare) is often less adequate than is coverage for younger persons. Thus, those with the greatest need for medical care, the highest medical expenses, and the least ability to pay have the poorest insurance coverage of any group.

Alcoholism is also a big problem for the elderly. Dr. Robert Butler formerly of the National Institute of Aging estimates that 20% have a significant alcohol problem. These problems are also ignored for many of the same reasons that sex in the elderly is dismissed without a further thought. "That nice old lady drinks too much (or is interested in sex)!" "Never!" Some of these elderly have had a long history of alcohol use and abuse; they may have been alcoholics for a good long time, but with adequate medical care have somehow lived to old age. However, with the overall deterioration of physical functioning, the alcohol use may

begin to take a heavier toll and become an increasingly difficult problem. Also, among the elderly are persons who do not have a prior history of alcohol abuse; their alcoholism may be described as late onset. The stresses of aging may have been too great or come too fast and at the wrong time. They have turned to alcohol as a coping mechanism. The subgroup of the total population with the highest risk for alcoholism is widowers over age 65. Whatever the variety of alcoholism present, intervention is important. All too often we are likely to dismiss the elderly with "what do they have to live for anyway…they have been drinking all these years, they'll never stop now…I don't want to be the one who asks them to give up the bottle." The *quality* of any amount of life left to any of us would better be the paramount concern. We would not hesitate to assume that a 35-year-old man ought to get treated for his problem even though he could easily be killed in an auto accident next year. The elderly deserve just as much, if not more, consideration.

Depressive illness is very prevalent among the elderly. There may well be a physiological basis for this. The levels of neurochemicals (serotonin and norepinephrine) thought to be associated with depression change in the brain as people get older. These depressions, then, are not necessarily tied solely to situational events. However, because so many things are likely to be going on in the surrounding environment for the elderly, it is too easy to forget the potential benefits of judiciously prescribed antidepressants. Malnourishment is all too common in the elderly. This can cause several syndromes that may look like depressions. Many physical ailments, due to disease processes themselves, manifest as depression.

Depression in the elderly may not present like depression in younger persons, with tearfulness, inability to sleep, or loss of appetite. Some of the tips for recognizing depression in the elderly are an increased sensitivity to pain, refusing to get out of bed when physical problems don't require bed rest, poor concentration, a marked narrowing of coping style, and an upsurge of physical complaints. Often, the poor concentration leads to absent-mindedness and inattentiveness, which are misdiagnosed as defective memory and ultimately as "senility," while the depression goes unrecognized and untreated. Senility is really a useless clinical term. The proper phrase should be *dementia*, which means irreversible cognitive impairment. However, all cognitive impairment should be considered reversible (delirium) until proven otherwise. It should also be remembered that alcohol abuse, as well as sometimes creating problems itself, can, in patients with dementia make the confusion worse. The elderly deserve an aggressive search for potentially treatable, reversible causes of organic brain syndromes by qualified medical personnel.

Suicide among the elderly is a very big problem. Twenty-five percent of those who commit suicide are over age 65. The rate of suicide for those over 65 is five times that of the general population. After age 75, the rate is eight times higher. In working with the elderly, a suicide evaluation is not to be neglected, because so many depressions are masked in their appearance.

Let us eat and drink; for tomorrow we die.

I CORINTHIANS 15:32

Iatrogenic stresses. Unfortunately, the medical problems of the elderly may be aggravated by the medical profession's insensitivities to the psychological and basic physiological changes in the elderly. All too often there is overprescription of medication in attempts to keep behavior controlled rather than diagnosed. Too few clinicians take into account the dramatically altered way the elderly metabolize medications, which means that fewer medicines in combination and lowered doses of any drug are required. There is also a tendency by everyone concerned to ignore the fact that alcohol, too, is a toxic drug. The combination of alcohol with other medications in light of the altered metabolism for both can create serious problems. Rarely is there any thought of whether the client can afford the medicine prescribed. Also, there is an overestimate of the client's ability to comply with directions for taking medications. A poignant example of this was the case of an elderly woman who was discharged from the hospital with a number of medications. She had been admitted in severe congestive heart failure but had responded well to chemical treatment of hypertension and fluid retention. Within 2 weeks of her return home, her condition began to deteriorate, which was a source of dismay and consternation to her physicians. The client was thought surely to be purposefully causing her ailments, and a psychiatrist, who was asked to consult on the case, decided to make a home visit. The woman knew which medications to take, when, and for what conditions. However, there was one problem. As she handed the bottle of capsules to the psychiatrist, with her crippled arthritic fingers, the "diagnosis" became obvious: the child-proof cap! She had been unable to open the bottles and therefore unable to take the medicine. This is a vivid reminder of the need to consider all the available information in assessing the problems of the elderly.

Practical treatment suggestions

1. If the elderly have some symptoms of psychological problems or physical problems, including a problem with alcohol, provide the same treatment you would for someone younger. Too often, problems of the elderly are dismissed under the assumption that the elderly are just complainers, "senile," unlikely to benefit, will die soon anyway, or are incapable of appreciating help.

2. In making an evaluation of an older person, do a comprehensive assessment rather than just a symptom-oriented search. Pay attention to the social, financial, emotional, medical, cognitive, and self-care status. The latter is often overlooked. Is the person able to do the daily activities required for well-being, such as preparing meals, getting groceries, taking medications as prescribed?

Portrait of an old man who gets drunk on sacramental wine

3. Recent literature suggests that signs of alcohol abuse in the elderly may be less obvious. For example, DWI is an unlikely occurrence if the elderly no longer drive. Instead of accepting self-neglect, confusion, or repeated falls as the vicissitudes of aging, they should prompt questions about alcohol use, just as they would in a younger person.

4. Because many elderly persons are reluctant to seek or receive professional help, a family member is often the person to make the first contact. This will initially be your best source of information about the person. Be sure to find out the family's views of the situation, their ideas, and fears. Whatever the problem, the chances are good that something can be done to improve the picture. Let the family know about this optimism. It often comes as a surprise to them that their elderly relative may get better.

5. Sometimes the family will appear to you as unhelpful, unsympathetic, or uncaring. This may be infuriating and annoy you. Even if this happens, do not alienate the family. Whatever problems there may be with the family, it is possibly the only support system the client has.

6. In dealing with the elderly, remind yourself that you are working with survivors. The fact that they have made it even this far means they have some strengths. These people have stuck their necks out in the past and taken risks. Find out how they have done it, and see if you can help them replicate that. Also, raise their expectations that indeed they can "make it" again, just as they have before.

7. Use all the possible resources at your disposal. In many instances the elderly need to become reinvolved in the world around them. Meaningful contacts can come from a variety of people, not just from professional helpers. The janitor in the client's apartment building, a neighbor, or a crossing guard at the street corner may all be potential allies. If the person was once active in a church group, civic organization, or other community group, but has lost contact, get in touch with the organization. There is often a member who will visit or be able to assist in other ways. Many communities have senior citizen centers. They offer a wide range of resources: everything from a social program, to Meals-on-Wheels, to counseling on Social Security and Medicare, to transportation. If there is a single agency to cultivate, this is the one.

8. In your interviews with the elderly, the importance of reaching out, showing interest, and having physical contact has already been mentioned. Also be active. Do not merely sit there and grunt from time to time. Your quietness may too easily be interpreted by them as distance and dislike. Another very important thing to do is to provide cues to orient the elderly. Mention dates, day of the week, current events. For anyone who has had any cognitive slippage, good cues from the environment are very helpful. In conversation with the elderly, don't stick with neutral topics like the weather all the time. Try to engage them in some topics of common interest to you both (such as gardening or baseball), as well as some controversial topic, something with some zip. This stimulates their egos, because it implies that you not only want *their* opinions, but you want *them* to listen to yours.

9. If you give specific information to the client, also write it down for him in legible handwriting. This makes it much easier for the client to comply. If family members are present, tell them the directions, too. In thinking about compliance and what can be done to assist the elderly in participating in treatment, take some time to think about how your agency functions. What does it mean for an elderly client coming to see you? Are there long waits at several different offices on several different floors? Does it require navigating difficult stairs, elevators, and hallways in the process? Are there times of day that make the use of public transportation easier? Consider such factors, and make adjustments to make it much easier for your elderly clients. In specific terms, make every

Drink because you are happy, but never because you are miserable.

G.K. CHESTERTON

effort to do things in as uncomplicated, convenient, nonembarrassing, and economical a fashion as possible.

10. Separate sympathy and empathy. Sympathy is feeling sorry for someone. The elderly don't want that; it makes them feel like children. Empathy means you understand, or want to understand. This is what they would like.

11. Be aware that you may be thought of and responded to as any number of important people in your client's long life. Also, you may alternately represent grandchild, child, parent, peer, and authority figure to them at various points in treatment, even in the same interview, and at the same time.

12. Display integrity with the elderly. Do not try to mislead them or lie to them. They are too experienced with all the con games in life. If they ask you questions, give them straight answers. This, however, does not mean being brutal in the name of "honesty." For example, in speaking with a client you might well say, "Many other people I talk with have concerns about death, do you?" The client responds, "No, I have pretty much come to terms with the idea of dying." You don't blurt out, "Well, you better think about it, you only have 6 months to live." That is *not* integrity.

13. In working with elderly clients, set specific goals. Make sure that the initial ones are easily attainable. This means they can have some surefire positive experiences. With that under their belts, they are more likely to take some risks and attempt other things.

14. Make home visits. Home visits are the key to working with this group. It may be the only thing that will break down their resistance and help them get treatment. Very few will seek help on their own initiative. So, if someone is not willing to come to your office, give him a call. Ask if you can make an appointment to see him at home. If the response you get is, "I don't want you to come," don't quit. Your next line is, "Well, if I'm ever in the area, I'd like to stop by." And try to do that. Bring some small token gift, such as notepaper or flowers. After your visit, you may well find the resistance has disappeared.

    The home visit can be vital in making an adequate assessment. Seeing the person in his own home, where security is at its peak, provides a much better picture of how the person is getting along, as well as the plusses and minuses of the environment. It also allows the client to be spontaneous in emotions and behavior.

If you regularly make home visits, beware of making the person "stay in trouble" in order to see you. Don't just visit in a crisis. Instead, stop in to hear about successes. Your visits may be a real high point for the person, who may not like to think of losing this contact. Make a visit the day after the client's first day on a new volunteer job, for example.

15. Beware of arranging things for the elderly that will be seen as something trivial to occupy their time. If there is a crafts class, the point ought to be to teach them a skill, an art, not to keep them busy. Many of the elderly also have something they can teach others. The carpenter who is no longer steady enough to swing a hammer and drive a nail will be able to provide consultation to do-it-yourselfers who want to remodel their homes. The elderly have a richness of life experiences and much to contribute.

16. Thoroughly evaluate symptoms of memory loss, disorientation, and behavioral changes to uncover potentially treatable causes of organic brain syndrome. Have clients show you all their medicines, including over-the-counter types. Coordinate medical care to avoid duplication of prescriptions.

In closing, the task in working with the elderly is to assist them in rediscovering strengths, getting involved with people, and discovering life is worth living, at whatever age.

SUICIDE EVALUATION AND PREVENTION

Alcohol use and suicide go together. Recall from Chapter 1 that in 65% of all suicide attempts the individual had been drinking, and that 40% of all successful suicides are related to alcohol. The suicide rate in alcoholics is fifty-five times that of the general population. Before we all commit suicide ourselves over these statistics, we should consider why suicide and alcohol are related, and what we can do about it.

Types of suicide: succeeders, attempters, and threateners

For practical purposes, there are several different groups to be considered when examining suicide. First are the succeeders, those who succeed and *intended to*. Classically, these are lonely white men over 50 years of age or lonely teenagers. They use violent means such as a gun or hanging, and their methods are calculated and secretive. Second are those who succeed but did *not* intend to. These are the attempters. Classically they are white women, ages 20 to 40, often with interpersonal conflicts, whose "method" is pills, and whose action is an impulsive response. Attempters die by mistake or miscalculation. For example, they lose track of dosage, or something goes wrong with their plans for rescue. The attempter's intent is not so much to die as to elicit response from the environment. Emergency-room psychology, which dismisses this client with a firm kick in the pants, is inappropriate. Someone who is trying to gain attention by attempting suicide is in reality quite sick and deserves care. Third are the threateners, who use suicide as a lethal weapon: "If you leave me, I'll kill myself." They are often involved in a pathological relationship. These people usually do not follow through, but are frightened and guilt-ridden. It is a good idea for the therapist to challenge the threat and quickly remove the deadlock it has created.

Statistics and high-risk factors

The real statistic to keep in mind is that suicide is the second leading recorded cause of death in people under 18 or over 65. Sixty percent give some prior indication of their intent, thereby making it preventable. Typical indications might be "I have a friend…," "What would you think if…," stockpiling drugs, or giving away possessions. Take note of new behaviors as cues. People doing things they have never done before may often indicate they have suddenly decided to commit suicide and are now at peace. Examples might be *suddenly* playing cards, dancing, or taking out the garbage when they have never made a practice of this before.

Melancholy should be diverted by every means but drinking.
—Dr. Johnson

Certain high-risk factors should be identified if present: recent loss of a loved one; single, widowed, and/or childless people; people living in urban areas; being unemployed, nonreligious, or "oppressed." High-risk emotional factors include anger plus hopelessness, broken or pathological family/friend communications, and marital isolation. Verbal high-risk cues take the form of both direct statements: "I'm going to kill myself," or indirect indications: "I won't be around to give you any more trouble." People entering and *leaving* a depression are especially vulnerable, as are those with chronic illnesses like arthritis, high blood pressure, ulcers, and malignancies.

Recall that 65% of all suicide attempts are related to alcohol. Several reasons explain this correlation. First, the chemical nature of alcohol tends to release certain brain areas from control. The guarding mechanisms are let down. Hidden thoughts and impulses are released. (You may have witnessed incidents such as the intoxicated guy calling the boss an S.O.B.) Second, because of the chemical action of alcohol, a state is created wherein the integrative capacity of the brain is diminished. It is a condition in which aspects of memory and concentration are lost. Third, when alcohol is used as a medicine, it is unfortunately a good one to initially produce a mood of relaxation and pseudostability. In this state, people may think things are just the way they should be. They feel cool, calm, and collected. Suicide at this point may seem relevant and a good idea: "I'll just jump. It's the rational solution." More alcohol acts as a true depressant with obvious potential consequences. Finally, alcohol may also bring out psychological weakness. It may place people on the edge of reality, tip the scales, lead to loose associations, bring out psychosis, loosen normal fears, produce voices saying: "The thing to do is rid the world of you," or "The world is better off without you." In all these cases, alcohol acts as a catalyst, both physically and psychologically.

The most fertile ground for suicide is in cases of clinical depression. Most people who have the "blues" are not suicidal. They might think, "Gee, I wish I were dead, things are going so badly," or "I don't know how I'll make it. I might just drive off the road if things don't get better." Things usually do get better, however. On the other hand, a clinical depression is characterized by a consistently low mood over a period of weeks, plus weight changes, sleep problems, and other physical symptoms. Pessimism is a part of the illness, just as fever is a part of the flu. Feelings of how bad things are are part of the depression. Depression, therefore, is bad enough alone, but combined with alcohol, it is a potent mix. "There is no way out." "I'm a bad person—the only way out is to kill myself."

How to ask

The therapist should *always* ask about suicide with any person who is depressed. The thing to remember is that we have never killed anybody by asking. We have certainly missed helping people we could have helped by not asking. There is no way to instigate a suicidal attempt by common-sense asking. It will come as a relief to your clients if you do ask them. Use your own emotional barometer to find out whether they are depressed or whether they are sad. Check yourself in an interview every so often. Block out the client for a moment and ask, "How am I feeling right now? Am I sad, angry, scared? What am I feeling?" It is probably a pretty good barometer of how the client is feeling. The client often says he feels great; check your own gut reactions and trust them.

Ask every client about suicide, but let rapport develop first. Do not just have the client come in and immediately ask him intimate questions like "I'm Dr. G., how's your sex life?" or "Been hallucinating lately?" or "Hi—Wanna kill yourself?" He will probably want to kill *you*. Let rapport develop, and later say, "Now, we've talked about a lot of things these last 20 minutes. Have any of them ever gotten you to the point of feeling you couldn't go on any longer?" Don't leave it there; explain that when you say that, you mean suicide. Always say the word "suicide." Do not just ask clients if they ever thought of "throwing in the towel" or some other euphemism. They can take you pretty literally and might say, "Well, no. I dried myself pretty well this morning." You have to get yourself to say "suicide." Practice. It is not so easy to come right out and say it. The first few times it bombs something like this. "Gee, we've talked about a lot of things. Have any of them ever gotten you to the point of thinking about committing s—s-ah—s-th—." It's almost the kind of thing you need to practice in front of a mirror. "Su-i-cide. Suicide."

Clients may say, "Boy, you're kidding!" but it's not a hostile response. If anybody does say "Yes"—and he probably will tell you if he has been thinking about it—obtain as much information as you can. Then go on to say, "Well, when was the time you thought of it last?" "How about today?" Whenever the client was thinking of it last, find out what he was doing, how he thought about it, when he thought of it, and ascertain his plans for it as specifically as possible. In cases of most serious intent, the client will probably say, "Well, not only have I been thinking of it today, but I've been cleaning my gun, it's in my car, my car's outside." In other words, get all the data.

What to do

Try to diffuse the situation psychologically and in a practical way. For instance, offer alternatives. Say something like, "On the other hand, what specific reasons do you have for living?" Try to get to a positive thing. Start initiating reasons to live. The more seriously depressed the client, the fewer reasons he will see to live. Remember, that is part of the illness. He will say, "Nothing," and cry. At that point, try to reiterate things he told you earlier about himself that are reasons to live—a child, a spouse, a business. Give him the reason to live: "That child really needs you." If he doesn't come up with anything, give him 60 seconds to think of something—one reason—then support that enthusiastically: "You're right. Tremendous!" Back the client up! Fill in the picture, and lead him into ways he can do this practically. If it is

a child, for example, ask where the child is now. How can the parent be of help?

Another important thing is to make a referral, whenever possible, to a mental health clinic or mental health specialist. As a counselor, you have a key role in identifying potential suicides. You cannot expect yourself to single-handedly treat and manage the situation. Request a consultation for further evaluation. Possibly the person is in a real depression and needs the supervision of an inpatient facility and/or medications. So, call and make an appointment *before* the client leaves the office. In conjunction with the mental health clinic, a decision can be made about how quickly the person should be seen—immediately, later today, or tomorrow. If the client is already being seen by a therapist, contact the therapist. A therapist who is unaware of the situation will want to know and will also be able to provide guidance for you, so that you are working together. Don't be afraid you are stepping on anyone's toes. Anybody contemplating suicide cannot have too many people in his corner.

In passing, maybe here we can lay to rest any discomfort that arises from the philosophical debates on whether someone has a right to commit suicide. Looking at it from the practical side of the issue, anyone who thinks he does would just go ahead and do it. He wouldn't be in your office. Anyone who "happens" into a counselor's office, or phones, and acknowledges suicidal thoughts, directly or indirectly, is not there by chance. They are seeking help in settling their internal debate over life versus death. The counselor, as do other helping people, must come down clearly on the side of living. Similarly, when depressed, a client cannot *rationally* make this decision. Once the depression clears, most clients are very pleased you prevented their action on suicide plans.

If a client has a weapon, ask him to check it at the reception desk (or elsewhere on the premises). If it is at home, ask him to have someone else take possession of it and notify you when that is done. *Never* let a client who is suicidal (he usually improves during the interview) leave your office without your double-checking all the great plans he has for the rest of the day. Be specific. Call home to make sure someone will be there if that is the expectation. Give the client chores and support. Get something for him to do. Have somebody there to watch him around the clock and to give him the attention he needs. Set up another appointment to see him within 48 hours. Have him call you to check in later that day, or you call him. Be specific. Say, "I'd like to call you between 4 and 5," or at least "this afternoon." It is better not to give an exact time because that is often hard to meet. This kind of paternalism is needed at this time. The weaning and fostering of independence come later. Give reinforcements. "What do you like to do?" "What do you have to do?" "Do it and let me know how it goes."

The only times in talking with a client that you may precipitate something going wrong are the following three situations. It's simple logic, but it's also a trap.

1. If the client's theme is rejection and loss, for example, he feels his mother's death shows she did not love him, be careful you do not reject him or put him off.
2. If you agree with the client about how bad things are— for example, the client says, "I am a worthless person. I beat my child"—you may easily get into your own negative feelings about this. You might communicate "Well, you are right, that was a horrible thing to do." Do not crucify clients. Do not support their punitive guilt response.
3. The client says how bad he feels. You are tempted to say "I understand how badly you feel. I often feel that way myself." You're trying to sympathize and share his misery, but the client interprets this as permission to feel the way he does. You are getting away from the reasons the client has to live and are underscoring his pessimism. It is better to reinforce his reasons to live.

Other thoughts about evaluation and prevention come to mind. Get histories of previous suicide attempts. Anyone who has tried it once has a poor track record. A family history of suicide plus a broken home in childhood also increase the risk. With someone who has either attempted suicide or is thinking about it, reduce isolation from family and friends. Consider hospitalization under close supervision if supports are lacking. Remove guns, ropes, pills, and so on. Have him give you the weapon personally. Shake hands with the client as he leaves the office, and give him "something of yourself" to take with him to put in wallet or pocket, such as a piece of paper with your name and phone number. Try to make sure the client has only a 1-to 2-day supply of medication and no barbiturates such as glutethimide (Doriden), ethchlorvynol (Placidyl), methyprylon (Noludar), methaqualone (Quaalude), meprobamate (Equanil, Meprospan, Miltown), or chloral hydrate. A 7-day supply of tricyclic antide-

pressants (1000 mg) or a 5-day supply of meprobamate (Miltown) (8000 mg) can be lethal.

Now consider a special situation. If you happen to get involved in an emergency where someone is about to shoot, jump, or do something else rash, try to be calm. Keep your voice down. Do not ask philosophical questions, but ask practical questions: "What's your name?" "Where are you from?" Try to have a nonthreatening conversation. This is a grueling situation and can last for hours. Wear the person down. *Do not ever be a hero.* Do not rush a person with a gun. Stay alive to help the people who can be helped.

Trust your gut reactions. Don't feel that if you are unsuccessful, it is your fault. Don't ever forget that your job with suicidal clients is not to be God. Being God's helper is enough.

MENTAL STATUS EXAMINATION

The mental status examination is one of the techniques used by psychiatrists and other mental health workers. The purpose is to guide observation and assist the interviewer in gathering essential data about mental functioning. It consists of standard items, which are routinely covered, insuring nothing important is overlooked. The format also helps mental health workers record their findings in a fashion that is easily understood by their colleagues.

Three aspects of mental functioning are always included: mood and affect, thought processes, and cognitive functioning. Mood and affect refer to the dominant feeling state. They are deduced from general appearance, what the client reports, posture, body movement, and attitude toward the interviewer. Thought processes zero in on how the client presents his ideas. Are his thoughts ordered and organized, or does he jump all over the place? Are his sentences logical? Is the content (what he talks about) sensible, or does it include delusions and bizarre ideas? Finally, cognitive functioning refers to intellectual functioning, memory, ability to concentrate, comprehensions, and ability to abstract. This latter portion of the mental status examination involves asking specific questions, for example, about current events, definitions of words, or meanings of proverbs. The interviewer considers the individual's education, life-style, and occupation in making a judgment about the responses.

If the alcohol counselor can get some training in how to do a simple mental status examination, it can be helpful in spotting clients with particular problems. It can also greatly facilitate your communication with mental health workers. Just telling a psychiatrist the fellow you are referring to him is "crazier than a bedbug" isn't very useful.

ALCOHOL PROBLEMS AND PSYCHIATRIC ILLNESS

Understanding the relationship between alcohol use and behavior is one of the most challenging and essential components of anyone's work in the alcohol field. At some point, part of this will be separating which problems result from alcohol abuse from those that do not, especially those that result from other psychiatric conditions. This is difficult on two counts. First, alcohol abuse can be a part of other psychiatric conditions. Second, the symptoms of alcoholism can resemble many other psychiatric disorders. For this reason, psychiatry, perhaps more than any other medical discipline, must respect alcoholism as "the great mimicker." Interestingly, alcohol/substance abuse is the most common psychiatric disorder for those between the ages of 18 and 65. It is twice as prevalent as the second most frequently occurring condition. Because of this, the following rule of thumb is suggested for all mental health workers: When a thorough alcohol use history shows that alcohol abuse is present, the starting assumption needs to be that the alcohol consumption is causing the symptomatology observed, rather than the symptoms being due to a separate psychiatric condition. Furthermore, if alcohol abuse is present, even if there is another psychiatric disorder, it is imperative that the alcohol abuse be treated aggressively. Otherwise, it is highly unlikely that the client will be able to comply with what is required to treat other psychiatric disorders.

We have placed considerable emphasis in this text on the fact that psychological problems are not the cause of alcoholism, per se. However, in trying to get that message across, it is important not to lose sight of the fact that an individual may have *both* alcoholism and another psychiatric condition. It is estimated that 20% of persons entering alcohol rehabilitation programs also have a primary psychiatric disturbance. Although certainly a minority, 1 out of 5 clients is still a significant proportion. Whether alcoholism grows in the soil of some other psychiatric condition (sometimes termed secondary or reactive alcoholism) or whether it coexists alongside another psychiatric problem, when present, it develops a momentum of its own. Thus, it is imperative to tackle the alcohol problem. On the other hand, the client's ability to establish and maintain sobriety may be dependent upon actively treating other pscyhiatric conditions as well. The clinician confronted by clients with psychiatric disorders faces both diagnostic and treatment challenges.

Attention now turns to some of the major classes of psychiatric illness as they relate to alcoholism and alcohol abuse.

Affective disorders

Affect refers to mood and emotion, what you feel and how you show it. There are two extremes: people who are depressed, and those who are manic. People can fluctuate between these two extremes; this is called *bipolar* illness. People who are manic show characteristic behavior. Often they have grand schemes, which to others seem quite outlandish. Their conversation is very quick and pressured. Often they jump from topic to topic. If there were a conversation about the state of the union, a manic person might say, "and, yes, New Hampshire is a very pretty state. Governor Thomson was the governor of the state, and the governor of my car is out of kilter. The left tire is flat, out of air like a balloon Suzy got at the circus...." Although there is a logical connection between these thoughts, there is an inability to concentrate on one. This pattern of thinking is termed "loose associations." Each thought is immediately crowded out by the next. Someone who is manic is often aggressive and irritable. They may feel themselves very attractive and sexually irresistible. Individuals who are manic are perpetually in high gear and have difficulty sleeping. Simply being in their company might well make you feel exhausted.

Depression, which is the other side of the coin and is far more common, has all the opposite characteristics. Rather than being hyped up, these people grind to a halt. Depressed people feel very down. Speech is slow, movements are slow. Rather than a flood of things, they say little. Biological changes can accompany depression: disturbances of the normal sleep pattern, constipation, retarded motor activity, loss of appetite. In extremes, the depressed person stops eating, is unable to rest, experiences a complete depletion of energy, and expends available motor energy in repeated, purposeless motions such as hand-wringing and pacing. Such depression typically creates a sense of self-reproach, irrational guilt, hopelessness, and loss of interest in life. In full force these phenomena may culminate in suicidal thoughts, plans, or actions. Severe depression often involves disturbed biological function as well as pervasive guilt and is a life-threatening disorder.

Dear, Are you sure this is just A Scotch and soda?

Most depression and mania are believed to have a biological basis. They are also episodic disorders. Between episodes, the mood states typically return to a normal state. This is *not* to imply that one simply sits back and waits for the manic or depressive episode to pass. With the seriously biologically depressed individual, suicide is an ever-present possibility. The manic individual can incur phenomenal life problems that can wreak havoc for himself or herself as well as for the family. These conditions are highly treatable with medications (see the following section). Talking therapies are of little use when someone's perception of reality and thought processes are so seriously altered.

Alcohol use and alcoholism are intertwined with affective disorders in several ways. The most important one is that the vast majority of alcoholics experience some symptoms of depression. Depression as a feature of alcoholism has been frequently described. Depending on the diagnostic criteria used, depression may be seen in over one half of those participating in alcohol rehabilitation. Alcohol can produce a toxic depression that embraces the full range of depression's symptoms including anorexia, insomnia, somatic complaints, suicidal thoughts, and despair. Experimental studies have demonstrated that heavy drinking can induce depressive symptoms in both alcoholics and nonalcoholics. Beyond the effects of the drug alcohol, chronic alcohol abusers often must confront deteriorating social relations, associated trauma, and loss of health. The literature suggests that women more often than men experience depression while drinking abusively. Otherwise, no demographic or personality features distinguish those who get depressed from those who do not.

As mentioned in the section on suicide, any alcohol use by someone in a depression is contraindicated. This is an additional concern for alcoholics. It is estimated that 7% to 21% of alcoholics commit suicide. Although suicidal behavior in general increases with alcohol consumption, active alcoholics attempt suicide far more often than nonalcoholics when drinking. Several factors contribute to this. Alcoholism may be an indicator of a suicide-prone individual; alcoholism itself can be considered a form of chronic suicide. Also, the loss of cognitive function resulting from alcohol abuse will create an increasing gap between personal expectations and actual performance, resulting in despair. The multiple losses mentioned above can compound a sense of hopelessness. In assessing an alcoholic's suicide potential, further risk factors to consider are the loss of a close interpersonal relationship within the previous 6 weeks, the presence of hopelessness, and negative attitudes toward the interviewer. The alcoholic with suicidal thoughts, above all, needs to be taken seriously whether he is inebriated or not.

As an important aside, alcohol-related depression may also be seen in the family members of a substance abuser. Alcoholism is a family illness and 1 out of 3 American families have direct contact with an alcoholic. These people may develop depression as their defenses are overwhelmed by the constant stress of dealing with emotional and physical abuse, economic instability, and their perceived impotency to change their loved one's behavior. Obviously, for most, referral to Al-Anon will be far more appropriate than the use of antidepressant medications for this population.

Because depression is often a result of alcoholism, representing a reactive or secondary depression, usually the depression seen in alcoholics does not require separate treatment. But research suggests that 10% to 15% of females and 5% of males seeking alcoholism treatment have a major affective disorder that *preceded* the alcohol abuse. In these instances, it is likely that the depression will not lift with abstinence and alcohol treatment. These clients will meet DSM III criteria for depression after 3 months of abstinence. At the point of entry into treatment, it may be difficult to get the information needed to distinguish initially between an independent, primary depression and depression that results from alcoholism. The client may have difficulty providing an accurate chronology of events, due to cognitive deficits that are a part of both alcoholism and depression. The most reliable information is often provided by family and friends. The type of depression present may only become apparent over time. Ideally, if there is a question, the person should remain abstinent for 3 months and be observed. If the depressive symptoms lift with abstinence, then one can be comfortable that the affective disturbance was secondary to the alcohol abuse.

If signs and symptoms of an affective disturbance persist with abstinence, for example, insomnia, anorexia, loss of interest, hopelessness, suicidal thoughts, then treatment for depression is indicated. This is critically important, because these people are likely to see themselves as treatment failures. For them, things have not gotten better with sobriety. Also, they may unwittingly be urged by AA friends or treatment personnel "to work the program harder." In fact, they have been giving it their all. Treatment must include a lot of education about depression, its biological basis, and why medications are required. These clients will also need extra support. A point of discomfort for them may surface about the use of medications, especially because many alcohol treatment programs caution clients about the dangers of psychoactive drug use. Clients need to be reassured that the medications prescribed for depression are not those associated with abuse.

A period of sobriety prior to making the diagnosis of depression, though preferable, may not always be posssible. On occasion, the clinician may be so impressed with the severity of depressive symptoms that waiting for several months cannot be justified. In these rare instances, use of medications (tricyclic antidepressants) along with the alcohol treatment is warranted.

There is also an association between bipolar affective disorders (manic–depressive illness) and alcohol abuse. Research indicates that about 20% of bipolar patients report excessive use of alcohol during the manic phases of their disorder. It is unclear whether this is to reduce disturbing manic symptoms or as a result of poor judgment associated with this phase. Other studies suggest a decrease in alcohol use during the depressed phase in this population. The focus of therapy for those bipolar clients with alcohol abuse is twofold. The primary disorder may require medication (lithium and/or antipsychotic agents), while counseling and education are necessary to address alcohol use issues.

Disorders involving psychosis. Psychosis refers to a disorder of perceptions with resulting disturbances in function. The term *psychotic* is often used to describe clients with schizophrenia. The schizophrenic disorders are a group of chronic remitting disturbances that are among the most incapacitating of the mental disorders. These are often referred to also as "thought disorders." These disorders are thought to have a biochemical basis.

Schizophrenic disorders are typically manifested by hallucinations (a sensory perception with no corresponding stimulus), delusions (a fixed, false belief), or incoherence of thought. Individuals with a psychosis due to schizophrenia or other conditions may be in significant disagreement with others as to what is reality. The psychotic individual has his own idiosyncratic notions of reality. Sitting in a room full of people, he might claim to be alone. Possibly, if we think of the statement in philosophical or poetic terms, it could make sense. However, as a statement of "fact" on which to base further interaction, it breaks down. Attempts to communicate are very difficult because the psychotic perceives reality very differently. This altered perception can be very subtle or very marked. The preference here is to think of it as a very gross disturbance. For example, suppose you were to see someone undressing in the parking lot outside your office, and then jumping on a car roof. Were you to ask why, a logical explanation might be given, yet it wouldn't be an adequate explanation to get you to do it, too. If the person is psychotic, the lingering question after the explanation would be: "But why are you doing *that?*" If only the perception of reality were disturbed, then such people would rarely come to our attention. However, there is also a disturbance of function. Because we observe strange behavior, we inquire about someone's perceptions and beliefs about the world. Ordinarily, we simply do not challenge one another. For someone to qualify as psychotic, you should expect fairly uniform agreement among others that he is not on the same wavelength. The treatment of schizophrenic disorders as well as other disorders with psychosis includes medications (see following section) as well as ongoing supportive counseling.

Some conditions associated with alcohol abuse closely resemble psychotic disorders. One study found a history of psychotic symptoms in over 40% of alcoholics presenting for treatment. One such condition that may be misdiagnosed and lead to the inappropriate use of antipsychotic medication is that of alcoholic hallucinosis. Although seen in less than 3% of chronic alcoholics, it is so easily confused with schizophrenia that it should be considered in all cases of acute psychosis. It is often part of withdrawal states. But it can occur in an actively drinking individual. Symptoms include auditory, tactile, or visual hallucinations. The person will typically develop delusions of a persecutory nature related to these hallucinations. Several features help to distinguish alcohol hallucinosis from schizophrenia. There will be the history of heavy alcohol use. The majority of alcoholics with this condition will have their first episode after the age of 40, while schizophrenia typically appears earlier in life. There is usually no family history of schizophrenia, and there may be a family history of alcoholism. Unlike schizophrenia there is little evidence of a formal thought disorder, for example, loose associations and disorganization of thinking. The content of the hallucinations is fairly simple, unlike the less understandable or bizarre hallucinations of schizophrenia. In alcohol hallucinosis, the resolution of these symptoms is usually quick, occurring over the course of 1 to 6 days. Management should include hospitalization, close observation, some sedation, and the limited use of antipsychotic medications. Wernicke-Korsakoff syndrome (see Chapter 5) also includes psychotic symptoms. This is an irreversible organic brain syndrome resulting from chronic alcohol abuse ; it is characterized by prominent memory impairment and striking personality changes.

Aside from the psychotic symptoms that may result from alcohol, studies have suggested that up to 35% of schizophrenics will, as part of that illness, encounter difficulties with alcohol. The combination of schizophrenia and alcohol abuse when it occurs will likely result in a rocky clinical course and a poor prognosis. These individuals may have difficulty complying with any treatment regimen. They will frequently not take medications as prescribed and are unwilling or unable to follow recommendations for abstinence from alcohol. Efforts to control drinking in this population must be based on an assessment of what alcohol provides for the individual. If drinking is used to reduce anxiety around hallucinations, then increasing antipsychotic medication may be appropriate. If drinking is used to reduce uncomfortable side effects from medication, then a reduction or substitution of medications may be warranted. For these clients, the need for compliance with medication cannot be overemphasized. Abstinence for this population may be indicated not because they are alcoholic, but because even moderate drinking may, for them, be disruptive. Standard alcohol interventions may be seen as threatening. Schizophrenics tend to do poorly in group settings. Thus, they cannot avail themselves of AA or many other alcohol treatment services. Specialized inpatient treatment settings for this dual diagnosis population are ideal, but in most areas are unavailable.

Anxiety disorders. These disorders involve incapacitating anxiety. This symptom may appear episodically, as in panic attacks, or it may be unrelenting. Physical concomitants of arousal, such as diaphoresis (sweating), tremor, diarrhea, pallor, rapid pulse, shortness of breath, headache, and fatigue are common. The anxiety may be unattached to a particular situation, person, or thought (free-floating); or it may be associated with a specific object (simple phobia). Some people fear being alone or in a public place (agoraphobia). For others it may take the form of a recurrent idea (obsession). In contrast to other mental disorders, which may show a significant amount of anxiety, the anxiety disorders do not involve major disturbances in mood, thought, or judgment. In relation to alcoholism, a longstanding albeit controversial contention has been that some people drink heavily in an effort to control disabling anxiety. In 1979, researchers in

Great Britain reported that one third of patients studied also had agoraphobia, which preceded their alcohol abuse; another one third had less disabling anxiety disorders. Investigations in this country have confirmed that association. This research has further fueled the controversy. The studies are criticized for their retrospective format; and the authors concede that the sequence of anxiety and drinking was highly variable between individuals.

The stakes in this controversy are high. If one treats anxiety disorders with medication, that will introduce the risk of substitute dependencies. It will also make management of the alcoholism itself far more difficult. The antianxiety agents are among the medications most likely to invite abuse and pharmacologically most similar to alcohol. The conservative approach is that long-term use of medications not only invites drug dependence, but is in itself ineffective with anxiety disorders and less effective than behavioral approaches.

Personality disorders and alcohol abuse. Everyone has a unique set of personality traits that they exhibit in a range of social situations. When these traits repeatedly interfere with social or occupational functioning, they constitute a personality disorder. People with these disorders have the capacity "to get under everyone's skin." One type is called antisocial personality. A person with this disorder is frequently in trouble—getting into fights, committing crimes, and having problems with authority. Although a high percentage (80%) of people with an antisocial personality disorder have a history of alcohol abuse and a high percentage of alcoholics appear antisocial, the assumption of a causal link between these two disorders is not supported. Antisocial personality disorders appear to be inherited as does the predisposition to develop alcoholism. However, these two disorders are *not* linked together. Chronic alcohol consumption can lead to personality changes that closely resemble the antisocial personality. However, these behaviors may well disappear following abstinence. Studies have found that from 10% to 20% of men and about 5% to 10% of women in alcohol treatment facilities meet the criteria for antisocial personality, which appears to predate their alcoholism. For this group the prognosis is poor. All their social problems will not disappear with cessation of alcohol consumption. They are generally resistant to any type of intervention and will frequently alienate caregivers and peer support groups.

Attention deficit disorders. It has been recognized that some children are unable to remain attentive in situations where it is socially necessary to do so. This is often most apparent in school, but also in the home. In the past these conditions were termed *hyperactivity* or *minimal brain dysfunction*; they are now known as attention deficit disorders (ADD). Follow-up studies of children with ADD have noted a tendency for the development of alcoholism in adulthood. The examination of alcoholics' childhoods also shows a higher incidence of ADD. A hypothesis exists that a subgroup of alcohol abusers began to drink in order to stabilize areas of the brain that are "irritable" due to damage earlier in life. For them alcohol can be considered a self-medication. Alcohol may improve performance on cognitive tasks, allow better concentration, and offer a subjective sense of stability. Such a response to alcohol would be highly reinforcing and thereby increase the risk of addiction. With adults, it is very difficult to sort out the cognitive impairment caused by alcohol from a preexisting, underlying deficit. Prolonged abstinence is once more desirable. On the other hand, these clients may be unable to achieve and maintain sobriety.

When confronted with an individual who has been through treatment several times and never been able to establish sobriety, take a careful childhood history. If there is evidence of difficulties in school, or other problems suggesting ADD, further evaluation and treatment with medication may be warranted. The medication prescribed in such cases belongs to the stimulant class; however, for such clients it has a paradoxical "calming" effect. In addition, the above data suggest it would be useful to discuss, with parents of children currently diagnosed as having ADD, steps that might be taken to reduce future risk of alcohol problems.

Other addictive disorders and alcohol abuse. The abuse of alcohol in those who are primarily abusing other licit and illicit substances is frequently overlooked. In one study, 70% of clients entering treatment for benzodiazepine abuse (minor tranquilizers) also met criteria for alcohol abuse. 20% to 35% of opioid addicts in treatment were found to have alcohol-related problems. The danger here is that an alcohol problem is mistakenly treated lightly with this population without any real assessment of the potential risks. The cocaine abuser who routinely uses alcohol to offset the stimulant's effects may not be aware of a developing alcohol dependence.

The concept of addiction is now being extended to behaviors that do not involve substance abuse. These range from gambling to running and include eating disorders. Some people refuse food intake because they believe they are too fat, although the scales say differently (anorexia). Others stuff themselves and vomit,

Eat not to fullness; drink not to elevation.

BENJAMIN FRANKLIN

over and over (bulimia.) Case reports of associations between eating disorders and alcohol abuse are increasing as recognition of each illness improves. A striking phenomenon is the frequency of referral for alcohol treatment of individuals who had eating disorders in earlier years. There appears to be a higher incidence of a positive family history for alcoholism in anorexics, which also increases their risk for developing this dependency. Although prospective studies are needed, the potential risk of alcoholism among those with eating disorders should be recognized.

Organic mental disorders. A disorder is diagnosed as organic when it is caused by a known defect in brain function. The causes can vary. For example, organic mental disorders can result from traumatic or toxic insult to the central nervous system, or the effects of a brain tumor, or the effects of a stroke. These impairments of brain function lead to a limitation of the ability to think and respond to the environment meaningfully. Usually there are significant changes in cognitive function. Hence, there may commonly be problems with memory, loss of intellectual capacity, and an inability to concentrate.

These disorders can represent permanent impairment or can be almost completely reversible. Which of these outcomes occurs depends mostly on whether there has been only temporary interference with the brain's function (e.g., through ingestion of drugs, or a blow to the head) or there has been permanent damage to brain tissue. Reversible organic mental disorders are referred to as *delirium*. Typically it is rapid in onset and usually resolved within days. *Dementia* generally refers to irreversible organic brain syndromes, which most typically have a more gradual onset with gradual deterioration of function over years. In addition to the limitations these disorders create for an individual, an equally significant factor may be how the individual perceives them. If the symptoms appear slowly, the individual may be able to compensate—appear normal— especially if in a familiar environment with no new problems to solve. On the other hand, if the symptoms appear rapidly, the person may understandably be extremely upset. As the individual experiences a reduction in thinking capacity, anxiety may be very prominent. Another not uncommon component can be visual hallucinations, especially at night, which can be particularly terrifying.

The treatment of organic mental disorders attempts, where possible, to correct the underlying cause. If it is a tumor, surgery; if it is drug-induced, withdrawal. If permanent impairments are associated with organic mental disorders, rehabilitation measures will be initiated to assist the person in coping with limitations. In relation to alcohol use, there are a variety of organic mental disorders—from acute intoxication, which clearly impairs mental functioning, to withdrawal states, which can occur in the person physically dependent on alcohol, to permanent brain damage associated with longstanding heavy alcohol use.

Severe cognitive deficits in a chronic alcoholic may lead to the diagnosis of alcoholic dementia. This presenile dementia develops insidiously and typically presents during the drinker's fifth or sixth decade. The symptoms include a deteriorating memory and often dramatic personality changes. Mood swings are common and range from anger to euphoria. CAT scans will show widespread damage and shrinkage of brain tissue. With abstinence there may be some cognitive recovery over the first 6 weeks, as well as improvements seen by CAT scan. But generally some degree of dementia persists. Abstinence, however, is difficult to achieve due to impairment in thinking, which doesn't allow the standard counseling and educational approaches to take hold.

The elderly are particularly susceptible to mental disturbances caused by alcohol. Metabolism slows with age leading to higher blood levels of alcohol with similar consumption in the geriatric population. Their increased use of prescribed medication also increases the likelihood of a drug/alcohol interaction often leading to episodes of confusion. Older people have an apparent heightened sensitivity to all psychoactive compounds leading to greater cognitive changes while drinking. Sometimes frank organic brain syndromes occur. As demographic changes result in a higher percentage of older people, practitioners will be increasingly challenged to identify alcohol-related cognitive deficits and not chalk them up simply to aging. The diagnosis is often missed in this population because they tend to be protected by their friends and family. They may not meet strict DSM III critieria for alcohol abuse or alcohol dependence; but they still may be drinking pathologically. In one study, 36% of alcoholic elderly presented as confused to emergency rooms compared with 11% of an age-matched nonalcoholic control group.

Clinical considerations. When confronted with a possible dual diagnosis of alcoholism and other psychiatric conditions, alcoholism treatment personnel should always feel free to seek consultation from a psychiatrist or mental health worker. Often the key to making the diagnosis is through careful history taking. When a question remains, alcoholism treatment will be initiated with an eye to conducting an ongoing assessment for other psychiatric disorders. Treating both conditions simultaneously may require a balancing act, entailing extra support and education. The individual needs to appreciate that he is being treated for two very different conditions. Other clients during the course of alcohol treatment may learn of medical conditions that require attention, for example, hypertension or diabetes. This is the kind of framework that should be employed in helping the alcoholic client come to grips with the presence of a psychiatric disorder.

MEDICATIONS

Alcoholism does not exist in a vacuum. Alcoholics, as do other people, have a variety of other problems, some physical, some mental. They may be receiving treatment or treating themselves. The treatment probably involves prescribed or over-the-counter drugs. The more one knows about drugs in general, the more helpful one can be to a client. Alcoholics in particular tend to seek instant relief from the slightest mental or physical discomfort. The active alcoholic may welcome any chemical relief and use psychotropic medications in a way that can lead to problems. The recovering alcoholic, on the other hand, may be so leery of *any* medication that there may be a refusal to use any, including those that are very much needed and would probably not lead to difficulties. Thus, some familiarity with the types of psychotropic medications and their appropriate use is important. They are not alike, either in terms of their actions or in their potential for abuse.

Taking a good drug history (even though it might be done conversationally) is a definite must in dealing with alcohol problems. Following are some of the questions you would want to have in mind: "What?" "Is it prescribed and when was it prescribed?" "Is the client following the prescription?" "Is he afraid of the drug?" "Is the drug having the desired effect or are the side effects canceling out the benefits?" "Should the physician be notified if the client is misusing the drug or mixing it with alcohol and possibly many other medications from several other physicians?" This is only a sample of the kind of information to be elicited.

Tremendous confusion may arise from a communication gap. The physician prescribes a medication intended to have a particular effect on a particular patient. The patient is unclear (and usually doesn't question) what the purpose is. He takes the drug without letting the physician know, in fact, what is occurring.

Every drug has multiple simultaneous actions. Only a few of these effects are being sought when any drug is prescribed.

These intended effects are the *therapeutic effects*. All other effects would be the side effects in that instance. In selecting a medication for a patient, the doctor seeks a drug with the maximum therapeutic impact and minimal side effects. Only feedback from the patient enables the doctor to make adjustments, if necessary. The regimen for taking a drug is important, also. There is a good reason for specifying before or after meals, for example. Often, as the patient begins to feel better, he stops or cuts the dosage of prescribed drugs. One danger in this is that he has taken enough of a drug for relief of symptoms, but not enough to remove the underlying cause. Any patient should be encouraged to consult with his physician *before* altering the way he takes his medications. Because treatment requires good communication, one should help the client to ask questions about the treatment and the drugs involved.

Psychotropic drugs. The group of medications of particular interest in relation to alcohol are the psychotropic drugs. Any drug influencing behavior or mood falls into this category. These drugs are likely to be of the greatest concern to the counselor. At the same time, they may be the most widely misunderstood. There is no denying that psychotropic drugs are widely prescribed and often *over*prescribed. Because of their mood-altering properties, such medications may be candidates for abuse. "Down with drugs" is not apt to be an effective banner for a counselor, however. All psychotropic medications are not alike. Not all are uniformly potential problems for clients. However, in no instance should they be used in combination with alcohol (see Chapter 5).

A discussion of the three major categories of psychotropic drugs follows. Each has a different combination of actions and is properly prescribed for different reasons. These are the antipsychotic agents, antidepressant agents, and antianxiety agents.

The *antipsychotic drugs* are also called the *major tranquilizers*. These drugs relieve the symptoms of psychoses. In addition to the antipsychotic effect, they also have a tranquilizing and a sedative action, calming behavior and inducing drowsiness. Different drugs in this group have differing balances of the three actions. The drug prescribed is selected on the basis of the client's constellation of symptoms. Thus, a drug with greater sedative effects might well be selected for a person exhibiting psychotic and agitated behavior.

The antipsychotic medications most frequently encountered are listed below.

Brand name	Generic name	Daily dosage range (mg)
Thorazine	Chlorpromazine	100-1000
Mellaril	Thioridazine	30-800
Stelazine	Trifluoperazine	2-30
Trilafon	Perphenazine	2-64
Navane	Thiothixene	6-60
Haldol	Haloperidol	3-50

These drugs interact with alcohol. Some possible effects include raising the seizure threshold and slowing the metabolism of alcohol.

On occasion, an antipsychotic agent will be prescribed, not to relieve psychotic symptoms, but for its sedative or tranquilizing properties. This is because they are less likely to be abused than the usual sedatives or antianxiety agents, because they are not chemically similar to alcohol and are therefore not subject to cross-tolerance or addiction.

The *antidepressants*, another major class of psychotropic drugs, are used to treat the biological component of depression. A period of time of regular use for these medications is necessary to have their full benefit. Therefore, an initial complaint of patients is that the medicine isn't helping. Common side effects are sedation and tranquilization. These are most pronounced when the person first begins taking the drug. The physician may choose to have the patient take the drug at bedtime, so the sedation effect will not interfere with daytime function.

The most common antidepressants follow.

Brand name	Generic name	Daily dosage range (mg)
Tricyclics		
Tofranil	Imipramine	75-300
Elavil	Amitriptyline	75-300
Aventyl	Nortriptyline	75-200
Sinequan	Doxepin	75-200
Norpramin	Desipramine	75-200
Vivactyl	Protriptyline	20-60
Asendin	Amoxapine	150-600
Ludiomil	Maprotiline	75-300
Desyrel	Trazadone	150-600
MAOIs*		
Nardil	Phenelzine	45-90
Parnate	Tranylcypomine	10-30
Marplan	Isocarboxazid	10-30

*Ingestion of alcoholic beverages with a high tyramine content (such as chianti, sherry, beer) while taking MAOIs can possibly lead to severe hypertension as well as increasing the CNS depression.

There is no clear evidence that antidepressant agents are addicting. Again, in combination with alcohol, problems can rise with additive effects.

Lithium carbonate is worth special mention. Though dissimilar to the antidepressants in chemical composition, it is the mainstay of treatment in manic–depressive illness. It controls and levels the wide mood swings. The dosage is geared to body weight, and the level of lithium is monitored periodically through blood samples. Lithium is unlikely to be abused by the client. The contrary behavior is the more common danger. Feeling greatly improved, those on lithium may decide it's no longer necessary. However, maintaining this improvement depends upon continuation of the medication.

The final group of psychotropic drugs are the *antianxiety agents*. Drugs in this class, along with barbiturates, are the ones most likely to be troublesome for alcoholics. The major action of these drugs is to promote tranquilization and sedation. Quite properly, alcohol can be included in any list of drugs in this class. The antianxiety agents are also called the *minor tranquilizers*. They have no antipsychotic or significant antidepressant properties. The potential for abuse of these antianxiety agents has become far more broadly recognized. Accordingly, the total number of prescriptions written has been dropping.

Alcohol and the minor tranquilizers in combination potentiate one another. Because of their similar pharmacology, they are also virtually interchangeable. This phenomenon is the basis of cross-addiction. For these reasons they are used for detoxification and to manage withdrawal from alcohol. This interchangeability with alcohol is what makes them very poor drugs for alcoholics except for detoxification purposes.

The most common antianxiety agents follow.*

Brand name	Generic name	Daily dosage range (mg)
Librium	Chlordiazepoxide	10-100
Valium	Diazepam	6-40
Equanil, Miltown	Meprobamate	600-1200
Atarax	Hydroxyzine	30-100
Xanax	Alprazobam	2-4
Tranxene	Clorazepate	15-60
Ativan	Lorazepam	2-10
Serax	Oxazepam	30-120

Continued.

---

*We have lumped the antianxiety agents together for the purpose of this discussion. However, differences among them, based on chemical composition, have significance if abuse occurs. These will be elaborated on in the following section.

Brand name	Generic name	Daily dosage range (mg)
(Hypnotics)		
Restoril	Temazepam	15-30
Dalmane	Flurazepam	15-30
Halcion	Triazolam	.125-.5

In the main, Americans are very casual about drugs. Too often, prescribed drugs are not taken as directed, are saved up for the "next" illness, or are shared with family and friends. If the attitude toward prescription drugs is so casual, over-the-counter preparations are treated as candy. The fact that a prescription is not required does not render these preparations harmless. Some possible ingredients of over-the-counter drugs are antihistamines, scopolamine, and, of course, alcohol. These can cause difficulty if taken in combination with alcohol, or they may themselves be targets of abuse. (For specific alcohol–drug interactions see Chapter 5.)

In working with clients, a good drug history is imperative.

MULTIPLE SUBSTANCE ABUSE

We're all out of hash and reds, but we have some fine coke and some vintage TCP.

Multiple substance abuse refers to simultaneous abuse of different mood-altering drugs, either one with another, or in combination with that all-time favorite, alcohol. Many who work in the alcoholism field have come to believe that addiction is addiction regardless of the substance being abused. For these people basic principles of treatment for drug abuse vary little from alcoholism treatment. Despite this view, the stereotype remains of drug abusers as different from alcoholics and more difficult to help. Thus, a tendency among some who work with alcoholics is to shy away from drug abusers or those who are cross-addicted to drugs as well as alcohol. Nevertheless, those working with alcoholics must become more knowledgeable and comfortable in working with clients who are also involved with other drugs. "Pure" alcohol abuse is less common than it used to be. A recent survey conducted by AA of its members revealed that 30% of those surveyed considered themselves addicted to drugs as well as alcohol. This was an increase of 7% from a similar survey 3 years earlier. Of AA members under 20 years of age, a whopping 76% said they were addicted to drugs as well, a 16% increase in just a 3-year period! Alcohol treatment units report that the number of clients being admitted who also abuse other drugs is increasing. Once again, the younger clients are more likely to use and abuse multiple substances.

Major substances of abuse

A complete listing of all the drugs of abuse and their effects is beyond the scope of this book. However, it is not necessary to be intimately familiar with every compound, if one is aware of the general classes into which psychoactive drugs or substances fall. Within each of the major classes there is similarity as to the drugs' effects and the problems that may be encountered with use. The major classes of "abuse-able" drugs are as follows:

Depressants

examples: benzodiazepines (Librium, Valium, etc.); barbiturates, chloral hydrate, paraldehyde, meprobamate.

action: not completely understood, in general produce a reversible depression of the central nervous system, some more selectively than others.

desired effects: similar to alcohol; elation or excitement secondary to depression of inhibitions and judgment or reduction of anxiety.

common problems: tolerance; physical dependence; respiratory depression with overdose.

withdrawal syndromes: physical symptoms similar to alcohol withdrawal, including seizures; psychological withdrawal.

Stimulants

examples: amphetamines, cocaine, methylphenidate (Ritalin).

action: stimulation probably due to increased levels of norepinepherine and/or dopamine in central nervous system.

desired effects: increased alertness; feeling of well-being; euphoria; increased energy; decreased appetite; rapid onset of mood change with cocaine.

common problems: tolerance; anxiety; confusion; irritability; psychosis; with cocaine-delusions, some data indicating physical dependence.

withdrawal syndromes: depression (possibly suicidal); loss of ability to enjoy ordinary pleasures.

Opiates

examples: heroin, morphine, methadone, opium, codeine, Demerol, Percodan.

action: affect central nervous system, probably by mimicking or blocking normally occuring opiate-like substances in the brain, thereby causing mood changes and mental clouding.

desired effects: "the rush" (feeling of intense pleasure immediately following injection); state of mental and physical relaxation with decreased mental awareness and reduction of drives.

common problems: production of tolerance and both physical and psychological dependence; death by overdose or as result of injection.

withdrawal syndromes: psychological (drug craving); physical symptoms (chills and sweats, abdominal pain, diarrhea, gooseflesh, tears).

Hallucinogens

examples: LSD, mescaline, psilocybin, DMT.

action: alteration of normal functioning of central and peripheral nervous systems, central nervous system excitement.

desired effects: modification of perception of all sensory input (hallucinations, distortions); temporary modification of thought processes; claims of "special insights."

common problems: acute anxiety and panic reactions; depression; flashbacks (post-LSD).

withdrawal syndromes: generally believed not to occur.

Cannabinoids

examples: marijuana, hashish, THC.

action: acts on the brain as a foreign substance.

desired effects: euphoria; detachment; modification of level of consciousness; relaxation; reported sexual arousal; altered perceptions.

common problems: psychomotor impairment; impairment in memory, comprehension, thinking, learning, and general intellectual function; respiratory problems with prolonged use; reproductive system problems with prolonged use; paranoia and psychosis in large doses; possible long-term psychological impairment with chronic use.

withdrawal syndromes: psychological dependence suggested; no physical withdrawal demonstrated.

Phencyclidine

examples: Phencyclidine (PCP).

action: nonspecific central nervous system depressant; anesthetic; psychedelic (multiple proposed actions on various neurotransmitters in central nervous system).

desired effects: visual illusions and distorted perceptions; depersonalization; distortion of body image; hallucinations; feelings of strength, power, and invulnerability; claims of "special insights."

common problems: feelings of severe anxiety, doom, or impending death; bizarre behavior; outbursts of hostility and excitement.

withdrawal syndromes: potential for both psychological and physical withdrawal reported, but not well documented.

Inhalants

examples: aerosol sprays, paint, model cement, adhesives, gasoline, amyl nitrite, butyl nitrite, nitrous oxide, benzydrex inhalors, asthma inhilators

action: central nervous system depression, generally secondary to access through respiratory system.

desired effects: immediate effects—euphoria, excitement (also often inexpensive and legal).

common problems: impulsive and destructive behavior; slurred speech; ataxia; impaired judgment; development of tolerance; "Sudden Sniffing Death"; possible long-term central nervous system damage and damage to multiple physical systems.

withdrawal syndromes: psychological documented; physical, not clinically established.

In respect to the drugs of abuse, there are clearly trends as to what is and is not popular, or "in," at any particular time. For example, the interest in psychedelics has waned. Cocaine use has become very widespread. Also apparently true is that drugs, though often touted as being nonaddictive when they are becoming popular, generally turn out *not* to be as universally benign as thought. Current terminology refers to "recreational" drug use, which by analogy is the counterpart of "social drinking." Controlled studies of the effects of "recreational" drug use are for the most part nonexistent. The problems that can accompany "casual use" are the same as for "casual use" of alcohol, for example, auto accidents from driving in an impaired state. Or there is the possibility that casual use may not remain casual. Any use of illicit substances invites a host of other difficulties.

For the counselor, the importance of distinguishing between legal and illegal substances is less a matter of pharmacology than it is "quality assurance." Inevitably, illicit drugs are pharmacologically of unknown strength and purity. And a safe, reliably available supply can never be assured. Also, the illicit drug use can invite social and legal problems. For example, while the price of cocaine may be coming down, it remains a very expensive drug. Therefore, large sums of money are spent for even "recreational" use. Heavy users may find themselves borrowing money, going into debt, or stealing. Or they begin to sell to others to cover the costs of their own coke use. Cocaine has thus been called the "Amway drug."

The observation has been made that for illicit drug users, because the substance is not legally available, some of the behaviors common in the later stages of alcoholism are present virtually from the beginning of the drug use. Early on with the drug use there is a need for the secretiveness, concern about supply, and feelings of guilt and apprehension.

Patterns of multiple drug use

Different patterns of use may be identified. One pattern might be considered as *"risk taking"* drug use, similar possibly to another generation's drag racing and "playing chicken" on the highway. For example, several years ago, there were reports of teenage parties with "fruit salad," a bowl of pills, with each guest contributing whatever he could glean from the family medicine cabinet. In what sounds like chemical roulette, the experimenters would take a handful of pills and "turn on" for the evening. From time to time, emergency rooms would be confronted with sick adolescents who had ingested unknown drugs in unknown

quantities. This is one form of multisubstance abuse, although admittedly not a common variety.

For many younger people alcohol may be an incidental but integral part of any other drug taking, whether the other drug use is experimental, or risktaking, or recreational. If one is in a situation in which drugs are being used, the beverage served is not likely to be lemonade! And if supplies of other drugs are limited due to their cost or availability, if one wants some mood alteration, there is always the old standby, alcohol. Therefore, if problems develop with drug use, it is not unlikely that alcohol will be one part of that picture (see section on adolescents).

Some use multiple drugs in an *effort to engineer moods*, to achieve different and particular feeling states. You name the mood, and they have a formula of drugs in combination to achieve it. This may mean uppers in the morning, downers to unwind later in the day, drugs to counteract fatigue, drugs to promote sleep, drugs to feel "better." Among those most likely to get into this drug use pattern are people with relatively easy access to drugs: nurses, physicians, pharmacists, and their spouses. This does not imply the medications are being stolen. Easy access can mean asking someone to write you a prescription as a favor. In all probability this pattern of use starts out innocently. The aim is not to get high, but to cope. Accustomed to the use of medications, often working at a pace beyond reasonable expectations, people may try a little chemical assistance to get by. Despite their knowledge of pharmacology, before they know it, they are in trouble. The drugs are no longer something to be used in special situations; they are essential for simply existing. Alcohol may well become a part of this picture. Alcohol workers are not immune. The intake worker who relieves the incoming client of his booze and pills may very quickly acquire an impressive and tempting stash in the desk drawer.

Alcohol and cross-addiction

When alcohol is involved, multiple drug abuse may not involve illicit drugs or fit the patterns just described. A portion of multiple drug abuse begins when people in the early stages of alcoholism start to ride "the doctor circuit" in search of a physical answer to their problems. Their complaints may be "nerves," "headaches," or "sensitive stomach." These people do not go to their physicians deliberately trying to obtain drugs. They truly want relief for their distress. If a careful alcohol history is not taken, their drinking may not initially appear to be different from that of other clients the physician treats. Quite possibly the budding alcoholic may openly tout alcohol as a godsend, given how he feels.

PHYSICIAN: How much do you drink?
PATIENT: Oh, not too much, mostly when I go out socially.
PHYSICIAN: How much is that, and how often?
PATIENT: Oh, not much, a couple of drinks at a party, occasionally a cocktail before dinner. But I tell you, these headaches have been murder. And I've sometimes said, "I may not be a drinker, but I will be if they continue."
PHYSICIAN: They're that bad...

It all sounds straightforward. Our friend has tests done; nothing emerges to pin the headaches on. He is reporting stress at work, and eventually he walks out of the physician's office with a prescription for a minor tranquilizer. This fellow may be headed for trouble. There is an increasing sensitivity within the medical community to prescribing minor tranquilizers for vague, nonspecific problems and awareness of the potential for abuse. Nonetheless a persistent client may often prevail.

Multiple drug use clearly has an impact on the drinking career. Depending on the drugs involved, there can be difficulties of a more acute nature on any drinking occasion. The effects of multiple substances taken together may be additive or synergetic (an effect greater than the summed actions of the drugs), resulting in increased central nervous system depression. This can be a life-threatening situation.

In addition to physical problems that can occur, there are other potential difficulties for the active alcoholic. One is the use of other drugs to maintain and control the drinking. Though alcohol is the drug of choice, somewhere along the line, the alcoholic may have learned the warning signs of alcoholism. By using pills, alcohol consumption may be maintained within what the drinker has decided are safe limits. What would *really* hit the spot would be a nice stiff drink. Instead, the drinker settles for a capsule. He doesn't drink during the day, so he doesn't consider himself an alcoholic. Thus, drug use can help the alcoholic keep alcohol use within "acceptable" limits. The drinking career can thereby, in his mind, be managed and extended.

Other drug use can prevent the reality of the alcohol problem from sinking in. The minor tranquilizers are also known as the antianxiety agents. Anxiety is what will eventually move the alcoholic near treatment. This happens when problems are such that one cannot explain them away or successfully drink them away—when the pain is no longer alcohol soluble. The antianxiety agents, by turning off anxiety, can create a false sense of well-being. The individual using antianxiety agents will still intellectually know what is happening, but the emotional impact is blunted. The active alcoholic has plenty to be anxious about. Although pills may help turn it off, they will be unable to alter the source of the anxiety, which is the drinking and its consequences.

Some anxiety seems necessary to produce change. The observation has been made that, "No one ever changes until it's too painful not to." Removal of the alcoholic's pain can be a block to recovery. In the mildly mulled state of minor tranquilization, it may seem much easier to the alcoholic simply to continue the life pattern as before, including the drinking.

Withdrawal

Just as tolerance develops for alcohol, so can it also develop for some other psychotropic medications. The list of abuse-able drugs mentioned earlier included a number of drugs that produce tolerance. These include the barbiturates, sedatives, and the minor tranquilizers. Just as with alcohol, as use continues, more of the substance is required to keep doing the same job. This is reinforced by the all-American viewpoint that discomfort is pointless when chemical comfort is only a swallow away. When tolerance develops, withdrawal symptoms may accompany abstinence. Several of these will be briefly described.

Barbiturates have been around since the beginning of this century. Central nervous system depressants like alcohol, they have an abstinence syndrome very similar to that of alcohol. At lower doses, withdrawal symptoms will most likely be limited to anxiety and tremulousness. At high levels, more serious withdrawal symptoms may develop. These can include convulsions and a "DT-like" syndrome of delirium, disorientation, hallucinations, and severe agitation. Barbiturate withdrawal presents a medical situation as serious, and potentially as life threatening, as that accompanying alcohol withdrawal.

Drugs included within the category of minor tranquilizers can be subdivided into different groups depending on their chemical compositions. These differences are important when it comes to withdrawal and potential problems of abuse. Librium and Valium both belong to the subgroup known as the benzodiazepines. When drugs of this subgroup are abused, withdrawal symptoms may be present if use is abruptly stopped. Withdrawal symptoms can include anxiety, tremulousness, sweating, insomnia, nausea and vomiting, muscular weakness, confusion, psychosis, and possibly convulsions. A full-blown "DT-like" picture is generally *not* associated with the benzodiazepines. However, it is increasingly recognized that physical dependence is not a casual issue. Clinically, more individuals are presenting for treatment following a longstanding use of Librium or Valium and more recently Xanax. Even if the symptoms of physical withdrawal associated with these substances are not as dramatic as those of alcohol or barbiturates, getting off these medications is no easy matter. For other subgroups of drugs in the minor tranquilizers category, withdrawal can be much more serious. Be particularly alert to abuse of Miltown or Equanil (the brand names for meprobamate) and Doriden (glutethimide). Withdrawal symptoms for these can be as dangerous as those associated with alcohol or barbiturates. (Doriden may have been prescribed for sleep. Don't overlook "just a few sleeping pills" in pursuing a drug history.)

Clincial considerations

Polydrug use and abuse should be suspected when any drug, including alcohol, is being used. Younger people are at especially high risk for multiple drug abuse. When physical dependence on alcohol is combined with dependence on another drug, the problems of detoxification are increased. The task that then confronts the physician is sequential detoxification or withdrawal of one drug at a time. Medical management can be a very delicate process in these situations. It is critical for multiple dependencies to be identified when someone first enters treatment. If alcohol detoxification is not going smoothly, the first question to be asked is: "Are other drugs involved?"

In respect to treatment, if a program is primarily oriented to alcoholism, it still needs to offer some individualized education for those using other substances—e.g., discussing the drug's actions and how it interacts with alcohol. Also to be considered for some clients is a referral not only to AA, but to NA (Narcotics Anonymous) or CA (Cocaine Anonymous). For all clients, discussing the dangers of using any chemicals "recreationally" is warranted.

RESOURCES AND FURTHER READING

Adolescents

Isralowitz, R., and Singer, M. (Eds.): *Adolescent substance abuse: a guide to prevention and treatment.* New York: Haworth Press, 1983.

Levine, B.C.: Adolescent substance abuse: toward an integration of family systems and individual adaptation theories. *American Journal of Family Therapy.* 13(2):3–16, 1985.

Macdonald, D.I.: *Drugs, drinking and adolescents.* Chicago: Yearbook Medical Publishers, Inc. 1984.

Mayer, J.E., and Filstead, W.J. (Ed.): *Adolescence and alcohol.* Cambridge, MA: Ballinger, 1980.

Smart, R.G.: *The new drinkers: teenage use and abuse of alcohol* (2nd ed.). Toronto: Addiction Research Foundation, 1980.

The Elderly

Atkinson, R.M. (Ed.): *Alcohol and drug abuse in old age.* Washington, D.C.: American Psychiatric Press, 1984.

National Clearinghouse for Alcohol Information: *Alcohol and the elderly,* Alcohol Resource List: Update. May 1985. (PO Box 2345, Rockville, MD 20852).

Sherouse, D.L.: *Professional's handbook on geriatric alcoholism.* Springfield, IL: Charles C. Thomas, 1982.

Alcohol Problems and Psychiatric Issues

Solomon, J. (Ed.): *Alcoholism and clinical psychiatry.* New York: Plenum Press, 1982.

Multiple Substance Abuse

AA surveys its membership: a demographic report. *About AA.* Fall, 1984.

Bennett, G., Vourakis, C., and Woolf, D.S.: *Substance abuse: pharmacologic, developmental, and clinical perspectives.* New York: John Wiley & Sons, Inc., 1983.

Gold, M.S., and Verebey, K.: The psychopharmacology of cocaine. *Psychiatric Annals* 14:714–723. 1984.

Kern, J.C., and others: Comparison of pure and polydrug alcoholics: its implications for alcohol detoxification in the 1980s. *Journal of Psychiatric Treatment and Evaluation* 5:263–267, 1983.

Wilford, B.B.: *Drug abuse: a guide for the primary care physician.* Chicago: American Medical Association, 1981.

Odds and ends

11

Jack Fin
e could
drink
NO Wi
Ne — H
iS WiF
E Could
drink
NO liquo
R — BUT ST
ill they both
goT drunk each nig
ht — though he got'd
runk much quicker...

La pauvre Presse

Brattleboro, Vt.

from the Collected Do
ggerel of 18ᵗʰ Century
France - by J. ANzolone

BEYOND COUNSELING

There are other topics we consider relevant for alcohol counselors. Space and time limitations prevent us from doing little more than just mentioning them here. Counselors frequently discover that although their formal job description is centered around serving clients, there are often other expectations. Such duties fall into the general area of *indirect services*, an awkward phrase used to cover all the other things a counselor is often required to do, in addition to directly serving clients. Public education, case consultation, and planning for community programs are just a few examples. These indirect services are vital to the overall success of alcohol treatment efforts. We would like to touch upon these aspects of a counselor's work.

Educational activities

Counselors are often called upon to participate in public and professional education programs. The former might include presentations to high school students, or the church group, or being a panelist on a radio talk show. The latter might take the form of in-service training for other professionals, supervision of trainees or students, or workshops.

Do's. In any educational endeavor, plan ahead—don't just "wing it." An effective presentation takes some thought ahead of time. Find out from those organizing the program what they have in mind for a topic (you may wish to suggest an alternative), who will be in the audience and its size, how long you are expected to speak, and if there are others on the program. In choosing a topic consider what would be of interest, ask yourself what kinds of questions are likely to be on the audience's minds. Do not be overly ambitious and try to cover everything you think someone ought to know about alcohol. If your audience goes away understanding three or four major points, you can consider yourself successful. Pick a subject about which you are more expert than your audience. A counselor might effectively talk about alcohol's effects on the body to a group of fifth or sixth graders.

Any counselor who would attempt to lecture a group of doctors about medical complications is asking for trouble. However, by sharing with physicians practical tips on how to interview an alcoholic or how to tell a patient about a suspected alcohol problem, you can make a big contribution. On that topic you are clearly the expert and able to provide them information they can use and do not already have. Leave time for questions and save some of your choice tidbits for a question-and-answer period.

Feel free to develop several basic spiels. Use films or videotapes. A film can be an excellent vehicle for stimulating conversation, but be sure it is appropriate. Three questions for sparking a discussion afterward are the following: "What kind of response did you (the audience) have?" "What new information did you learn?" and "What surprised you?"

Don'ts. Avoid crusading, "drunkalogs," or horror stories. These approaches may titillate your audience; however, most audiences will not identify with what you are saying. The presentation will be unconnected to their experience and you are likely to leave them with a "Not me!" response. Clinical vignettes, too, are usually inappropriate with lay audiences. With professional audiences, if case material is used, great care must be taken to obscure identifying information. Avoid using jargon. Instead, look for everyday words to convey what you mean, or use examples.

Professional training. Counselors have a special contribution to make in training of other professionals. A common complaint of many counselors is how ill-equipped other professional helpers may be to work with alcoholics. However, this situation is not likely to change unless and until the alcohol experts, such as counselors, begin to participate in the education of others. So we would urge you to consider this a priority activity.

The general do's and don'ts already listed apply. Here it is especially important to stick to your area of expertise. To our minds, your single unique skill is your ability to interact therapeutically with alcoholics. This is the thing you can share. Often this is most effectively communicated by example rather than by lecturing. However, one trap you should avoid is giving the impression that what you do and know is a mystery that others could never hope to learn. This can come across to your students in subtle ways, through statements such as "Well, I've been there so I know what it's like," or the offhanded comment that "If you really want to know what alcoholism's all about, what you have to do is (1) spend 2 weeks working on an alcohol unit, (2) go to at least twenty AA meetings, (3) talk firsthand to recovering alcoholics, (4) and so on." Any or all of these might be advisable and valuable educational experiences; however, you ought to be able also to explain in very concrete terms what this might provide, *why* it is valuable.

A few words on supervision of trainees or students may be helpful. Do not be fooled by the notion that the arrival of a student or a trainee is going to ease your workload. It shouldn't. Doing a good job of supervision requires a big investment of your time and energy. Whether the student is with you for a single day, several weeks, or a semester, you will need to give some hard thought to what can be provided to insure a valuable experience for the student. There are some basic questions you need to consider in planning a reasonable program. Do you want the trainee to acquire specific skills or just become "sensitized" to alcohol treatment techniques? What are the student's goals? What will prove most useful to the student later on? What is the student's background in terms of academic training and experience with alcoholism? The social worker trainee, the clergy member, the recovering alcoholic with 10 years of AA experience—each is starting from a different point. Each has different strengths and weaknesses, different things to learn and unlearn. In planning the educational program, consider how you will incorporate the trainee. In what activities will the trainee participate? Generally, you will want to have the student at least "sample" a broad range of agency activity but also have a more in-depth continuing involvement in selected areas.

Probably the single most important thing is to allow the trainee ample time to discuss what goes on, either with you or with other staff. The idea is not to run a student ragged with a jam-packed schedule and no chance to sit down with anyone to talk about what has been observed. If a student is going to be joining you for an interview, be sure you set aside at least 10 to 15 minutes ahead of time as a preinterview briefing. Also at the conclusion spend some time to review the session, to respond to questions. Do not expect that what the student is to learn is obvious.

Be sure to introduce or discuss with clients the presence of trainees. Clients do not need to be provided a student's resume, or a brochure describing in complete detail the nature of the training program. However, they do need to be told who the trainees are and to be reassured that they are working with the staff in a trainee capacity. Clients have every right to be uncomfortable and apprehensive at the thought that either the merely curious are passing through to observe them or they are being used as guinea pigs. In our experience, most clients do not object to being involved with students if the situation is properly presented and if they recognize they have the *right* to say no.

Prevention activities

Prevention has been receiving increased attention at the national, state, and local levels. Certainly, anyone involved in the alcohol field would like to see fewer people caught up in alcohol problems. However, the real impetus came about 10 years ago when the NIAAA first earmarked funds for prevention programs. Since then, various programs have been initiated using a variety of techniques, and the topic has been a "hot" one in the alcohol field.

Before commenting on some of the approaches, some background on prevention and terminology may be useful. Activities directed at preventing the occurrence of disease have been the mainstay of all public health efforts. This is true whether it is the notion of vaccination to prevent smallpox, polio, or measles, or efforts to assure that the town water supply is uncontaminated so as to prevent cholera outbreaks.

However, the emphasis on prevention within the alcohol field is probably more closely linked to prevention efforts as they developed in the community mental health movement in the 1950s and early 1960s. Attempts at primary, secondary, and tertiary prevention were first widely introduced in that context. What these three different kinds of prevention activity all have in common is that each is intended to reduce the total numbers of people who suffer from a disease. If you think about it for a moment, you will realize that can be accomplished in only three ways. One way is to prevent the illness in the first place; thus no new cases develop. This is *primary* prevention. A second way is to identify and treat as quickly as possible those who contract the disease. By restoring to health those having the disease, you reduce the number of existing cases. This is *secondary* prevention. Third, you can initiate specific efforts to avoid relapse and maintain the health of those who have been treated. This is *tertiary* prevention.

Apply this framework to problems associated with alcohol. In respect to alcohol*ism*, primary prevention efforts are activities directed to reducing the numbers of people who develop alcoholism. Secondary prevention is essentially early detection and early intervention. Tertiary prevention efforts include follow-up and continued monitoring after active intensive treatment to avoid relapse and reactivation of the disease. Prevention efforts can also be targeted to acute problems of alcohol use, which most frequently involve intoxication. Here primary prevention is directed toward achieving moderate alcohol use. Secondary prevention would be the steps taken to prevent problems if intoxication occurs. And any efforts to avoid repetition of such situations in the future is tertiary prevention.

In the early days of alcohol prevention programming, it was not fully appreciated that programs that may be effective for prevention of acute problems could not be expected to automatically be effective in dealing with the problems of chronic use. Furthermore, the most successful programs at one level of prevention may not work well at another level. Not being especially clear as to exactly what it was that they were trying to prevent, folks tended to lump both alcohol problems and alcoholism together. We've taken a step forward as these necessary distinctions are just beginning to be made. Take as an example, SADD. This program may be effective in reducing the toll associated with teenage driving and alcohol use. However, it probably would not be a promising method by which to prevent alcoholism in teenagers now or as they grow to adulthood.

Until very recently, primary prevention of alcoholism got the lion's share of attention. Without question it sounds like a very attractive and laudable goal. To question the idea may be almost synonymous with bad-mouthing Mother and apple pie, but let us raise some questions. Any effort directed at preventing alcoholism has to make some assumptions about the causes. A brief review of the presentation in Chapter 4 on etiology reminds us that there is no simple, single cause of alcoholism. The best that can be said is that alcoholism results from a complex interaction between a drug, the individual (both biochemical and psychological makeup), and the culture. If you are designing a prevention program, which of these elements do you zero in on? Do you really know enough to do something that has a reasonable chance of making a difference, or are you going on the basis of hunches and common sense?

Ironically, much of the prevention effort was directed at the single element that we have since come to recognize as carrying the least weight; that is, the individual's psychological makeup and functioning. Realistically this is probably the only point at which most agencies or individual clinicians are equipped to in-

tervene. A counseling center is not set up to do biomedical research to uncover the genetic basis of alcoholism! Nor is the
agency likely to be able to undertake a massive campaign to
change U.S. drinking practices! However, it is not unlikely that
the clinician or agency will be asked to lobby for or against
changes in public policy, be it around legal drinking age or tax
rates or public expenditures for treatment. While public policy is
not a cure-all, various measures can be predicted to have a de-
monstrable impact upon the rates of alcohol problems. A slim volume by the National Research Council (NRC), *Alcohol in America: Taking Action to Prevent Abuse*, is a summary for the layperson of a federally funded study. It is highly recommended for its
summary of various public policy approaches to prevention.

What has been the effectiveness of prevention efforts? Too
frequently those who initiated a program felt that its merits were
obvious. There was all too little evaluation. Programs tended to
be replicated based on the enthusiastic reports of those who
started them. However, now that evaluation reports are becoming available, some of the earlier assumptions are being questioned. The domino theory of knowledge leading to attitudes that
result in behavior does not hold up. One can increase knowledge
only to discover that this has no effect on the other two. Similarly, one can provide the facts, change attitudes, and still leave
behavior unchanged. At this point it appears that broad-based
educational approaches, by themselves, have little impact upon
drinking behaviors. And they have the least impact upon those at
greatest risk. They may, however, be useful in providing a "back-
drop," that is, fostering a climate in which other targeted programs can be more successfully conducted. It is now recognized
that one must be quite specific in targeting programs. For example, a program for adolescents was found to have opposite results
depending upon whether its participants were or were not already into alcohol. The response by those who were not drinkers
was a confirmation and strengthening of the decision not to use
alcohol. However, for those who were already drinkers, the program was dismissed and did not lead them to question their alcohol use. Another new targeted prevention approach is work
with peer groups, such as an athletic team or a church youth
group. Through discussion and problem-solving sessions, the
group is assisted in articulating and defining the rules that its
members want their "crowd" to follow, and that they are willing
"to enforce" among themselves. There have also been programs
specifically addressing children in alcoholic homes. The

CASPAR program from Cambridge, Massachusets is among the best known. It has developed a multipronged program incorporating teacher training, education–discussion groups and peer-facilitated programs.

With the spotlight on primary prevention of alcoholism, unfortunately, less attention has been paid to secondary and tertiary prevention. Those in the field of alcohol treatment might well have more complete knowledge of these areas and be better able to develop programs. If you are in a position to be involved in planning prevention efforts, consider the following before jumping into just anything. Are there particular groups with whom you already have contacts who might be at special risk to develop alcoholism? Children of alcoholics, the elderly, the participants in drinking–driving schools are some of these groups. Do you have any natural opportunities to do early detection? For example, if you are located in an agency that is not exclusively devoted to alcohol treatment, can you develop screening programs for the general client population to identify early alcoholism? In terms of tertiary prevention, are there subgroups of clients for whom either more intensive or special follow-up arrangements might be appropriate to help avoid relapse? If you are going to become involved in prevention efforts, spend some time investigating programs that have already been developed.

Professional development

Part of the work life of any professional is properly directed, not to serving clients, nor to developing programs or promoting the broad interests of the alcohol field, but to nurturing your own professional growth. This can take many forms, for example, attending workshops, going to conferences, seeking consultation from colleagues, visiting other programs, or reading. It is time that you allocate to provide for your own continuing professional growth.

It has been said that the "half-life" of medical and scientific knowledge is 8 years. This means that half of what will be known 8 years from now has not yet been discovered. On the other hand, half of what is now taken as fact will be out of date. Consequently, education must be a continuing process. What can so easily happen is that in the press of day-to-day work, you find you do not have enough time to keep up. Sadly, what can occur is that a counselor may have a resume with 10 years' job experience, but it is the first year's experience repeated nine more times.

As with any specialty, the daily pressures make keeping current a real problem. Get on NIAAA's mailing list, subscribe to a journal or two, and then make the time to read them. Area meetings of alcohol workers of all disciplines are also a way to keep posted.

You need to know about the efforts to certify and/or license alcohol counselors and may also wish to be actively involved with them. Within virtually every state, efforts are underway to establish minimum standards for counselors in alcohol treatment. In some states, the effort is being led by an alcohol counselors' association. In others, the impetus is coming from the state alcohol programs. Reaching a consensus on what alcohol counselors need to know and what skills they must possess to be credentialed has not been easy. Yet despite the difficulties, there is growing agreement that this is essential for protection of clients, agencies, and workers. One of the characteristics of any profession, be it physicians or lawyers or teachers or alcohol counselors, is that its members take responsibility for defining the standards that they will follow and expect one another to uphold.

Being a professional colleague

Historically the alcohol field developed outside the mainstream of medicine and the other helping professions. Alcohol treatment programs initially developed for the very reason that alcoholics were excluded or poorly served by the traditional helping professions. The first alcohol treatment programs were often staffed by recovering alcoholics. The basic therapeutic program consisted of providing sober time and attempting to orient clients to the Fellowship of AA.

With the establishment of the NIAAA, alcohol treatment as we now know it began. Although no longer functioning in isolation, separate and outside the mainstream, some tensions need to be dealt with because of that history. The different professions are just now learning how to work together collaboratively. Being the "new kid on the block" it may fall to the alcohol professionals to work a bit harder at this. One of the difficulties, which may go unrecognized, is problems in communication. Each profession has its own distinctive language, terminology, and jargon, which often are not understood by the outsider. For example, a counselor reports to the client's physician that the client has "finally taken the First Step." The counselor shouldn't be surprised if the physician has no idea what is meant. In such situations it may be tempting to get a little testy, "well, doggone it, doctors should know about AA, etc, etc." Of course they should, but they'll not learn if you don't use language they can understand. Remember, you expect them to use language you can understand when discussing your client's medical condition. Return the favor.

Be sensitive also to the fact that many other professionals have a distorted view of alcohol treatment's effectiveness. In large part this is because they never see the successes. However, the client who comes in again and again in crisis, though only a very small minority of clients, is all too memorable. In fact, Vaillant found that as few as half of one percent of all the clients at a detoxification center accounted for as many admissions into the program as did 50% of the clients who only entered once. Of the 5,000 clients seen in a 78-month span it seems that the 2,500 who never returned were easily forgotten while the 25 who were admitted sixty times or more were always remembered! So encourage recovering clients to recontact the physician, social worker, or nurse who may have been instrumental in their entering treatment, but who have no idea of the successful outcome.

Also make yourself available to other professionals for consultation. One of the surest ways to establish an ongoing working relationship with someone is to have been helpful in managing a difficult case. Consider offering to join a physician during an appointment with a person he thinks may be alcoholic. Or similarly, sit in with a member of the clergy. Your availability may make their task of referral far easier. They may be reluctant to make a referral to an alcohol treatment program because that would imply they had already made a definitive diagnosis. Alcohol clinicians should be sensitive to the fact that in "just making a referral," the counselor, physician, or clergy is being forced to deal with the alcoholic's denial, resistance, and ignorance of the disease. That's the hard part, especially for someone who doesn't do it day in and day out! So anything you can do at that stage will be very helpful.

THE REAL WORLD

Selecting a professional position

In seeking and selecting a position in the alcohol field, there are a number of points to consider. By analogy, accepting any employment is almost like entering into a marriage. When it works it's marvelous and when there's a "mismatch," it's quite the opposite. Many positions may have the title of "alcohol counselor" or "alcohol therapist," but there will be considerable variation among them, depending on the agency setting and its clientele. Beyond looking closely at the facility, it is equally important to look closely at yourself. Take a professional inventory. What are your clinical strengths and what are areas of lesser competence? What are you most comfortable doing and which things are more stressful? Is "routine" a comfort or is it likely to invite boredom? Because of the differences between people, one person's perfect job is another person's nightmare.

In considering agencies, you are your own best counsel. But at the same time, speak with colleagues and use the grapevine. What should you give thought to? There is a long list of things worth considering, among them: What is the work atmosphere like? Does the agency have a staff turnover or is it fairly stable? Why do people leave? Is there a sense of camaraderie? How do the various disciplines interact if there are diverse professions on staff? How does the alcohol counselor fit into the hierarchy? What are the opportunities for professional development, both formal and informal? How is clinical supervision handled? Does the agency support and encourage continuing education? Will it help cover costs of attending conferences and workshops? What are the routes for promotion? To what are promotions tied— formal credentials, experience, certification? Is the position part of a well-established program or a new venture just getting off the ground? What kind of security does the position provide? How much security do you want and need? Where do you want to be professionally 5 years from now; how will the position you are considering facilitate attaining that? Are there skills that you would like to develop and can that be accomplished in the position being considered?

Then there are always the nuts and bolts of personnel practices. Is the salary appropriate for the position and can you live on it? Are the benefits comparable with those for other professional staff? What are the hours? Is there "on call" or evening or weekend work? How many hours a week do comparable staff typically work? In both alcohol and human service agencies there is too often chronic understaffing. So conscientious workers pitch in, work extra hours, and somehow never have the opportunity to take that time off later!

Being a professional—what it is...

Alcohol counseling is a growing profession. The professional counselor has mastered a body of knowledge, has special skills, and has a code of ethics to guide in the work. Being a professional does not mean you have to know it all. Do yourself a favor, right now. Give yourself permission to give up any pretense that it is otherwise. Feel free to ask questions, seek advice, request a consultation, say you don't know. Alcohol treatment requires diverse skills and talents. Treatment programs are staffed by people with different training, for the very reason that no one person or specialty can do the job alone. Being a professional also means constantly looking at what you are doing, evaluating your efforts. There is always more than one approach. You cannot make sober people by grinding drunks through an alcohol treatment machine. Being open to trying new things is easier if you aren't stuck with the notion that you are supposed to be the big expert. And of course you will make mistakes—so what else is new?

And what it isn't...

Overwhelming numbers of alcoholics need and ask for help out there. The tendency is to overburden yourself because of the obvious need. Spreading yourself too thin is a real problem and danger. One needs also to develop assertiveness to resist agency pressures to take on increasing responsibilities. In either instance it creates resentment, anger, frustration, and a distorted view of the world. "No one else seems to care! Somebody's got to do it." It's a trap. Unless you're an Atlas, you'll get mashed. You are important as a person and must keep that in mind. Save your own space. Collapsing might give you a nice sense of martyrdom, but it won't help anybody. Better to be more realistic in assessing just what you can do productively, devoting your energy to a realistic and limited number of clients, and giving your best.

Keep a clear eye on your own needs for time off, trips, visits to people who have nothing to do with your work. The people who live with you deserve some of your attention, too. It is hard to maintain a relationship with anyone if all you can manage is "What a day!" lapse into silence, and soon fall asleep. It is not going to be easy to handle, but some rule of thumb must be set in your own head to handle the calls that come after working hours. Some workers ruefully decide on unlisted home phone numbers. Drinking drunks and their upset families are notoriously inconsiderate. "Telephone-itis" sets in with a few drinks. You may decide you do want to be available at all hours. Whatever rules you set, however, try to be consistent. Take a good look at the effects on the important people in your life. Some compromise may be necessary between your "ideal counselor" and your own needs. Give it some thought. State your rules clearly to your clients, preferably when they are sober, and then stick to them. If you said no calls when a client is drinking, then don't get caught listening to a "drunkalog" at 3 AM for fear he'll do something rash. Being inconsistent may be more dangerous in the long run. When you have had some experience, you will be able to tell when you must break your own rules. Then you can say that to your clients: "I did say I don't take home phone calls, but you do seem to be in a real bind..."

You cannot take total responsibility for clients. Rarely does someone make it or not because of one incident. This does not mean that you should adopt a laissez-faire policy; however, just as you cannot take all the credit for a sober, happy alcoholic, neither can you shoulder all the blame when it doesn't work out that way.

CONFIDENTIALITY

For the counselor, as for anyone in the helping professions, confidentiality is a crucial issue. Most of us simply do not consider how much of our conversation includes discussion about other people. When we think about it, it can be quite a shock. It is especially difficult when we are really concerned about someone and are looking for aid and advice. There is only one place for this in a professional relationship with a client. That is with your supervisor or therapist coworkers. It is *never* okay to discuss a client with spouse, friends, even other alcohol workers from different facilities. Even without using names, enough usually slips out to make the client easily identified some time in the future. Unfortunately, this standard is not kept all the time. There are occasional slips by even the most conscientious workers. You will do it accidentally, and you will hear it from time to time. All you can do is try harder in the first instance and deliberately forget what you heard in the second. What your client shares with you is privileged information. That includes where he is and how he is doing. Even good news is his alone to share.

If you are heading up an outreach office, rather than functioning within a hospital or mental health clinic, it is up to you to inform your secretary about confidentiality. The same is true for any volunteers working in the office. They have some knowledge about the people being seen, at least who they are. It must be stressed that any information they acquire there is strictly private. You do not need to get huffy and deliver a lecture, but you should make the point very clearly and set some standards in the workplace.

There are also federal statutes with respect to confidentiality of client information and records in alcohol services. Information cannot be released to any outside party without the client's permission. This means friends, physician, employer, or another treatment facility. Generally, one always has a client sign a statement agreeing to release information before anything written is sent out. This then becomes part of the client or medical record. Similarly, if you want to get information from another facility or party, you would seek the client's permission and get a written release to forward to those from whom the information is being requested.

ETHICS

Being a professional means being allied to a set of ethical standards. These might not be written down, but they are nonetheless understood by your professional coworkers. They are there as guidelines. They have a history and have developed from experience. This discussion is intended to point out some of what is expected of helping professionals that may not be expected of others. Maintaining confidentiality, for example, is one standard of behavior taken for granted. In general, helping professionals are expected to avoid romantic entanglements with clients. If a romantic inclination on the part of either client or counselor begins to show up, it should be worked out—and not in the nearest bed. This is the time to run, not walk, to an experienced coworker. It may be hard on our egos, but the fact is that people with problems are as confused about their emotions as everything else. They may be feeling so needy that they "love" anyone who seems to be hearing their cry. It really isn't you personally. If they had drawn Joe or Amy, then one of them would be the object of the misplaced emotion right now. So talk it over with a supervisor, guide, or mentor, not just a buddy. Then, follow their advice. It may have to be worked through with the client, or referral to another counselor may be necessary. The ethical standards are not arbitrary no-nos set up by a bunch of Puritans. They are protections designed to keep both you and the client from any needless hurt. The hurts can be emotional or range all the way to messy court actions. The counselors who have walked the road before you have discovered what keeps upsets to a minimum, your sense of self-worth realistic, and your helpfulness at its optimum level.

Clients will occasionally show up with presents. While they are actively working with you, the general guideline is no gifts. This is especially true if something of real monetary value is offered. In such cases it is important to discuss what is being said by the gift. Use your common sense, though; there are times when clearly the thing to do is accept graciously. (If you have a fantasy of an MG being delivered anonymously to your door, and it comes true…unfortunately, our experience doesn't cover that.) Similarly, social engagements with the client alone or his family are not recommended. It could be a "plot" to keep you friendly and avoid crunchy problems that have to be worked out. In the office time, deal with the invitation and gently refuse. Hopefully, in your first years of counseling, you will have a supervisor to help you through such sticky wickets. Use him or her. The real pros are the ones who used all the help they could get when they needed it. That is how they got to be pros.

Another ethical concern is directed at keeping professional life and private life separate. Don't do your counseling number on your friends. You are likely to end up with fewer of them if you do. When you see a friend exhibiting behavior that you think indicates he is heading for trouble, it is hard not to fall into your professional role. Don't. Bite your tongue. He knows what business you're in. If he wants help, he'll ask. Should that day come, refer him to see someone else. And stay out of the picture. Counseling friends and relatives is another no-no. Vital objectivity is impossible. No matter how good you are with your clients, almost anyone else will be better equipped to work with your family or friends. Or if confronted with concern about a close friend, then *you*, see a counselor, as the client, to see, as an individual, if you want or can, become part of an intervention process.

COUNSELORS WITH TWO HATS

Many of the workers in the alcohol field are themselves recovering alcoholics. Long before national attention was focused on alcoholism, private rehabilitation centers were operated, often staffed by sober alcoholics. In the evolutionary process of recovery, many alcoholics find themselves working in many capacities, in many different types of facilities. We must say here that we do not believe that simply being a recovering alcoholic qualifies one to be a counselor. There is more to it than that. That view ignores the skill and special knowledge that many alcoholics working in the field have gained, on the job, and often without benefit of any formal training. They have had a harder row to hoe and deserve a lot of respect for sticking to it.

Being a recovering alcoholic has some advantages for a counselor but also some clear disadvantages. Being a counselor may at times be the most confusing for the recovering alcoholic who is also in AA. Doing AA Twelfth Step work and calling it counseling won't do, from the profession's or AA's point of view. Twelfth Step work is voluntary and has no business being used for bread earning. AA's traditions are clearly against this. AA is not opposed to its members working in the field of alcoholism, if they are qualified to do so. If you are an AA member and also an alcohol counselor, it is important to keep the dividing line in plain sight. The trade calls it "wearing two hats." There are some good AA pamphlets on the subject, and the AA monthly magazine, *The Grapevine*, publishes articles for two-hatters from time to time. A book, *The Para-Professional in the Treatment of Alcoholism*, by Staub and Kent, covers a lot of territory on two-hatting very well.

A particular bind for two-hat counselors comes if attending AA becomes tied to their jobs more than their own sobriety. They might easily find themselves sustaining clients at meetings and not being there for themselves. A way to avoid this is to find a meeting you can attend where you are less likely to see clients. It is easy for both you and the clients to confuse AA with the other therapy. The client benefits from a clear distinction as much, if not more, than you. There is always the difficulty of keeping your priorities in order. You cannot counsel if you are drinking yourself. So, whatever you do to keep sober, whether it includes AA or not, keep doing it. Again, when so many people out there seem to need you, it is very difficult to keep from overextending. A recovering alcoholic simply cannot afford this. (If this description fits you, stop reading right now. Choose one thing to scratch off your schedule.) It is always easy to justify skimping on your own sober regimen because "I'm working with alcoholics all the time." Retire that excuse. Experience has shown it to be a counselor killer.

Another real problem is the temptation to discuss your job at AA meetings or discuss clients with other members. The AAs don't need to be bored by you any more than by a doctor member describing the surgical removal of a gallbladder. Discussing your clients, even with another AA member, is a serious breach of confidentiality. This will be particularly hard, especially when a really concerned AA member asks you point-blank about someone. The other side of the coin is keeping the confidences gained at AA and not reporting to coworkers about what transpired with clients at an AA meeting. Hopefully, your nonalcoholic coworkers will not slip up and put you in a bind by asking. It is probably okay to talk with your AA sponsor about your job if it is giving you fits. However, it is important to stick with *you*, and leave out work details and/or details about clients.

Watch out if feelings of superiority creep in toward other "plain" AA members or nonalcoholic colleagues. Recovery from alcoholism does not accord you magical insights. On the other hand, being a nonalcoholic is not a guaranteed route to knowing what is going on, either. Keep your perspective as much as you're able. After all, you are all in the same boat, with different oars. To quote an unknown source: "It's amazing how much can be accomplished if no one cares who gets the credit."

Counselor relapse

We have alluded to a variety of situations that may spell potential trouble: counselor burnout, inappropriate relationships with clients, slackening AA attendance, overinvolvement with the job, unrealistic expectations. For the counselor who is a recovering alcoholic, all of these can lead to a relapse. Becoming a counselor in no way confers immunity to relapse. Unfortunately, this fact of life has not been very openly discussed by the alcohol counseling profession. It is the profession's big taboo topic. On the occasions where it has occurred, the situation has too often been dealt with poorly. There is either a conspiracy of silence or a move to drive the counselor out of the field. The coworkers can very readily assume all the roles of "the family," and the counselor's coworkers can get caught up in functioning as "coalcoholics."

What suggestions do we have? Ideally, the time to address the issue of possible relapse is at the time of a counselor's hiring. To our minds, both the counselor and the agency have a mutual responsibility to be alert to possible danger signs and agree to address them openly. This does not mean the counselor is always under surveillance. It simply is a means of publicly acknowledging that relapses can and do occur, and that they are too serious to ignore. We would suggest that if drinking does occur, it is the counselor's responsibility both to seek help and to inform the agency. The job status will be dependent on evaluating the counselor's ability to continue serving clients and to participate in treatment for himself or herself. The time to agree upon an arbitrator/consultant or referral is before the possible event, not in the midst of a crisis.

Some people favor an arbitrary ironclad rule: any drinking and you're out of your job. However, that seems to miss the point. There is the recovering alcoholic, who is also a counselor who buys a six-pack, has one and a half beers, sees what is going on, picks up the phone, and calls for help. Another case is the counselor who "nips" off and on for weeks, who subsequently exhibits loss of control, and shows up at the office intoxicated. Though it is important not to treat the former case lightly, nonetheless the disease process has not been wholly reactivated as it has in the latter case. Interestingly, counselors we have known who have had a single drinking incident, as in the example given, have tended to take sick leave and enter a residential program. They have interpreted the drinking as a very serious sign that something in their life is out of balance, warranting serious attention. What is essential in any case is securing adequate treatment for the counselor and not jeopardizing care of clients.

If you as a counselor are known to your clients as a recovering alcoholic, and if your counseling style draws heavily upon your personal experience, your relapse will have a profound effect on your clients. If you are off the job and enter treatment, you can count on the news rapidly becoming public knowledge. It is our belief that the agency and the coworkers dealing with your clients have a responsibility to inform your clients. Certainly, any details are a private matter, but that a relapse has occurred cannot be seen as none of their business.

A word to coworkers providing coverage for a relapsed counselor: if you are the coworker, be prepared to deal with clients' feelings of betrayal, hopelessness, anger, fear. You will need to provide them extra support. Be very clear on who is available to them in their counselor's absence. Also recognize that this can be a difficult painful experience for you and other coworkers, who may well share many of the clients' feelings. Be prepared to call upon extra reinforcements in the form of consultation and supervision.

If you are a counselor with a relapse and you return to work after a leave, there is no way you can avoid dealing with the fact of the relapse. How this is handled should be dealt with in supervision and with lots of input from more seasoned colleagues. You will be trying to walk along a difficult middle ground. On one hand, your clients do not need apologies, nor will they benefit from hearing all the details or in any way being put in the role of your therapist. Yet neither can it be glossed over, treated as no big deal and of no greater significance than your summer vacation. In short you have to, in your own counseling, come to grips with the drinking or relapse, so that you do not find yourself working it out on the job with your clients.

A different but similar situation is posed by the clinician who enters the alcohol field as a nonalcoholic but who comes to recognize a budding alcohol problem. In the cases of which we are aware, the individuals were in very early stages of the disease. This raises interesting questions. Since there has been ample evidence of the wisdom of not having recovering alcoholics enter the field until sober a minimum of 2 years, how does the "2-years-of-sobriety-principle" apply in such situations? Does that automatically mean that those who have been good clinicians must exit from the field for the same length of time? To jump to that conclusion is premature. As a profession we need to determine what the dynamics in this situation are, when an extended leave is needed and when it is not. In the meantime, common sense dictates that this situation needs to be carefully evaluated and monitored. Possibly a brief leave of absence might be indicated, not necessarily because the counselor has to enter a residential program. On the other hand, residential treatment might be wise; it provides an opportunity to work intensely on personal material which then reduces the risk that it will be dealt with inappropriately in sessions with clients! At the very least it will be imperative that lots of clinical supervision at work, and both a sponsor and a counselor, for the counselor, be an integral part of the recovery.

The foregoing may seem a very grim note on which to conclude this text. It is sobering, but it is reality, too. Maybe one of the hardest things to learn in becoming a counselor is how to take care of yourself. Like everything else, that takes a lot of

practice too.

Be good to yourself. Treat yourself to a movie tonight and on your way home, remember to look at the stars!

RESOURCES AND FURTHER READING

Kalb, M., and Propper, M.S.: The future of alcohology: craft or science? *Am J Psychiatry* 133:641–645, 1976.

Kinney, J.: Relapse among alcoholics who are alcoholism counselors. *J Stud Alcohol* 44(4):744–748, 1983.

Kinney, J., Price, T.R.P., and Bergen, B.J.: Impediments to alcohol education. *J Stud Alcohol* 45(5):453–459, 1984.

Miller, P., and Nirenberg, T. (Eds.): *Prevention of Alcohol Abuse.* New York: Plenum Press, 1984.

Valle, S.K.: *Alcoholism counseling: issues for an emerging profession.* Springfield, IL: Charles C. Thomas, 1979.

Valle, S.K.: Burnout: occupational hazard for counselors. *Alcohol Health and Research World* 3(3):10–14, 1979r.

Publications

Alcohol Clinical Update (bimonthly newsletter). Project Cork Institute, Dartmouth Medical School, Hanover, NH 03756.

Alcohol Health and Research World, NIAAA (quarterly). Superintendent of Documents, U.S. Government Printing Office, Washington, DC 20402.

DATA: Digest of Alcoholism Theory and Application (quarterly review of literature). Johnson Institute, 510 First Avenue North, Minneapolis, MN 55403.

Drug Abuse and Alcoholism Newsletter (ten issues per year). Vista Hill Foundation, 3420 Camino del Rio North, Suite 100, San Diego, CA 92108.

NIAAA Information and Feature Service. (Available through National Clearinghouse for Alcohol Information, Box 2345 Rockville, MD 20852.)

The Journal (monthly newspaper). Addiction Research Foundation, 33 Russell St., Toronto, Ontario, Canada M5S 2S1.

The U.S. Journal of Drug and Alcohol Dependence (monthly newspaper). 1721 Blount Road, Suite 1, Pompano Beach, FL 33069.

Index

Credits

1. From Baruch, Dorothy. *New Ways of Discipline: You and Your Child Today.* New York: McGraw-Hill Book Co., 1949. Used with permission of McGraw-Hill Book Co.

2. From Siegel, R., Strassfeld, M., and Strassfeld, S. *The Jewish Catalogue.* Philadelphia: The Jewish Publication Society of America, 1973.